# Religious Fundamentalism

How does a religious fundamentalist come to embrace a counter-cultural world view?

Fundamentalism can be analysed from a variety of perspectives. It is a type of belief system that enables individuals to make sense of their lives and provides them with an identity. It is a social phenomenon, in which strictly religious people act according to the norms, values, and beliefs of the group to which they belong. It is a cultural product, in the sense that different cultural settings result in different forms of fundamentalism. And it is a global phenomenon, in the obvious sense that it is to be found everywhere, and because it is both a reaction against, and also a part of, the globalising modern world.

*Religious Fundamentalism* deals with all of these four levels of analysis, uniquely combining sociological and psychological perspectives, and relating them to each other. Each chapter is followed by an in-depth case study, and these range from a close textual analysis of President George W. Bush's second inaugural speech through to a treatment of al-Qaida as a global media event.

This book provides a comprehensive social scientific perspective on a subject of immense contemporary significance, and should be of interest to both university students and to students of the contemporary world.

**Peter Herriot** has been an academic and consultant throughout his working life. Most of his work has been in the field of organizational psychology, specializing in personnel selection, career management, and the employment relationship. Since retirement he has concentrated on the application of social scientific theory and research into the profoundly important current issue of religious fundamentalism. He was himself brought up in a fundamentalist family.

# Religious Fundamentalism

Global, Local and Personal

**Peter Herriot**

Routledge
Taylor & Francis Group

LONDON AND NEW YORK

First published 2009 by Routledge
27 Church Road, Hove, East Sussex BN3 2FA

Simultaneously published in the USA and Canada
by Routledge
270 Madison Avenue, New York, NY 10016

Reprinted 2009

*Routledge is an imprint of the Taylor & Francis Group,
an Informa business*

© 2009 Psychology Press

Typeset in Times New Roman by
RefineCatch Limited, Bungay, Suffolk
Printed and bound in Great Britain by
TJ International Ltd, Padstow, Cornwall
Cover design by Jim Wilkie

This publication has been produced with paper manufactured to
strict environmental standards and with pulp derived from
sustainable forests.

*British Library Cataloguing in Publication Data*
A catalogue record for this book is available from the British Library

*Library of Congress Cataloging-in-Publication Data*
Herriot, Peter.
  Religious fundamentalism : global, local, and personal /
Peter Herriot.
      p. cm.
  Includes bibliographical references and indexes.
  ISBN 978-0-415-42208-6 (hardback) – ISBN 978-0-415-42209-3
  (pbk.)
  1. Religious fundamentalism.    I. Title.
  BL238.H475 2008
  200.9′04–dc22                                            2008003040

ISBN 978-0-415-42208-6 (hbk)
ISBN 978-0-415-42209-3 (pbk)

# Contents

# Introduction

## Religion: the big issue

Religion has recently become a central topic of debate in the West. Twenty years ago, it was relegated to the back pages of the quality press, or limited to sex scandals in the tabloids. Terrorist assaults and their repercussions have added to religion's recent prominence. There is nothing like the perception of constant threat to heighten awareness. However, the issues thrown up by the debate are far from being answered. Indeed, on some of them discussion has hardly begun.

For example, are we to attribute the increase of religiously inspired conflict to religion in general, or only to its extremist fringes? Some commentators, for example Huntington (1996) have argued that religion is a key feature of each of the different historic civilisations of the world. Conflict, when it occurs, is primarily between, rather than within, civilisations. Hence religion *in general* often inspires and justifies such conflict. Others maintain that it is *specifically* fundamentalism that is responsible for religion-related conflict. Fundamentalism, they feel, should be distinguished from mainstream religion as a perversion of its central message of peace and justice.

Other issues and debates are also pressing. For example, in a democracy, should appeals to religious observance carry more weight than other criteria in determining what is legally acceptable? Is the law the only criterion for what is acceptable behaviour in a multi-cultural society, or should there be an attempt to foster a unifying national identity? What happens when religious people seek to challenge the Western liberal consensus that religion is a matter of private choice for the individual, and should not intrude institutionally into the political arena?

Responses to such questions have been vehement. There has been a recent spate of books attacking religion in general, often from an evolutionary perspective (e.g. Dawkins, 2006). However, most hostility has been reserved specifically for fundamentalism, demonstrated both in the media and in the results of opinion polls. I will seek to demonstrate in this book that such hostility is sometimes ill-informed, and, furthermore, exactly suits the purposes of fundamentalists. Rather, we need to develop a rounded understanding of the phenomenon of fundamentalism before deciding how to respond, both personally and politically.

## What is fundamentalism?

First, however, we have to establish that there is a phenomenon to understand. Is there really a category of religious movements that we can term 'fundamentalism', or is the term simply used pejoratively for people who take their religion too seriously for the liking of the rest of us? The social scientist has to reply that such a category can only be established if some religious movements can be distinguished from the rest because they uniquely possess certain features in common. Extensive sociological research has indeed identified five such features (Almond, Appleby, & Sivan, 2003).

The first and most basic distinguishing feature of fundamentalist movements is that they are *reactive*. Fundamentalists believe that their religion is under mortal threat from the secularism of the modern world, and they are fighting back. They may resist in different ways, but they are all essentially oppositional; they have to have an enemy.

The remaining four distinctive features are all means to aid the ultimate task of resistance. First, fundamentalists are *dualist*. That is, they conceive of the world in binary opposites: God and the Devil, good and evil, truth and falsehood, etc. Such thinking aids the task of resistance, for it justifies the development of an in-group versus out-group social dynamic and all that follows from such a dynamic. Second, fundamentalists believe that their *holy book*, through its interpreters or read directly, has supreme authority over what to believe and how to act. It reveals God's will for mankind. However, third, fundamentalists' interpretation of the holy book is *selective*. They choose specific ideas from it and emphasise them, often changing their traditional meaning when they do so. Such selective adaptation of the holy book provides justification for resistance strategies and tactics. Finally, they hold to a *millennialist* view of history, expecting God to fully establish His rule over the world at some future time. Some believe that they can hasten the arrival of this glorious event by fighting, literally or spiritually, on God's behalf. The cosmic range of millennialist thinking motivates and inspires the faithful, and provides a structure and significance to their lives.

*Fundamentalism is a twentieth century phenomenon.* Many have used the term more generally to denote movements, throughout the ages, which have reacted to political, social, or religious changes by fighting for traditional religion. Certain societies, such as the Jesuits within the Roman Catholic church, and stern Islamic sects, such as the Wahhabis in Saudi Arabia, are historical examples of such self-styled defenders of the true faith. However, fundamentalism is *by definition* a modern phenomenon, because it is reacting against modernity. I will argue that modernisation, and its latest expression, globalisation, is a unique historical process. It offers new threats to traditional religion, but it also provides new opportunities for reactionary religious

movements to flourish. We are therefore justified in distinguishing fundamentalisms from older reactionary religious movements, because they are
fighting against new and different enemies. We are seeking to understand
a modern phenomenon: today's religious movements, which are currently
helping to create today's world.

Note that all the five defining features have to be present if a religious
movement is to be called fundamentalist. There are many movements, for
example, which give great authority to their holy book. Indeed, this could
probably be said of the Muslim faith as a whole. However, these movements may not be hostile to the modern world, and thereby signal that they
are not fundamentalist. There are other movements that are primarily political rather than religious in their inspiration. For example, the Protestant
and Catholic enemies in the conflict in Northern Ireland should rather be
labelled Loyalist and Republican. These too do not justify the label of
fundamentalist.

Moreover, we should not assume that all members of fundamentalist movements are fundamentalist individuals, although there is, as I will argue, strong
pressure to conform. Likewise, there are many individual fundamentalists
who are members of non-fundamentalist movements. For example, there
are many members of the mainstream Anglican Communion who are fundamentalist believers. Indeed, conflict between fundamentalists and mainstream believers occurs in many religious movements, including many of the
Christian denominations.

It follows from this definition that fundamentalist movements and individual fundamentalists are not always easy to distinguish from other religious
movements or individuals. There are a great number of traditional believers
whom it would be easy to mistake at first sight for fundamentalists. We have
to be confident that all five criteria are present, in particular, the first and core
criterion: hostility to aspects of modernity. Their specific enemies may vary:
fundamentalist Muslims may target apostate Muslim governments or the
degenerate West, whereas fundamentalist Christians attack specific groups
that defy their moral agenda. However, to repeat: labelling groups and people
'fundamentalist' requires analysis of their beliefs and practices. The term
cannot simply be used to describe people who are unusually religious or who
claim to represent the true and traditional faith. In the nine detailed case
studies that complete each chapter, I will repeatedly point up the features
of movements or individuals that place them firmly within the definition of
fundamentalism.

Given the basic criterion of hostility towards modernity, I am not placing
fundamentalism within a context of postmodernity, for reasons that are
presented in detail in Chapter 1. In brief, fundamentalisms are unashamed
grand narratives, competing with other such grand narratives as secular
humanism and religious pluralism. Their key characteristic is their hostility
to modernity, and they are likely to prefer theocracy to democracy, and
universal moral laws to respect for minority rights. Globalisation is better

construed as possibly the final flourish of late modernity, and it is primarily modernity, rather than postmodernity, against which fundamentalisms are reacting.

## Different from us, and different from each other

Reference to the five distinctive features of fundamentalism will recur throughout the book. They serve to point up how very *different and unusual* fundamentalists appear to other people. Often, fundamentalists signal these differences visibly by their appearance and behaviour. They lead many to conclude that there is something unique and peculiar about them. Observers suppose that they cannot be understood in normal terms, but require new explanations. For example, many have assumed psychological abnormalities or personality defects. Others have developed unique theories to cope with what they believe to be a unique phenomenon.

However, I will take an entirely contrary perspective. I will seek to demonstrate that fundamentalism consists of religious movements that can be understood using well-established concepts from the social sciences, and from *social psychology* in particular. Fundamentalists are indeed different; they seek to establish their difference at every available opportunity. But only sound theory and research can hope to answer the core question: *How do fundamentalist movements succeed in attracting, retaining, and motivating people who live in modern societies on the prospectus of a pre-modern world view?*

It is, of course, also immensely important to understand why a very few fundamentalists act violently. However, this question is logically secondary to the question of why they are fundamentalists in the first place, and I will not seek to address it in this book. Fundamentalists vary in many other ways too, while all sharing the same five definitive characteristics. For example, some fundamentalist movements are highly politicised; others are totally preoccupied with saving souls or keeping pure. The huge and growing charismatic Christian movement is far more concerned with spiritual experiences than with winning political victories (Coleman, 2000). Of those fundamentalisms that are politicised, the vast majority seek to achieve their objectives by political rather than by violent methods.

Such differences between fundamentalisms need explanation, and the approach I will adopt is to relate them to differences in cultures. But the hardest question to answer is the key mystery of fundamentalism in general. How can we explain why, in the late-modern world, fundamentalists can successfully propagate a set of pre-modern beliefs, values, and practices. This book seeks, unusually, to address this question at a variety of levels. It is only by understanding the cultural context at global, national, religious movement, organisational, and cell-group levels that the power of fundamentalist belief and the attraction of fundamentalist identity in the lives of individual people can be properly understood.

## A social psychological approach

Thus a *social psychological* approach characterises my treatment of fundamentalism. This is because, uniquely, social psychology attempts to relate social structures at all levels to individual identity and to a variety of psychological constructs such as beliefs, values, attitudes, and behaviour. This is not to deny the contributions of other academic disciplines. Sociologists have done a superb job in explaining fundamentalisms as social movements; psychologists and pollsters have thoroughly analysed fundamentalists' beliefs, attitudes, and norms of behaviour; political scientists have demonstrated how fundamentalist movements have achieved and exercised power; historians have pointed to the origins of fundamentalisms in reactionary religious movements down the ages; and theologians and philosophers force us to constantly re-examine the nature and status of the concepts we use in our analyses of the fundamentalist phenomenon. All these other disciplines have informed this book, and as a consequence are likely to have been misrepresented as a result of my ignorance. Without doubt, my own identity as a Western liberal Christian social/organisational psychologist has markedly skewed the contents towards Christianity in particular and the three 'religions of the book', Judaism, Christianity, and Islam in general. Sikh, Hindu, and Far Eastern fundamentalisms receive far too little attention.

However, it is, unusually for books about fundamentalism, the *social psychological* approach that determines this book's purpose and structure. In particular, I want to emphasise the *social* origins of fundamentalism. Although the Western preference is to treat religion as a matter of private and individual choice, fundamentalism can only be understood in terms of the social context in which it has developed. The book therefore moves from the broadest context of all, the globalising world, through national cultures, to fundamentalist movements as social movements. Then the unit of analysis becomes smaller, as I analyse fundamentalisms from the perspective of their local organisations and small groups. Such a range of perspectives is essential if we are to comprehend fundamentalism in a sufficiently nuanced way to do justice to its complexity (Percy, 2002).

Only half way through the book, in Chapter 6, does the individual appear. Thereafter the account moves from the inner to the outer aspects of the person. We start with the self, the identity, and then move on to the belief system of fundamentalism. From beliefs follow values, attitudes, and behaviour. The sequence is thus from the outside in, i.e. from the context to the person, and then from the core of the person, the self, out to his or her visible behaviour. And if books were circular rather than linear, fundamentalist behaviour would feed back into the context, for it is a truism to state that fundamentalism has profoundly changed the world.

## Core concepts: culture and identity

The analysis that I will present depends heavily on two key concepts: *culture* and *identity*, and on the relationship between them. These are very broad-ranging concepts, but breadth is a necessary feature if they are to bear the explanatory weight that is placed upon them. *Culture* is used to analyse the various levels of context for fundamentalist belief, with cultures at a lower level of analysis sometimes forming sub-cultures of those at higher levels. American Protestant fundamentalism, for example, is treated as one of the sub-cultures of the American culture.

*Identity*, on the other hand, explains how cultural categories are internalised into the mind of the believer, together with the beliefs, values, and norms of behaviour that constitute the major elements of cultures. The two concepts, culture and identity, are treated more as *process* than as *content*. This is because fundamentalist movements have only succeeded in surviving so successfully in the rapidly changing late modern world by adapting to their social environments. Their cultures and their social identities are always on the move.

In particular, it is the process of change in symbolic meanings, often initiated by fundamentalist leaders, which create revised ideologies. These in turn motivate new strategic directions. The new and aggressive meaning of jihad, for example, developed by radical Islamic theorists, provided the justification and motivation for attacks on nominally Muslim governments, and ultimately on Western nations. These attacks, in turn, gained immense symbolic significance, confirming and further developing the idea of jihad in the minds of militant Islamists.

I will argue, then, that there is a continuous process of changes in beliefs and values justifying and motivating new behaviour, which accrues symbolic meaning and thereby affects beliefs and values to motivate new behaviour, etc., etc. This analysis contradicts the self-presentation of fundamentalist movements, which usually argue that they are returning to the immutable and traditional truth from which mainstream religion has strayed.

## Organisation of the book

I have adopted a specific format within each chapter. The first and major part of the chapter is primarily theoretical in purpose. It introduces those concepts that are appropriate to the level of analysis of the chapter, for example, the global, organisational or behavioural levels (Chapters 1, 4, and 9). Brief examples derived from fundamentalism are used throughout to exemplify and support the theory.

Then at the end of each chapter a detailed case study is provided, which demonstrates the chapter's key theoretical points. These case studies aim to provide a level of detail that will enable the reader to 'get inside' a particular group or to become 'properly acquainted' with individuals. Theory is allowed to become grounded in detail, even if the detail does not always illustrate the full range of the theory.

The book is intended as an academic text, and therefore is concerned to develop theoretical understanding on the basis of complex and often conflicting evidence. I make no apologies for this approach, which does not appeal to those looking for a lively and opinionated polemic, such as Dawkins' 'The God Delusion'. However, I hope that general readers may find it of use in helping them address one of the most important issues of our times. Such readers might find it useful to read the case studies at the end of each chapter before tackling the theoretical account in the main portion.

Rather than summarise each of the chapters here, I refer the reader to the summaries located between the theoretical and case-study elements of each chapter.

# 1 Fundamentalism is global

## Modernisation

### A selective enemy

The most basic characteristic of fundamentalism is that it is reactionary. Its basic stance is oppositional, as it is always hostile to an Other, whom it perceives as threatening. Moreover, it defines itself by that opposition; it depends upon the Other's existence for its own *raison d'être*.

But who or what is the Other? At different times, and in different places, fundamentalists have come up with a variety of enemies. We should pay careful attention to this choice of enemy, whether it be the Great Satan, religious apostates, the New World Order, the feminist movement, or secular humanism, to name but five out of many. For fundamentalists' own statements about whom or what they are fighting are an important source of evidence for what it is that they are reacting against, and why. However, while we should listen to what fundamentalists say, and respect it as an honest statement of what they think and feel, we should not adopt their account as an explanation. We have to search for the origins of their reactionary fervour within our own understanding of its social and psychological context.

That context is *the modernising world*. The term 'modernising' implies an ongoing process, which has reached different stages in different nations and cultures. Some are still even now essentially feudal in nature. Others are in the early-modern stage, being engaged in the initial process of industrialisation. Many have reached the turbulent stage of late modernity, characterised by their involvement in, and acceptance of, *globalisation*. However, it does not necessarily follow that those societies currently in a feudal or early-modern condition will follow the same course of change as those now termed 'late modern'. The history of the West is not necessarily the destiny of the world. Their future is not already determined for them.

The use of the term 'modernising' also indicates a stance on an issue that has preoccupied many sociologists for some time: whether recent changes are so radical that the world has become a qualitatively different place as a result (Bauman, 1987, 1992). The use of the term 'postmodern' expresses a belief that nothing less than a revolution has occurred in our institutions, cultures, and consciousness. Such arguments may be partly a matter of semantics. However, I have chosen to use 'modernisation' as a label for the entire process because I wish to emphasise the way in which early features of modernity are at the root of its latest manifestation in globalisation (Habermas, 1987). The seeds of globalisation were sown in the eighteenth and nineteenth centuries. It is nevertheless unarguably true that modernisation is rapidly increasing in pace, having acquired the characteristics of a positive feedback system (Castells, 1996).

It is useful to adopt three different levels of analysis when seeking to understand modernisation; these are *institutional and technical, cultural and world-view*, and the level of *the self*. All three levels, however, are dynamically inter-related. For example, changes in world-view both inform and are shaped by changes at the institutional and technical level. Thus modern people tend to play down a supernatural world-view because of the capacity of modern human institutions to explain, and to a considerable extent control, the natural world.

To return to our initial question of what it is that fundamentalists are reacting against, one answer might be 'the process of modernisation' or 'the modern world'. Popular commentary sometimes argues that fundamentalists seek to return the world to the middle ages, if not earlier. However, this broad response immediately requires qualification. There are many features of modernisation that fundamentalists positively embrace, despite their repeated re-affirmation of ancient tradition. Some of these features they have adopted consciously, and others perhaps unawares. For example, Protestant Christian fundamentalists try to apply modern scientific and historical truth criteria to the Bible (Armstrong, 2000a). They are also experts at using the modern political process. Fundamentalists in general are second to none in their

*Table 1* Features of modernisation

| Institutional and technical | Cultural and world-view | Individual and self |
| --- | --- | --- |
| Rationalisation | Rationality | Alienation |
| Organisation | Control | Identity |
| Instrumentalism | Mobility | Personality |
| Power of capital | Pluralism | Lifestyle |
| Mobility of capital | Relativism | Self-development |
| Mobility of labour | Risk and fear | Uniqueness |
| Information | Public vs. private | Authenticity |
| Global vs. local | Consumerism | Brief relationships |
| Mediated experience | Commodification | Insecurity |
| Networks | Minority rights | Multiple roles |
| Inequalities | | |

skilful use of communication technologies. As I will demonstrate in the following case study, al-Qaida are consummate exploiters of the global media. In the light of such selectivity, we should therefore be asking: *Which* features of modernity are they opposing, and why?

## The modernisation of institutions

### *Early modernity*

The early development of capitalism and its embrace of the profit motive were closely related to industrialisation and manufacture. This in turn both stimulated and was formed by technologies that were derived ultimately from developing scientific knowledge. The increased cheapness and availability of energy was a major driver. Early industrialists emphasised the rationalised division of work into manageable units: 'scientific management' as Frederick Winthrop Taylor (1911) termed it. Technological systems and processes rapidly superseded craft knowledge, and roles within organisations became more and more specialised. According to Weber (1947), roles were depersonalised and bureaucratised, so that anyone with the appropriate training and aptitude could fill them. The job, rather than the person, became the key element of organisation.

Organisations themselves became more and more specialised, both in the public and private sectors. Whereas in pre-modern times the church had assumed responsibility for a wide range of services and governance, now institutions or organisations competed for control over the provision of each. The Reformation was a stimulus for this decline in the institutional church's authority, since it encouraged individuals and social classes to develop a variety of religious structures to suit their needs. A wide range of Protestant denominations resulted.

The dominant operational mode became one of establishing the best means of achieving specified objectives; and observing, and if possible measuring, outcomes to check that they had indeed been achieved. This essentially instrumental and pragmatic approach did not encourage questions regarding the value of objectives. Furthermore, it paid little attention to other outcomes than those intended. Thus the migration from the country to the city, and the development of class structures based on occupation and ownership, caused (and continue to cause) apparently unforeseen societal conflict and individual problems. The only too visible inequalities that resulted created (and still create) a sense of injustice and the demand for rights. So powerful are these responses to modernisation that two countervailing ideologies have already been spawned, both of which have convulsed the world: fascism and communism.

Of course, feudal society had also been grossly unequal. However, feudal institutions and the social order were seldom questioned. It was simply assumed that they were the natural state of affairs, ordained by God. The new capacity of institutions to reflect upon themselves, and to re-design and improve themselves as a consequence, was a direct outcome of the rational approach to the world that was the product of the Reformation and the Enlightenment. It was to become one of the major drivers of modernisation.

### Globalisation defined

Indeed, so effective and powerful have modern institutions and organisations become that they presently dominate the modern world. One prominent account (Rugman, 2000) of globalisation describes it largely in terms of the increased power and reach of multinational corporations. The power of capital relative to that of other institutions, such as nation states and organised labour, has increased immensely.

Before we consider the impact of globalisation, however, we should try and define it. *Globalisation* is characterised by a huge increase in the world's wealth, achieved by capital reproducing itself through investment (Reich, 1991). Much of this consists of foreign direct investment, with multinational corporations and investment funds seizing opportunities for profit across the world. This creation of wealth has been driven by the essential feature of globalisation: the new-found mobility of capital, labour, and information. It is primarily information technology that has made such mobility possible. And it is the mobility of capital, in the form of financial instruments, investment capital, and currency speculation, which creates not only opportunities for wealth creation, but also uncertainty for national economies and corporations. Indeed, even the global economy itself can feel threatened by capital flows.

The centrality of *information technology* to the process of globalisation cannot be exaggerated (Castells, 1996). It is pervasive because every organisational activity involves the use of information. Moreover, information technology permits the action of knowledge on other knowledge, creating a dynamic in favour of innovation. 'What has changed', argues Castells (1996, p. 92) 'is not the kind of activities humankind is engaged on, but its technological ability to use as a direct productive force what distinguishes our species as a biological oddity: its superior capacity to process symbols'.

The global reach of capital, enabled by information technology, has bypassed nation states, which in early modernity were the most powerful institutions of the modern world (Ohmae, 1995). Investors can profoundly impact a national economy by removing their investment to another location that offers cheaper labour, less protection for labour, higher subsidies, and lower taxes. The power of the nation state has consequently been eroded. So has its legitimacy in the eyes of its citizens as the provider of social protection in fulfilment of the social contract between government and governed. National politics and politicians are discredited. Meanwhile, supranational organisations with an agenda of trade liberalisation, such as the World Trade Organization, succeed in influencing or even controlling national economic policies.

However, the notion that globalisation is by now all but complete is mistaken. The supposed triumph of political democracy and liberal economics has not resulted in 'the end of history', as Fukuyama (1992) predicted. Many governments protect their economies by tariffs on imports and by subsidies. These governments are not only those of poor nations being forced to liberalise. On the contrary, the rich nations, which are most vociferous in urging liberalisation on others, protect their own industries such as steel and agriculture (Greider, 1997). Moreover, groups of rapidly developing nations, such as Brazil, India, and China are organising themselves to resist what they perceive to be the imposition of a Western capitalist model in cultures and economies where it is inappropriate.

## *Mediated experience*

Capital's power and reach has expanded to the extent that the world is apparently becoming a global market. However, this expansion is balanced by a new emphasis on the local. As corporations and other institutions strive for competitive advantage in the global market place, they realise that unique features make certain regions or localities attractive to capital investment. Silicon Valley was the ideal cultural setting for the initial development of the information technology industry, while Bangalore currently provides a growing hub for the development of technological services.

This contrast between the global and the local is also exemplified in the *global media*. Ownership of the global media is concentrated in a relatively few giant media organisations, with the consequence that their products such as film, music, video, and news bulletins, which are often American in origin, are available world-wide. The possibility of a global mediated culture appears real (Robertson, 1992). Media products are marketed to a diverse and highly segmented market, and the opportunity to choose from among a customised portfolio of products is presented, giving the appearance of almost infinite choice. One of the consequences of this globalised marketing of media products is the blurring of distinctions between such modes of communication as information and entertainment; drama documentaries and 'reality' TV are examples.

However, local media outlets, such as talk radio, also flourish, expressing levels of populist discourse that national and international cultural elites would not countenance. Furthermore, the interactive nature of media such as the internet, together with their global reach, ensure that the big media corporations do not control their use and content, although they may be censored by certain governments (e.g. China). Virtual internet communities across national boundaries may develop, but they are usually ephemeral in nature, and there is no assurance that participants are who they say they are. Indeed, media experience for many consists of a world of make-believe. As Castells (1996, p. 373) puts it 'appearances are not just on the screen through which experience is communicated, but they become the experience': real virtuality rather than virtual reality.

If they are to prosper in the globalised world, institutions have to engage with the global media. They have to compete with other commodified products, such as entertainment, pornography, and sport, for consumers' attention. In their efforts to do so, they run the risk of changing their nature. Religion and politics, for example, can easily become entertainment. The public domain now reveals the private and personalised; the distinction between 'backstage' and 'frontstage' becomes ever more difficult to maintain for anyone in the public eye. Social and cultural distinctions become blurred, as when middle-class British television presenters give the illusion of being 'one of the people' by affecting mock cockney (working-class London) accents.

## *The global corporation*

Meanwhile the *corporations* at the cutting edge of globalisation have changed radically in recent years in their structure and in their organisation of work processes. In contrast with the machine-like bureaucracies typical of early modernity, with their predictability, functional divisional structures, and multiple levels of accountability, many late modern organisations are becoming hollowed out structures (Clarke & Clegg, 1998). At the top are senior managers and professionals, who are often global travellers on behalf of their employers. At the bottom are groups of employees engaged in those tasks that are not (yet) automated, such as call-centre staff or fast-food providers. These groups are often on temporary contracts, or work for a sub-contractor. Their employment often depends upon the retention of contracts, and they suffer from a chronic lack of employment protection.

The upper level of employees has seen its real income increase rapidly in the last decade or two, whereas the lower has frequently been rewarded at a rate little above the minimum legal wage (if one has been set). Undoubted increases in productivity have not resulted in major increases in wages for the mass of employees in the richer nations. Inequalities of wealth within late-modern societies have increased as a consequence, as has the social segregation of the wealthy from the rest in terms of location and lifestyle. Yet even the higher-level employees suffer from increased employment uncertainty. Corporate takeovers and mergers are more frequent, and the pressure to deliver shareholder value in the short term makes cutting costs by means of redundancies an attractive strategic option.

Rather than the traditional hierarchy, with its promotional structure and single lines of accountability, late-modern multinational organisations are becoming *temporary networks* of individual employees. Employees frequently associate virtually more than they do face-to-face, and it is the flow of information that determines the identity and nature of relationships between employees. Their work is often organised around projects, rather than jobs, with the consequence that relationships with colleagues, and indeed, the employment relationship itself, are temporary (Herriot, 2001).

Because of their increased power relative to that of labour and of the professions, both public and private sector organisations are able to demand more from their rank-and-file employees (Noon & Blyton, 1997). Many of them can wield the threat of re-locating the work to a country where wages are lower; others simply affirm that they will fail to survive unless they increase productivity and cut costs. As the work of their managers and professionals is of high value to organisations, and because they reward these employees handsomely, they feel able to demand ever more from them too. They want them to take initiatives and to seek responsibility. And as the work of their lower level employees often involves interaction with customers, they come to expect these people, usually women, to invest their selves fully in 'emotional labour' (Hochschild, 1983). 'Have a good day' is simply not good enough today. You have to really empathise with the customer.

Thus the recent increase in the pace of the modernisation process, which we term globalisation, is pervasive. It adds to the impetus of those various trends which were set in motion in early modernity:

- The power of capital is enhanced, but now at the expense of the nation state.
- Wealth is increased, but distributed unevenly within and between nations.
- The marketing of commoditised goods and services is ever more pervasive, as it spreads globally.
- Organisations and institutions are changing even more rapidly so as to meet the new global challenges that face them.
- The media are more available, and more and more of everyday experience is mediated rather than direct.

In sum, globalisation is the ultimate acceleration of the process of modernisation. All of these accelerated trends are reflected both in *cultural perspectives* and in *individual selves*.

## The modernisation of culture and world-view

### Humankind the master of its fate?

The relationship between institutional and cultural aspects of modernisation is just one more version of the chicken-and-egg dilemma. New ways of acting upon the natural and social worlds both depended upon, and also created, new ways of thinking about them. The continuing empirical discovery of causal relationships between means and ends naturally results in a preference for natural rather than supernatural explanations for events. If one believed that outcomes are determined by God, then the only way to achieve one's objectives would be to pray in an effort to influence the Almighty. Given that rational efforts to achieve objectives appeared to work better than praying for them, the idea became popular that humankind, not God, was in charge of its own destiny.

Once again, we may attribute some of this change in world-view, at least in Europe, to the Reformation. For that great religious and cultural transformation demythologised the everyday life of medieval people, inhabited as it was by a whole range of saints and other spiritual beings, such as angels and demons. Instead, the Reformation located the one true God outside the everyday world, His people's spiritual King enthroned in heavenly splendour. This theological distancing left believers free to investigate and seek to control the natural and social worlds (while still acknowledging the existence of the Almighty, their creator).

The control exercised by means of technological and organisational systems and processes enabled modern people to escape many of the dangers that had afflicted their medieval ancestors. For example, many diseases were no longer a threat, and the growth of the insurance industry permitted financial risk to be controlled. As a result of the taken-for-granted management of everyday life, what remains as essentially uncontrollable becomes a fearful threat (Giddens, 1991). Natural disasters are today the stuff of nightmare, whilst the apparently uncontrollable vagaries of the market create job insecurity and fears for one's social status.

Globalisation has rendered these fears yet more acute. Ever larger and more impersonal forces appear to hold our futures in their hands, and the scale of potential disaster feeds apocalyptic imaginations. The world financial system could collapse; terrorists could destroy whole populations; ecological catastrophe could strike at our very survival as a species.

### Cultural diversity

Another characteristic of modernisation is its *physical and social mobility*. People increasingly move geographically within and between nations, and, until recently in late-modern societies, up and down the social status hierarchy. This results in increased social contact between people of different cultures or sub-cultures and beliefs. At first, people find it hard to believe that there could be other cultures so different from their own. Soon, however, cultural diversity leads to pluralism, the recognition that no-one has a monopoly of the truth, and that different cultures or sub-cultures are, and have a right to be, different from one's own. Consequently, it becomes very hard to continue to maintain that one's own beliefs, values, and practices are the only correct ones. Indeed, it is then only a fairly short step to complete relativism: the refusal to recognise any belief system as preferable to any other.

One consequence of such cultural diversity within any national culture is the sharp *distinction between the public and the private spheres* typical of modern nation states. Religion in late-modern societies has largely, but not entirely, been relocated into the private sphere, the personal choice of each individual citizen. For no particular religion can claim dominance in a multi-cultural society. Instead, one's religion, if one has one, becomes part of sub-cultural experience as a member of a synagogue, temple, mosque, or church, or of a sect or cult. Such sub-cultural experience is separate from the state. Alternatively, religion loses any social anchor at all, and becomes yet another commodity for personal and private consumption only. Individuals can act in their customary modern role as consumer, picking and mixing from among the spiritual products on the market and enjoying them in the privacy of their own homes (Roof, 1999).

### The world as a market

The recent extended power and reach of capital across the world has created a new world-view: *the world as a market*. Every product and service, every experience and relationship, can be packaged as a commodity for consumption (at a price). Our use of language reveals the extent of this commodification. We speak of spending, and saving time, of having sex, of getting work, of the market for spirituality, and so on. The view of the world as consisting of billions of potential individual customers/consumers clearly enhances the importance of individualism at the expense of community. Backed by the power of capital, it over-powers such alternative views of the world as a planet or as a global society.

Clearly, the organisational practice of segmented marketing creates subsets of consumers. It is the marketers who determine the portfolio of offers from which individuals can 'choose'. Their social status, geographical location, or spending power determines what is on offer. Consumers can be persuaded that the purchase meets their needs, or indeed, that they thoroughly deserve the reward it brings. But the main driver is the promise of gratification. It is the pleasure principle rather than any social obligation or moral imperative that motivates consumption (Bauman, 1987).

However, the gratification may not be direct sensual pleasure. Increasingly, consumers are targeted in terms of the symbolic value of the commodity in question. The challenge to the marketer is to persuade consumers to imagine themselves as different people. It is what their possession of the commodity in question says about them as individuals which matters to them. How, they ask, will it differentiate me from others and make me unique? How will it enable me to be recognised by others as a unique person, with real personality and status? How will it help me to feel good about myself? It is all in aid of the construction of the self. Many commodities in the late-modern era are thus cultural goods that constitute a lifestyle (Lasch, 1985).

### Threats to patriarchy

A final cultural feature of the process of modernisation is the increasing threat it presents to patriarchy. In early modernity, the recognition of the ideal of human rights and dignity extending to all challenged the subordinate status of women. Many modernising nations passed legislation granting women the right to vote, to work, to earn the going rate for the job, and so on. However, continued failure in many societies either to pass, or else to properly enforce, such legislation, together with an appreciation that women were often abused and exploited in other ways too, led to a sense of community and shared identity among women.

Women started to challenge the patriarchal institutions and values that characterised early modernity, and many of them celebrated what they perceived as their uniquely female identity. A set of alternative cultural values were promoted, in which masculine emphases on power, competition, and hierarchy were replaced by solidarity, co-operation, and non-violence. Various sub-identities were also assumed by some, particularly in late-modern societies, such as lesbian woman, black woman, or black lesbian woman. However, many women all over the world are still fighting for basic rights and respect without necessarily having developed a feminist consciousness.

Women were not the only threat to the traditional patriarchal family and culture. Other people who felt themselves to be unfairly treated in terms of the proclaimed values of modern societies also joined together to fight for their rights as equal citizens. The most notable group in terms of its threat to patriarchy is gays and lesbians. Like feminists, they too established a distinct social identity, and celebrated it in ways that enhanced their self-esteem and their visibility and legitimacy. Like feminists, they presented a threat to traditional gender and family roles. These roles clearly depend for their continuance on the assumption of heterosexuality, for homosexuality threatens the very categories of man and woman, let alone those of husband and wife, or father and mother.

The development of feminist and sexual identities derives from the late-modern emphasis on the creation of the self by the individual, which we consider shortly. However, these identities are not solely individual. Rather, they are oppositional *social* identities. They constitute membership of a perceived category of people opposed to traditional patriarchal society. And, even in late modernity, patriarchy still retains much of its power.

## Modernisation and the reflexive self

### From inherited to personal self

The same capacity for self-examination and change that characterises modern institutions and cultures is also typical of modern individuals. Modernisation has resulted in *the reflexive self*. Instead of simply assuming the position and roles in society decreed by a fixed traditional structure, modern people see their selves as capable of change and development. They use their selves as working mental models, which constantly regulate and adapt to the interactions they have with others (Baumeister, 1999). Selves, in other words, direct people's social behaviour, and are in turn shaped by it. Moreover, people believe that they themselves can effect personal change. Instead of being inherited as a set of given social identities (e.g. peasant, villager, carpenter), the emphasis is on the self as under the control of its individual 'owner', and indeed, to a considerable extent, as their own creation.

However, it is only part of the picture to see the reflexive self as the outcome and expression of modernisation. We must also recognise that the new modern self is in dynamic relationship with that process. People construct modernisation as well as being constructed by it. They can now create not only their selves, but also the changing world of which that self is a part.

The self, together with the social identities it incorporates, is a central theoretical idea in this book. The self of the fundamentalist is in dynamic relationship with each of the different levels of analysis: the late-modern world, national cultures, religious movements, religious organisations, and religious groups. All these social constructs both create, and are created by, the self.

The historic transition from fixed and inherited selves to changing and personal ones was not easy. The first great movements from country to city, from agriculture to manufacture, famously resulted (and still result) in *alienation and anomie*, defined as 'a crisis in the moral order of a social group resulting in the inability of the group to provide order and normative regulation for individual members' (McGuire, 2002, p. 335). The anchors of time and place, of family and ritual, were lost, and there was little to put in their place. Traditional rural life was all of a piece; you were essentially the same person whatever you were doing. And what you did depended predictably on the recurring seasons of the year. Urban living and factory jobs, however, created a dislocation between work and home. Different roles played out in different settings, each with their own values and norms of behaviour, often resulted in 'the divided self' and the loss of social identity and support.

Gradually, during early modernity, the idea of a *personal*, as opposed to a *social*, identity gained currency. Ordinary individuals started to consider themselves to be unique, and, later still, to have chosen their own uniqueness. Social identity, by way of contrast, refers to the belief that one belongs to this or that category of persons (Turner, 1985). This idea of choosing who you are soon led to the high value placed on personal authenticity. In order to be authentic, you have to have chosen who you are yourself, rather than have others choose for you.

The modern commercial emphasis on the marketing of products and experiences as commodities catered for this desire for choice. The providers of commodities – whether fashion items and automobiles, holidays and therapies, or political loyalties and religious experiences – can offer a wide range of alternatives (Rifkin, 2000). Indeed, segmented marketing has resulted in the tailoring of products and services to suit the individual consumer's wants. However, commodification is also limiting, in the sense that it is the providers who determine the range of choices and how they are packaged. Such commodification is based ultimately, of course, on their need to make a profit.

The same motive requires them, in an age of over-production, to create demand for new products and services that people did not realise that they 'needed'.

Thus, even in wealthy countries, the opportunities to design and develop one's self may be more illusory than real. To define oneself in terms of products and experiences, or 'lifestyle', may result in dissatisfaction, particularly as the marketing of commodities requires a continuous replacement of one satisfied 'need' with a new unsatisfied one. Even therapies, designed as they are to enable one to directly manage or change one's self, outdo each other in their claims of yet more profound insight or personal development (Rieff, 1966). This use of commoditised products or services to constitute the self omits any personal or societal moral obligation. It ignores the possibility of a bigger picture. On the contrary, it tends towards narcissism, the obsession with creating one's self and with getting assurance from others of the beauty of one's own creation (Lasch, 1980).

In reaction against such a context, the opportunity is clearly present for the return of the *grand narrative*. Anyone who offers a convincing and all-embracing story that accounts for one's life and one's position in society and in history can offer competition to the 'pick and mix' consumerist culture. Obedience to a single authority can relieve one of the burden of choice. Enter stage right, among other actors, *fundamentalism*.

### Temporary relationships

The mobility and transience of people and jobs, which has characterised modernisation throughout its history and which has increased further in the period of globalisation, has also had profound effects on the self. I remarked above how it led to pluralist societies and relativist world views. However, it also had an impact upon social relationships. Many relationships that used to be more permanent are now transitory passages with employers and work colleagues, spouses or partners, and institutions and localities. We exchange each one of these 'items' for the next with increasing frequency and decreasing regret. The institutions of civic society that used to provide social glue are in decline (Puttnam, 2000).

Mobility and the decline of social institutions in a 'civil society' have thus combined to destabilise relationships and hence increase individuals' dependence on themselves. They now need to present themselves in such a way as to form new relationships quickly. In both senses of the word, they are under pressure to 'perform' socially and at work. The presentation of self thus becomes a dominant task (Goffman, 1959, 1971). Instead of developing the traits of *character*, such as persistence and reliability, which are required to sustain longer-term relationships, the late-modern emphasis is on *personality* and the making of a sufficient impression to initiate a relationship (Sennett, 1998).

In late modernity, relationships are no longer determined so much by family, locality, or social obligation. Rather, many of them are 'pure relation-ships', that is, ones which 'exist solely for whatever rewards that relationship as such can deliver' (Giddens, 1991, p. 6). Instead of confidence in the reliabil-ity of established social ties, much late-modern social life generates anxiety about one's capacity to be acceptable to others.

This transitory nature of relationships, and of experience in general, has another effect. It diminishes the probability of being able to construct a convincing identity for oneself in terms of the life-cycle. When family and employment relationships followed a predictable course, everyone could tell the story of their lives in terms of a sequence of roles played out in turn, often in the same place and marked by rites of passage. At work one followed a career path through a structure, and at home one played a sequence of generationally determined roles.

Today, however, traditional marriage is a less successful institution, and responsible (or irresponsible) parenthood may extend well into middle age. Working lives no longer consist of a period of continuous employment until retirement, and old age provides a multitude of alternative scenarios. Thus, individuals can create their own life story by making some sense out of what may be a fairly disjointed sequence of experiences. If they have failed to achieve success in material terms, they may well blame themselves, maintain-ing an internal locus of control that mirrors their society's belief that success is the result of one's own effort. Or they may create a brilliantly successful project out of their lives, mastering their social environment by choosing and controlling their relationships. However, either way they are less likely to fall back on a template based on traditional life-cycles.

Thus, the search for a unique and satisfying personal identity, which has characterised the late-modern world, has proved frustrating for many. Their narrative is often fragmented and incoherent, a pastiche of fashions and trends, of meetings and partings. Such narratives mirror the extraordinary rate of change in the world. They are a far cry indeed from the orderly story of a predictable life-cycle, typical of bygone eras.

### Injustice and the self

However, there are other parts of the world, less studied and theorised by sociologists, which have not reached late modernity. These societies are the victims of the inequality generated by globalisation, which does indeed have its 'discontents' (Stiglitz, 2002). They are joined by those within late-modern societies who themselves have individually suffered from inequality. Gross and increasing personal and national inequality results in feelings of injustice, and such feelings have profound effects upon the self.

The most obvious form of injustice is *distributive* injustice: the unfair allo-cation of wealth and resources. Their disproportionate share of these goods gives rich nations power to control the process of allocation. This process is anything but fair and transparent; many as a result feel *processual* injustice.

In particular, the perceived failure of rich Western nations to abide by the same rules that they seek to impose on others grates on the sensibilities of other nations and cultures. Specific examples are rich nations' retention of protectionist trade policies, and their development of their own military capability while seeking to control that of others. Finally, when national and personal worth is gauged on the basis of economic, political, and military power, poorer societies and individuals perceive *interactional* injustice; they are treated without respect (Folger & Cropanzano, 1998).

The impacts of perceived injustice on the self are profound. Facing the threat of low self-esteem and decreased status, many poorer societies and individuals now define themselves by their hostility to their more powerful rivals, whom they characterise as oppressors. They create alternative selves, based upon traditional social identities of race and religion. And they become very angry.

Thus, in both early-modern and late-modern societies, social identities derived from resistance to perceived injustice have been developed. The resistance movements from which these identities are derived are both the product of modernity and, at the same time, are reacting against certain features of it. They are modern products in the sense that they are derived from the modern cultural assumption of the human right to justice. However, they are reacting against its failures to live up to its manifesto. They have set the cultural climate for oppositional social movements buttressed by powerful social identities. *Such a climate is clearly conducive to the development of fundamentalism, characterised as it is by profound reactivity and dualism.*

## Modernisation and fundamentalism

### *Modernisation as fundamentalism's opportunity*

So why are fundamentalists so hostile to certain aspects of modernisation whilst at the same time embracing other of its features as golden opportunities? Has the ever-increasing pace of modernisation resulted in less demand for traditional religion, and indeed, as they argue, threatened its very existence? Is all that is left New Age spiritual gifts on offer in the market for lifestyle commodities? Or, on the contrary, has modernisation created greater psychological and spiritual needs, which the fundamentalist brand of traditional religion can claim to meet? Its current success relative to more mainstream forms of religion certainly requires explanation.

In the sociological study of religion, these questions have often been presented as mutually exclusive alternatives. One side argues that the process of modernisation leads inevitably to secularism, which is irretrievably reducing traditional religious affiliation, as modern people no longer feel the need for supernatural explanations (Bruce, 2002). There is highly convincing evidence that this generalisation is correct, for *in general* traditional religious observance is highest in agrarian societies, lower in industrial ones, and lower still in post-industrial ones (Norris & Inglehart, 2004, p.57). Thus, fundamentalists are justified in being hostile to aspects of modernity as threatening their faith. The fall of traditional religion is the cue for the rise of fundamentalisms in its defence.

The second theoretical position, increasingly popular in the last decade, argues against the onward march of secularism. It proposes that the need for religion remains constant, but the effectiveness of its provision varies enormously. The growth of fundamentalism is due to the fact that fundamentalists happen to be particularly effective providers (Stark & Finke, 2000). America, for example, although a post-industrial nation, is one of the most religious nations in the world. The reason is its free and varied market in religious provision.

In economic jargon, the dispute is about whether demand or supply is the driver. However, as McGuire (2002) convincingly argues, this is a false antithesis, arising from the praiseworthy academic desire to set up alternative theories in order to test them against each other. It is likely to be more fruitful to concentrate upon the central definitive feature of fundamentalism, *its reactionary and oppositional nature*. Then we may seek to disentangle those elements of modernisation that form a useful context for the growth of fundamentalism from those against which it is reacting. In most cases, as I will argue, the existence of something to react against provides both the opportunity and the opposition. In other words, modernisation's real threat to traditional religion is at the same time fundamentalism's motive force and, indeed, its very reason for existing.

The first and most obvious early modern development is the *alienation and anomie* resulting from the migration from country to town, from agriculture to manufacture. The removal of the cultural props of family, religion, and social identity left a gaping void, famously filled historically by communism or other forms of political association. The need of the alienated for a substitute belief system, together with their social need for affiliation, presents fundamentalists with a major opportunity. Their clear and simple doctrines and warm welcome give them a head start in meeting such needs. It is no accident that converts in the newly industrialising nations are more frequently fundamentalist.

However, many in late-modern societies experience a similar feeling of being uprooted. This arises not only from the physical re-locations in their employment, but also from their social mobility as they form and exit from relationships. In such a social situation, one is likely to suffer anxieties about one's acceptability to others on the basis of one's personality and social skills. This can be assuaged by membership of a group that accepts one on the basis of membership alone. Of course, membership has its costs, but at least anxiety is reduced.

Another source of anxiety concerns *risk*. If the risks of late-modern life become ever bigger and more uncontrollable, then one solution is to

reconstrue them as acts of God, sent to punish this perverse and evil generation. The benefit of such a fundamentalist construction is that the believer
escapes this retribution. He or she can be safely raptured from the earth
before catastrophe occurs (Boyer, 1992) or received into heaven as a martyr,
having made real his or her apocalyptic imaginations (Wheatcroft, 2004).

In late-modern society, the failure of *consumerism* to bring lasting satisfac-
tion, together with its lack of any moral anchor or social affiliation, renders
the creation of a coherent self very difficult. Further, the late-modern task
of building one's identity from a huge range of possible choices, creates a
similar anxiety about bringing everything together. What better than to be
presented with a life story based on a simple account of one's relationship
with God, together with a clear view of one's place in the world and in the
broad sweep of history? It must be a huge relief to hand over responsibility
to an authority who comes up with unequivocal answers to one's questions
regarding who one is, what to believe and value, and how to behave (Tamney,
2002).

Fundamentalism provides not just a clear and simple *meaning system*,
however; it can also meet the needs of those whose *self-esteem* is low. Those
who perceive themselves to be unjustly treated and suffer from a lack of
respect are frequently casualties of the headlong rush of modernisation. They
may live in nations or whole ethnic/religious cultures that feel patronised or
threatened by nations richer and more powerful than themselves. Or they may
be members of late-modern societies who are the victims of organisational
restructure. Even if they have retained a job, those in the middle ranges of
occupational incomes in the USA, for example, have seen their real income
increase moderately if at all, whilst the rich have become very much richer
(Greider, 1997). If one blames oneself for this 'failure', one loses one's
self-esteem. And if one blames others, the search for a scapegoat can be
made easy.

In both cases, fundamentalism can provide an answer. The Other, whoever
or whatever it may be, can serve as a scapegoat. And self-esteem can recover
if one's identity becomes that of a servant of God who will one day rule with
Him, or a soldier of Allah who will be honoured in heaven as a martyr.
Indeed, the very fact of being distinctively different from the Other strengthens one's identity and therefore one's self-esteem (Turner, 1985). Add to these
benefits the more mundane blessing of becoming a welcomed and valued
member of a tightly knit group, and it is clear that low self-esteem is easily
boosted by fundamentalism.

The opportunities for fundamentalism presented by the process of modernisation do not occur only at the level of *the self*. They also embrace the
*institutional* level of change. The large-scale mobility of labour characteristic
of globalisation helps fundamentalism break out of the boundaries of its
local origins. The richer nations of the West, for example, have received many
immigrants from North Africa and the Middle East, not a few of whom are
fundamentalist Muslims. The global reach of some fundamentalist media

messages, such as the latest tape from Osama bin Laden, has its local counterpoint in the folksy gospel channels and chat shows on American radio. And the openness and ubiquity of the internet make it possible to create virtual networks of like-minded believers.

However, it is modern *organisational sophistication* that provides the most important vehicle for fundamentalism. Fundamentalist movements solicit donations from both wealthy benefactors and humble members. They also demonstrate sophisticated public-relations and lobbying skills. Both their fundraising and their public-relations activities indicate fundamentalists' skills in using that iconic product of modernity, management and organisation. For example, the Institute on Religion and Democracy is a fundamentalist lobbying and pressure group operating from Washington DC, busily trying to gain control of the few liberal Protestant denominations that survive in America (see pp. 53–55); and al-Qaida, as the following case study will demonstrate, is a sophisticated late-modern organisation.

### Modernisation as fundamentalism's opposition

Many features of modernity, then, provide a fertile soil for fundamentalism. Some of these features are actually welcomed, or at the very least ignored, by fundamentalists. Others, however, become the source for many examples of the Other (i.e. whichever out-group currently differs from, and yet defines, fundamentalists). Most of these are at the *cultural/world-view* level of analysis.

The most profound feature of the modern view of the world has been to *put humankind rather than God at its centre*. Humankind is responsible for its fate, and natural and human explanations for events have replaced supernatural and divine ones. Moreover, the institutions of society, including law and government, are understood to have been created by human beings. It is this feature of the modern world-view which fundamentalists challenge the most.

However, except in the writings of radical Calvinist theologians (see Chapter 7), or the Muslim cleric Sayeed Qutb (see Chapter 6), one seldom finds the enemy defined in such abstract terms. True, 'secular humanism' has sometimes been targeted, but usually the Other has been a more concrete foe. The key to understanding their specific choice of opponent is the fundamentalists' selective emphasis on the holy book as the word of God. For fundamentalists are, as Ralph Hood and colleagues assert (Hood, Hill, & Williamson, 2005), *intra-textual* in their belief systems. That is, they believe that all that they need to know is to be found in their holy book or books, and that all other claims to knowledge are to be judged in terms of their compatibility with its contents.

Hence, *cultural pluralism* and its frequent consequence, *moral relativity*, are anathema to fundamentalists. They are necessarily *particularists*, that is, they believe that there is only one true faith, their own, since God has revealed it to them in His holy Word. His laws and commandments are clearly stated and binding, and therefore the modern separation between church and state, and the relegation of religion into the private sphere, is an affront to God's majesty. On the contrary, they believe, theocracy and obedience to God's law are the ideals towards which they should strive.

Given the centrality of God's law as revealed in the holy book in fundamentalists' belief systems, it is hardly surprising that *feminists and gays* are among their favourite out-groups. The Qu'ran, Torah, and Bible were of course written by members of patriarchal societies, at a time when any threat to male authority was not tolerated. If the holy books, written in pre-modern times, are taken as inerrant expressions of God's law, then a supernatural world-view with a patriarchal God as its ruler will necessarily follow. Whilst feminists and gays are holding modernity to its prospectus, fundamentalists are re-affirming God the Father's eternal patriarchal verities.

The same internal consistency within fundamentalist belief, given its basic assumptions, lies behind the choice of others of their enemies. Fundamentalists have sometimes targeted *the state*, since it fails fully to embrace God's law. In America, the hostility is towards the Federal government rather than the nation as such (Durham, 2000), whereas in Arab countries and in Israel, fundamentalists seek to overthrow or eject secular governments and replace them with theocracies. In America, supra-governmental entities have also been cast as the enemy, but only in the shadowy and conspiratorial forms of the New World Order or the Evil Empire.

Thus fundamentalists' holy book contains God's laws, which promulgate enough prohibitions to enable them to select from a wide variety of out-groups whom they can accuse of breaking them. It is an important theoretical issue whether belief in the holy book is the motivator for their reactive opposition to aspects of modernity, or whether it merely focuses their opposition on certain specific targets. Either way, perceived threat to the true faith creates the fear and the anger that characterise fundamentalist movements, and are used by their leaders to motivate action.

I will argue later that fundamentalists define themselves as opponents of these perceived threats, and consequently gain their social identity and self-worth from their fundamentalist allegiance. I will also maintain that the nature of the Other varies, depending upon the main strategic purpose of the fundamentalist leadership. That purpose may be to *mobilise the faithful* to take action against specific groups or institutions. The out-group will then, for Christian fundamentalists, consist of gays or feminists or liberal churches, for example. For Islamic fundamentalists, America the Great Satan may be selected as the out-group, or women who fail to dress strictly according to *sharia* law. For some, but not all, Jewish fundamentalists, Palestinians are the enemy.

Alternatively, the strategic purpose of fundamentalist leadership may be *to emphasise the oppositional nature* of the fundamentalist movement. The greater and more inclusive is the foe, the more exclusive and heroic is the movement, and the more powerful and rewarding the social identity that results from membership becomes. In the case of certain Christian and Muslim fundamentalisms, the enemy has sometimes appeared to be the whole of the rest of the world other than themselves.

So, to conclude, the picture of fundamentalism in its global context of modernisation is a complex one. Fundamentalist Islam's claims to fear for its future at the hands of its secular enemies are understandable in the present geopolitical environment. However, it is not the survival of their institutions and organisations so much as the threat to their world-view that motivates fundamentalists everywhere. They appear to ignore the fact that many of those features of modernity that they themselves embrace, actually underpin modern world-views. For example, their perception of a need for a scientific argument to support the Biblical account of creation undermines the supernatural world-view that they maintain. *We may infer that it is difficult for modern people to hold a consistently pre-modern world-view, but that the fundamentalists' attempt to do so is an outcome of modernity itself. And we must acknowledge the power of this attempt, providing as it does a unique world-view, boosted by powerful authority, and a detailed rule for life and conduct, God's law.*

## Summary

- The modernising world forms both a context for, and an object of, fundamentalist opposition.
- Modernisation is an ongoing process of ever-increasing pace, which has reached different stages in different parts of the world. Its most recent phase is globalisation.
- Modernisation may be analysed at three levels: institutional and technical, cultural and world-view, and the self.
- At the *institutional level* of analysis, early modernity was characterised by rationalisation and organisation. However, the nature of work and organisation has recently changed radically in the face of change in the global environment.
- At the *cultural level*, early modernity permitted people to think that they were masters of their own fate.
- Mobility led to a greater diversity of populations, resulting in pluralism and moral relativity.
- The increasing power of capitalism led to a consumerist market morality, in which individualism triumphed over community.
- Finally, individual rights for minorities threatened the patriarchal family.
- At the *level of the self*, inherited social roles were displaced by a personal self, which could be created by its owner.
- The building blocks for the personal self were often lifestyle commodities, which created new needs to satisfy.

- Relationships became more temporary as institutions and organisations changed. Anxiety increased.
- Societies that were less far along the modernisation path, and individuals within late-modern societies who were relatively poor, felt unjustly treated.
- Thus modernisation promised control but, for many, produced anxiety and anger.
- Is modernisation an opportunity or a threat to fundamentalism? For fundamentalists, modernisation is overwhelmingly an opportunity.
- First, it increases the needs that fundamentalism can meet. Anomie, anxiety, dissatisfaction with consumerism, low self-esteem, and feelings of injustice are for many people the outcomes of modernisation. By means of its grand narrative, fundamentalism can help to meet some of these needs.
- Second, modernisation, or at least some features of it, presents an ideal enemy, a 'them' against whom to define an 'us'.
- The Enlightenment notion that humankind is responsible for its own institutions, and the recognition that in a pluralist society there are different but valid points of view, are clear ideological enemies for fundamentalism.
- But modernisation works itself out in more concrete ways, for example, in the development of minority movements. These form ideal enemies.

## Further reading

Bauman, Z. (1992) *Intimations of Postmodernity*. London: Routledge.

Bruce, S. (2002) *God is Dead: Secularisation in the West*. Oxford: Blackwell.

Castells, M. (1996) *The Rise of the Network Society*. Oxford: Blackwell.

Giddens, A. (1991) *Modernity and Self-Identity: Self and Society in the Late Modern Age*. Cambridge: Polity Press.

Greider, W. (1997) *One World, Ready or Not: The Manic Logic of Global Capitalism*. London: Penguin.

McGuire, M.B. (2002) *Religion: The Social Context* (5th edn.) Belmont, CA: Wadsworth.

Puttnam, R.D. (2000) *Bowling Alone*. New York: Simon & Schuster.

Reich, R. (1991) *The World of Nations*. New York: Random House.

Robertson, R. (1992) *Globalisation: Social Theory and Global Culture*. London: Sage.

Sennett, R. (1998) *The Corrosion of Character: The Personal Consequences of Work in the New Capitalism*. New York: Norton.

Stark, R. & Finke, R. (2000) *Acts of Faith: Explaining the Human Side of Religion*. Berkeley: University of California Press.

Stiglitz, J. (2002) *Globalisation and its Discontents*. London: Penguin.

## CASE STUDY: AL-QAIDA: A GLOBAL FUNDAMENTALIST MOVEMENT

*This case study illustrates several key features of the previous theoretical account. First, al-Qaida clearly sees the products of modernity, such as nationhood, religious pluralism, and secular social institutions, as threats. However, it also considers some of the outcomes of modernity, and especially of globalisation, as an opportunity. For example, widespread perceptions of injustice permit al-Qaida to present itself as the champion of the oppressed. Moreover, the movement has the opportunity, presented by globalised media, of organising and communicating at the global level. Such an ambitious scope presents al-Qaida with two dilemmas typical of global organisations: how to maintain control while adapting to local circumstances; and how to outsmart rival organisations at the geopolitical level.*

### Religious and fundamentalist

Al-Qaida is perhaps the best-known current example of a fundamentalist religious organisation (Kepel, 2006; Wright, 2006). Al-Qaida perfectly illustrates the fundamentalist paradox: on 9/11 it assaulted the iconic symbols of globalisation whilst itself developing as a global organisation (Juergensmeyer, 2005). The reason al-Qaida is so well known is that it was unique among Islamic jihadi movements in treating the USA and its allies as its primary target, rather than specific secular governments in Muslim

Ayman al-Zawahiri                    © Corbis Sygma

nations. It is thus primarily global in its geopolitical reach, rather than local (Gerges, 2005).

The above description of al-Qaida as a fundamentalist religious organisation is certainly controversial. Is it really at heart a religious movement, or is it more a political or criminal conspiracy? Is it part of a fundamentalist sect derived from mainstream Islam, or is it merely using religious language to legitimise its activities? And can it justifiably be called an organisation, or is it largely a media creation? Perhaps it is just a revolutionary brand created by that world celebrity, Osama bin Laden, and given credence by the response of the West? The answers to these questions reveal al-Qaida's late-modern organisational structure, but at the same time its pre-modern assumptions and beliefs.

*The basic motivation of al-Qaida is religious.* The fact that its immediate objectives are political does not argue against this assertion. Indeed, it is the close relationship between Islamic doctrine and political objectives that distinguishes fundamentalist Islam in particular from mainstream Muslim, Jewish, and Christian faiths (Armstrong, 2000b). The principle of *tawhid* affirms the absolute unity of God, so that there is no distinction between faith and doctrine, adherence to *sharia* law, and the implementation of conservative social and political principles. Belief and practice at both individual and communal levels are one. Fundamentalist Islam is therefore an all-embracing religious, political, and social system (Blanchard, 2006).

Bin Laden and his associates have regularly repeated their statements of religious doctrine. These have changed relatively little in their tone and content since his startling revolutionary announcement in 1996 of a defensive jihad against the USA, whom he accused of an attack upon Islam. In particular, he alleged, the Americans had desecrated the two most holy places of Islam by stationing their troops in Saudi Arabia (bin Laden, 1996). This announcement of jihad against America was a radical change of focus, and met with the disapproval of the majority of jihadis, who had treated their own secular or nominally Muslim governments as the real enemy (Gerges, 2005). However, subsequently, there has been a continuous ideological consistency in all al-Qaida's communications. This ideological consistency is in marked contrast to the adaptability and flexibility of its political strategy and tactics over the same period.

The announcement of jihad was followed in 1998 by the promulgation by bin Laden of a *fatwa* against the 'Jews and Crusaders' (bin Laden, 1998). He had no religious authority to pronounce a *fatwa*, which, as a formal decision on a matter of *sharia* law, is the prerogative of a cleric. However, in a skilled use of religious imagery, he appeared in front of a cave, thereby associating himself with the exiled Prophet Mohammed and acquiring symbolic authority.

After 9/11, the *defensive* justification for that powerful expression of militant jihad was repeatedly stressed. Al-Qaida had been responding to initial American aggression against Islam, it argued. Moreover, the targeting of civilians was justified on the basis that they elected the governments that were guilty of that aggression. In a clear example of the persuasiveness of this justification, Shezhad Tanweer, aged 20 and one of the London bombers of July 2005, said in his martyrdom video to the non-Muslims of Britain: 'Your government has openly supported the genocide of 150,000 innocent Muslims in Fallujah. You are directly responsible . . .' (Taylor, 2006). Further, argued al-Qaida, given that America's 'bombs and its embargo killed millions of Iraqi Muslims', it would be in accord with *sharia* law to kill Americans proportionately, i.e. no more than four million of them. The clerical authorities were actually consulted (Cullison, 2004), and some were found who were willing to support this self-justifying rhetoric. Al-Qaida certainly needed to justify itself; the vast majority of jihadis, let alone mainstream Muslims, disapproved of the 9/11 assaults and rightly feared the consequences (Gerges, 2005).

In 2003, bin Laden condemned the global Muslim establishment as traitors for failing to support his 1996 pronouncement that jihad was a religious duty incumbent upon all Muslims (Karmon, 2006). This tilt at the establishment was calculated to appeal to young Muslims, and it was certainly successful in this respect. Both the successful and failed bombings in London in July 2005, and the discovery of a possible plot to blow up several aircraft in flight from Britain to the USA in August 2006, testify to the appeal of this militant message. An opinion poll commissioned by the BBC found that a small but not insignificant proportion of British Muslims supported the aims of al-Qaida (Anthony, 2006).

Further pronouncements by close associates of bin Laden re-affirm the central religious message of al-Qaida (Blanchard, 2006). Ayman al Zawahiri, bin Laden's second-in-command, contrasted this message both with statements by the US government in favour of democracy, and also with other Muslim ideologies. The first and most important of the three principles that al Zawahiri pronounces is the creation of an Islamic state governed solely by *sharia* law. Democracy is unacceptable because it empowers human rulers and legal systems in opposition to God. Abu Musab al-Zarqawi, the leader of an Islamic resistance group in Iraq, condemned Muslims for participating in the Iraqi democratic elections of 2005. Sayf al-Adl, another senior leader of al-Qaida, repeated the central tenet of *tawhid* as the inspiration for all the group's strategic objectives. Abu Bakar Bashir, the head of Jemaah Islamiah (the Indonesian Islamic organisation reportedly affiliated to al-Qaida), said: 'The democratic system is not the Islamic way. It is forbidden. Democracy is based on people, but the state must be based on God's law – I call it Allahcracy' (Sheridan, 2006). All these pronouncements share the same central theological thrust: the purpose of jihad is to defend and assert Islamic theocracy, and therefore all those seeking to establish or maintain other forms of government should be resisted.

Perhaps the most convincing affirmation of religious motivation, however, can be found in the instruction manual used by the 9/11 hijackers (Lincoln, 2002). This document contains 89 references to Allah, and 25 to the Prophet Mohammed. The key religious themes, recurring throughout, are: first, purification and the martyrdom for which it is a preparation; and, second, jihad, the struggle against infidels, a sacred duty that the hijackers are fulfilling. There are verbatim quotations from the Qu'ran on 22 occasions, and different prayers suitable for different stages of the hijacking operation are recommended.

The *religious motif of struggle against the infidel* pervades al-Qaida's every public, and many of its private (but subsequently discovered) communications. Hostility towards the 'near enemy', secular Muslim states, such as Egypt or Jordan, and more recently towards the 'far enemy', America and its allies, can be explained primarily in religious terms. These nations are treated as enemies because they stand in the way of the establishment of theocratic rule. They assault and diminish the true faith, both by their military, political, and economic policies, and also by their cultural excesses.

This emphasis on moral rigour derives largely from the second of the two ideological strands motivating al-Qaida. The first strand is primarily political in nature, and is informed in particular by the writings of Sayeed Qutb (see Chapter 6). The second is Saudi in origin, emphasising the moral purity and stark simplicity of Islamic belief and practice. It derives from the Wahhabi sect, long established as the dominant branch of Islam in Saudi Arabia. Immoral behaviour breaks the law of God and threatens young Muslims with its temptations. The contrary example of a truly obedient and morally pure regime was that of the Taliban, which bin Laden much admires (Al Jazeera, 1999).

It is clear that this religious position is *fundamentalist* in character. The basic hostility towards some of the elements of modernity is encapsulated in the doctrine of jihad (Gerges, 2005). This idea has always been present in mainstream Islam, but it has traditionally been taken to mean the commitment required to be steadfast in the faith and defend it against its enemies. It does not feature among the five pillars of Islam: the testimony of faith; prayer; the giving of alms; fasting; and making the pilgrimage. Radical clerics of the twentieth century, Abu Ala Mawdudi and Sayeed Qutb, elevated it to become the central tenet of the faith, and re-interpreted it as a 'universal all-embracing revolution' (Mawdudi, 1976).

Futhermore, they re-defined the infidel, the object of jihad, as *jahiliyyah*. The Other, the *jahili*, in this dualistic world-view, is 'any system in which the final decisions are referred to human beings and in which the sources of all authority are human' (Qutb, 1981); in other words, any political system that is not an Islamic theocracy. To quote: '. . . any society is a *jahili* society which does not dedicate itself to submission to God alone, in its beliefs and ideas, in its observances of worship and in its legal regulations. According to this definition, all the societies existing in the world today are *jahili*' (Qutb, 1981). Originally, the term was used to refer to the uncivilised peoples before the birth of the Prophet.

Given these theological assumptions, the choice of enemies made by al-Qaida is perfectly understandable. Moreover, in addition to the *reactivity* and *dualism* evidenced above, the other three key elements of fundamental-ism are also present in al-Qaida's ideology. It is based upon the authority of the *holy book*, although this is interpreted highly *selectively*. And the *millen-nial* hope is present that God's law will ultimately be supreme, but only after apocalyptic struggles in which martyrdom will lead to heavenly reward for the true believer.

Because all-embracing religious belief is relatively rare in late-modern societies, there is a temptation for Western commentators to interpret al-Qaida's religious statements as post-hoc justifications for actions under-taken for other reasons. Alternatively, they are sometimes seen as cynical attempts to manipulate malleable Muslim youth. Yet there is no reason why we should not take them at face value, as sincere statements of an all-embracing belief system that motivates extreme action. Of course, this does not preclude the possibility of other motives also directing and energising their activities, or other psychological needs being met. It does, however, point to the nature of fundamentalist belief as a self-contained world-view, which, associated with group membership and identity, motivates their actions (Hood et al., 2005).

It is interesting to note in passing that the reaction to 9/11 of the American government has been to embrace a similar dualistic meta-narrative. Instead of dealing with specific movements or groups individually, taking into account their particular history and context, President George W. Bush has collapsed them all into a single enemy ('terror'), and confirmed with a mirror image al-Qaida's own dualistic analysis of the world as engaged in a war between good and evil (with, naturally, the roles reversed).

In summary, we may say that al-Qaida retains pre-modern elements in its belief system. The replacement of human by divine authority regarding mat-ters of law and morality, and the selective reliance on the holy book as the source of these precepts, are both examples of pre-modern thinking. But the use of these ideological elements as a reaction against modernisation is by definition a modern phenomenon. The essential modernity of al-Qaida is most clearly demonstrated in its organisation.

## Al-Qaida: A late-modern organisation

Most analysts of today's organisations (e.g. Clarke and Clegg, 1998) argue that the increasing pace of globalisation frequently renders such metaphors for organisations as 'smoothly functioning machine' and 'biologically adap-tive organism' inappropriate. After all, machines have to be re-designed and re-engineered if they are to change, whereas organisms take a long time to adapt to their environment in Darwinian terms. Rather, continuously changing networks of information, innovation, personal relationships, power shifts, and organisational alliances are more useful descriptions of late-modern organisations.

In these terms, al-Qaida has indeed embraced the process of modernisation in its mode of organising. Its political flexibility and rapid response to a changing environment have been outstandingly successful. The very foundation of al-Qaida in 1988, when the Russian occupation of Afghanistan was nearing its end, was an act of *political opportunism*. Bin Laden and others had organised the Arab volunteers who aided the Afghan mujahedeen in expelling the Russians. In a post-war dispute about how best to use this organisational 'base' (the translation of 'al-Qaida'), bin Laden won out. The aim now was to disperse these skilled Arab activists back to their own countries to foment rebellion against their pro-Western secular governments (Katzman, 2005), using terrorist tactics. I take the term 'terrorism' to refer to 'the use or threat of use of violence as a means of attempting to achieve some sort of effect within a political context' (Horgan, 2005, p. 1). Often, but not always, the victims are random, and the immediate purpose is indeed to induce terror in the short term and anxiety subsequently.

Opportunism particularly characterises al-Qaida's subsequent actions towards Saudi Arabia. Terrorist attacks in Saudi were only sporadic during the 1990s, despite the American presence there since 1991. There is speculation (Karmon, 2006) that bin Laden had an unwritten agreement with the Saudi rulers not to attack their country, particularly as Saudi Arabia was one of only three countries to support the Taliban regime in Afghanistan. However, sensing the growing unpopularity of the regime, al-Qaida and its affiliates made the Saudi regime and the resident Americans their targets for a major bombing campaign in 2003 and subsequently. They clearly felt that the downfall of the Saudi royal family would lead not to a secular takeover, but to the sort of chaos that followed the overthrow of the Saddam regime in Iraq. Such chaos might tempt Western intervention, and present the opportunity for the recruitment and training of yet more jihadis in yet another applied university of conflict and insurrection.

Indeed, the American and British invasion of Iraq in 2003 provided another opportunity for al-Qaida to represent itself as fighting for the *ummah*, the true people of Allah. 'The whole world', said bin Laden:

> . . . is watching this war and the two adversaries; the *ummah* on the one hand, and the United States and its allies on the other. It is either victory and glory, or misery and humiliation. The *ummah* today has a very rare opportunity to come out of the subservience and enslavement to the West and to smash the chains with which the Crusaders have fettered it.
>
> (bin Laden, 2004)

In addition to seizing this propaganda opportunity, in 2004 bin Laden opportunistically allied with Abu Musab al-Zarqawi, who had arrived in Iraq with his band of jihadis, having anticipated the invasion. The immediate outcome of the invasion has been conflict between Sunnis and Shi'ites, rather than a unified *ummah* battling with the Great Satan. On the other hand, a wide range of Islamic institutions world-wide, many of them hostile to al-Qaida, have united in condemnation of what they perceive to be American imperialism.

The most recent, and possibly the most noteworthy, example of al-Qaida's flexible opportunism occurred in 2006. Following the invasion of southern Lebanon by the Israeli army, Hizbollah, the Shi'ite military and political movement, gained considerable prestige in the Arab world by its strong resistance to the powerful Israeli forces. Likewise, Hamas, a similar resistance movement, has enhanced its reputation in its constituency by its continued opposition to the Israelis in Palestine.

Very soon, Ayman al-Zawahiri issued a video in which he urged: 'Oh Muslims everywhere, I call on you to fight and become martyrs in the war against the Zionists and the Crusaders' (*The Guardian*, 2006). Al-Qaida 'cannot just watch these shells as they burn our brothers in Gaza and Lebanon and stand by idly, humiliated'. Al-Zawahiri was seeking to muscle in on the successes of Hamas and Hizbollah, whose popularity was eclipsing that of al-Qaida.

Al-Zawahiri's call to all Muslims who are unjustly treated to unite against the oppressors is considerably more inclusive than many of al-Qaida's previous broadcasts. In an effort to establish al-Qaida as the focus of resistance for all radical Muslims, he ignores the historic differences between Sunnis and Shi'ites, despite having recently called the latter infidels (Whitaker, 2006). Such differences had hitherto kept al-Qaida's profile low in predominantly Shi'ite Palestine and Lebanon. He also ignores the continuing killing of Shi'ites in Iraq by people loyal to Abu Musab al-Zarqawi, his recently deceased ally. Al-Zawahiri delivers his message in front of pictures of the twin towers of 9/11 and of Mohammed Atta, thereby reminding his audience of the major part already played by al-Qaida in the war against 'the Crusaders'. Polls taken in Arab countries indicate that sympathy for al-Qaida is based more on its record against the Americans than on a popular desire for a theocracy (Telhami, 2006).

The flexible opportunism exemplified above is facilitated by al-Qaida's *network of allied organisations*. Alliances permit initiatives or rapid responses to local situations in which the allied organisation operates. Early announcements proclaimed that specific Islamist organisations had actually joined or allied with al-Qaida. However, more recently it has become evident that ad-hoc groupings, often consisting of groups of friends and relatives in a locality, have joined together under their own volition to undertake violent action in their own country (see Chapter 5). This is in marked contrast to the hijackers of 9/11, for example, who volunteered to al-Qaida to serve in Chechnya, but were instead sent to America for their momentous mission. The new type of local group has usually been radicalised in the first place by an Islamist organisation, however (Sageman, 2004). Moreover, they are organised into cells consisting of an organiser, a quartermaster in charge of weapons and training, and a few volunteers (Cowan & Norton-Taylor, 2006). Such groups have no previous history as cells, however, although individuals may be known to the authorities for having been trained in an al-Qaida camp or engaged in other radical action. This was true of the plotters of the Madrid bombings of 2004 and those of the London bombings of 2005. Many of these recruits have been radicalised by the invasion of Iraq in 2003 (US Director of National Intelligence, 2006).

What appears to be happening is that al-Qaida is responsible for these attacks, but in a different way to 9/11. It has now succeeded in achieving what late-modern commercial organisations have so often striven for: the ability to attain their objectives by instilling an ideology into the minds of their followers, and then letting them get on with the job. This may mean that the job is sometimes performed inadequately (for example, the abortive second London bombing of July 2005 and the Casablanca bombing of 2003), but al-Qaida need only claim its successes. Commercial organisations today use evangelical metaphors in an effort to engage the hearts and minds of their employees (Willmott, 1993), but do not often succeed. Al-Qaida, by contrast, can subsequently claim responsibility for actions that it only indirectly inspired. Such loose networks are typical of many late-modern organisations.

Central to its success in inspiring its followers is another modern feature of al-Qaida's organisation: its *use of the internet* and the media in general. Its public-relations strategy has had two main aims: first, *to spread the ideology*; and second, to make known its *specific political objectives* at particular times. The centrality of ideology is demonstrated in almost every media communication from al-Qaida or its agents. The duty of jihad, the unity of God to encompass all areas of life, and the virtues of martyrdom are frequently re-asserted, together with denunciation of the enemy. The internet is an ideal medium for such ideological outreach, for it allows the communication of abstract dualistic ideas, such as the *ummah* versus the secular enemy. Participants can feel themselves part of a virtual global community, participating in a cosmic struggle between good and evil. This socialisation through chat rooms and websites into the jihadi ideology can then lead to face-to-face encounters, which in turn can establish potential for active membership.

However, the political as well as the ideological objectives are clearly specified, as can be seen from the following extract from an alleged e-mail from Ayman al-Zawahiri to Mullah Mohammed Omar, the leader of the Taliban, dated 3 October, 2001 (Cullison, 2004):

> Conduct a media campaign to fight the enemy's publicity. The campaign should focus on the following important points:
>
> a)   Attempt to cause a rift between the American people and their government, by demonstrating the following to the Americans:
>
>     –   That the U.S. government will lead them into further losses of money and lives

- That the government is sacrificing the people to serve the interests of the rich, particularly the Jews
- That the government is leading them to the war front to protect Israel and its security
- America should withdraw from the current battle between Muslims and Jews.

This plan aims to create pressure from the American people on their government to stop its campaign against Afghanistan, on the grounds that the campaign will cause major losses to the American people.

b) Imply that the campaign against Afghanistan will be responded to with revenge blows against America.

There are, however, several other uses to which al-Qaida have put the internet (Thomas, 2003). The first is the *planning and co-ordination* of a plan for action. When those who are going to take part in an attack are geographically dispersed, the internet is an ideal communication tool. The second is to establish a *database of profiles* indicating those who may be radicalised, recruited, or sympathetic enough to give a donation. A third is more psychological than organisational: it is to establish a *climate of fear* of an organisation that presents itself as having capacities to inflict much worse damage than in fact it can.

So, for example, al-Qaida has claimed responsibility for attacks that it may not have carried out itself; it has posted threats of actions that it has not yet carried out; and it has imputed to itself clever motives for previous attacks. For example, in 2005 it claimed that, before the assault on the twin towers, it intended America to respond aggressively to 9/11, thereby uniting Muslims against the infidel (Blanchard, 2006). Finally, and most important of all, al-Qaida has succeeded in establishing and nurturing a *self-perpetuating cycle* in which the global media repeat the scenes of 9/11 and other violent operations whenever they can find a justification for doing so (Jenkins, 2006).

However, those who live by the internet can also die by it. The monitoring of al-Qaida messages via computer and cell phone, and the seizure of their laptops, has resulted in the capture of several of their key operatives and the prevention of planned assaults. When virtual communication becomes disrupted, then the co-ordination of virtual networks becomes difficult. This is why the operational use of groups of locally based friends who meet face-to-face is now a frequent tactic.

So al-Qaida resembles late-modern organisations in its sophisticated use of information technology and public relations. It also spends much of its time seeking *sources of finance*, again a late-modern pre-occupation (Levitt, 2002). Al-Qaida uses a network of charitable and humanitarian organisations, front companies, unregulated banks, and crime, especially the drugs trade (Scarborough, 2003). These sources help to supplement the gifts of wealthy and other radical supporters. Moreover, it has financial links with Hamas and Hizbollah involving money-laundering. The cost reductions that late-modern organisations carry through in order to be more competitive are effortlessly achieved by al-Qaida. The more recent devolved structure results in locally based groups making their own explosives at minimal cost. The Madrid train bombings are estimated to have cost only $10,000.

However, al-Qaida should not be considered an unqualified success in its own terms. It could be argued that the reason for the extension of the jihad to fight the West was the failure of the strategy of fighting secular governments in Muslim countries. On the one hand, all the subsequent flexible manoeuvres described above can be seen as reactive attempts to regain prominence. Moreover, the apocalyptic success of 9/11 has not been accompanied by the development of a social and political movement to secure more general polit- ical support; political power still seems a very long way off. On the other hand, the considerable number of volunteers who wish to become jihadis has enabled al-Qaida to dispense with active recruiters, and select only some- where between 10% and 30% of applicants (Sageman, 2004). Continued violent assaults upon the West appear guaranteed.

### The control issue: Reining in al-Zarqawi

Both its network of affiliate organisations and also its capacity to control by inspiration facilitate al-Qaida's global reach. For by these means it is enabled to operate locally yet maintain a global profile. However, as the following case study within a case study will demonstrate, there is still a *control issue* to be addressed. The issue of control is central for all global organisations. It is inherent in their need to have a single global strategy and profile, yet exercise flexibility in their local operations (Bartlett & Ghoshal, 1990).

The specific issue that I will now explore in detail is the attempt by al-Qaida, in the person of Ayman al-Zawahiri, to control the activities of Abu Musab al-Zarqawi. The key evidence for this episode is a letter from al-Zawahiri, dated 9 July 2005, and released by the USA Office of the Director of National Intelligence in October 2005. Assuming the letter is genuine, it gives unparalleled insight into the efforts of the al-Qaida leader- ship to bring back into line one of its more difficult associates.

After the fall of Baghdad in the American and British invasion of Iraq in 2003, al-Qaida recommended guerrilla warfare as the most effective way of continuing the conflict with 'the Crusaders'. An effective insurgency did indeed materialise, but over the course of the next two years, its prime targets changed. Rather than the occupying troops and their associated civilian con- tractors, it was Shi'ite Iraqis who suffered the brunt of the casualties in bomb- ings, which included attacks on sacred Shia shrines and religious pilgrimages. The Shi'ites were represented as traitors to Islam, since some of them were collaborating with the Americans in establishing a democratic government and national security forces.

Responsibility for much of this development has been attributed to al-Zarqawi, who had founded his own group, Monotheism and Jihad, composed mostly of non-Iraqi Arab volunteers. Although he had had previous connections with al-Qaida, it was only in October 2004 that he made a formal statement of allegiance to bin Laden. To signal this new allegiance, he renamed his organisation the al-Qaida Jihad Organisation in the Land of the Two Rivers. Apart from his assaults on Shi'ite Iraqis, al-Zarqawi was notorious for beheading his captives and hostages and showing such actions to the world on video-tape.

Not only had al-Zarqawi attacked Shi'ites and broadcast gruesome executions. He had also quarrelled with other jihadis fighting in Iraq regarding religious matters, denigrating those who followed any other tradition than the Salafist version of Sunni Islam (his own belief system). All of these activities were contrary to al-Qaida's overall strategic intent. This was to unite Muslims in a jihad to expel the Crusaders from the Middle East and establish theocracy. The revolutionary vanguard of al-Qaida needed to receive the tacit, if not the active, support of the masses. How could it do so if it was killing other Muslims?

How did al-Zawahiri set out to bring al-Zarqawi into line with this strategic intent? He had a major problem, because not only was al-Zarqawi acting unilaterally, he was also putting out theological justifications for doing so, and angrily refuting critics, such as his spiritual mentor, al-Maqdisi. In May 2005, al-Zarqawi broadcast a decision by Muslim clerics that the evil of infidels' heresy was greater than the evil of the accidental killing of Muslims, and therefore collateral damage in the war against the Crusaders was justified. In the same video, however, al-Zarqawi announced the intended execution of a leader of the Shi'ite Badr movement, hardly 'collateral damage'. In July, he claimed that it was a duty to wage jihad against the Shi'ites, who were apostates and traitors, and later in the same month he attacked clerics who criticised him from afar. They were not engaged in the jihad in Iraq, he argued, and therefore had no right to criticise him. They were even helping the enemy.

Nevertheless, al-Zawahiri needed to keep al-Zarqawi sweet, since he provided most of the manpower in Iraq. Iraq was an arena in which al-Qaida needed to perform well to bolster its flagging reputation in the Muslim world. This perhaps accounts for the placatory tone of the following letter.

After lengthy greetings, which pray that God will protect al-Zarqawi, al-Zawahiri's letter goes on to praise him for his historic battle, fought in the heart of the Islamic world (Iraq), and says that he would join him if he could. He then broaches the delicate subject of al-Zarqawi's activities carefully. He requests information about what is going on in Iraq, and asks that al-Zarqawi will explain his situation in a little detail, 'especially in regards to the political angle. I want you to express to me what is on your mind in regards to what is on my mind in the way of questions and inquiries'. Having introduced the control issue in the guise of an exchange of information, al-Zawahiri immediately reverts to congratulating al-Zarqawi on his operations in the heart of Islam, and also on the purity of his doctrinal beliefs.

He then outlines al-Qaida's strategic plan for Iraq once the Americans have left, as follows: Having expelled the Americans, establish an Islamic authority in Sunni areas of Iraq at first, and then by struggle throughout Iraq. Next, extend this 'caliphate' to neighbouring countries. And finally, fight the war with Israel, which such success will undoubtedly precipitate. The plan is to build a nation for Allah, not just to win a war.

In order to achieve these objectives, al-Zawahiri maintains, 'the strongest weapon which the mujahedeen enjoy – after the help and granting of success by God – is popular support from the Muslim masses in Iraq, and the surrounding Muslim countries'. This support must be maintained and increased, provided, of course, that 'striving for that support does not lead to any concessions in the laws of the *sharia*'.

Thus al-Zawahiri anticipates al-Zarqawi's religious justifications for his killings of Muslims, and now feels free to elaborate on the need for popular support. He says that the support of the masses is not only necessary for the establishment of a caliphate in Iraq, but also 'if the jihadist movement were obliged to pursue other methods, such as a war of jihad or an intifada, then popular support would be a decisive factor between victory and defeat'. He further alleges that the aim of the secular apostates who rule nominally Muslim countries is to separate the jihadis from popular support.

The whole argument leads to the carefully qualified conclusion that 'the mujahed movement must avoid any action that the masses do not understand and approve', provided that there is no contravention of *sharia* law, and as long as there are other options. Al-Zawahiri then goes on to insist that the caliphate can only be established in Iraq if there is an appeasement of Muslims, and if they share in the governance of the country. He hastens to add that he is sure that al-Zarqawi has no intention of establishing governance without the participation of the Iraqi people (indicating by his very mention of the issue that he has just such a concern). We must avoid the mistake of the Taliban, he argues, who restricted participation in governance by the Afghan people, who as a result disengaged themselves. 'Therefore, I stress again to you and to all your brothers the need to direct the political action equally with the military action, by the alliance, cooperation and gathering of all leaders of opinion and influence in the Iraqi arena'. Immediately, however, he stresses that he is not prescribing a specific course of action, since 'you are more knowledgeable about field conditions'.

Next, in a lengthy passage full of theological justifications, al-Zawahiri urges al-Zarqawi not to quarrel with fellow groups of jihadis who follow the teachings of different sects from the Salafi. Finally he arrives at the most delicate topic of all: al-Zarqawi's attacks on Shi'ites.

He desperately tries to disarm objections by stressing again that he is viewing matters from afar only, and admitting that the Shi'ites have indeed collaborated with the Americans. He agrees that the Shi'ites are in theological error, which will in the end be rooted out. However, he suggests that the 'common folk' do not understand this at present, 'and are wondering about your attacks on the Shia'. He puts into the mouths of others questions that he himself would like to ask al-Zarqawi: Are such attacks unavoidable and in self-defence? Why were they directed against ordinary Shi'ites rather than their leaders? And why incur the hostility of Iran (a predominantly Shi'ite state) by these attacks? Repeating his distance from the scene, al-Zawahiri now more boldly asserts the constant refrain of those at the corporate centre: 'monitoring from afar has the advantage of providing the total picture and observing the general line without getting submerged in the details, which might draw attention away from the direction of the target. As the English proverb says, the person who is standing among the leaves of the tree might not see the tree' (sic). Success must not make us merely reactive, he argues; we have suffered from being reactive before. Rather, 'one of the most important factors of success is that you don't let your eyes lose sight of the target'.

The broadcasting of scenes of slaughter is therefore counter-productive. Al-Zarqawi is in danger of being deceived 'by the praise of some of the zealous young men and their description of you as the sheikh of the slaugh-terers'. Here is apparent the age-old fear of the young bloods who work at the cutting edge of the organisation (in this case, literally as well as metaphoric-ally) in the minds of the older men who try to control it from the centre. Al-Zarqawi must realise that more than half of the battlefield is in the media, and that there is a race to win the hearts and minds of Muslim people.

Then, in an astonishing revelation of al-Zawahiri's motivations, he gives some personal news to end the letter. The most central element of this news is six paragraphs regarding his recent publications. Here is the 'professor of Islamic history and theology' boasting about his academic productivity. Yet he is also a revolutionary activist who threatens world order! Western people cannot imagine a current world leader adding diligently to his pub-lications list. This may have been possible for Renaissance man, but surely not today, we feel. However, this response fails to realise that al-Zawahiri is simply living according to his religious beliefs. The doctrine of *tawhid* argues for the unity of God: the faith, the law, and its implementation, are indivis-ible. Al-Zawahiri is acting out his faith by seeking to contribute to all these three elements. Indeed, he is the real ideological brain behind al-Qaida. If we needed a further indication of his basic religious motivation and his indispensability to the organisation, it is to be found in this apparently unimportant end to a very important letter.

In summary, al-Qaida demonstrates clearly the ambiguity in fundamental-ism's response to modernisation. It is a thoroughly modern organisation with a pre-modern ideology. Indeed, it might be described as post-modern, given its reliance on its media profile sometimes at the expense of grass roots organ-isation and support (Kepel, 2006). Even though the radical clerics have put a selective modern interpretation on the ancient scriptures, the underlying assumptions are still pre-modern.

Why do modern people embrace an ancient world-view? There are several answers to this question, the first of which was explored in this chapter. *Fundamentalism is a reaction to certain aspects of modernisation and globalisation.* The second answer is at the cultural level of explanation. They also do so because *the world-view in question is historically embedded deep in their national or ethnic culture.* The next chapter explores this latter explanation at length.

# 2 Cultures and fundamentalisms

## Fundamentalist differences

The first chapter dealt in some big concepts. The process of *modernisation*, culminating in globalisation, seems to dominate our world. It implies an increasing homogeneity of culture, with Western consumerism appearing on the surface to be seducing the rest of the world away from its own varied cultural heritages. Further, the current importance of *fundamentalism* as a forceful reaction against aspects of modernisation led us to consider it as a general category, rather than as a set of different religious movements. The grand scope of Chapter 1, therefore, necessarily resulted in an over-simplified analysis, which ignored the differences between cultures and between religious movements. We need to avoid 'the widespread and parochial conceit that the European civilisation of the West is now the universal civilisation of the world' (Huntington, 1996, p. 55). This chapter seeks to redress the balance, as it addresses two questions. The first is: Why are fundamentalist movements different from each other? Or, putting it another way, why do we need to talk about fundamentalisms as well as about fundamentalism? Why, for example, do some fundamentalisms violently assault their perceived enemy, others engage in political activity in an effort to change the moral climate, and yet others seek to avoid all contact with the sinful world (Almond et al., 2003)? And the second question is this: Why are fundamentalisms to be found more in some parts of the world than in others? Why are there many more fundamentalists in America than in Europe, or in the Middle East than in the Far East?

These questions can be addressed by reference to the concept of *culture*. Before we venture into the intellectual minefield of the definition of culture, however, we must examine ways of differentiating between fundamentalisms. Only when we are familiar with the differences between the religious movements subsumed under the label 'fundamentalism' will we be able to appreciate those elements of the host cultures that gave each of them birth and sustenance.

There are three dimensions along which fundamentalisms differ, which, taken together, will form the basis for a theoretical account in Chapter 3 of their individual development as social movements. These are, first, the *identity of their Other*: who is their favourite enemy? The second dimension is their *mode of operation*: how do they engage with the world? And the third is their *ideology*: what are the key beliefs, values, and norms of behaviour (BVNs) that motivate and justify their actions?

### *Fundamentalisms' enemies*

Fundamentalisms have *varied enemies* (Almond et al., 2003, p. 246). The identity of the enemy differs both between fundamentalisms and within each fundamentalism as it develops. Almost all fundamentalisms treat the *religious establishment*, the representatives of mainstream religion, as an enemy, especially in the earlier stages of their development. American Protestants started off by defending the fundamentals of their faith against the increasingly liberal religious establishment of the early twentieth century. Militant Muslims first attacked mainstream Islam, particularly as represented by the nominally Muslim nationalist governments that emerged in the mid-twentieth century. Haredi Jews criticised Judaism for its inadequate observance of the Torah. Moreover, these enemies continue to be attacked today, particularly when fundamentalist leadership judges it tactically appropriate to do so.

While in some cases *the state* is reviled as being insufficiently religious, in others it is opposed because it is perceived as actually assaulting the faith and its adherents. There are some areas where their own government or another state has actively put down fundamentalist groups, for example Egypt, Palestine, Algeria, Afghanistan, Iraq, and India. In these cases, a nation state is the enemy, and violent opposition is usually the option, especially where fundamentalists' peaceful constitutional opposition is overridden by the authorities (e.g. in Algeria). Militant movements such as Hamas and Hizbullah hold Israel to be their most important enemy. Sikh fundamentalists fight against the secular Indian government, and Hindu fundamentalists, in their turn, have attacked the same enemy, criticising it for being too secular and too tolerant of other religions.

Other fundamentalisms have chosen *civil society* as their prime target. This is a convenient foe, because it can be sectioned into different out-groups, each of which can provide a concrete Other against whom to mobilise. So, for example, the Moral Majority of the 1980s in the USA could choose between feminists, abortionists, gays, pornographers, rock musicians, the film industry, and so on (Lienesch, 1993). Haredi Jews rail against the decadent habits of secular Israelis. The perceived moral failings of modern societies are useful targets because they point up the authority of the holy book and the purity of its teachings, and enable fundamentalists to feel separate from, and superior to, the sinful world that surrounds them. In some cases the enemy is hated both because it is perceived to persecute the faithful and violate their shrines, and also because it represents an unholy decadence. The hostility of radical Islam to the USA embraces both these attitudes.

Yet another enemy is to be discovered in *rival fundamentalisms*. Radical

Islamists seek to set up such oppositions by harking back to historical wars between Christians and Muslims. The Americans are labelled infidel 'Crusaders', a title inadvertently accepted by George W. Bush when he spoke of setting forth on a crusade for democracy. Sometimes the split is within a fundamentalist movement itself. As we saw in the last chapter, al-Zawahiri had to restrain al-Zarqawi from fighting his co-religionists as well as the Americans.

### *Fundamentalisms' mode of engagement*

A second dimension along which fundamentalisms differ is in terms of their *mode of engagement* with the enemy, whoever it may be at the time. Almond et al. (2003) distinguish four different reactive responses, which they call world conqueror, world transformer, world creator, and world renouncer. These labels speak for themselves. The *world conqueror* uses all means available to conquer the world for his God, including violence. The *world transformer* engages with the world politically in an effort to gain power on God's behalf. The *world creator* offers an alternative world to the sinful one that has rejected God, and invites others into it. The *world renouncer* simply withdraws from the world to preserve his precious purity, yet frequently is in the humiliating position of depending on that outside world for his very existence and protection.

Some fundamentalisms adopt different modes of engagement at different stages of their development. For example, the Muslim Brotherhood in Egypt initially sought to gain political power constitutionally, but later, under the influence of Sayeed Qutb, became *world conquerors* rather than *world transformers*, and tried to assassinate President Nasser. In America, the historical sequence is more complex still, representing a series of aggressive advances by Protestant fundamentalists against the enemy, interspersed with strategic withdrawals (Carpenter, 1997; Wuthnow, 1988). Their initial stance in the 1920s was that of *world transformer*, as they sought to engage the liberal enemy by argument and persuasion. Defeated and ridiculed after the Scopes 'Monkey' trial, they withdrew. Then, adopting a *world creator* mode, they recruited and organised, culminating in the glorious 1950s, when it looked as though revival had returned at last. The counter-culture of the 1960s and its associated interest groups persuaded them to adopt a *world transformer* mode again, as they united to form the Moral Majority in the 1980s. Elements of civil society rather than the apostate church were now the enemy, but relatively little legislative and political success was enjoyed. Soon, financial and sexual scandals forced another withdrawal into *world creator* mode. However, the election of George W. Bush and the assault of 9/11 encouraged an emergence into *world-conqueror* mode. The 'war on terror' may be construed by some American fundamentalists as a Judaeo-Christian war on militant Islam, just as, for bin Laden, America is the Great Satan.

*Fundamentalisms' ideologies*

A third dimension along which fundamentalisms differ is that of *ideology*. Each movement's choice of ideology is a function of its position on the other two dimensions: its mode of engagement and the identity of its enemy. Its beliefs and practices are selected so as to best support its mode of engagement with its enemy, and they are devised with the enemy's identity in mind. Thus *the five defining features of fundamentalism* (see p. 2) *are differentially emphasised in different fundamentalist ideologies*. However, the presence of all five features distinguishes fundamentalisms from other movements.

For example (Almond et al., 2003, p. 248), the possibility of hastening by our actions the coming rule of God on earth is strongly emphasised by interventionist American Protestant fundamentalists who support Israel against Palestine, Hamas, and Hizbullah. It is also a dominant ideological feature for Gush Emunim, who believe that final redemption will only occur when the Jews have conquered all of *Eretz Israel*, the territory that God promised to Abraham (see Chapter 3). In other fundamentalisms, however, such as the radical Sunni Muslims and the radical Sikhs, millennialism plays a lesser ideological part.

Similarly, fundamentalisms place a different emphasis on evangelism, depending on whom they perceive their enemy to be. Where the Other is a nation state that they perceive to be persecuting them, the response is largely local. Hamas and Gush Emunim, for example, are consumed with hostility towards Israel and Palestine, respectively. They are interested in financial support, but they do not proselytise abroad. Pentecostals, on the other hand, in full world-creator mode, evangelise eagerly world-wide. This is because they believe their enemy to be the Devil of secularism, from whom the whole world needs saving (Cox, 1995).

## Culture defined

*Cultures exist at varied levels*

So fundamentalisms differ and flourish more in some parts of the world than others. Why do these differences in form and influence occur? The answers have to lie hidden somewhere in the theoretical undergrowth that has grown over and around the concept of *culture*.

Culture is an abstract concept. It subsumes a wide range of other concepts, the instances of which are more observable (Schaller, Conway, & Crandall, 2004). These other concepts include customs, traditions, beliefs, values, social norms, language, symbols, religion, various institutions (for example, governmental, educational, and legal systems), arts, sciences, technologies, leisure activities, media, everyday habits and automatic social behaviour such as greetings and farewells, the whole created environment including cities, and so on. The concept of culture therefore embraces both subjective psychological constructs, such as beliefs and values, and also objects, such as buildings and sculptures. There has been a tendency to concentrate more on subjective than on objective features. And when objective features are considered, more attention is paid to surface than to deeper features (for example, Western consumer products as opposed to Western institutions of government) (Bruner, 1990).

Culture is essentially *a group product*; people have to share these elements in common for the term to be applied. Hence, we usually speak of culture as belonging to *a category of persons*: Arab culture, for example, or the Appalachian culture, or Victorian culture. But in order to be able to say that a culture exists, we have to demonstrate that it exhibits a particular pattern of features, such that some features are shared almost universally within it, whereas others are extremely rare. And second, we have to show that the particular pattern of features it exhibits differs from the pattern observed in other cultures. So, for example, it is legitimate to speak about a fundamentalist culture, since fundamentalisms demonstrate five features that, taken together, are not shared by any other religious movements.

Cultures vary incredibly in nature and size. We can speak of cultures located in *historic times*, for example, classical culture, eighteenth-century culture, or 1960s culture. Different *civilisations* can be said to have their own culture, and Huntington (1996) enumerates nine distinct civilisational cultures: Western, Latin American, African, Islamic, Sinic, Hindu, Orthodox, Buddhist, and Japanese. At a slightly lower level of generality, Hofstede (1980) distinguishes between *regional cultures*, such as those of Southern Europe and the Nordic countries. Of course, many have proposed the existence of *national* cultures: the American culture, for example. But cultures can also belong to *social categories* of persons: working-class culture, for example, or the accountancy culture, or the US Marine culture.

Given this immense range of cultures, it is not surprising that in some cases sub-cultures can nest within super-ordinate cultures: Southern Baptists are a sub-culture of American Protestant fundamentalists, for example, who are in turn a sub-culture of fundamentalism as a whole. To fulfil the empirical criterion, however, we must demonstrate that each of these sub-cultures demonstrates a unique pattern of features: Southern Baptists must differ from other American fundamentalist denominations, whilst retaining a central core of Protestant fundamentalist features; American Protestant fundamentalists must differ from other fundamentalists, whilst demonstrating the five definitive features of fundamentalism in general; and fundamentalism must differ from other types of religious movement, whilst remaining religious at heart.

The existence of these *multiple levels* of culture immediately rules out the identification of culture with any one level. 'Nation' and 'culture' are not synonymous, and it is perfectly possible for a nation not to have a distinctive culture of its own. Similarly, civilisational cultures are not the only sort of culture around, nor are ethnic ones (e.g. Serb, Arab).

### Cultures are dynamic human products

Despite the sometimes immense power of cultures, however, especially large-scale cultures such as the civilisational ones listed above, we should not forget that they are all human products. Rather than determining our destinies, they both shape, and are shaped by, individuals and groups of people (Adams & Markus, 2004). It is people who *reproduce* culture in their everyday behaviour, their beliefs and values, and their institutions. It is people who *maintain* their culture by consciously resisting efforts to change it, especially by those from outside the culture. It is people who *select* aspects of their culture for retention and jettison others. And it is people who *import* or create new cultural elements (Holland, Lachicotte, Skinner, & Cain, 1998). Very often, such changes occur through the existing institutions of a culture. So, for example, Western technology developed the contraceptive pill, which put women in control of their reproductive capabilities and consequently changed the institution of marriage and the roles of men and women within it.

Cultures have therefore to be construed as fluid patterns of features, in which *people and cultures are in dynamic relation*, continuously both influencing and being influenced by each other. Thinking of a culture as a static entity rather than as a continuous process has several dangerous consequences. First, it becomes very easy to treat the category of persons whose culture it is as a *homogeneous stereotype*, different from one's own culture (from the perspective of which one is making the judgement). Second, it is tempting to go further and say that this category is *naturally* like it is, an 'essential' rather than a socially derived category. And finally, a static notion of culture can result in the *solidifying of a cultural tradition* into permanence, the 'law of the Medes and the Persians'. Often, such hardening up of a tradition is a conscious ideological choice by the leaders within a culture.

### Cultures are historically derived

This dynamic view of cultures as a long-term process allows us to construe them as *historically derived*. The present pattern of cultural features may be very different to that of two thousand years ago, but features that were prominent then may still have an indirect and perhaps unnoticed effect today. Similarly, there exists the possibility of cross-cultural fertilisation. The individuals and groups who create cultural change also belong to other cultures, and may import features from them. For example, it could be argued that political culture in the West has been considerably affected by the importation of various beliefs, values, and practices from the business/managerialist culture. Later in this chapter I will seek to show that religious cultures and national cultures are sometimes connected.

In the light of this analysis of culture, we can easily think of a range of possible cultural influences upon fundamentalism. Some cultures are more likely to support fundamentalism than others. And those that do will be sufficiently different from each other to generate different fundamentalisms. First, however, we need to examine the ancient historical cultural roots from which fundamentalisms are derived. Such an examination will be concerned with culture at the *civilisational* level of analysis, and will therefore help us more with the first of our questions: why are fundamentalisms more likely to occur in some parts of the world than others?

## Civilisations: The sacred and profane

### Sacred and secular: The first split

In early human history, the world was a holy place. The sacred was immanent in the spaces in which people lived and moved. However, during the Axial Age, in the first millennium BC (Jaspers, 1965), the sacred and the secular, the transcendental and the mundane, became separate and distinctive categories of experience (Weber, 1922/1993). Perhaps this cultural revolution occurred because, in several different civilisations, people had gained sufficient control and predictability of their daily lives to cease to be continually anxious. Things that had previously caused them to feel awe, wonder, or fear were now tamed and had become mundane.

Different historical civilisations treated the divide between the transcendental and the mundane in different ways. The Greeks, the Romans, and the Chinese, for example, sought to bring the transcendental into the realm of the mundane: the classical deities even wandered around on earth. Some Eastern civilisations, on the other hand, and Buddhism in particular, treated the transcendental as highly abstract.

However, Judaism, Christianity, and later, Islam, took a different path. They worshipped a single transcendent God, holy and separate. As a consequence, the mundane and secular sphere, in comparison with the Almighty, came to be seen as incomplete, inferior, and impure. Human beings and human institutions seemed fatally flawed. Fundamentalism has its deep historic roots in the various subsequent efforts to deal with this gulf between the sacred and the secular.

Compromise soon became one solution, as Christianity early demonstrated. 'Give unto Caesar the things that are Caesar's, and unto God the things that are God's', the Bible reports Jesus to have said (Mark 12.17). And, as Christianity became acceptable to the Romans, St Augustine could imagine the City of God and the City of Man existing together in mutual tolerance. However, it soon became apparent that the mundane world of human politics and institutions could only practically deliver but a part of the demanding and holy transcendental vision. Fundamentalism derives from the continuing effort to actually implement this utopian vision in full.

Judaism, Christianity, and Islam are all 'religions of the book'. As a consequence, they rapidly developed formal doctrines based on their holy book. For Christians and Jews, the doctrine is abstracted from the book, whereas for Islam it is based on the description in the Qu'ran of the life and times of the Prophet Mohammed, a golden age of faith. As Almond et al. (2003, p. 169) observe, the explicit formalisation of belief into orthodox doctrine has always given the opportunity for heterodoxy to rear its head, arguing that the original vision has been polluted. So, in Islam, Hambalites and Wahhabis offered an even more orthodox alternative to orthodoxy, while the ultra-orthodox Jews reacted against orthodox and reformed Jewry. In the case of Christianity, it was the Calvinists and Anabaptists of the Reformation who rebelled against the compromises between the City of God and the City of Man that the official church had enforced.

### Sacred versus secular: Early utopias

These early 'proto-fundamentalisms' (Eisenstadt, 1999) were the forerunners of fundamentalisms. The historical transmission of these heterodox utopian ideas to the present was facilitated in the West by those great political upheavals that ushered in the modern era: the English, French, and American Revolutions. The English and American Revolutions both had a strong religious component, whereas the French one had the established (Catholic) church as an enemy. In all three cases, the utopian vision was of a reconstructed society, the achievement of which justified the use of any means available, including violence. So profoundly affected were the revolutionaries by the power of their vision that they believed that it had universal application, and therefore they should seek to make it happen for others too. The Puritans believed they were a city on a hill, an example to show to the rest of the world.

Revolutionary violence and evangelical fervour were not the only features of these radical changes to find echoes in fundamentalism. The revolutionaries' sectarian origins and non-establishment roots enabled them to create new political and religious institutions and organisations. These new forms soon resulted in conflict and schisms within sects. Those exercising political leadership found it impossible to implement fully the utopian vision of the intellectuals and clerics who had done such a good job in its formulation. The vision was doomed to failure. But the legacy of equality, radical reform, protest, and the proliferation of organisations and sects remained as part of civil society.

The same revolutionary upheavals did not usher in modernity in the other civilisations where the religion was that of the book (Judaism and Islam). However, there were still repeated historical episodes in which the proponents of the pure utopian vision sought to bring back their compromising leaders and politicians to the path of righteousness (Armstrong, 2000a).

So we have a paradox. The long tradition of utopian radicalism ushered in the process of modernisation by its revolutionary achievements. Yet that same tradition, now embodied in fundamentalisms, is reacting violently against modernity. Modernisation, clearly, has failed to follow through on the promise of utopia. But the physical location of fundamentalisms confirms our historical analysis of civilisational cultures and religions. For they are primarily to be found in the birthplace of the religions of the book, the Middle East, and also in the nation to which the Protestant sects were banished, America.

## Nations and civil religion

### Foundation myths and civil religion

Having addressed the question of why fundamentalisms are found more in some areas of the world than others, we now need to ask why fundamentalisms differ from each other in the ways described above. To answer this question, our analysis of culture at the civilisational level has to give way to one primarily at the level of the nation.

It is worth making a distinction between *nation* and *nation-state*. A nation is a construct, a category to which people believe they belong, and usually claims a culture. A nation-state is a political institution, and thus by definition is only one of the elements of a national culture. Nations have varied degrees of relationship with religion. In some cases, nations resemble religions in that they share some features typical of religion but none of its content. So, for example, avowedly secular states can nevertheless have historic myths (stories with a transcendental meaning), saintly heroes or heroines, sacred objects, annual festivals, and so on, just like religions. In other cases, nations actually incorporate elements of religion into their culture. God appears frequently, together with such religious myths and symbols as the promised land, the true Israel, God's chosen people, the *ummah*, the holy book, the ten commandments, the Hidden Imam, prayer in schools and in government institutions, religious leaders as rulers *ex officio*, etc.

A national culture with religious similarities or with actual religious content is known as *civil religion*. One definition reads 'any set of beliefs and rituals, related to the past, present, and/or future of a people ("nation") which are understood in some transcendental fashion' (Hammond, 1976, p. 171). This definition clearly leaves open whether these elements of culture are religious in origin or not. Another definition (Demerath, 2003, p. 353) implies that they *are* religious: 'any society's most common religious denominator which consecrates its sense of nationhood and pivots around a set of tenets and rituals forged in the fires of a shared history'.

Either way, the function of civil religion is to strengthen the idea of the nation as a category to which people belong, and with which they can identify. It is therefore of great use to leaders who wish to legitimate a nation, and to transcend other categories that can be constituted within it, such as ethnicities, class divisions, religions, or denominations/sects. The more transcendent the concept of nation can be made to appear, the more likely people are to perceive themselves as belonging to it, to identify with it, and to fight for it.

Of particular importance are the *foundation myths* of a nation, and, together with its other key historical myths, they constitute the national tradition. When the founding myth emphasises the single religion shared by the founders, as in the USA, then it is highly likely that the nation's civil religion will contain a great deal of that 'real' religion, i.e. radical Protestantism. Modern France, on the other hand, treats the Revolution as its foundation myth, and therefore resolutely excludes 'real' religion from its civil religion. When a religiously founded nation subsequently becomes much more pluralist and secularist, as has occurred in the USA, the civil religion loses some of its original religious cutting edge.

In other cases, for example in modern India, the secular foundation of the newly independent nation led to a civil religion, nurtured by the Congress Party. However, Hindu nationalist fundamentalism gained considerable impetus during the 1980s and 1990s, energised by an ideology of *Hindutva* (Hinduness) which harked back to a golden age free from the West and from competing religions (Almond et al., 2003). In this case, fundamentalist religion reacted *against* civil religion.

Fundamentalists are, of course, opposed to pluralism and secularism, both elements of the modernisation project. However, rather than reacting against the nation, they may critique it for betraying the founders' intentions. This allows them to appear as patriotic as the next person. They present their own interpretations of the foundation myth in support of their critique of modern national decadence, and they carefully select other features of the tradition. So, for example, Islamic fundamentalists bring up the Crusades whenever they can. Haredi Jews revere the medieval introduction of the *kabbala*. And American fundamentalists seek to re-write the history of the founding fathers as they contest the separation of church and state.

### America and Islam

The historical origins and foundation myths of national cultures had a profound effect on the nature of the fundamentalisms they nourished in the twentieth century. In particular, *they determine the way in which their native fundamentalism reacts to the world*. So, for example, in the USA the nation dates its origins from the Pilgrims and the Puritans, religious sectarians who, despite persecution, were determined to establish their own godly community separate from the mainstream Christian churches of their time. Religious freedom and choice was written into the constitution, as was the separation of the institutional church from the state.

Multiple Christian denominations, sects, individual 'ministries', and parachurch organisations developed in America, mirroring the individualism, entrepreneurship, and mistrust of government typical of the national culture. The nation had nurtured religious people without seeking to control them and, as a consequence, they almost invariably operated within the democratic institutions. Hence the American fundamentalists of the twentieth century mainly employed a *'world transformer'* mode of operation; they sought to achieve their objectives via the political process. When the compromises necessarily involved in democratic politics appeared periodically to be blurring their distinctiveness and polluting their purity, they retreated into *'world creator'* mode.

This embeddedness of American fundamentalists in society renders it unthinkable for them violently to assault their nation. The social and economic linkages they have with their fellow countrymen, together with their patriotism, prevent them from doing so. Their only enemies who are the targets of their violence are usually representatives of specific out-groups, such as doctors who perform abortions. Footloose global jihadis, on the other hand, have no such cultural embeddedness. Their loyalties are to their movement, and so they find no difficulty in casting either apostates within their countries of origin or Westerners as enemies to be destroyed.

The Islamic world, unlike the West, had always been ruled in a relatively authoritarian manner. Periodic suppression of the people and corruption by the rulers had stimulated resistance by those 'proto-fundamentalists', who argued that the *sharia* law was being broken. Then, after the Second World War, the United Nations, other supra-national organisations, and the victorious allies imposed government by secular nation-states, in such historically Muslim countries as Egypt, Syria, Iran, and Tunisia. Given this authoritarian context, and the absence of truly democratic processes, the only stance open to Islamic fundamentalists was that of *world conqueror*. When they did try the *world transformer* mode, operating within the system as in Egypt and Algeria, they were rejected and persecuted.

In the Islamic world, the attempt to separate the civil religion of the secular nation-state from Islamic theocracy by the use of external power instigated a violent reaction by fundamentalists. In Judaism, some of the ultra-religious reacted in a similarly violent way to secular Zionism, although most played by the democratic rules.

In the USA, however, civil religion and 'real' religion were closely intertwined. Hence, when the traditions and meanings of the civil religion became increasingly contested, this contest naturally spread into the religious arena. Commentators such as Hunter (1991, 1994) and Wuthnow (1988) noted that the growing political divide between liberals and conservatives, which Hunter termed 'culture wars', was mirrored in many of the church denominations and other religious organisations that flourish in the USA. Indeed, on many occasions political and religious agendas merged, as the following detailed example demonstrates.

### *The IRD: Merging political and religious agendas*

The Institute on (sic) Religion and Democracy (IRD) is one of the many lobbying and pressure groups that flourish in Washington DC. Like most of its rivals in this highly politicised arena, it is small, quick on its feet, well funded, media savvy, legally astute, and smoothly marketed. It has cultivated a wide variety of contacts and alliances with voluntary organisations and government agencies. In sum, it is an archetypical twenty-first-century instrument of political influence. What is not so typical about it, however, is that, in the words of the *New York Times*, it 'is now playing a pivotal role in the biggest battle over the future of American Protestantism since churches split over slavery at the time of the Civil War' (Goodstein & Kirkpatrick, 2004).

The IRD is one of several conservative politico/religious pressure groups funded in large part by a dozen conservative charitable foundations (Weaver & Seibert, 2004). The purpose of the wealthy families who established these foundations is to shape the direction of American public policy. A major strategy is to undermine those institutions in American civic life that still maintain some liberal values. Such institutions include the judiciary, academia, media, Congress, and charities themselves. The final example of such an institution is the 'mainstream' American church, consisting mostly of the following three denominations: United Methodists, Episcopalians, and Presbyterians. These churches have in fact been decreasing in membership, both overall and in comparison to the charismatic Pentecostals and the conservative Southern Baptists (Almond et al., 2003, p. 127). They are the supposed bastions of secularism and modernity at which the IRD is targeted.

The 'case of the unpatriotic bishops' is an example of an opportunistic assault on the patriotism of the leadership of United Methodism. The 9/11 attacks on America provided an ideal opportunity. The item of news upon which Mark Tooley, an IRD journalist, chose to hang his commentary was itself a media event: a column in the News Service of the United Methodist Church by Bishop Ken Carder, entitled: 'God Bless America ... and the World'. After a snide comment: 'Shouldn't he have taken political correctness to the next level and retitled the article "God Bless the Universe"?', Tooley goes on to make the observation upon which the rest of his article is based (IRD, 2004). Everywhere he goes, Tooley reports, he sees the American flag flying proudly. But at all the national United Methodist meetings he has attended, he saw only one individual who displayed the flag. There seemed an absence of emotion:

> There was no singing of 'God Bless America' or any other patriotic song, needless to say ... These church leaders apparently understood the events of September 11th as merely a 'tragedy' – one among many in this sad world – involving the deaths of several thousand people. Either they did not perceive a direct assault upon their own nation and its people, or they felt no outrage about it ... Why is there such unease, if not distaste, with the notion of love of country among United Methodist leaders? ... Why has this not aroused more heart-felt revulsion among the United Methodist officials who are fellow citizens of our country? Are they so

cold toward their native land, and are they such ardent citizens of the world, that they cannot express any special love for their own country?

After all, Tooley goes on to argue, they should be eternally grateful to God for what He has done for America. 'Who but the most blind can fail to admit that God has blessed our own country in ways and on a scale never seen before in the history of humanity?'

So not only are the Methodist leaders lacking in patriotism; they are also ungrateful to God. Even black Americans, who historically have much to complain about, are more patriotic, says Tooley. And now come the crocodile tears:

> The blindness and ingratitude of our United Methodist officials when it comes to our country should cause us sorrow . . . On the issue of patriotism, as on so many other issues, they have divorced themselves from the mainstream of our church. As such, they cannot really enjoy our church any more than they enjoy our country, because inwardly they feel superior to most of its members.

The usual populist dig at those unrepresentative and superior people up there concludes a highly partisan piece.

Such political and religious polarisation remains within the boundaries of democratic institutions, and represents an attempt to manipulate public opinion typical of late-modern society. However, the combination of civil and 'real' religion becomes more threatening when the conflict is physical and violent rather than ideological and verbal. In such recent arenas of conflict as Ireland, India/Pakistan, and the Balkans, civil and 'real' religions have combined to create apparently intractable conflicts. This dangerous combination easily transforms a world transformer fundamentalist into a world conqueror. I will argue in the following case study that this is what may have happened in the USA post-9/11.

### Different enemies, different strategies, different ideologies

There are, of course, many other differences between cultures that lead to differences between their respective fundamentalisms. As well as their *mode of reacting to the world*, fundamentalisms also differ in terms of who *their enemy* is and in the nature of *their ideology*. For example, given the political history and institutions of Islam, Islamic fundamentalists are more likely to choose governments as their out-group than are Protestant fundamentalists. Given their history of exile, fundamentalist Jews will treat their nearest Arab neighbours as a threat to their redemption, which can only occur when they repossess *Eretz Israel*. And given the wave after wave of immigrants from different cultures into the USA, Protestant fundamentalists will attack pluralism, tolerance, and moral relativity.

Moreover, the *holy books* from the different cultures present a different repertoire of concepts for fundamentalist leaders to reinterpret and emphasise in their ideology. The Qu'ran offers, for example, the concept of jihad, which Sayeed Qutb transformed into the leading element of revolutionary Islamic ideology. The Torah allows for a reading of God's promise to Abraham that justifies the annexation of the whole of *Eretz Israel*. And the Book of Revelation permits a variety of programmes to allow Protestant fundamentalists to hasten God's coming rule on earth.

Finally, the *nature of authority* differs between fundamentalisms as a consequence of cultural differences. The individualist values of American culture result in a theology in which God speaks directly to the believer through His word the Bible. Anyone is considered capable of making sense of God's word, which the Holy Spirit interprets for all. There is no need of a priest or a theologian; everyone is their own theologian. The result is, for example, the unusual spectacle of thousands of devotees arguing about eschatological doctrine on the internet. In authoritarian Islam, on the other hand, it is the imam's interpretation of the Qu'ran that matters, and although there are different schools of thought exemplified in the various traditions, ordinary Muslims are certainly not considered theological experts. One of Osama bin Laden's early attempts to increase his authority involved the claim to priesthood. He certainly could not pronounce a *fatwa* without such authority.

Thus, we may conclude that the historic cultures of the world still differ in many ways from each other. Their historical origins in the Middle East separate out those cultures that produced the religions of the book from other cultures. It was their utopian idealism that ultimately prepared the ground for modern fundamentalisms. And it was their location in different societies under different forms of governance that resulted in their different enemies, ideologies, and ways of reacting against the modern world. The global analysis from the perspective of modernisation emphasises the family resemblance of fundamentalisms; the more local analysis from the perspective of culture highlights their differences.

### Selves and identities – again

A major unifying theme relates the analyses of Chapters 1 and 2; it is *the concept of social identity*. I argued in Chapter 1 that modernisation and globalisation were not inevitable forces, but rather the results of human action. These huge historic movements both form, and are formed by, individual selves (in collaboration). In the same dynamic fashion, cultures are continuously evolving patterns that interact with people's selves and their identities.

The psychological process through which selves and identities develop in interaction with their cultural environment is the key to understanding the growth of fundamentalisms. The analysis of the concept of culture at the beginning of this chapter emphasised that culture is shared. A culture exists only if a category of persons 'owns' it. However, the possible range and nature of such categories is immense. The important feature of social categories is that they can be *internalised* by individuals, so as to become part of their selves (Turner, 1985). The category of jihadi warrior, born-again believer, or ultra-orthodox Jew becomes a social identity, a part of the self. Hence, those powerful motivations, such as self-esteem, which derive from the self are brought into play whenever the category in question becomes salient (Hogg & Abrams, 2003): If others denigrate my religion, then it is I whom they are diminishing; if we win a glorious victory, then it is my own self that is enhanced. Thus, those who perceive themselves to be members of a persecuted or a triumphant category of persons can be motivated to effective and dedicated individual or group action. For it is their self-esteem that is being diminished or increased.

If we apply this psychological level of analysis to cultures, its explanatory power becomes evident. When civil religion (aspects of the national culture) and 'real' religion are closely intertwined, the two categories of nationality and religion overlap considerably. So, therefore, do the two social identities that result when the categories are internalised into the self. Hence, in those situations where the national identity is salient, for example in times of perceived threat to the nation, the religious identity is also likely to be active. For fundamentalist Americans, the mutual interdependence of these two identities is not difficult to embrace. For fundamentalist Muslims and Jews, however, nationhood is a much more complex issue, as the nation-states that govern them may fail to generate a social identity for them. Rather, they have to rely on the categories of the *ummah*, the whole nation of Islam, or of Israel, defined not as the nation-state but as the chosen people of God.

It now becomes clearer how fundamentalists can be in dynamic relation with national cultures. Their 'native' culture has historically provided fundamentalisms with the soil they need to grow, and has planted the ideological seeds from which they have sprung. But they themselves have changed the cultural climate by their own actions. American culture will never be the same after the Moral Majority of the 1980s or the ongoing campaigns against abortion and gay rights. The laws and institutions of the secular state of Israel nevertheless include religious elements. And there is an ever-changing panoply of heroes and martyrs to add to Islamic mythology as battles are waged against the infidel. Some fundamentalisms are hostile to *the nation-state* as a product of secular modernity. However, the active public role of religion should not be underestimated (Casanova, 1994). Even fundamentalists value the concept of '*the nation*' as the cultural soil from which their religion has sprung, whether that 'nation' is characterised as the *ummah*, *Eretz Israel*, or the land of the free.

## Summary

- There are many different fundamentalisms, which have differing enemies, engage with the world in different ways, and create different new ideologies.
- Their enemies may be the religious establishment, nation-states, secular society, or other fundamentalisms.
- Their mode of engagement may be as conquerors of the world, as its transformers, as creators of their own world, or as renouncers of the world.
- Fundamentalisms may alternate between enemies and between modes of engagement.
- They develop their ideology so as to best fit their choice of enemy and mode of engagement.
- Active modes of engagement emphasise millennialist ideologies, as the fundamentalism justifies its political programme in terms of hastening the arrival of God's rule on earth.
- Fundamentalisms can be seen as sub-cultures, set within national and religious cultures. They tend to flourish in civilisations that, early in their history, embraced a concept of a holy and distant God.
- This resulted in repeated utopian attempts to re-instate the original purity of the founding fathers, and these attempts represent the forerunners of fundamentalisms.
- At the level of the national culture, many nations have developed a 'civil religion'. This is often based on the nation's foundation myth, and serves to legitimise the nation and its rulers.
- Fundamentalisms may seek to restore its purity and vitality. However, they are frequently hostile to the nation-state as a product of modernism.

## Further reading

Almond, G.A., Appleby, R.S., & Sivan, E. (2003) *Strong Religion: The Rise of Fundamentalisms around the World*. Chicago: University of Chicago Press.

Armstrong, K. (2000) *The Battle for God: Fundamentalism in Judaism, Christianity, and Islam*. London: HarperCollins.

Bruner, J. (1990) *Acts of Meaning*. Cambridge MA: Harvard University Press.

Casanova, J. (1994) *Public Religions in the Modern World*. Chicago: Chicago University Press.

Himmelfarb, G. (1999) *One Nation: Two Cultures*. New York: Random House.

Hunter, J.D. (1994) *Culture Wars: The Struggle to Define America*. New York: Basic Books.

Huntington, S.P. (1996) *The Clash of Civilisations and the Remaking of World Order*. New York: Simon & Schuster.

Schaller, M. & Crandall, C.S. (eds.) (2004) *The Psychological Foundations of Culture*. Mahwah NJ: Lawrence Erlbaum.

## CASE STUDY: CIVIL AND FUNDAMENTALIST RELIGION IN BUSH'S AMERICA

*America provides an excellent example of civil religion embedded deep in the culture of a nation founded by religious dissidents. Although this origin resulted in a legal separation of established church and state, the religious element is nevertheless of profound political and cultural importance. This case study demonstrates the degree of influence of religious fundamentalism on elections, the cornerstone of democratic politics. It explores how civil religion and fundamentalism can overlap in the context of a specific political platform. And it points to the policy changes that can result.*

### The context: Bush's re-election

Civil religion and the idea of nationhood in America have always been closely related to Protestant religion (Beaman, 2003). President George W. Bush is a self-confessed born-again believer. During his presidency he has sought to ensure that this relationship between nation and faith is strengthened, and that patriotism, conservatism, and fundamentalist religion are seen as natural bedfellows. This aim is in direct contrast with another American tradition, which favours secularism, tolerance, and multi-culturalism. So marked is this distinction that Himmelfarb (1999) has argued for the existence of two distinct American cultures.

However, overall, the Americans are an extremely religious nation. By

George W. Bush                                            © Brooks Kraft/Corbis

some criteria, they are second only to India in their degree of religiosity (Tickle, 1997, p. 189). We would therefore expect that religion would play at least some part in a presidential election. In 2004, the biggest determinant, equally with race, of which way an individual voted was, for the first time in recorded American history, a religious factor:

> Whether a person regularly attends church (or synagogue or mosque) was more important in determining his or her vote for president than such demographic characteristics as gender, age, income and region, and just as important as race . . . By far the most powerful new reality at the intersection of religion and politics is this: Americans who regularly attend worship services and hold traditional religious views increasingly vote Republican, while those who are less connected to religious institutions and more secular in their outlook tend to vote Democratic.
>
> (Pew Forum, 2005)

The evidence is extraordinarily powerful. Of the 16% of Americans who attend church more often than once a week, 64% voted Republican and 35% Democrat. For weekly attenders, the percentages were 58% and 41% respectively; for monthly attenders, 50% and 49%; for occasional attenders, 45% and 54%; and of the 15% of the electorate who never go to church, 36% voted Republican and 62% Democrat.

The same sort of pattern emerges when citizens' degree of religious orthodoxy is investigated. Orthodoxy was assessed in terms of belief in traditional doctrine and in interpretation of the Bible. Those who held the most orthodox religious beliefs, whether they were White Evangelical Protestants, White Roman Catholics, or Mainline Protestants, were most likely to be Republican in their affiliation; doctrinal modernists were more likely to be Democrats. Thus, old allegiances based on religious *denomination* have to some extent lost their grip. As recently as 1960, 71% of Roman Catholics supported the Democrats. Degree of orthodoxy has now become more predictive.

However, a huge majority of White Evangelical Protestants voted for Bush. This religious group comprised 23% of the overall electorate, and were:

> . . . by far the single most potent voting bloc in the electorate last year . . . The 2004 campaign showed once again that White Evangelicals are by far the most important component of the GOP [Republican Party] coalition. This group makes up nearly a quarter of the electorate, and votes Republican by increasingly lopsided margins. The president garnered 78% of all White Evangelical votes in 2004, a 10 percentage point increase over what he received four years earlier.
>
> (Pew Forum, 2005)

Why were these religious factors so much more predictive even than in Bush's 2000 victory? Then, for example, race was the most predictive factor, with gender the third most predictive, after church attendance. An answer is to be found in the range of 'moral' issues that have become increasingly important to religiously engaged voters, especially Evangelicals, since the formation of the Moral Majority in the 1980s. These issues include abortion, homosexuality, and prayer in schools. For some 22% of voters, these issues were the most important reason for them voting as they did. They outnumbered even those for whom national security was the most important issue. The association of such 'wedge' moral issues with religious commitment is indeed close. Highly committed religious voters were 12% in favour of gay marriage in 2003, those of average commitment 35% in favour, and those of low religious commitment, 50%.

What is more, Americans are in general in favour of their churches expressing their views on political matters, by a majority of 52% to 44%. Those aged 18 to 29 are 59% in favour and 36% against, whereas those aged over 65 are 38% in favour and 54% against. Clearly, American politicians will find it increasingly worthwhile to play the religious card; and religious leaders will find that they are increasingly expected to play the political one. Civil religion and 'real' religion are increasingly overlapping. In 2004, some religious leaders went so far as to recommend a Republican vote.

## The second inauguration speech

### *Its major themes*

If the 2004 re-election of a born-again Evangelical president was a watershed in the political power of the Christian Right, Bush's inaugural address to the nation was proof that the President not only recognised that new power, but was prepared to act as the *de facto* leader of the Christian Right himself. Careful textual analysis is required to reveal the message that religious constituencies would receive from the speech.

The President's speech begins with the defining event of his first term: the attacks of 9/11.

> At this second gathering, our duties are defined not by the words I use, but by the history we have seen together. For a half century, America defended our own freedom by standing watch on distant borders. After the shipwreck of communism came years of relative quiet, years of repose, years of sabbatical – and then there came a day of fire.

> We have seen our vulnerability – and we have seen its deepest source. For as long as whole regions of the world simmer in resentment and tyranny – prone to ideologies that feed hatred and excuse murder – violence will gather, and multiply in destructive power, and cross the most defended borders, and raise a mortal threat. There is only one force of history that can break the reign of hatred and resentment, and expose the pretensions

of tyrants, and reward the hopes of the decent and tolerant, and that is the force of human freedom.

We are led, by events and common sense, to one conclusion: The survival of liberty in our land increasingly depends on the success of liberty in other lands. The best hope for peace in our world is the expansion of freedom in all the world.

America's vital interests and our deepest beliefs are now one . . . So it is the policy of the United States to seek and support the growth of democratic movements and institutions in every nation and culture, with the ultimate goal of ending tyranny in our world.

(White House, 2005)

The war on terror is to be followed by the war on tyranny, since tyranny, in the President's analysis, is the origin of terror. He then asserts, however, that this task is not primarily a military one, nor does it involve the imposition of the American style of government. America will, nevertheless, not avoid the task of ending tyranny. In a passage designed to be noted by governments throughout the world, the President promises: 'We will persistently clarify the choice before every ruler and every nation: The moral choice between oppression, which is always wrong, and freedom, which is eternally right'. The President goes on to affirm his belief that freedom has a universal attraction. Then, speaking even more directly to different categories of listener, he says:

The rulers of outlaw regimes can know that we still believe as Abraham Lincoln did: 'Those who deny freedom to others deserve it not for themselves; and, under the rule of a just God, cannot long retain it'. The leaders of governments with long habits of control need to know: To serve your people you must learn to trust them. Start on this journey of progress and justice, and America will walk at your side.

(White House, 2005)

Then the President addresses Americans. He asks them to join him in this battle for freedom, both abroad and in America itself. He states that America itself is not totally free, referring to 'the unfinished work of American freedom'. He goes on to make clear what it is that he means by freedom for Americans (and, by implication, for others too):

In America's ideal of freedom, citizens find the dignity and security of economic independence, instead of labouring on the edge of subsistence. . . . To give every American a stake in the promise and future of our country, we will bring the highest standards to our schools, and build an ownership society. We will widen the ownership of homes and businesses, retirement savings and health insurance – preparing our people for the challenges of life in a free society. By making every citizen an agent of his or her own destiny, we will give our fellow Americans greater freedom from want and fear, and make our society more prosperous and just and equal.

In America's ideal of freedom, the public interest depends on private character – on integrity, and tolerance towards others, and the rule of conscience in our own lives. Self-government relies, in the end, on the governing of the self. That edifice of character is built in families, supported by communities with standards, and sustained in our national life by the truths of Sinai, the Sermon on the Mount, the words of the Koran, and the varied faiths of our people. Americans move forward in every generation by reaffirming all that is good and true that came before – the ideals of justice and conduct that are the same yesterday and today and forever.

(White House, 2005)

The President then calls upon the nation to unite, in the way that it did after 9/11. It should continue to unite in the fight for freedom. As for the future:

We go forward with complete confidence in the eventual triumph of freedom. Not because history runs on the wheels of inevitability; it is human choices that move events. Not because we consider ourselves a chosen nation; God moves and chooses as He wills . . . History has an ebb and flow of justice, but history also has a visible direction, set by liberty and the Author of Liberty.

(White House, 2005)

The speech concludes with a reference back to the Declaration of Independence, and to the sounding of the Liberty Bell, both key elements of the foundation myth:

America, in this young century, proclaims liberty throughout all the world, and to all the inhabitants thereof. Renewed in our strength – tested, but not weary – we are ready for the greatest achievements in the history of freedom.

May God bless you, and may He watch over the United States of America.

(White House, 2005)

The President is reported to have begun to plan the speech almost immediately after his election victory had been confirmed. It is said to have gone through at least 20 drafts (Balz & VandeHei, 2005). It is therefore important to recognise that its ideas and construction are more complex and carefully crafted than may appear at first reading. There are at least three levels of meaning to which it can be analysed.

### The speech as civil religion

At the most basic level, most commentators considered the speech in the context of previous historic inauguration speeches. 'The President is expected to deliver an address that emphasises the basic principles that united the country', affirmed the *New York Times* (2005). 'On that count, George W. Bush did his job . . . Mr Bush's declarations about promoting global democracy ring true as a statement of American ideals'. The speech, after all, was consciously following such outstanding rhetorical performances as those of Presidents Truman and Kennedy.

'Not since JFK in 1960 has an American President provided such an ambitious and unabashed case for the promotion of liberty at home and abroad', announced the *Wall Street Journal* (2005). The *Washington Post* contented itself with remarking that the speech was 'one of the most expansive manifestos ever offered from an inaugural podium', offering a little gentle criticism of 'an inaugural address of expansive idealism, breathtaking ambition – and uncertain relevance to the policies he will pursue in a second term' (Balz & VandeHei, 2005).

At this first level of analysis, the speech can be construed simply as an attempt to unify and inspire the nation behind the archetypal American values of liberty and freedom (the words 'free', 'freedom', and 'liberty' were repeated no fewer than 49 times). There were the usual references back to the founding fathers, the Constitution, and the Declaration of Independence. There were several references to God, but certainly no more than in previous inaugural speeches. And there was the usual hint of the domestic programme that the President intended to pursue, a hint that all knew would be fleshed out in the forthcoming address to Congress. In sum, the speech rehearsed the key themes of American civil religion.

### The speech as political promise

However, the speech was also a political event. It can be construed, at a deeper level, as a series of messages to the various constituencies who voted the President into office. In particular, we can clearly see the influence of the neo-conservatives, who seized the political initiative after their publication of the document 'Project for a New American Century' in 1997, and whose ideas dominated American political discourse for nearly a decade.

The first part of the speech argues that America's security can only be secured if the rest of the world is free. The tone of warning to other nations clearly reflects a willingness to exercise American power throughout the world, unilaterally if necessary. 'This is not primarily the task of arms, though we will defend ourselves and our friends by force of arms when necessary' (White House, 2005). Although the President did not refer to any other nations by name, his Secretary of State elect, Condoleeza

Rice, shortly thereafter mentioned no less than five states that should take particular note of the President's message. Later, the President installed two neo-conservatives, John Bolton and Paul Wolfowitz, to key positions in multinational institutions (the United Nations and the World Bank). The President was thus re-affirming the interventionist programme of the neo-conservatives, that he had already promoted in his first inaugural address in 2001: 'Through much of the last century, America's faith in freedom and democracy was a rock in a raging sea. Now it is a seed upon the wind, taking root in many nations' (White House, 2001a).

In the second part of the 2005 speech (White House, 2005), referring to American affairs, the President makes further gestures to his conservative support. We are told that just as the rest of the world does not, in many places, enjoy freedom, even America itself has some way to go before it achieves freedom. Just as foreign nations need freedom from tyrannical governments, so the American people need to be free from government constraint. Freedom means 'the dignity and security of economic independence, instead of labouring on the edge of subsistence'. In a nation that has already decreased state social provision in various areas, the aim is to 'build an ownership society'. This 'ownership' includes the privatisation of retirement savings and health insurance. For, says the President, 'the public interest depends on private character'. Character is built in families, supported by communities, and sustained by religious faith. The President is referring back to his first inaugural speech again, where the word 'character' occurs several times. Clearly, the second part of the speech, too, is crafted to please conservatives, since it defines freedom as the citizen's freedom from government, a classic conservative theme.

However, the President is also gesturing to the Christian Right throughout the speech. He does not do so by frequent overt references to God, but rather by coded references, which have resonance only for the Christian Right (Rothschild, 2005). He starts by describing 9/11 in apocalyptic terms as 'the day of fire'. This fiery theme is echoed in the phrases 'the untamed fire of freedom', and 'hope kindles hope', which draw from passages in the books of the biblical prophecies to be found in Jeremiah (17.27, 50.32) and Isaiah (33.14). He also refers to a prominent biblical theme when he says that unity and pride are felt when 'the captives are set free'. When he says 'Freedom is the permanent hope of mankind, the hunger in dark places, the longing of the soul', he is quoting almost directly from Psalm 107: 'For he satisfieth the longing soul, and filleth the hungry soul with goodness. Such as sit in darkness and the shadow of death, being bound in affliction and iron'. When he affirms that 'History also has a visible direction, set by liberty and the Author of Liberty', he is echoing a favourite evangelical text from Hebrews (12.2): 'Let us fix our eyes on Jesus, the author and perfecter of our faith'. When, in his peroration, he proclaims 'America, in this young century, proclaims liberty throughout all the world, and to all the inhabitants thereof', he is repeating almost word for word Leviticus (25.10): 'And ye shall hallow the fiftieth year, and proclaim liberty throughout all the land unto all the inhabitants thereof: it shall be a jubilee unto you'. Knowing that conservative Christians favour the King James version of the Bible, Bush consciously retains one of its archaisms ('thereof').

The President reserves a particularly heavyweight biblical reference for a specific purpose. In a necessary concession to other religions, he had argued that character is built in national life not only by the ten commandments and the sermon on the mount, but also by the words of the Qu'ran and the varied faiths of our people. As the personification of the nation's civil religion, he has to include other faiths. Realising that this liberal note will upset many conservative Christians, he immediately refers to ideals of justice and conduct that are 'the same yesterday, today, and for ever'. The Biblical letter to the Hebrews refers to 'Jesus Christ, the same yesterday and today and for ever' (13.8). This text is on the walls of many conservative Christian homes. Its use signals that the President has them especially in mind, despite his inclusive reference to other faiths.

However, the conservative Christians will want and expect more than mere coded messages that indicate that the President is one of them and has not forgotten them. They voted for him largely because they thought that he would promote a conservative policy agenda with respect to the 'wedge' issues of social morality. The President does not forget these concerns. In a subtle reference to abortion, he announces 'even the unwanted have worth'. His repeated references to conduct and character also signal his recognition of the moral agenda. He follows a well-known world-view of the fundamentalist Christian right when he starts with the character of the individual, moves on to the family, then to local communities, and finally to the nation and the world. This world-view represents a series of concentric circles moving steadily outwards from the individual and his or her relationship with God (Lienesch, 1993). It is the aim of those fundamentalists who seek dominion for God in every sphere of life to introduce God's reign at all these levels.

### The speech as ideological statement

At one level of analysis, then, the President was simply making another speech of a high-flown rhetorical nature proclaiming America's virtues and following on in a sequence of equally inspirational orations. At a second, political, level, he was addressing his key constituencies, the neo-cons and the Christian Right, and promising that he would not forget them in his second term. But at a third level he was doing something much more profound. He was articulating a new ideology. Or, to be more precise, he was pulling together civil religion and fundamentalism and weaving them together into a single narrative. He was, to quote his speech, equating America's 'vital interests with our deepest beliefs'.

The first strand is the belief in America's *manifest destiny*. The Puritan leader John Winthrop had insisted during the passage from England that the settlers would be seen by the rest of the world as a city on a hill, with all eyes upon them. The implication was, that because they were establishing a new way of life, they had an obligation to make sure they fulfilled its charter and promise. They would be an example for the rest of the world to follow. They had to be virtuous. However, very soon into the nineteenth century this bold optimism tempered by a humble sense of obligation morphed into a much more expansionist rhetoric. America would lead the world until the whole earth was free. It was this expansionist belief in the export of liberty and freedom that informed the neo-conservatives' Project for the New American Century, although they themselves proposed the national interest as their motive.

The second strand of the President's ideological innovation is the fundamentalist belief that *God directs human history*: 'history also has a visible direction, set by liberty and the Author of Liberty'. This is a profoundly important belief for American Protestants. It underpins their understanding of history, of the present national and world situation, and of the future (Boyer, 1992). Many believe that the future course of history is already set by the Almighty, and that its details can be discovered in the Bible. Some are more concerned to establish God's reign on earth so as to inaugurate the millennium.

Bush weaves these two strands together in a subtle way, so that we come imperceptibly to the conclusion that the freedom and liberty, which it is America's duty to bestow on the world, are also God's plan for the world. Civil religion's Manifest Destiny is fundamentalism's Divine Destiny: America is God's agent, and God is a crusading God. There are at least three passages in Bush's inaugural speech in which American liberty and God are elided. First, where God is described as the Author of Liberty; second, where American ideals of justice and conduct are elided with Christ, since both are 'the same yesterday and today and for ever'; and third, where the call of freedom is said, like the call of Christ, 'to come to every mind and every soul'.

As America's task is to spread freedom throughout the world, it is also by definition to spread God likewise. In Christ's 'great commission', which is not quoted but which underlies the reworked ideology, he enjoins his disciples (Matthew 28.19,20): 'Go ye therefore, and teach all nations, baptising them . . . Teaching them to observe all things whatsoever I have commanded you'. In a word, spreading freedom to nations, not just to individuals, is God's work. And, as we have seen, the President was clear about the nature of freedom. It is essentially radical free-market capitalism. The corollary is that those who reject this version of freedom are thereby rejecting God.

## Faith-based initiatives

Textual analysis can take us only so far. If an ideology based on a fusion of civil and fundamentalist religion is being used to justify and motivate action, then we should be able to discern it at work in a political programme. There are several arenas in which the President has indeed acted in accord with the agendas of his first and second inaugural addresses. The prosecution of wars abroad is one obvious example. A more domestic one is the attempt to influence the administration of justice through judicial appointments, and by other means. However, the example that best demonstrates the President playing to his Christian conservative support can be found in his *faith-based initiatives*. These serve both to reward the faithful for their support and also to further the neo-conservative agenda of privatising social provision.

Faith-based initiatives were nothing new for the President (Farris, Nathan, & Wright, 2004). When he was elected Governor of Texas in 1995, and fairly soon after he had undergone his conversion to evangelical Protestantism, he had come under the influence of Marvin Olasky. Olasky was intellectual leader of a group that argued that the causes of poverty, such as joblessness and drug abuse, were best tackled by faith-based groups. Such committed workers can avoid the bureaucratic constraints of secular government, ran the argument, and change people's hearts and lives. The Personal Responsibility and Work Opportunities Reconciliation Act (1996) contained a provision championed by Senator John Ashcroft (later Bush's Attorney General), which stated that government could no longer exclude faith-based groups from receiving federal grants because of their religious character. Bush was the first state governor to apply this new provision at the state level, saying:

> Government can hand out money, but it cannot put hope in our hearts or a sense of purpose in our lives. It cannot bring us peace of mind. It cannot fill the spiritual well from which we draw strength day to day. Only faith can do that.
>
> (Farris et al., 2004)

Campaigning under the slogan 'compassionate conservatism' for his first term, Bush said in his first inaugural speech 'compassion is the work of a nation, not just a government'. Within 10 days, on 29 January 2001, the President established the White House Office of Faith-Based and Community Initiatives, together with five centres within key federal agencies: Education, Health and Human Services, Housing and Urban Development, Justice, and Labor. In December 2002 and June 2004 he added five more. The initiative has also been promoted in many other government agencies, where programmes relating to business ownership and development, and home ownership, are supported.

The task of these centres is essentially to penetrate the operations of the federal government agencies in a co-ordinated and purposeful way to further the President's initiative and ensure that funds go to faith-based providers of services. This centralised executive action by the President is thus, ironically, aimed at reducing federal involvement and bureaucracy. However, the reach of his programme extends down to state and city level, with the President's office estimating that, at the beginning of 2005, 20 state governors and 180 mayors had opened faith-based offices or programmes.

These structural changes were accompanied by legislative proposals aimed at providing incentives to faith-based organisations and at permitting them to retain their own discriminatory employment policies, even though they were receiving federal funds. However, Congress did not approve the legislation in 2002, and the President instead took executive action. He justified this step by arguing that he was preventing the faith-based agencies from being discriminated against by government because of their faith:

> I believe in the power of faith in people's lives. Our government should not fear programs that exist because a church or a synagogue or a mosque has decided to start one. We should not discriminate against programs based upon faith in America. We should enable them to access Federal money, because faith-based programs can change people's lives, and America will be better off for it.
>
> (White House, 2001b)

Or, as the White House 'fact sheet' entitled 'America's Compassion in Action' puts it: 'regulations protecting the religious integrity of faith-based organisations and the religious freedom of beneficiaries have been put into place ... The Federal government does not fund religion', the fact sheet hastens to add: 'instead, the President's Faith-Based and Community Initiative enables some of America's most effective social service providers to compete fairly for Federal funding to make a difference in the lives of our most vulnerable citizens without diluting the providers' religious identity'. By 'religious identity' is meant the practice of discriminating against gays and other minority groups when hiring employees.

The regulations do indeed overtly maintain the ruling of the United States Supreme Court that faith-based organisations may not use government funding to support 'inherently religious' activities. In its advice to potential applicants, the White House says that this refers to religious worship, instruction, or proselytism. But these are slippery terms; 'Although you may invite participants to join in your organisation's religious services or events', advises the White House, 'you should be careful to reassure them that they can receive government-funded help even if they do not participate in these activities'. We should also note that the regulations refer to direct funding only. Indirect funding, for example by means of vouchers, may be spent on such things as training to be an evangelist.

Having made it easier for faith-based organisations to apply by 'creating a level playing field' by these regulations, the President also ensured that teams were available to train such applicants in how to apply. All these measures certainly had an effect on the disbursement of funds. For example, in 2003 the number of Department of Health and Human Services grants to faith-based organisations rose by 41%. Overall funding rose by 19% to $568million. The money has gone to a wide range of projects. For example, the Commerce Department's Technology Opportunities Program gave the Ekklesia Development Corporation of the Corinthian Baptist Church in Cincinnati a $510,000 award to establish the nation's first online service linking more than 2000 faith congregations and more than 100 religious organisations and faith-based agencies to their clientele.

There appears, however, to be a certain selectivity about the allocation of grants. For example, 'abstinence only' programmes of sex education have received an increase in funding at the expense of comprehensive programmes (Farris et al., 2004). Some 90 grants for 'abstinence-only' programmes, ranging from $250,000 to $800,000 were made in 2003. This trend is also evident in grants made by USAID for programmes in developing countries. Such selectivity in grant allocation is doubtless encouraged by the involvement of faith-based organisations in the evaluation of applications by other faith-based organisations.

## The President among friends

The privatisation of social provision into the care of faith-based organisations is clearly a long-standing and fundamental plank of the Bush presidential programme. We can get a further insight into the President's mind on this issue, and that of his Christian Right constituency, from his remarks when he is speaking to them largely off the cuff. These are, perhaps surprisingly, available from the White House itself. The occasion was the first White House National Conference on Faith-Based and Community Initiatives, held in Washington in June 2004 (White House, 2004).

The first notable feature of the President's remarks is his continuous denigration of the federal government: *his* government:

> Listen, I fully understand there are people in the faith community who have said, why do I want to interface with the federal government? (Laughter). Why would I want to interface with a group of people that want to try to get me to not practice my faith? It's hard to be a faith-based program if you can't practice faith. And the message to you is we're changing the culture here in America (Applause) . . . Listen, what I'm telling you is, is that I told our government, the people in my government, rather than fear faith programs, welcome them. They do a better job than government can do (Applause). So the federal government wants to curtail religious freedoms, and is incompetent to boot. It's a process debate that takes place up on Capitol Hill rather than a results-oriented debate. If you're a results-oriented debater, you say, all I care about is making sure that the addict receives help. And if it takes changing a person's heart to change addiction, we ought to welcome the power that changes a person's heart in our society (Applause).

The same bureaucratic enemies are to be found at the state and city levels:

> Now, look, one of the – part of the feedback we've gotten is that there's a bottleneck at the state and local governments. Some of the money – (Applause) Yes, see what I mean? (Laughter). Some of the money is block-granted to states. And therefore, if there's not a governor who has a faith-based office who understands the vast potential of changing their state, you'll be frustrated. I know that. So part of our mission is to work with you to help change the attitude at the state level. We got our hands full here, by the way, too. Don't get me wrong. (Laughter). There's a bureaucratic mindset that we're working to change in Washington. But we also want to help you with the governors and mayors.

Faith-based programmes can work miracles:

> Governments can hand out money. But governments cannot put love in a person's heart, or a sense of purpose in a person's life. The truth of the matter is, that comes when a loving citizen puts their arm around a brother and sister in need and says, I love you, and God loves you, and together we can perform miracles (Applause).

Of course, this does not constitute an 'inherently religious activity'. Among the souls saved, (and I am echoing the President's own words here) was one Brad Lassiter:

> . . . the youngest of 17 children. He spent most of his childhood without a home. His education ended in the 4th grade – essentially he was abandoned and left on the street – got addicted to drugs, took a bullet in the mouth, actually, at one point in his life, went to prison. And Gospel Rescue Ministries gave him a place to live when he came out of prison. See, he started reading the Bible in prison. It is a powerful change agent when you start reading the Bible in prison (Applause). America changes one heart at a time, one soul at a time.

This is a classic story of the salvation of the lost soul, typical of traditional evangelical discourse. What is more, it is a re-assertion of the individualistic American culture: salvation occurs not at the social, but at the individual level of analysis. It is also worth noting in passing that the President still observes some of the legal proprieties: Brad started reading the Bible himself. Gospel Rescue Ministries are not credited with sowing this seed.

The money is in fact going to religious businesses. The word 'ministry' in America has largely lost its original meaning of 'serving', and now refers to the businesses that evangelical religious leaders such as Jerry Falwell and many others have established. Falwell at one stage had a 'ministry' of $23million per annum (Harding, 2000). Says Bush:

Remember, a faith-based program can be a mega-church – and by the way, there's some fantastic churches in our country who spread faith throughout their ministry – or it can be a five-person staff . . . [Tony Evans] is willing to help young churches, and faith-based programs in inner-city Dallas, Texas, as to how to accomplish the mission, how to grow from little to big, how to grow from wanting to be vibrant, to successful. And that's what the faith-based initiative is meant to do. It's meant to allow for access of federal money, but at the same time spawn the entrepreneurial spirit, what I call social entrepreneurs, and encourage their growth.

Thus the faith-based initiative is intended to enable little businesses to become bigger businesses. As synagogues and mosques are not in the habit of calling themselves businesses, or ministries for that matter, the intended recipients seem likely to be Protestant evangelical churches.

The above analyses of 2004 voting patterns, the second inaugural speech, and the faith-based initiative all point to a profoundly important fact for America and the rest of the world. President Bush was, probably uniquely among American presidents, willing to merge civil religion with Protestant fundamentalist belief to the extent that they are not always distinguishable.

# 3 Fundamentalisms as social movements

## The Western religious context: Early theories

The globalising world is a fruitful context for the development of funda-mentalisms, challenging as it does so many local assumptions and affiliations, and creating uncertainty and threat for many (see Chapter 1). National or regional cultures, likewise, can provide the backdrop of civil religion from which fundamentalisms may emerge (Chapter 2). But to explain properly the growth, development, and historical course of fundamentalisms, we have to construe them as *social movements*, which all arise in response to their local religious and political contexts. Those changing contexts, and the effectiveness of fundamentalisms in shaping them and reacting to them, will determine their success or failure. This chapter owes a special debt to the Fundamentalism Project, the findings of which are summarised by Almond et al. (2003).

Some fundamentalisms appear mainly to be responses to changes in their *religious* context. The obvious example here is American Protestant funda-mentalism. Others arise primarily as a result of *political* developments, for example fundamentalist Islam. Some Jewish fundamentalisms (for example, Gush Emunim, the subject of the case study in this chapter), and Khalsa Dal, the major Sikh fundamentalism, also appear to have mainly political origins. In order to simplify the account, I will discuss the *religious context of Western Protestant fundamentalisms* in the first two sections, and the *political context of fundamentalist Islam* in the third. Of course, in reality religion and politics are not so easily distinguishable.

### Western Christianity: Decline and fall, or balanced market?

There are several different theoretical accounts of recent religious develop-ments in Western Christianity. McGuire (2002) distinguishes four such accounts: *secularisation, reorganisation, individualisation*, and *market supply*.

The *secularisation* thesis represents the Christian church as in permanent decline in the face of secular modernity (Bruce, 2002). The *reorganisation* account notes the structural changes away from established denominations

(Johnson, 1993), especially in America. Others go further, suggesting that churches as institutions are no longer the main arbiters of belief. Rather, each *individual* selects their own beliefs and values to meet their personal needs (Roof, 1999). And the logical conclusion is, using the analogy of economics, a *market-place* where suppliers of religion differentiate their product so as to meet a relatively constant demand for spiritual goods (Stark & Finke, 2000).

Some of these accounts present themselves as alternative and mutually exclusive theories. However, McGuire helpfully suggests that the four accounts are better understood as meta-narratives of the Western Christian scene rather than as fully fledged theories. Each account highlights features of that context that the others largely ignore.

In terms of the different levels of analysis used in this book, the *secularisation* thesis clearly best relates to the global level of analysis, since secularisation is a global phenomenon (see Chapter 1). Paradoxically, the secularisation of mainstream religion may have provided the initial motivation for the world-wide growth of fundamentalisms in angry reaction. The *reorganisation* narrative sits squarely in the present chapter, since it is within the context of structural change in religion that specific Christian fundamentalist movements arise. The *market* approach is best dealt with at the organisational level of analysis (see Chapter 4), as different congregations of the faithful compete for adherents. Finally, the *individualisation* account fits into an analysis at the level of the person (see Chapter 6).

### Church and sect

How, then, are we to understand the ongoing structural reorganisation of Western Christianity, and why should fundamentalisms occur as a part and product of these changes? The analysis of structural change has been dominated by the theory of *church and sect*, inspired by Weber (1919/1946, 1922/1993) and developed by Troeltsch (1981).

Weber distinguished the utopian purity of an original religious movement from its subsequent institutionalisation, naming the former condition 'sect', and the latter 'church'. He used the foundation of Christianity to exemplify sect, and the Roman Catholic Church as an instance of church. Church institutionalised sect by such means as professional clergy hierarchically organised, dogmatic doctrine, and formalised ritual. Further, it compromised with secular authorities in its search for power and influence. Weber also distinguished asceticism from mysticism, the former indicating a strict regime for personal living and the latter spiritual experience, sometimes of an ecstatic nature.

Troeltsch combined these two binary distinctions into a single tripartite distinction: church, sect, and mysticism. He noted that church was likely to be politically conservative, in alliance with the secular power to legitimate their authority over the people. Sect, in his view, was a separate community of people who had a personal relationship with God and treated each other as equals. Mysticism referred to a radical religious individualism, which was hostile to creeds, sacraments, and organisation.

Both Weber and Troeltsch saw church and sect as mutually inter-dependent in promoting religion. Sect continually renews religion by reminding it of its utopian ideals, whereas church provides the structure to spread the faith. Hence the repeated occurrence of schisms in religious history was not necessarily disastrous, but rather a means of survival and sometimes of growth.

Clearly, the ideas of Weber and Troeltsch were based on the historical example of the Catholic Church in Europe. They were not particularly appropriate for the analysis of twentieth-century religion, especially as it developed in America. America has been the major source in the West of new religious movements in the modern and late-modern periods. Moreover, the huge preponderance of social scientific research into religion has been conducted by Americans, and most of it is about America. There may be a danger that unwarranted generalisations regarding European Christianity may be derived from American research. For example, the thesis that religious vitality is a function of the number and variety of suppliers of religion is not generalisable to Europe, where in many countries suppliers have increased but vitality decreased. However, America is an ideal example, since its proliferation and variety of Christian movements, together with its demanding religiosity, combine to bring about constant reorganisation of religious structures. Such flux, I will argue, is a fruitful context for fundamentalisms.

### Religious dynamism in America

One cannot exaggerate the extraordinary number and diversity of religious movements in America. There are a large number of denominations, within which disputes and conflicts result in frequent schisms and the birth of *new sects*. These, in their turn, often spawn further sects, as soon as some adherents perceive them to have departed from the pure ideals that prompted their foundation. For example, the Methodist Episcopal Church in America was itself originally a sect. In the early 1900s a schism occurred, and the Church of the Nazarene was formed in Los Angeles, while the Holiness Church of Christ started up in Texas. In the 1950s, the Church of the Nazarene itself suffered schism, spawning two sects, the Voice of the Nazarene Association of Churches and the Wesleyan Holiness Association of Churches (Bainbridge, 1997).

The schismatic process of sect formation, however, is not the only source of religious movements. Religious entrepreneurs invent and popularise entirely *new movements*, which do not derive from a schism with existing movements. These are often labelled cults, at least when they are first invented. Successful examples are Jehovah's Witnesses, Seventh Day Adventists, Church of Jesus Christ of Latter-Day Saints (Mormons), and Christian Scientists. Because they require adherents to grasp and embrace new ideas, cults tend to attract more educated followers than do sects (Stark & Bainbridge, 1985).

Finally, huge *suburban congregations*, which are only distantly, if at all, affiliated to a denomination, develop and plant further congregations, led by charismatic pastors. As I will demonstrate in Chapter 4, these enterprises become highly developed and sophisticated organisations.

## The Western religious context: Recent developments

### *Tension with society*

Although the early sociological theories of religion are not clearly applicable to today's religious scene, they nevertheless provide some useful pointers to aid our understanding. In particular, the church/sect distinction highlighted differences in the relationship of religious movements with their secular environment. Johnson (1963) expressed this in binary terms, defining a church as a religious group that accepts the social environment in which it exists, and a sect as one that rejects it. Thus he defined modern-day sects in terms of the central feature of fundamentalisms: hostility to aspects of modernity. Johnson's definition enabled the term 'church' to be freed from any connotation of establishment or political power. Instead of 'church', a more useful label might rather be 'denomination' (Niebuhr, 1929), denoting an organised and established religious movement (which was probably a sect early in its history). If members of established denominations are accepting of their social environment, it is likely to be because they find that environment rewarding and comfortable. It is therefore no surprise to find that adherents of established denominations are generally wealthier and better educated than those of sects (Bainbridge, 1997, Chapter 2).

More recently, the dichotomous categorisation of movements by their acceptance or rejection of their societal context has given way to the idea of a *continuum of tension* between a movement and its context (Stark & Finke, 2000). Thus some denominations known for their liberal theological approach are considered to be at a low level of tension, since they have accommodated to the societal context by, for example, appointing gay priests and bishops. Traditional conservative denominations and most sects, on the other hand, would be at a much higher level of tension. Thus those schisms that are the result of a desire for renewed purity of doctrine and practice, or for a more fervent relationship with God, create a new movement with a higher level of tension. Religious movements that lack support because they are either at a low or at a high level may increase or decrease their level, respectively. In this way they approximate more closely to the mean, thereby appealing to more people.

However, this idea of a single dimension, 'tension', relating religious movements to a single entity, 'the societal context', cannot do justice to the complexity of the organisational restructuring of Western, and specifically American, Christianity. For example, there are two very different historical strands in traditional American Protestantism: the *dissenting* and the *Calvinist* traditions. The *dissenting* tradition is essentially anti-establishment, libertarian, democratic, enthusiastic, and, above all, individualistic. The individual's relationship with God is central, and to some extent he or she is their own religious authority, provided that their understanding is Bible-based. The various Pentecostal movements reflect this strand. The *Calvinist* tradition, however, is far more concerned with formalised doctrine and ascetic practice in obedience to the laws of God. Southern Baptists and some Reformed denominations exemplify this tradition. Clearly, the nature of the tension that a sect or denomination will have with its context will differ, depending upon which of these two historical strands dominates in its culture. A primarily dissenting movement will tend to be in tension regarding any perceived threat to its religious freedom; a primarily Calvinist one will attack perceived violations of God's law.

Moreover, '*the societal context*' is similarly far too inclusive a concept to explain the complexity of the relationship of traditional conservative religion to other institutions and sub-cultures. For example, underlying the tension thesis outlined above is the assumption that 'the societal context' is necessarily more liberal in its beliefs, values, and attitudes than even the liberal Christian denominations that approximate closely to it at a low level of tension. It is far more liberal than more conservative denominations and sects. Yet today's pluralist American society consists of a huge variety of sub-cultures, many of which are just as conservative as conservative religious movements, but are not religious in nature. The group of neo-conservatives who dominated the early years of the George W. Bush presidency are a case in point.

### Different sub-cultures

Rather than using inclusive constructs and a one-dimensional relationship to gain a theoretical understanding of Western Christianity, we need to develop a more nuanced account. The approach adopted here uses the concepts of cultural analysis outlined in Chapter 2. This account treats religious movements as related *sub-cultures*, and their social context as a number of varied cultures.

To construe a religious movement as a sub-culture implies that it possesses a unique set of beliefs, values, and norms of behaviour (BVNs), some of which it shares with other religious movements. Comparisons with other religious and non-religious sub-cultures may then be made along the dimensions of BVNs. These are not the only possible dimensions of sub-cultural comparisons, however. Such cultural features as the nature of the movement's organisation, and its authority structure and leadership, together with sub-cultural artefacts such as documents and buildings, are also of potential relevance.

Consider, for example, some of the questions asked of referees regarding student entry to Tennessee Temple University, ('Where Truth is Taught'):

2    Is the applicant born-again?
4    Does the applicant attend church regularly?
5    What is the applicant's position on speaking in tongues?
10   Does the applicant have any personality weaknesses?
12   What is the applicant's denominational affiliation? (Temple University, 2002)

Comparison of this sub-cultural artefact with the application requirements for other religious and secular universities would reveal a complex set of differences in BVNs.

When we compare religious movements in sub-cultural terms, some interesting recent developments become apparent. All traditional conservative Protestant movements hold fast to certain core *beliefs*, such as the supreme authority of the Bible for belief and practice, and the existence of a supernatural realm from which God constantly intervenes in the natural and social worlds. Indeed, in the early 1960s, approximately 90% of 'high-tension' American Protestant believers held that the Devil actually exists, that Biblical miracles happened, and that Jesus will return to earth in a literal sense (Glock & Stark, 1965). However, near the beginning of the twenty-first century, in several traditionalist movements the Bible is not taken entirely literally, and while its authority is not questioned, alternative interpretations on some issues are countenanced between which the believer may choose (Tamney, 2002). Furthermore, increasingly informal and enthusiastic forms of worship are being practised (Coleman, 2000).

At the level of *values and attitudes*, a similar accommodation is increasingly being made. Whereas traditionalist believers hold the family in high regard, and are generally solid on flagship issues such as abortion and homosexuality, they may revise the traditional position regarding the patriarchal headship of the family by the husband and father, and be more understanding of divorce (Smith, 2000). They are not now so hostile to 'worldly' professionals as to ignore the need of many for individual therapy or counselling, nor do they attribute all their problems to their sin. Further, they do not regard many of the activities made possible by their increasing affluence as sinful. Former strict *norms of behaviour* have frequently been revised to permit dancing, fashionable dress, drink in moderation, and visits to the theatre and cinema.

These developments are of great interest, for they help us to understand why conservative Christianity embraces some features of modernisation but reacts angrily to others. We may characterise the above concessions in general as a recognition of the increasing individualism of Western society. Individualism is undoubtedly a feature of modernisation; it is also part of the historical strand of dissent at the root of American Protestant religion. The Reformation, after all, gave a kick-start to the process of modernisation. The concessions have clearly been made shrewdly.

### Tradition revived: But why?

Tamney (2002) categorises the current Christian flux in America into four types of religious movement: traditional, modernised traditional, modern, and late-modern movements. *Traditional* movements have made few of the compromises exemplified above, *modernised traditional* ones have made more. *Modern* movements constitute the 'mainstream' denominations such as the United Methodist, Presbyterian, and Episcopalian churches, but although the central governance of these denominations is fairly liberal in its theology, each contains strongly traditional elements and the potential for, or the actuality of, schism. Finally, *late-modern* churches reflect the pluralism and eclecticism of the late-modern age. They give a home to people who are happy to remain uncertain about their faith, regarding it as a journey in an unclear direction and to an unknown destination.

Research has pointed to an important general trend. *Those churches that are traditional, but especially those that are modernised traditional, appear to have flourished relative to the other two types.* The various Pentecostal denominations increased their membership from under 2 million in 1960 to 12 million in 2000. In the same period, the Southern Baptists went up from 10 to 17 million. However, the United Methodists dropped from 10 to 8 million, and the Episcopalians from 3.5 to 2 million (Sherkat, 2001). Other indices of vitality in addition to membership numbers, for example, extra time and money spent on the church, have been developed. They confirm the relative strength of traditional denominations such as Southern Baptists and Assemblies of God (Olson & Perl, 2001), and of the more traditional congregations within denominations (Iannacone, 1994).

How are we to explain this trend? Traditional and modernised traditional churches are by definition more exclusive than modern and late-modern churches, in that they require a greater level of conformity in terms of BVNs, including the expenditure of time and money, from their members. Thus in both their recruitment of new members and in their maintenance, these movements would be expected to exclude individuals whom others would include (Bibby, 1978). Yet their membership and vitality has actually increased relative to that of the others.

Kelley (1972) argued that the explanation for this paradox lies in the *'strictness'* of these churches. By this he meant that they require membership to be a costly commitment, and then enforce that commitment. For example, they regulate members' behaviour, require conformity to authoritative leadership, punish dissent, and discourage leisure association with non-believers. No 'free riders', who enjoy the benefits but do not pay the costs, are permitted. They therefore attract adherents by persuading them that this is indeed a movement worthy of respect, because it takes its faith seriously.

Stark and Finke (2000) argue further that although the costs of belonging to these movements are greater, so are the rewards. If the most attractive religious 'firm' (their term) is the one that offers the most advantageous cost/

benefit ratio, then the rewards offered by 'strict' movements will have to be greater than those offered by their competitors by a considerable order of magnitude. This is because they will also have to compensate for the greater costs they demand. Stark and Finke argue that these rewards are generally spiritual in nature: the assurance of forgiveness and salvation, for example, and the promise of eternal life. Clearly, this cost/benefit analysis makes untested psychological assumptions about what people in general find rewarding and costly.

### Traditional churches are fundamentalist

A more fruitful theoretical approach construes Western Christian religious movements as social movements that are sub-cultures of the religious culture in general. The *traditional* and *modernised traditional* categories of religious movement appear to be characterised by the five features of fundamentalisms. They are *reacting* against certain aspects of modernisation and globalisation, in particular the pluralism of Western society and the elevation of humankind as the creator and maintainer of social institutions and mores. Thus they hold fast to a God who is in charge of the world, and the Bible as the only *authoritative* source for belief and practice, although *selectively* so. They are still *dualist* in their world-view, distinguishing the religious from the secular and treating the latter as ungodly. And finally, they are *millennialist*, working towards the establishment of God's Kingdom on earth, either by evangelising so that enough people are converted to change the world, or by actively seeking to gain control of other religious and secular institutions. The evangelisation route is assumed to work because the world's problems are all believed to be the result of sin at the individual level of analysis. The political approach seeks to expedite and enlarge God's rule by more direct means.

Thus, since traditional and modernised traditional movements are fundamentalisms, we may conclude that Christian Protestant fundamentalisms are succeeding relative to other religious sub-cultures. But why is the Western, especially the American, religious context such a fertile source of fundamentalisms?

First, that context is profoundly affected by the historic *dissenting and Calvinistic strands* of Protestant belief and practise. Both of these strands emphasise the utopian idealism of the Reformation, the former in terms of the purity of the believer's personal relationship to God, and the latter in terms of the perfect rule of God over sinful lives and institutions.

Second, the development of fundamentalisms is supported by the *absence of an established or state church* in America, and the decreasing influence of such churches in Europe. Third, the *flux and dynamism* of the American religious scene encourage the growth of sects and cults which emphasise utopian purity. Fourth, many fundamentalist movements have successfully *embraced certain features of modernisation* and, as a result, are more attractive to modern people. Finally, fundamentalist religious movements take a *firm stance on social developments* that threaten the values and attitudes of conservative Americans. They therefore attract the more conservative citizens of one of the most religious nations in the world.

## The Muslim political context

### *A glorious past, a humiliating present*

Jesus Christ is reported to have said that his kingdom was not of this world (John 18. 36) and to have urged his followers to render to Caesar the things that are Caesar's and to God the things that are God's (Mark 12. 17). The Prophet Mohammed, however, was much more involved in political action, and indeed in military conflict (Qu'ran, chapters 8 and 9; Armstrong, 1991). Ten years after starting to preach the message of the Qu'ran, the Prophet led about 70 families in emigration from Mecca to Medina (622 AD). From 624 to 628 AD, he was involved in warfare with the Meccans, before making a peace treaty with them. At this point, the confederacy of clans that he led was dominant in Arabia. When the Meccans broke the treaty, he captured their city without bloodshed (630 AD), and did not force the inhabitants to become Muslims. Two years later, he died.

During the next two centuries, and despite constant internecine quarrels, Muslims gained control of most of the Middle East and parts of North Africa and Spain, under the rule of the caliphs. The first Crusade captured Jerusalem in 1099, but Saladin restored Jerusalem to Islam in 1187. Crusader occupation of parts of the Near East continued until the end of the thirteenth century, but the Crusades were of little importance to the vast majority of Muslims, whom they did not touch. It was only in the twentieth century that the symbolic significance of the Crusades as the archetype of Western aggression was emphasised by Islamists (Armstrong, 2000(b)).

From the thirteenth to the sixteenth centuries, the conquering Mongols from the East, having converted to Islam, laid the basis for the subsequent great Muslim Empires, the Safavid, Moghul, and Ottoman Empires. The Ottoman Empire reached from Algeria in the West to Hungary in the North, the Persian Gulf in the East, and Yemen in the South (Wheatcroft, 1995).

However, in the nineteenth and twentieth centuries, the industrialising and modernising West sought to colonise the agrarian economies of the East, both as markets for its products and as sources of raw materials (Lewis, 2001). The colonisers divided the colonised, educating the privileged classes in the ways of modernity and imposing new secular legal codes which the mass of the people found alien. In the nineteenth century, much of the Islamic world was reduced to a state of dependency, with Algeria, Aden, Tunisia, Egypt, and Sudan becoming French or British colonies. The final collapse of the moribund Ottoman empire at the end of the First World War resulted in the partitioning of the Muslim heartlands of Syria, Lebanon,

Palestine, Iraq, and Jordan. In the meantime, Balkan, Russian, and Central Asian Muslims became part of the new Soviet Union. Only Turkey, under the aggressively secular Mustapha Kemal, retained its independence.

This abject descent from medieval glory to the modern status of colony was a religious disaster. It was Islam that was humiliated in the eyes of all but the Westernised elites, not national, regional, or even ethnic pride (Ruthven, 2000). Politics and religion are one, according to the central doctrine of *tawhid*, literally 'making one'. *Tawhid* denotes 'The divine unity, which Muslims seek to imitate in their personal and social lives by integrating their institutions and priorities, and by recognising the overall sovereignty of God' (Armstrong, 2000b, p. 174).

Hence the forcible replacement of their religiously inspired legal, educational, and political systems by secular institutions was perceived as a devastating assault upon their faith and their God. Further, this time Allah had not come to their rescue, as He had in times past when Islam suffered temporary reverses. The *ummah*, the world-wide Muslim community, clearly needed radical religious revival under holy leadership to battle successfully against the overwhelming power of the infidel and restore *sharia* law and other Islamic institutions. Only by living in accordance with God's will and redeeming the course of history would the *ummah* be saved from a humiliation which was political *and therefore spiritual*.

### Secular nationalism and the fundamentalist reaction

After decolonisation during the mid-twentieth century, the regimes in control of the newly independent nation states took a variety of stances regarding Islam. The progressive socialist states, such as Egypt, Syria, Iraq, Algeria and Libya, controlled religious institutions carefully and sought to use them for their own propaganda purposes. States allied to the West ranged broadly in their relationship with religion, from Turkey's aggressive secularism to Saudi Arabia's embrace (Kepel, 2006). Moreover, the modern idea of a nation with territorial boundaries was foreign to Islamic culture, which was centred on clans and their relationships at the micro level of politics, and on the *ummah* at the macro level. Furthermore, the new nations failed to uphold the honour of Islam, with the defeat of Egypt by the Israelis in 1967 appearing an iconic failure. The humiliation of the *ummah* seemed doomed to continue.

It was at this historical point that the *fundamentalist ideologies* that have inspired radical Islam for the last fifty years were developed. Abud Ali Mawdudi and Sayeed Qutb had re-defined Islamic theology to suit the revolutionary aims of Islamic fundamentalism (Armstrong, 2000a). Their ideology was starkly dualist in nature. Allah and His law, the *sharia*, were sovereign, as opposed to the legal and political sovereignty of human beings: the rule of God versus the rule of man. Any human institution, including the governments of nominally Muslim nations, was *jahili*, i.e. typical of the benighted pagan era before the time of the Prophet. Those who obeyed the laws of these governments were simply slaves. They had lost their freedom, which can only truly be found in obedience to the law of Allah. The traditional duties implied by the five pillars of Islam were merely preparation for jihad, re-defined as war against all apostates (Akbar, 2002). The various traditions of scholarly and mystical Islam were down-played. The ideological stage was set for religiously inspired revolution.

Moreover, the more moderate opposition to colonialism had failed to save the *ummah*. The Muslim Brotherhood in Egypt became radicalised, while in Algeria, Islamic political parties that played and won the democratic electoral game found the result over-turned by what they perceived as hypocritical Western cynicism. The same pattern occurred in 2006, when the West refused to accept the democratic election of Hamas as the Palestinian government. The West has been seen to prop up corrupt regimes that abuse the ordinary people and enjoy opulent Western lifestyles. And most important, the West, particularly America, has invaded parts of the Muslim world and given continuous support to the arch-enemy, Israel. The corrupt and repressive nature of the regime of the Taliban in Afghanistan is forgotten, and local theocratic successes in Iran and Sudan give continued hope.

The example of revolutionary Iran is instructive (Riesebrodt, 1993). The Ayatollah Khomeini, who ruled from 1979 to 1989, ultimately took complete authority himself, justifying this step by a selective adaptation of Islamic theology. He appointed himself the 'Just Jurist', the representative and guardian on earth of the 'Hidden Imam', who would shortly reappear to redeem Islam (according to Shi'ite theology). The traditional Islamic model of learned clerics administering the *sharia*, to whom even the ruler was subject, was thus overturned. The aim of revolutionary Islam was now to concentrate on jihad, in order to establish theocracy. The traditional political/religious duties of *dawa* (preaching and social assistance) and *hijra* (separation or emigration), modelled on the life of the Prophet, were down-played relative to the overwhelming obligation of jihad. The survival of Islam would soon be perceived to be dependent on the outcome of a battle against the godless secular culture of the West with its decadent morality. Local theocracies became the immediate aim, buttressed by a radical ideology that promised the ultimate victory of Allah and the establishment of a world-wide caliphate.

Thus, in summary, the entire history of Islam, culminating in the overwhelming dominance of the West in the twentieth century, provides the political back-drop for the recent growth of Islamic fundamentalisms. So great is the perceived threat to Islam that it would be astonishing if there were not a fundamentalist reaction. Yet we fail to understand these movements unless we recognise that any notion of a politics divorced from religion is foreign to Islam, although such separation is a key feature of Western modernisation. Political impotence constitutes, for Islam, religious failure.

However, Allah cannot be blamed for such failure, since by definition He defends the faithful against their enemies. Therefore the explanation has to lie in the failure of His people to obey His law to the letter. They must purify their practice and clarify their vision. They must identify the secular enemy, separate utterly from him, obey God's law, especially those parts that can be used to justify struggle, and hope for complete and final victory when God will reign. They must, in other words, embrace fundamentalism and its five key features.

The actions of suicide bombers now become explicable. It is a religious duty to defend the faith with one's life. Killing the enemies of the faith is necessary if it is to be saved. And using one's body in martyrdom is to use spiritual weapons against the secular foe. Recall that the 9/11 hijackers were proud to use knives against the technological might of the Great Satan. If one's central identity is that of Islam, then an attack on Islam is an attack on the self. Fear of the overwhelming aggressive power of the West, and rage at the impotence of Islam to resist, are likely to motivate fundamentalist belief and violent action (Juergensmeyer, 2003). When allied to a starkly simple but inspirational ideology, these emotions can motivate anyone, from a rural peasant schooled in a *madrassah* to a sophisticated technologist with a PhD, to embrace jihad as their religious duty.

Thus both in the West and in Islam, the context of the twentieth century was such as to render the development of fundamentalisms highly probable. It is fairly arbitrary to label the Western context 'religious' and the Middle Eastern one 'political', as I have in this chapter. Protestant fundamentalisms have increasingly sought to intervene at the political level to further their social and moral agenda, while for Islam the very distinction between politics and religion is meaningless. For Muslims, 'salvation did not mean redemption from sin, but the creation of a just society in which the individual could more easily make that existential surrender of his or her whole being that would bring them fulfilment' (Armstrong, 2000b, p. 134).

## Social movements: Emotional *and* rational, social *and* individual

### *Deconstructing dichotomies*

Although the local political and religious contexts of the twentieth century made the development of particular fundamentalist movements more likely, we still have to explain how they started, why they took hold and developed, and why they have flourished or failed. Did huge tides of emotion sweep across America and the Middle East, or did people become fundamentalist believers because they thought fundamentalism made good sense? Did fundamentalisms begin as mass movements, or did they take shape in the minds of religious individuals?

Theory and research about social groups and movements have long been confounded by two binary distinctions: those between *emotion and reason*, and between *group and individual* (Worchel, 2003). Early theories stressed the highly emotional nature of crowds and mobs, so much so that the crowd itself was construed as a psychological entity and credited with such motives as rage and fear, or guilt and relief (Reicher, 2001). Archetypal examples are a lynch mob, or a revivalist gospel meeting.

However, emotion soon became an unfashionable topic in social psychology, with the emphasis moving towards *social cognition* as the preferred explanation for social behaviour. People joined social groups or movements, ran the argument, because they *believed* themselves to belong to the category of persons who formed the movement. They behaved aggressively towards an out-group because they *believed* that members of that category were inferior, corrupt, or generally bad. An example of the cognitive bias of modern social psychology as applied to religion is the theory of Stark and Finke (2000) described above (see pp. 76, 79–80), which proposes that people join churches on the basis of a rational cost/benefit analysis of the alternatives available.

The dichotomy between *group and individual* explanations followed a similar historic sequence. Early scholars focused on the collective level of theory, crediting groups or social movements with various attributes. However, following the arguments of Allport (1924) that collectives could not experience emotions or cognitions, which were essentially individual psychological processes, most scholars changed tack. They now examined such topics as conformity, social identity, and prejudice as individual internal psychological processes, which nevertheless had their origins and outcomes in interactions with others.

Thus, while *sociological* analysis focuses strongly upon fundamentalisms as social movements, much of the *psychological* research on fundamentalisms has adopted a predominantly individual level of analysis. Selecting beliefs, values, attitudes and norms of behaviour as their topics for study, psychologists have treated fundamentalism as a particular individual *religious orientation* (see, for example, Altemeyer & Hunsberger, 1992).

A general *social psychological* approach to fundamentalism has to succeed in reconciling these two sets of binary distinctions. It has to take account of both the emotional and the rational motivational springs of fundamentalist movements; and it has to treat the individual in the context of the fundamentalist movement, whilst acknowledging that groups are composed of individuals. An initial theoretical step to this end is to deconstruct the dichotomies.

The distinction between *the emotional and the rational* has all sorts of justification, not least extensive biological and physiological evidence (Ekman & Davidson, 1994). However, *from a social psychological perspective*, it is important to remember that both emotions and reasons are socially constructed (Berger & Luckmann, 1967). We jointly make sense of our experience, basing our accounts on the previous and current sense-making of others, as embodied in our language and symbols. We discover both how to feel and also how to explain by making *social comparisons* (Festinger, 1954). That is, we frequently look to others to find out the appropriate response, be it emotional or rational, particularly in complex or unusual situations. Moreover, the two types of response are themselves related: we usually find good reasons for our emotions subsequently, while religious beliefs have carried enough emotion to motivate both the torture and execution of many heretics and also the heroic pursuit of peace and justice.

Furthermore, we cannot clearly separate *the individual from the social*. The individual self is largely constructed from social interactions of one sort or another, since we continuously form a view of who we are on the basis of how others respond to us (Baumeister, 1999). Groups and movements, on the other hand, are the constructions of individuals who each attribute leadership qualities to certain members, embrace an ideology, contribute resources, and coordinate their actions to achieve agreed ends (Almond et al., 2003, p. 92).

### A social psychological account

So what might *a social psychological account of the formation, growth, and outcomes of a fundamentalist movement* look like? The central *emotions* of fundamentalisms are their fear for the future of their religion at the hands of secular modernity; their anger at the assaults that they perceive their enemies to be making; and sometimes, their frustrated rage and humiliation at their inability to fight back effectively. Because their religion is central to their selves, the perceived threat is not only institutional but personal. It is their group identity, internalised into their selves as their dominant social identity, which is at risk.

These strong emotions are often experienced in a social situation, where we may describe group, as well as individual, arousal as high (Reicher, 2001). The social situation allows people to share their *social representations* regarding the causes of their fear and anger (Moscovici, 1988). Objects of their anger and fear may be identified. Explanations of, and justifications for, those emotions may be learned. Indeed, an entire world-view may be constructed based upon the battle between God and the sinful world.

Initial emotional arousal, followed by social representations of the situation as a struggle against the enemy, may thus differentiate out into a complex set of BVNs, which forms part of the movement's sub-culture. The basic assumptions from which the rest of these BVNs are derived may strike many observers as irrational, for example, belief in the supernatural and in the infallibility of the holy book. However, BVNs are likely to be internally rationally coherent. Indeed, they will probably constitute a powerful ideology, capable of providing a *meaningful world-view* to counteract the uncertainty and risk of the modern experience (Hogg & Mullen, 1999). Moreover, the individual adherents' social identity and assured position in history as chosen by God will *enhance self-esteem*, which may have been diminished by their life experiences. Thus they will become primed to act individually and collectively to promote God's kingdom.

Included among fundamentalist BVNs we are likely to find potent historical myths, stories of current persecution, expressions of solidarity and homogeneity, hostile stereotypes of the enemy, and an overall account of the adherent's place in history, past, present, and future. To the extent that the BVNs of a movement are part of its sub-culture, they are not dependent for their survival upon the continued membership of individual adherents; therefore we may speak of a movement as having a cultural identity of its own (Brewer, 1991).

In the development of fundamentalisms, the initial emotional impetus is rapidly subsumed into a meaningful account of the situation capable of motivating individuals to take collective action in the interests of a movement. In other words, *any attempt to understand fundamentalisms must take account of emotional, rational, individual, and collective elements.*

## Fundamentalist strategy

### *Strategic alternatives*

Any social movement can only achieve its aims if it has a successful strategy for relating to its social environment. As the basic aim of fundamentalisms is to oppose aspects of modernisation, then their strategy should be directed towards achieving *effective opposition.*

Immediately, such oppositional movements are faced with *a series of dilemmas.* Should they seek to shape their environment so that it threatens them less, or should they seek to overcome and conquer it? Who or what should they identify as their targets or enemies within that environment? Where should they draw the boundaries between their environment and themselves: how inclusive or exclusive should they be? And how permeable should those boundaries be: tightly drawn and difficult to breach in either direction, or permitting a degree of exchange? Should they, for example, form strategic or tactical alliances with other religious or social movements, and to what extent should they make the inevitable compromises that such collaboration entails? How are they to explain and legitimate their existence and activities, both to their adherents and to the rest of the world? If this is to be achieved by means of their ideology, to what extent should this adhere to the mainstream orthodox tradition of the religion from which they are derived? And to what extent should their ideology be dualistic in nature, emphasising the distinctions between us and them, God and the world? Finally, how should they organise themselves structurally so as to most effectively achieve their objectives? Will a structured organisation result in the loss of the original purity of vision and oppositional zeal?

Different fundamentalisms have each arrived at different answers to these strategic questions. The strategic choices they have made depend upon a variety of factors. These include:

- The religious tradition from which the movement originally sprang.
- The specific circumstances of its foundation.

- Its changing religious, political, social, and demographic context.
- The nature and quality of its leadership.
- The psychological, social, and economic needs of its adherents.
- The resources actually and potentially available to it.

So, for example, *a Western Christian fundamentalism* may be based on the dissenting Protestant tradition, founded in reaction against liberal theology, and flourish within a democratic and secular political context. Its adherents may mostly be in employment and, demographically, be evenly distributed according to age. They have urgent concerns about the state of the institution of the family, and their own and their children's future in the unpredictable secular environment. Their leadership is both charismatic and organisationally and politically aware, and they have sufficient income from members and wealthy backers to use the sophisticated tools of organisation and communication which their late modern environment provides.

An *Islamic fundamentalism* may have sprung from Sunni or Shi'ite traditions. Both are theocratic in their beliefs and purposes, with Shi'ites historically more concerned that clerics should exercise authority. The precipitating context for its foundation may have been persecution by a nominally Muslim ruler, or interference or invasion by the secular West. The political and social context appears to be deteriorating, with Islam humiliated and on the defensive, and Islamic culture threatened by secular imports. There is a demographic surplus of young people, many of them without the jobs for which their education has fitted them. The potential adherents are low in self-esteem, and perceive themselves to be the victims of overweening power, arrogance, and injustice. Leaders make good use of the funds available from wealthy backers, directing their use flexibly. They take care to exemplify in their words and public behaviour the pure life required by the law of Allah. (Please note: a Jewish fundamentalism will be examined in the following case study.)

These two very different sets of contextual factors will result in different *strategic choices*. The Christian fundamentalism is more likely to seek to moderate its environment democratically, the Islamic one to overthrow it violently. The contrast is between the Moral Majority and al-Qaida. The Christian fundamentalism will probably identify elements of the secular culture, such as the media, the education system, the judiciary, or minority groups as the enemy; the Islamic movement is clear that their enemy is secular government itself, whether local or Western. The former will necessarily permit a degree of permeability of its boundaries as it deals with allies and opponents within the democratic process. The latter will keep close control in order to avoid detection, but will gladly recruit disaffected youth as operatives, and non-active sympathisers as contributors.

## The role of ideology

Both Christian and Muslim fundamentalisms are derived from religions of the book, and therefore will need to justify their strategy and tactics by *selective re-interpretation of ideology*. For example, the first fundamentalists, American Protestants, emphasised the pre-millennialist doctrine of Christ's coming to rapture his chosen saints away from the ever more powerful machinations of the Evil one, before Christ returned to conquer the enemy. Billy Graham, however, adapted this doctrine to a more activist post-millennial stance when strategy became interventionist. Christians, he argued, were even now suffering a minor tribulation, and could hasten the return of Christ by actively promoting his Kingdom on earth (Boyer, 1992).

Likewise, Mawdudi and Qutb selectively emphasised jihad, while Khomeini adapted the theory of the Just Jurist to apply to himself. However, while revolutionary Islam transforms the meaning of some traditional beliefs, such as jihad and *jahili*, and places them at the forefront of its ideology, fundamentalist Christianity prides itself on adherence to traditional Biblical doctrine. Nevertheless, the emphasis on the doctrine of atonement by evangelicals, and on obedience to the Old Testament law by Calvinists, indicates that even traditional orthodoxy is maintained in a selective way.

We cannot over-emphasise *the importance of ideology* in the creation and maintenance of fundamentalist movements. In pluralistic societies without, apparently, any fixed BVNs, some individuals solve their uncertainties by discovering in a fundamentalism a coherent account of themselves, their world, their place in it, and what they should do about it. An ideology is a belief system that explains and legitimates action.

## Modes of engagement

Thus different histories and contexts result in different strategic choices regarding fundamentalisms' engagement with the world and regarding the ideology they use to justify that engagement. How can we categorise these different sets of choices? Almond et al. (2003) suggest four distinct categories (already reviewed on p. 45). To recapitulate, the first is *world conqueror*, where the aim is to gain control of society and replace its present governments and institutions with theocratic ones. Violent revolutionary action is one tactical choice, as it is for al-Qaida and other Islamic movements, but control may also be gained by political means. For example, the American reconstructionists (see Chapter 7) seek to put sympathisers into important offices of state. Second, *world transformers* seek to influence societal institutions so that their secular opponents lose influence and become less formidable. The Moral Majority and the early Muslim Brotherhood are examples. Third, the *world creator* leaves the Almighty to conquer the world in His own good time. However, the world creator builds up the strength of the movement by keen evangelism, and creates an alternative religious world to the wicked one outside. Many charismatic and Pentecostal groups favour this strategy. Finally the *world renouncers* simply withdraw into their enclave, desiring only to be left alone to perform their religious rituals and live according to their laws. World renouncers often need assistance from outside to be able to maintain the degree of separation they desire. Certain ultra-orthodox Jewish fundamentalisms, and also the Amesh, are world renouncers.

Almond and colleagues say that they have difficulty distinguishing world creators from world renouncers, and admit that the latter are very rare. I therefore propose three strategic categories: *assault, engagement,* and *withdrawal*. These are action words, rather than categories of person, emphasising that while some movements regularly favour one type of strategy, others move from one strategy to another as their environment changes. So, for example, the Muslim Brotherhood moved from an engagement to an assault strategy when President Nasser started to persecute them, but before very long returned to working within the political framework. The original American Fundamentalists, however, moved in the other direction, wounded by their humiliation at the Scopes 'Monkey' trial of the teacher who taught evolution. They withdrew from engagement, and organised within their movement so as to engage more effectively in the 1950s (Carpenter, 1997).

Indeed, some argue that there is a typical *strategic cycle*, in which movements change from an interventionist strategy (assault or engagement) to withdrawal, and then back again. Withdrawal may have two purposes; first, to re-emphasise the boundaries between Us and Them by concentrating on what distinguishes the movement from the rest of the world; and second, to re-group and recover after a defeat. American Protestant fundamentalisms may have hitherto acted in such a cycle. Having re-engaged in the 1950s, the cultural revolution of the 1960s forced a withdrawal, from which re-engagement only fully occurred in the 1980s with the Moral Majority. Subsequent to scandal and defeat at the polls, the 1990s were a period of relatively quiet organisation. Then the election and re-election of George W. Bush (see pp. 59–72) gave a huge boost to the interventionist impetus. It remains to be seen whether Bush's appointment of conservative Supreme Court judges will result in a change in the laws on abortion and homosexuality, or whether the fundamentalists' high hopes of real political leverage on social and moral issues will be dashed yet again. Yet it is easy to judge success and failure from an external perspective. Those with a strong faith in God's coming reign can explain apparent setbacks as all part of the divine plan.

## Leadership

### *Leader as prototype*

Leaders of fundamentalist movements do not face only strategic dilemmas such as those described above. They also have *a legitimacy problem*. Many fundamentalisms are opposed to religious and secular authority, so authority has to be earned. How, then, can leaders acquire the degree of authority they need to determine the strategic direction of the movement? Popular stereotypes picture charismatic demagogues duping ill-educated and credulous followers into irrational beliefs and grandiose schemes. On the contrary, leadership is always a negotiated and delicate relationship between leaders and followers (Bryman, 1996). This is particularly true of such voluntary organisations as religious fundamentalisms.

We cannot adequately understand any form of leadership unless we construe it as *a social relationship*. The search for personal characteristics that define leaders has proved unfruitful. To separate out the role of leadership into various specific role requirements will help us to realise the enormity of the task facing leaders of fundamentalisms. Fundamentalist leaders have to be charismatic ideologues, pure saints, and political organisers, although not necessarily all at the same time. However, such a list will not explain from a social psychological perspective how leadership of fundamentalist movements actually works. We need, rather, to explain the nature of the relationship between these leaders and their followers. One such explanation might run as follows.

Fundamentalisms seek to distinguish themselves as sharply as they can from other religious and social movements. As a consequence, they emphasise their own internal homogeneity. They are a social category consisting of people who have the same characteristics and BVNs as each other. Thus there develops a *prototype*, an idealised picture of an adherent who demonstrates all of the valued criteria of membership (Turner & Haslam, 2000). Given that fundamentalisms are by definition attempts to recover the purity and zeal of 'true religion', these criteria are likely to be highly demanding and rarely found in a modern environment.

If a fundamentalist leader is to gain credibility and legitimacy, his first task (and it is almost invariably a *he*) is to be accepted as *prototypical*. He has to symbolise and represent the movement by exemplifying its prototype (Haslam, 2001). It is not an easy task to be attributed by others with a whole range of idealised virtues, but it is an essential first step. However, once this difficult first step has been taken, there then become available a variety of ways of enhancing the relationship.

This is why the choice of enemy is a very important strategic issue for any fundamentalist leader, apart from opportunistic tactical considerations. The nature of the ideal prototype is likely to vary with the identity of the enemy. So, for example, when the enemy is liberal theology, the prototype is that of sound and orthodox scholar. When it is gays or feminists, the prototype becomes righteous moral crusader. If the leader is to continue to be prototypical when the identity of the enemy changes, he has to adapt his own persona.

### Leader as chosen

A second step for the would-be leader is to establish God's imprimatur on his leadership by means of a story of *special selection or call* to leadership, over and above the initial call to the faith. These episodes are often characterised by a resemblance to the experience of iconic figures in the religious tradition. For example, both Pat Robertson and Jim Bakker, American evangelists, describe themselves as having been tried and tested to the limit in a spiritual or an urban wilderness (Lienesch 1993), just as Christ is reported to have faced temptation in a desert (Mark 1. 12–13). Osama bin Laden took care to be filmed at the mouth of a cave, an echo of the experience of the Prophet Mohammed during his struggle against the Meccans.

Indeed, leaders have to interpret the religious tradition in such a way as to suggest that they are its exemplars. They either, like Khomeini, explicitly claim a role played or foreshadowed in the tradition, or, like Robertson, undergo the call, temptation, ridicule, and suffering that its founder endured.

They may invent new symbols or rituals that add weight to the attribution of leadership by their followers, or they may re-interpret the holy book to provide a powerful ideology for intervention in the world. In the 1980s, Jarnail Singh Bhindranwale re-defined the enemies of Sikh fundamentalism as the secularism of the Indian state and at the same time the threatening growth of Hindu fundamentalism. This unlikely combination of foes radicalised his movement. A more down-to-earth route to leadership is the acquisition on the movement's behalf of necessary resources: funding, or recruits, for example.

All such activities gain a leader what has been called 'idiosyncracy credit' (Haslam, 2001, p. 64). That is, having paid his dues by being a model adherent, he has gained some leeway by additional leader-like activities. He can then use this idiosyncracy credit to take strategic decisions which are opposed by many in the movement.

So, for example, in helping to create the Moral Majority, Jerry Falwell allied his Fundamentalists with the 'soft and woolly' evangelicals. Fundamentalists typically castigated evangelicals as positive-thinking and easygoing betrayers of true Bible belief. Likewise, it was a huge strategic switch by Osama bin Laden to attack the 'far enemy' (the West) instead of the 'near enemy' (Muslim governments). This was utterly contrary to the accepted jihadist strategy, and even went against the advice of his own inner circle of advisers (Gerges, 2005).

It is nevertheless essential that a leader continues to have leadership qualities attributed to him by all his followers. Otherwise, internal dissension may cripple the movement, and result in decline or schism. Of course, any new movement formed out of schism may flourish in time, but all the hard work will have been wasted. There are many reasons why followers may stop attributing leadership to their leader. A first is the obvious one of his death, but often the faithful have already been prepared to accept the great man's successor, quite often his son. A second is when a leader forgets his need to remain a prototypical member, and succumbs to worldly temptation. Although some lose power as a consequence (e.g. Jim and Tammy Bakker), others succeed in persuading their followers that they too are human, and provided that they repent, are fallible but forgiven disciples and therefore continue to be prototypical.

Internal dissension can also occur when the leader becomes distant from the followers, whose access to him may be denied by an inner circle. Alternative leaders may claim to represent them. Moreover, fundamentalisms are in general *absolutist* movements, that is, they believe that there is only one truth (their own). Hence, there is major scope for dissent when a theological or moral dispute occurs, as, by definition, only one of the parties can be right. Leaders may trigger such disputes by over-ambitious re-interpretations of doctrine to legitimate their strategic plans.

Finally, of course, the leader may simply fail to make the right strategic decisions. He may lead the movement into an alliance that fatally weakens its boundaries and blurs its own identity. Or he may embark upon projects that demand too many sacrifices, even from adherents who are used to sacrificial giving of selves, energy, time, and money. In such cases, the relationship between leader and followers is ruptured.

We may conclude, with Almond et al. (2003, p. 142), that a variety of contextual features, such as those explored in the first three sections of this chapter, are necessary conditions for the existence of fundamentalisms. However, they are not sufficient without the actions of leaders and followers in relationship. This chapter therefore concludes, as do Chapters 1 and 2, with an affirmation of the importance for any fundamentalism of *social action by individuals in relation*. And that action is far more likely to occur if those individuals have internalised the fundamentalist movement as a *social identity*.

## Summary

- Fundamentalisms are unique social movements which arise in particular contexts.
- The religious context of Western Protestant fundamentalisms may be more explanatory than their political context, while the reverse is true of Islamic fundamentalisms.
- Protestant fundamentalisms have arisen in a period of extreme religious flux, with new movements being created, frequent schisms occurring within existing movements, and large autonomous congregations being formed.
- Nevertheless, two historic strands inform these structural changes: the dissenting and Calvinist traditions.
- The dissenting tradition has stimulated some modernisation of traditional Protestantism, making concessions to individualism while retaining such core beliefs as the inerrancy of the Bible.

- Fundamentalist groups that have modernised in this way are flourishing relative to other groups.
- Islamic fundamentalisms may likewise be attributed to historical events, in their case in the political context.
- To distinguish political from religious contexts is impossible for Muslims, however. God is one, and rules all areas of life, including politics. Hence the political fortunes of the *ummah*, the people of God, are also the fortunes of Islam.
- Until the nineteenth century, the great empires of Islam ensured that religion and people flourished. However the colonising activities of the modernising West resulted in the loss to infidel empires of control of many Muslim countries.
- These political and religious disasters were not ameliorated by the wars of independence. Independence resulted in the imposition of secular nationalist governments, which failed to restore Islam's former glories.
- These debacles prompted the invention of radical new Islamic ideologies, which were highly selective interpretations of traditional Islamic theology.
- They promoted the supreme importance of jihad, revolutionary struggle against all who were not Islamic theocracies.
- All social movements, including fundamentalisms, have to be explained in both emotional and rational terms; and at both individual and social levels of analysis.
- Individual adherents, as a result of group experiences, will internalise the movement as a social identity, part of the self, together with its beliefs, values, and norms of behaviour.
- They may thereby gain self-esteem and meaning, and will be motivated to action to save the world for God.
- There are some necessary conditions for fundamentalisms to flourish. The first is strategic direction. Three strategic options exist for fundamentalisms: withdrawal from the world, engagement with it, or assault upon it.
- A second necessary condition is a radical and creative change in religious ideology.
- A third is effective leadership, which is a mutual relationship between leaders and followers.

### Further reading

Almond, G.A., Appleby, R.S., & Sivan, E. (2003) *Strong Religion: The Rise of Fundamentalisms around the World*. Chicago: University of Chicago Press.

Armstrong, K. (1993) *A History of God*. London: Heinemann.

Armstrong, K. (2000) *Islam: A Short History*. London: Weidenfeld & Nicolson. (Paperback, 2001). London: Phoenix Press.

Bainbridge, W.S. (1997) *The Sociology of Religious Movements*. New York: Routledge.

Baumeister, R.F. (ed.) *The Self in Social Psychology*. Hove, Psychology Press.

Gerges, F.A. (2005) *The Far Enemy: Why Jihad Went Global*. Cambridge: Cambridge University Press.

Iannacone, L. (1994) Why strict churches are strong. *American Journal of Sociology*, 99, 1180–1211.

Juergensmeyer, M. (2003) *Terror in the Mind of God: The Global Rise of Religious Violence* (3rd edn.). Berkeley, CA: University of California Press.

Kepel, G. (2006) *Jihad: The Trail of Political Islam* (4th edn.). London: IBTauris.

Lawrence, B.B. (1989) *Defenders of God: The Fundamentalist Revolt Against the Modern Age*. Columbia, SC: University of South Carolina Press.

McGuire, M.B. (2002) *Religion: The Social Context* (5th edn.). Belmont, CA: Wadsworth.

Reicher, S.D. (2001) The psychology of crowd dynamics. In M.A. Hogg & R.S. Tindale (eds.) *Blackwell Handbook of Social Psychology: Group Processes*. Oxford: Blackwell.

Tamney, J.B. (1992) *The Resilience of Conservative Religion: The Case of Popular Conservative Protestant Congregations*. Cambridge: Cambridge University Press.

Worchel, S. (2003) Come one, come all: Toward understanding the process of collective behaviour. In M.A. Hogg & J. Cooper (eds.) *Handbook of Social Psychology*. London: Sage.

## CASE STUDY: GUSH EMUNIM: A NATIONALIST RELIGIOUS MOVEMENT

*Fundamentalist movements have their origins within their religious and political contexts. Gush Emunim was founded in response to a specific political situation, and has a nation-building agenda. It depended for its success on an ideology adapted from a long theological tradition. It benefited from an adaptive leadership, which resolutely maintained an engagement strategy, cleverly developing resources of political power and influence. The leadership did not permit this influence to be jeopardised by those who wished to change to a strategy of violent assault.*

### Historical context

In the ninth and eighth centuries BC, a group of clans collaborated to secure their safety as they sought to survive in the land of Palestine. Their separate tribal gods had become one God, whom they called Jehovah. God became distant and holy rather than local and tangible (Eisenstadt, 1999). Thus were the seeds of monotheistic religion sown. The Jews saw themselves as God's chosen people, the recipients of His favours (Armstrong, 1993). Their side of the bargain was to obey the Law that He revealed to them. The Torah became the symbol of the people's unity, and obedience to its every detail their first duty. Only if they kept the laws regarding worship and daily life would they continue in God's favour and ultimately be redeemed. But redemption, when

Moshe Levinger          © Milner Moshe/Corbis Sygma

it came, would not be confined to the chosen people. It would be extended to the whole gentile world.

These beliefs withstood some historic blows (Lustick, 1988). As Byron put it unforgettably, 'The Assyrian came down like the wolf on the fold', and a dreary exile in Babylon followed (sixth century BC) until the Jews returned to their land and holy city. However, in the second century BC, the Maccabees successfully rebelled against the Seleucid empire, which had by then Hellenised Palestine. By this achievement they provided the inspiration for subsequent doomed revolts by the Jewish Zealots against the Roman Empire. The conquering Romans were so oppressive that the Jews believed their pain could only be explained as the birth-pangs of their redemption as the Messiah came to save them. Moreover, the 'chosen nation' could not compromise with an alien power; the people had to be ruled by the anointed king appointed by God. The result of this uncompromising stance was the destruction by the Romans of Jerusalem and the Temple itself in the rebellion of 66–73 AD.

The dangers of seeking redemption by political action were subsequently preached to the Jews at home and in exile by their rabbis. God would only redeem His people if they were obedient to the Law. They had to pay particular attention to their religious observance, in the absence of the possibility of the worship in the Temple, which God required. This advice failed to head off a second equally disastrous revolt against the Romans (132–135 AD).

Throughout subsequent history, a latent Messianic fervour has occasionally broken through the faithful religious observance of the Jewish Diaspora (Lawrence, 1989). Obedience to the law was demanding and, particularly in Eastern Europe, Jews found the added inspiration they needed in the persons of charismatic *rebbe*. These spiritual leaders mediated between practising Jews and their God, and provided spiritual satisfactions that the Torah teaching of the rabbis failed to deliver.

There was always the danger, however, that such charismatic leaders would forget the dreadful lessons of history, and themselves seek to set in motion the process of the redemption of Israel. Shabbatai Zevi (seventeenth century) was one such false Messiah, and Jews everywhere started to prepare to return to Palestine. When he was captured, recanted, and converted to Islam, their disillusion was immense. The spiritual lesson of leaving redemption to the Almighty, rather than seeking to hasten it by one's own efforts, was re-inforced. The miniature Israels that flourished locally throughout the Diaspora should continue to observe the Law, and God would redeem them in His own good time.

Thus, in the nineteenth century, when the Jews of the Western European Diaspora began to take on board the ideas of the Enlightenment, the orthodox tradition held firm. As far as the *Haredim*, or pious Jews, were concerned, accommodation to the West was apostasy (Heilman & Friedman, 1991). Intermarriage with gentiles, new ideologies such as socialism and nationalism, failure to observe the *halakah* (religious law) in modern urban environments, and the dilution of the faith by Reformed Jewry, were all deeply shocking.

Thus, when the Zionist movement started in the late nineteenth century, pious Jews treated it as another product of secularism. Nationalism, even when it was the nation of Israel that was proposed, was unacceptable. They ensured that their children were educated in *yeshivot*, religious schools that excluded any secular content. And then, to make sure that they were not distracted by worldly concerns, they sent their young men on to *kollel* to advanced study of the Torah, while their wives earned them a living. They insisted that Zionism was a grievous error. It ignored the messianic hope, failed to install the *halakah* as the law of the land, and omitted any idea of the universal redemptive mission which is the duty of God's peculiar people.

Therefore, when the foundation of the state of Israel occurred in 1948, truly pious Jews decried the development as likely to delay the redemption of Israel (Ravitsky, 1996). This was because Israel's secular laws reduced the level of obedience to the *halakah*, and since only obedience could hasten the arrival of the Messiah, that arrival was less likely. They certainly did not join American Protestant fundamentalists in treating Israeli nationhood as the dawn of the redemptive era. Rather, they dwelt upon the Holocaust as God's punishment for His people's apostasy.

However, many religious Jews went along with the Zionists. They offered their support to the government in exchange for control over such matters as marriage, divorce, diet, and Sabbath observance. They formed the National Religious Party, and sought to maintain Judaism as civil religion within the body politic.

So far, so typical. Yet another historic religious tradition of law-keeping orthodoxy, with an admixture of populist fervour, is faced with modernity and secularism. A part of that tradition accommodates and liberalises, earning the vitriolic condemnation of the remnant. The remnant becomes an oppositional fundamentalism, hostile to any national identity other than theocracy. It embraces a strategy of separation, content to wait until God Himself chooses to redeem His people, send His Messiah, and establish His Kingdom. The reconciliation of pious religion with secular nationalism is beyond its capabilities. It continues in spiritual Exile, even though it is physically restored to its Promised Land. So much for the *Haredim*. However, there is one Jewish fundamentalist movement that has succeeded in making such a reconciliation: Gush Emunim (Sprinzak, 1981).

## The story of Gush Emunim: Early days

The story of the Gush Emunim movement well illustrates the key features of fundamentalisms as social movements (Aran, 1986, 1991). It has historic religious and cultural antecedents, as the previous section has demonstrated. It has, moreover, faced many of the dilemmas typical of fundamentalisms all over the world, for example: Should it engage with the secular Zionist political process or stand aloof until theocracy occurs? Should it use violent or non-violent methods of engagement? Who is its primary enemy: Islamic fundamentalist movements, Arab states, Palestinians, or secular Jews? Who are its friends and allies, and how inclusive or exclusive should its membership be? How can it adapt the Hasidic religious tradition for its ideological purposes? How and by whom should leadership be exercised, and how organised should it become? It has arrived at clear answers to some of these problems, whilst wavering ambiguously on others. Its longevity and continuing influence imply that its answers have been, at the least, adaptive to its changing environment.

The immediate story of Gush Emunim probably begins with the *political* refusal of many Jews to accept the boundaries of the new state of Israel (Lustick, 1988). They had been given to understand that Israel would extend West from the Jordan all the way to the Mediterranean coast. These 'Revisionists' established a military arm, the Irgun, a key member of which was Menachim Begin. When this movement was forcibly disbanded by the Labour government, they formed a political party, Herut. This formed an alliance with the right-wing Liberal party to gain, as a coalition, 21% of the vote in the 1965 election. There was therefore a sizeable group of the Israeli electorate wishing to re-open the question regarding what territorial boundaries were appropriate for the state of Israel.

A parallel but *religious* development was provided by two rabbis, father and son, Abraham Isaac Kook (died 1932), and Tzvi Yehuda Kook (died 1982). Kook the Elder argued that the Jews had a privileged vision of God, being capable of experiencing Him in a pure and spiritual way. They were exceptional, and because they were uniquely chosen, they had to obey God's laws rather than those of man. Others were likely to pervert the vision and engage in some form of idolatry. Indeed, the Jews themselves had been punished with exile in order to purify themselves, so that they could truly experience the pure spiritual light. However, the approach of nationhood would permit the commencement of the process of spiritual redemption, Israel's ultimate destiny.

Thus the establishment of the state of Israel was seen by Kook the Elder as a temporal means to a spiritual end. It would doubtless involve some breaking of the *halakah*, but this was to be tolerated, since the most important *mitzvah* (divine command) was to live and work in the land promised long ago to Abraham (*Eretz Israel*): 'And I will give unto thee, and to thy seed after thee, the land wherein thou art a stranger, all the land of Canaan, for an everlasting possession' (Genesis 17. 8). Such a selective and partial interpretation is an archetypal feature of fundamentalisms. Restoration to the land was the first step towards the Messiah's return and the salvation of the whole world. Kook the Elder was appointed Chief Rabbi by the Zionists, who appreciated that his teachings provided both legitimacy for nationhood and also a way of persuading religious Jews to collaborate with secular fellow citizens.

Kook the Younger developed his father's teachings into a more practical form. He specified what the stages were in the process of Israel's redemption, and how to achieve them. Diaspora Jews should all return to their promised land, but while they were still doing so, *Eretz Israel* should be reclaimed. This claim to (at least) Judaea and Samaria of course echoed the aims of the Revisionists, who had refused to accept the 1948 territorial boundaries. The land is capitalised as 'Land' in Kook the Younger's writings. It merits high spiritual status, since redemption can only be achieved if the People of God, the Land of God, and God Himself are reconciled in a three-way relationship.

The tasks, then, according to Kook the Younger, are return from exile, settling of the Land, and worship of God. The state of Israel was instituted by God as the instrument by which these tasks could be achieved, and so had cosmic, not merely secular, significance. All of its struggles with its enemies were of cosmic importance: they signified that the rest of humankind was resisting its destiny. And that destiny was to be redeemed by God's people Israel, restored to their Land at last. Only the people of God fully understand the pattern of history. The past is the preparation for the process of redemption, the future its fulfilment. And responsibility for bringing it about is to be shared between God Himself and his People.

Thus the political and ideological stages were set for the foundation of Gush Emunim. However, two other conditions typically have to be met before a fundamentalism can gain momentum. First, there usually has to be a *precipitating event*, which can energise potential leaders and followers and provide the basis for a foundation myth (Aran, 1991). And second, there have to be enough *immediate recruits* to make the initial push successful.

The two wars with Egypt, the Six Day War of 1967, and the Yom Kippur War of 1973, were the essential trigger. The Six Day War resulted in the Israeli conquest of the Sinai peninsula, the Gaza Strip, the West Bank (Judaea and Samaria), the Golan Heights, and the re-unification of Jerusalem. Observant Jews could now pray at the Wailing Wall, their most sacred site. An ideology to justify this expansionism was required (Lawrence, 1989, p. 141).

Then came the disaster of the Yom Kippur war, in which Egypt and Syria inflicted heavy casualties by their surprise invasion. The Labour government lost credibility, and attributed the defeat partly to the failure of the Jewish settlements on the Golan Heights to slow down the Syrian invasion. On the contrary, argued the Labour government, they had taken up valuable military time by having to be rescued, and Labour therefore sought to develop a policy of withdrawal from settlements. However, the secular and religious Right argued that a more extensively developed network of settlements would have provided a better defence.

The manpower for the foundation of Gush Emunim came from sources of highly religious young men. In the Yom Kippur war, for the first time, students from the *yeshivot*, the religious schools, served in the Israeli military. They returned determined to do whatever was necessary to prevent another such debacle. Some 25 to 30% of Israeli youth attended religious schools, and many of these, perhaps up to 30,000, had joined Bnei Akiva, a youth organisation with a strong emphasis on messianic themes.

More specifically, former students of Yeshivat Merkaz ha-Rav, the religious school led by Kook the Younger, had formed a group within the National Religious Party. They had been inspired in 1967 by Kook, who, in a lecture, loudly bewailed the partition of Israel. Three weeks later the Six Day War resulted in the restoration of the territory of *Eretz Israel* and more (depending upon how it was defined). The prophetic imprimatur had been given, they concluded. Redemption was already happening, since God's People had been reunited with their Land. Thus when the Yom Kippur War halted the process, they blamed the government. They formed Gush Emunim, literally 'the bloc of the faithful', one of several populist protest movements. All were intent on fighting the government's intention to withdraw from much of the territory gained in 1967.

So why, after their official foundation in 1974, did they flourish to the extent that they soon became the pre-eminent movement of protest? Several factors contributed to their success. First, *leadership was shared and recognised*. The elderly Kook the Younger served as a charismatic ideological figurehead, but a group of younger and able disciples played a variety of tactical and strategic leadership roles. Such men as Levinger, Porat, Druckman, and Waldman continued in these roles for many years, despite the inevitable disagreements regarding ideology and strategy.

A second success factor was their immediate and astute *formation of alliances*, in particular with politicians who wanted territorial expansion for political rather than religious reasons. Thus they formed relationships not only with members of the National Religious Party, their natural allies, but also with Likud, a secular right-wing party. They assiduously cultivated members of the Knesset, the Israeli parliament. Nevertheless, political progress was not rapid, due to the fact that the Labour government of Rabin was still in power (until 1977).

They therefore engaged in other activities, which were more loosely political (Sprinzak, 1981). Their use of *public protest* and the consequent publicity was masterly. The post-war agreements made by the Rabin government with Egypt and Syria were the target for hunger strikes, the blocking of streets in Jerusalem, and clashes with the police. Demonstrators deliberately disturbed intermediary Henry Kissinger's sleep outside his hotel. When Rabin shook hands with Yasser Arafat on the White House lawn, Gush mobilised some 200,000 demonstrators in Jerusalem. They also engaged in symbolic activities reminiscent of the tactics of the Old Testament prophets. They played cat and mouse with the military in order to reach the places in Judaea and Samaria where they argued that settlements should be established. However, they had no intention of staying there, nor of coming to blows with the army. This was a symbolic act. Symbolism was supplemented by holiday hikes across Samaria, joined by eminent politicians such as Menachem Begin.

Nevertheless, there stood firm and strong the real, if small, settlement at Elon Moreh near Nablus in Samaria, a symbol of settlers' determination, founded in 1973 before the formation of Gush Emunim. Realising its symbolic significance, Gush joined the original settlers, thereby gaining status and visibility as the vanguard of the settler movement. Facing opposition from the Rabin government in 1975, Gush took the opportunity for another publicity coup by gaining media support from a visiting American Jewish delegation for its settlement attempts. Thereafter, the movement flexibly concentrated on establishing more political contacts in Jerusalem. It succeeded in getting a group of Labour politicians onto its side, thereby making the government realise that the settlement lobby was stronger than they thought.

Gush never gave up its settlement aims, and in 1976 produced a plan that proposed to settle one million Israelis all over Judaea and Samaria. 'It is the right and obligation of the Jewish people to settle throughout the width of the land, and therefore it is forbidden that there should be any political obstruction of settlements in Judaea and Samaria' (quoted in Newman, 1982).

## The second phase: Consolidation and settlement

In 1977, Begin's Likud government came to power, in coalition with the National Religious Party. It seemed that all the earlier cultivation of Likud politicians, such as Begin and Ariel Sharon, would pay off. The second stage of the redemptive process would gain pace as the promised Land was regained. Indeed, Begin immediately engaged in a symbolic act of his own, visiting the settlement of Elon Moreh holding a copy of the Torah. Gush's plan for settlements in the heart of Judaea and Samaria was indeed pursued in Begin's first and second premierships (1977–1981 and 1981–1984). By 1984, nearly 60 settlements were instituted on the West Bank, increasing the number of settlers there to over 38,000. Settlements in the West Bank and Gaza received more than $1 billion in aid, and government jobs were provided for many of the settlers.

However, these settlement successes had to be fought for. The honeymoon with Likud and Begin came to a rapid and nasty end when, in 1978, the government entered into the Camp David accords, which sought to give the Palestinians a degree of autonomy within the territories occupied in 1967. Then it signed a peace treaty with Egypt, agreeing to withdraw from Sinai. The concessions to the Palestinians were anathema to Gush, since they delayed the second stage of redemption, the restoration of *Eretz Israel*. The dismantling of the settlement at Yamit in the Sinai in 1982 was a further body blow. Despite its political influence, Gush was powerless when push literally came to shove, and the Israeli army ejected the settlers. Although it appealed for supporters to go down to Sinai and offer (passive) opposition, unarmed soldiers removed the relatively few protesters, and the settlers of Yamit were resettled in the Gaza Strip.

Faced with these setbacks, some abandoned the tactics of political pressure allied to demonstrations and symbolic actions, and opted for a more violent and direct approach. This, they felt, would scupper any further progress in the peace process, but, more important, would hasten the process of redemption by claiming an iconic emblem of the Land for the People of God. There could be only one target for attack, which, if captured, would hasten the process of redemptive history: the Temple Mount, the site of Solomon's Temple but now an Islamic shrine, the Al Aqsa mosque.

In 1983, an attempt to seize the Mount was discovered, and some of the conspirators were shown to be Gush adherents. The next year, a carefully planned attempt to blow up the Mount was aborted, apparently because the plotters failed to gain the approval of eminent Gush rabbis for their enterprise. Many of the plotters were also involved in a foiled attempt to blow up Arab buses. The Gush leadership initially sought to distance itself from these violent actions, but its close ties with the perpetrators gave the lie to these efforts, and it subsequently sought to justify them as an understandable reaction to government failure.

However, the danger of losing control over their fringe extremists was clear from the justification for their violence which they offered: that God Himself had spoken *directly* to them instructing them to take violent action, thereby by-passing Gush ideology in one massive leap.

The failure of these aggressive initiatives gave further impetus to those in Gush who emphasised another explanation for the recent political debacles. Insufficient effort, they argued, had hitherto been put into cultivating powerful members of government, and into gaining the support of the broader mass of conservative Israeli voters. After all, the value of powerful friends in high places had been demonstrated as early as 1980, when the government promised support for a considerable expansion of settlements.

After Begin's departure in 1984, the coalition government of Likud and Labour under Shimon Peres turned a blind eye to the gradual expansion of the settlements. The settlers had organised themselves into a body called Yesha, an acronym for Judaea, Samaria, and Gaza (Etkes & Friedman, 2006). Its Council is controlled by Gush adherents or sympathisers, although it is composed of a wide range of members. Many secular Israelis had joined with the fundamentalists in developing settlements, but although they are represented on the Yesha Council, the religious nationalists still hold the power. Some of them are members of the Knesset, elected from the National Religious Party, or from the Tehiya party, a Gush creation. Others are activist settler heroes, and others again are Gush rabbis such as Druckman and Waldman. Yesha frequently opposes government policy, while receiving extensive government funding in the form of grants to the regional settlement councils.

The subsequent Palestinian intifadas have probably strengthened the hand of Yesha and Gush. The national response has been to seek to unite against a common enemy, and the settlers are seen by many as heroes in the struggle. They may have become, as Sprinzak (1981) argues, the tip of the iceberg, the underwater part representing their popular support throughout the nation. However, several recent government actions have provoked their opposition. The Oslo Accords of 1998, the building of the wall of partition, and the withdrawal from the Gaza settlements (2005), initiated by their erstwhile ally Sharon, are prime examples. Their opposition is motivated by their continuing religious imperative to settle the whole of *Eretz Israel*. If a wall is built and if Gaza is evacuated, then clearly this aim is being ignored by the government, however desirable these actions might appear from a security perspective.

Their failure, in 2005, to prevent these actions appears at first sight to be a setback for Gush and Yesha. However, the current further strengthening of the West Bank settlements is a compensatory sop to the settlers, and a tribute to their continuing political influence. The second stage of the redemptive process can still be construed as on course for success, whilst secular Israelis can feel that the settlers offer a degree of protection. Indeed, the settlers may now be seen as a more effective defence than the Israeli army, whose reputation for invincibility was dented by the doubtful success of the invasion of Lebanon in 2006.

## Strategy, leadership, and ideology

The as yet unfinished story of Gush Emunim illustrates well the various elements of the theoretical account of fundamentalisms as social movements outlined in the present chapter. They opportunistically seized the moment in the political and religious development of Israel to form their movement. Then, as the political context changed, they adapted their strategy accordingly, to the extent that they had a profound effect themselves upon those political changes (Sprinzak, 1981). However, there was still a degree of struggle within the movement. On more than one occasion they put all of the hard political work at risk by engaging in, or supporting, violent activities that neither the government of Israel nor most of its citizens could tolerate.

As far as *strategic direction* is concerned, the Gush dissociated themselves from the traditional ultra-orthodoxy of the *Haredim*. In terms of the three categories of strategic direction proposed on p. 90, – withdrawal, engagement, or assault – the approach favoured by the *Haredim* could best be described as withdrawal. The Gush strategy, on the other hand, was a judicious mixture of engagement and assault. Of course, by 'engagement' we are not referring to engagement with 'the enemy', but rather with the political process, which is dominated by those outside the movement itself. And 'assault' does not mean the use of violence, which is only one of the forms of tactic available to this strategic option. Rather, it refers to an uncompromising approach to completely defeating the enemy by all appropriate means.

*Engagement with the political process* is evident throughout the history of the Gush. At first sight, it seems unlikely that Gush would flourish in the complex political environment of Israel. The movement did not have a formal structure with membership lists, nor a detailed statement of its aims, objectives, and policies, or even of its ideology. Yet this apparent disorganisation was one of its sources of strength. Adherents could join established political parties, or indeed form new ones themselves, and spread their influence over a range of political groupings. Thus they avoided being limited to one small minority party, which would be doomed to acting as a mere irritant. Since the Israeli electoral system is one of proportional representation, this was a wise move. Geographic representation might have resulted in a number of Knesset representatives for a Gush party from the settlement areas, but this possibility was not open to them.

Political engagement necessarily results in compromises. Furthermore, this need to compromise politically puts a brake on the dangerous excesses of an assault strategy. Time and again in Gush's story the need to retain political influence has tempered the urge to go beyond the bounds of tolerance of its political allies and their electorates. The benefits of pursuing engagement and assault strategies simultaneously are clear. Engagement gains support, vitally important in a democratic political environment. Assault achieves goals, which those non-active supporters desire, while using methods that they are not willing to use themselves. We are all threatened together, says the Gush populist message, and we are doing something about it on behalf of all of us. And finally, assault also serves the purpose of enthusing the faithful.

Gush has also been astute in its *drawing of its boundaries* and in its *choice of enemy*. Its boundaries are cast wide, including secular nationalists with whom it has collaborated throughout its life. Pragmatically, these have the same aim as Gush, that is, to establish and defend the state of Israel in its traditional land. Although they do not embrace the theological meaning of this aim, they may be included among those who are God's instruments in his redemptive plan. It is just that they are not aware of their role. Thus the question of who is properly to be called a Jew receives a far more inclusive answer from Gush than from the *Haredim*, for whom even being religiously observant is certainly not enough.

However, the identification of the enemy, the Them against whom We struggle, ensures that boundaries are not excessively broad. The government is only an ally conditionally. As soon as it appears to turn away from its divinely ordained mission, to rule over *Eretz Israel*, then it certainly joins the ranks of the enemy, as do other secular and religious Jews. The evacuation of Sinai after Camp David, and the recent withdrawal from Gaza, have been such governmental apostasies. However, it is worth noting that even when the government had apparently put itself beyond the pale by these two decisions, Gush was prepared to bargain with it to gain compensatory concessions.

More generally, Gush have shown themselves to be hostile to *gentiles*, especially Western ones, who embrace such fruits of the Enlightenment as democracy. To quote Moshe Levinger (1985, p. 15): 'If in Europe and the United States a moral and democratic mission requires equality of rights for all, it is clear and obvious that in Israel what must determine rights to vote and to be elected to public office must be identification with, and participation in, the struggle of the people of Israel to accomplish its mission'. Such a position is in line with a theology that proposes that Israel's mission is ultimately to redeem the whole world to establish a theocracy. Any armed intervention by Israel is likely to be for the gentiles' own good, since it will promote their eventual redemption. More generally, the secular orientation imported from gentile societies is argued to have diluted the original Zionist culture formed in the early days in the kibbutzim. This period of national formation was, after all, ushering in the age of redemption.

The most obvious and immediate gentile enemy is *the Arabs*. Precisely which Arabs are to be identified as Them is ambiguous. Arab citizens and inhabitants of Israel, for example, are clearly to be distinguished from

Palestinians, who in turn are not all members or supporters of Hamas. Arabs are in a large majority in the West Bank and Gaza, and form a substantial minority within the state of Israel. As befits a fundamentalism, Gush has recourse to the holy book. Jews are there enjoined to treat well the stranger within their gates, and so Gush advocates treating individual Arabs with respect, while not according them the rights associated with the chosen people.

Palestinian attacks on the settlements are another matter. These have prompted violent responses by settlers, large numbers of whom are Gush adherents. Furthermore, demographic predictions suggest that Arabs will be in the majority well within the next century. These developments have inspired attempts to create an ideological justification for making a financial or forcible 'inducement' to Arabs to leave. This selective piece of theology involved the identification of the Arabs with the Amalekites, who are reported in the Bible to have harassed the Israelites in their journey to the promised land. God told the Israelites to wipe out the Amalekites because they threatened His people, runs the account (Exodus 17). However, this attempt to treat Arabs as a collective enemy has been disputed within Gush. Such a failure to agree on the precise identification of the enemy is an indication of internal disagreements between those who regard themselves as the vanguard of the movement and those who consider public and government support is vital (Lustick, 1988).

Nevertheless, despite this ambiguity regarding the exact identity of the enemy, the *leadership* of the Gush has succeeded in creating an iceberg of popular support. Skilful use of political resources and media publicity, together with the willingness to be flexible both politically and ideologically, has gained the movement far greater influence than its ultra-orthodox counterparts the *Haredim*. Gush adherents are perceived to be intelligent, idealistic, and modest professionals with a strong work effort and loyalty to the collective (Sprinzak, 1998).

Perhaps the most important predictor of leadership success has been the quality of *the leadership*. Gush was fortunate, in that the ideological foundation for the movement had already been provided by the Kooks. Thus Kook the Younger could be treated as the holy and charismatic founding father, while the young Turks got on with implementing his vision. Many of these early leaders have continued for a generation to guide the strategy of Gush. Their longevity can be attributed in social psychological terms to their high degree of prototypicality.

A *prototypical leader* is an individual who is an archetypal example of the membership of the movement. He (or, very rarely in the case of fundamentalisms, she) exemplifies all the characteristics of the ideal member, and none of those of the out-group enemy. All of the leaders of Gush have given clear indications of their commitment to the redemption of Israel and the world, not only by their words and writing, but also in their deeds. It was the leadership, including several rabbis, who were among the first pioneer settlers and who were seen to participate in the public actions. Thus they embodied the core aspect of the Gush sub-culture: the importance of the unification of People with Land. Because their leaders embody the attributes of the movement, followers are willing to attribute leadership to them.

*Ideology* is one of the key responsibilities of fundamentalist leaders. The Kooks had done most of the ideological work, their creative theology centring on active recovery of Eretz Israel, with the state of Israel as God's unwitting tool in His redemptive plan. Their highlighting of the process of apocalyptic redemption was a further creative stroke. However, further selective theological adjustments had to be made as strategic considerations dictated. The emphasis on the *mitzvoh* to take control of *Eretz Israel* as the overriding duty certainly came in useful when Gush leaders broke the Sabbath in order to drive to meet Ariel Sharon (Lawrence, 1989, pp. 145–146). The overall aim of occupying the land justified breaking a lesser *mitzvoh*. When such setbacks as the withdrawal from Sinai and Gaza were experienced, the immediacy and urgency of the redemptive process was readjusted. The faithful should certainly do all they can to make ready for the Messiah, but his arrival will be in God's good time. We cannot hasten the divine timetable: merely prepare the way and facilitate it (Almond et al., 2003, p. 71).

In sum, Gush Emunim represents an archetypal modern fundamentalism. It demonstrates the more recent trend towards activism that can be discerned in Protestant and Islamic fundamentalisms, and also in such other nationalist fundamentalisms as the radical Sikhs and Sinhala Buddhists. Like other active fundamentalisms, it employs both engagement and assault strategies to suit tactical needs. And also like others, when in assault mode it operates on the brink of violence, if not actually over the edge. Like all fundamentalisms, it needs an ideology that both justifies and motivates action, and it has made selective changes to the orthodox belief system from which it has its origins. Further, this change in belief has not only to be supported by a new interpretation of the holy book, it also has to tap into a historic sub-cultural strand of belief, in this case the mystical association of the People with the Land, and the charismatic *rebbes* who brought believers closer to their God.

The modern techniques of politics and public relations are embraced, but in aid of an absolutist belief system, which claims unique status for believers. Awareness of the global political scene is evident, yet the global is totally subservient to the local, the world to the tiny Land of Israel. Unlike the *Haredim*, Gush adherents are not distinguished by unique forms of dress or behaviour, but cultural relativism and pluralism are nevertheless anathema. Its boundaries are drawn fairly wide, but they are certainly held secure against out-groups. Truly, they are both ancient and modern.

In terms of the embryo theoretical account of fundamentalisms proposed on pp. 86–93, Gush certainly appear a typical case. They are afraid for the survival of their religion and their land, and angry at assaults upon it. They believe that assault and occupation are the only course of action available to them in response. The close and overwhelming atmosphere of political engagement in Israel provides the appropriate social context for people to recognise these emotions as their own. Further, their emotions are justified in the light of the interpretation of the situation with which their fundamentalist movement provides them. The sub-cultural BVNs that Gush provide give self-esteem and meaning, as they are incorporated as part of the social identity of Gush into the adherent's self. The close collective nature of this social identity, together with the psychological needs it meets, renders it central to the self. Hence it is a powerful motivator to action, since the achievements of the movement are one's own.

# 4 Fundamentalist organisations

## Organisational culture

### *Culture and identity*

The grass roots realities of fundamentalisms become visible at the local level of analysis. When we examine the Finsbury Park Mosque in London, where Abu Hamza preached to several of those found guilty of planning to bomb London in 2005, or Jerry Falwell's Thomas Road Baptist Church in Lynchburg, Virginia (Harding, 2000), or Rabbi Kook's *yeshiva* in Jerusalem, we are getting down to the practical details of how fundamentalisms work. However, the analysis will not be in terms of leaflets printed, donations secured, or systems put in place. Rather, I will continue to treat such local examples of fundamentalisms as *cultures*, in this case, sub-cultures of the particular fundamentalist movement of which they are part.

Of course, fundamentalist movements are themselves organised, and so organisation is not the definitive feature of local manifestations of movements. However, theories of organisation offer a great deal of explanatory power at this local level of analysis. They enable us to pursue in greater depth the themes that have emerged at the global, national, and social movement levels of analysis (see Chapters 1, 2, and 3). The two key theoretical themes that I have stressed hitherto are those of *culture* and *identity*.

Culture and identity are related because aspects of cultures become internalised as social identities. Not only do people consider themselves Americans, or the Islamic vanguard, or a graduate of Rabbi Kook's yeshiva, they also *internalise* as part of their selves the BVNs, the rituals, the myths, the peculiar language, and many other aspects of the cultures of these social categories.

We have also noted that levels of cultural analysis may be clearly *differentiated* from each other. For example, global culture appears to be becoming increasingly integrated with American culture. American culture has always included radical Protestant themes of dissenting and Calvinist traditions, leading to such movements as the first Fundamentalists of the 1920s (denoted with a capital F). And the Thomas Road Baptist Church was well integrated

Abu Hamza                                              © Reuters/Corbis

with that tradition. Thus, in the American case, there is a considerable degree of integration at all levels of analysis we have considered so far: global, national/regional, social movement, and, now, local organisation.

However, we should not ignore the considerable degree of *differentiation* also present in this example. Globally, national cultures are fighting what they perceive to be American cultural imperialism. Nationally, a long tradition of American liberalism is differentiated to a marked degree of polarity from religious conservatism (Boston, 2000). At the level of religious movement, several Protestant denominations and, of course, other faiths, would disassociate themselves from Fundamentalists. And many Fundamentalists looked askance at the strategic thrust of Jerry Falwell's church towards political involvement in the 1980s (Harding, 2000).

Thus there is a variable balance between differentiation and integration at the different levels of cultural analysis in America. The overall degree of integration may well be greater in America than in other cases, however. For example, the degree of integration of Jewish culture from a global perspective may be only moderate, and the sub-cultures of messianic religious groups such as Gush Emunim may be highly differentiated from the culture of the mass of secular Israelis.

The *integration* of different levels of cultural analysis, together with the *internalisation* of cultural features into the self in the form of social identities, suggests the importance of *nested identities* (Ashforth & Mael, 1989). That is, to the extent that sub-cultures are integrated into parent cultures, the corresponding social identities are compatible. At least some aspects of being an American subsume features of being a Fundamentalist, while being a Fundamentalist subsumes a great number of features of being a member of Falwell's 'ministry'. If social identities are nested within the self, they are mutually supportive in giving structure and coherence to the self, and in motivating social action.

### Organisation as culture

How, then, may an analysis in terms of organisational theory help us understand fundamentalisms in their local manifestations? Scholars of organisation have found it hard to theorise the phenomenon they study. Some, for example Morgan (1997), have drawn upon metaphor as a useful starting point. Taking organisation and management as typical products of modernity, Morgan selects different metaphors as expressing key aspects of organisational reality. For example, the *machine* metaphor stresses the bureaucratic features of organisation: organisation as designed by the principles of scientific management. The picture of organisations as *organisms* emphasises the importance of their adaptation to their changing environments if they are to survive. The *brain* metaphor reflects the view of organisations as systems for processing information, for learning, and for learning to learn. Organisation as *culture* implies that implicit assumptions, values, and norms of behaviour permeate organisations, and that sub-cultures may exist within them. When organisations are referred to as *psychic prisons*, the reference is to modes of managerial control that are internalised by employees so that they control and motivate themselves. Finally, the *chaos* metaphor suggests that organisations are often in a state of total flux, and that outcomes are dependent on opposing forces acting upon them.

Scholars have realised the danger of reifying the concept of organisation. The temptation is to speak of an organisation as though it were a person engaged in action. The use of the noun conceals the reality of the verb: organisations consist of people who organise. People use such metaphors as those listed above to construct and enact their organisation (Weick, 1979); they constantly create and recreate their organisation by their organising activity. According to the theory of the social construction of reality (Berger & Luckmann, 1966), people negotiate with each other in a variety of ways regarding the meaning they put onto their social experience and the metaphors they use to describe it. As organisation is not an entity, but rather the activity of organising, then we may ask whether some metaphors more than others inform the activities of those who organise in late-modern societies.

Different types of organisation are probably best viewed through different metaphors, for example, the metaphor of machine may still fit some bureaucratic public sector organisations well. However, the five differentiating features of fundamentalisms indicate clearly which perspective on organisations is most appropriate for understanding them. Fundamentalists are passionate oppositional ideologists with a dualistic world-view based on a selective reading of a holy text, and working for a millennial kingdom of God. Only an analysis of *organisation as culture* will do justice to the beliefs, values, norms, symbols, and artefacts that dominate fundamentalisms.

Ironically, the cultural perspective has been used as a tool by top managements to intervene in all sorts of organisations. They believe, usually mistakenly (Legge, 1995), that they can change their organisation's culture so as to achieve a desired end (for example, improved service to the customer) (Willmott, 1993). Indeed, during the 1980s and 1990s, culture change programmes were the most popular organisational intervention in the UK (Institute of Management, 1996). Moreover, they sometimes even use the language of fundamentalist Protestantism in these change programmes. Vision, mission, and values can change employees for the better, runs the message. They can be redeemed by a transforming experience of seeing visions and dreaming dreams. They can be inspired by charismatic leaders, who were just like them originally, and whose current stardom they can aspire to emulate. They can give public testimony to the radical change in their lives, and they can be welcomed into the inner circle of the elect. All this in aid of selling more perfume! (Hopfl & Maddrell, 1996).

Such misuse of cultural analysis merely indicates that the evangelical sub-culture has a powerful resonance for some business executives. The use of cultural analysis to understand fundamentalist organisations appears, on the contrary, entirely appropriate. However, it is important to guard against the danger of reifying what is a human activity. Hence we may end up mistakenly construing what is a continuously enacted process of organising as a static entity, an organisation; mistaking, in other words, active subjects for a structured object. 'Organisational change' is therefore a redundant use of two words where one will do. For all organisations are by definition continuously changing, since they are constantly being re-created and re-enacted by their members.

It follows that a cultural perspective on organisations has to give an account of a process: the *process of organising*. The concept of culture is highly suited to this task, since it is itself a dynamic concept. As Morgan (1997 p. 141) says: '[culture] must be understood as an active, living phenomenon through which people jointly create and recreate the worlds in which they live'. One of those worlds is the world of organisation.

## Interpreting organisational experience

### *How organisational meanings develop*

The members of a culture or sub-culture share particular *constructions of reality*, or *representations*. These representations are shaped by some, and shared by all. They take a great many forms, such as unstated assumptions, explicit world-views, attitudes towards others, and norms of behaviour. They are communicated by means of a wide variety of artefacts, including the behaviour of members. Others infer from what these members say or do how they themselves should believe and act (the process of *social comparison*). Stories, myths, rituals, routines, language forms, and images are all cultural artefacts that help members to communicate a particular representation of organisational reality.

In particular, the organisational culture provides the meaning and purpose of members' organising activities. For fundamentalists it can answer such questions as: How exclusive or inclusive are we: are we a proud bastion of the truth, or are we merely a temporary hostel for any Tom, Dick, or Harriet passing through? How are we led: does the existing authority structure appear the obvious and natural way? And what are we to make of our environment: is it full of dangerous enemies, or of potential allies, or is it mostly evil but containing a few like-minded others? How do we relate to that environment: is it to be feared as a threat, conquered as an enemy, or welcomed as a resource? Are the boundaries to be drawn tight and close, or loose and wide? What is the situation in which we currently find ourselves: is it a threat or an opportunity? Are the issues currently facing us a simple and obvious moral choice, or a complex tissue of conflicting rights and interests? And, therefore, what should we be feeling: pride for choosing good over evil, or hesitation at the complexity of it all?

All these organisational ambiguities are resolved when reality is clearly and simply defined. (Of course, no value judgement is implied here: clear and simple answers are not always good ones.) But how exactly does this occur? What are the cultural processes through which reality becomes defined for organisational members? It seems likely that, at the local organisational level of analysis, *symbols and artefacts* play a large role. Hitherto I have, with Schein (1985), stressed beliefs (assumptions), values, and artefacts as the key features of culture. However, following Hatch (1993), we may distinguish four major elements of organisational culture: assumptions, values, artefacts, and symbols. To distinguish symbols from artefacts, we define symbols as 'anything that represents a conscious or unconscious association with some wider concept or meaning' (Hatch 1997, p. 219).

A symbol has a tangible form, as an object, statement, or action, for example, but may stand for a broad meaning or meanings. Examples are the Christian cross, or the affirmation 'There is no God but Allah', which may have several meanings. Moreover, symbols may have different meanings for different people, and their meanings may change over time. In the organisational setting, they need to be actively interpreted by members. Artefacts, on the other hand, 'are the visible, tangible, and audible remains of behaviour grounded in cultural norms, values, and assumptions' (Hatch, 1997, p. 216). Thus symbols are a subset of artefacts: they are those artefacts that have acquired added meaning, having been used in communicating BVNs among organisational members.

Hatch (1997) models the development of organisational culture in terms of the dynamic interaction between its internalised elements (assumptions and values) and its external ones (artefacts and symbols) (see Fig.1). Assumptions and values direct actions, which are realised in artefacts. On the basis of their beliefs and values, people build synagogues, formulate statements of doctrine, or establish rules for male dominance. Some artefacts gain symbolic value because of their use to convey larger meanings.

*The relationship is dynamic*: artefacts that have gained symbolic meaning can change members' assumptions and values as they are used to communicate. Hence there is the usual dynamic, present in any form of learning or change, between the consequences of action and its internal drivers. The added emphasis from the cultural perspective is the importance of meaning and interpretation in the process. This is signified by the presence of symbols as one of the four elements of the model.

This brief account does less than justice to the model's complexity. The relationships between the four elements are themselves reciprocal. So, for example, artefacts may become symbols by being used to communicate added meaning; but existing symbols may affect which artefacts are so used. For example, the routine of marshalling communicants in queues to receive the bread and wine in a Christian service of communion will remain a mere administrative artefact unless the symbolism of communion suggests to some that equality in the eyes of God is not being observed in these routines. Worshippers of high status sometimes appear to be called before others. The routines themselves then gain symbolic significance: the queuing system becomes a symbol of the church's concern with status, and may be changed as a consequence.

### Leadership as the management of meaning

The cultural analysis of organisation in terms of the creation of meaning has implications for the exercise of *power and leadership*. From the interpretive

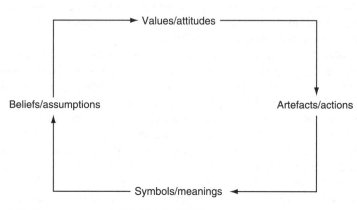

*Figure 1*  Culture as process (after Hatch, 1997).

perspective, power can be understood as the capability of defining reality and creating meaning for organisational members. To the extent that all share the same interpretations, the members are likely to be mutually committed and capable of cohesive action. So how is a leader able to define reality for other members? The tools for achieving such power are several. First, an *understanding* of people's current perceptions of reality is required, together with an appreciation of the history and traditions that have shaped those perceptions. Second, the capacity to *act out* those meanings, especially the beliefs and values, in one's own behaviour, and to interpret and communicate appropriately the existing symbols. This means becoming *prototypical* to a greater degree than others: being more of a model than them.

This successful enactment of the present culture enables the emerging leader to be attributed with leadership qualities by other members (Haslam, 2001). He or she is then in a position to influence the culture by creating artefacts and making them *symbolic*, and also by interpreting new events and situations as they occur. This capacity may be enhanced by providing *a frame* or a lens through which all new situations may be interpreted (Goffman, 1974). An example of a frame might be the fundamentalist view of society as a clash between two incompatible world-views. The environment may be represented as unstable and threatening (and therefore requiring firm leadership and complete conformity within the organisation).

Finally, a leader may actively seek to persuade members of *the nature of the organisation*. This interpretation may then become what the members internalise as their *organisational identity* (Albert & Whetten, 1985). As such social identities are part of the self, the leader has thereby acquired the ability to inspire commitment and motivate action in the organisation's defence. Osama bin Laden succeeds in defining al-Qaida as the revolutionary vanguard of Islam, thereby giving his followers an esteemed identity.

The interpretive approach to organising also sheds light upon the nature of *intra-organisational conflict*. Internal conflict is likely to be about meanings. As beliefs and values are internalised and seldom explicit, the first focus for conflict will often be at the surface level of observables: artefacts, and, especially, symbols, for example, a corporate logo. The explanation of conflict, however, will probably lie at the deeper level of values and assumptions. When only one detailed and explicit set of values and assumptions is considered to be correct, as in fundamentalist organisations, then the opportunity for conflict over small differences is considerable.

## Buildings and rituals

How may we apply this conception of organisations as cultures to fundamentalist organisations? Religions in general, and fundamentalisms in particular, are replete with symbolic meanings. Their artefacts are seldom without a deeper significance. However, if we are to understand how fundamentalist organisations survive and develop over time, we have to investigate the dynamic interplay between their artefacts and symbols on the one hand, and their beliefs and values on the other.

Three arenas illustrative of this dynamic process of cultural development at work are *the buildings and rituals* of Protestant fundamentalist churches, *the 9/11 violence* and martyrdom as a symbolic act, and *processes of social control*. I will analyse each in turn.

### Protestant buildings

Three fundamentalist Protestant churches in America differ in their *buildings*. The built environment of each lends itself to a particular form of symbolic ritual, and this in its turn shapes, and is shaped by, that church's assumptions and values. The churches are 'Spirited Church' and 'Truth Church' in Muncie, Indiana, described by Tamney (2002), and the Capstone Cathedral in Phoenix, Arizona, visited by Balmer (2000). Truth Church comes from the Calvinist tradition, whereas Spirited Church and the Capstone Cathedral are both from the enthusiastic dissenting tradition. Spirited is moderately enthusiastic in style; Capstone is ecstatic and apocalyptic.

#### Truth Church

*Truth Church* looks, inside and out, as one would expect a Protestant church to look. Its external notice board announces the denomination to which it belongs, and inside it has an organ, a choir, and a piano. The congregation arrives in good time, in relatively formal dress, and falls silent as the minister enters and walks slowly towards a lectern. The minister is male; there are no female ministers within the denomination. The entire service is conducted in an orderly, quiet, and reverent manner. There is no applause after any part of the service. There is little spontaneous participation by the congregation, except when the minister requests a response, and little overt emotional expression.

The symbolic meanings of the building and its accompanying rituals are clear. The purpose of the service is to worship God in His majesty. As one of Tamney's interviewees put it rhetorically: 'Are we genuinely worshiping an almighty God, or are we just here to make ourselves feel better?' (Tamney, 2002, p. 123). The concentration on the words of the Bible, the creed, and the minister's sermon (which is an exposition of a Biblical text), indicates that doctrinal belief is of central importance. To advertise the church's denominational affiliation proclaims its adherence to the doctrines and rules of the denomination.

These symbolic artefacts translate themselves into the assumptions and values of the congregation. God is a holy and majestic God. He has revealed His will through the Bible, which forbids women ministers, of whom we therefore disapprove. Indeed, this disapproval resulted in the denomination declaring itself to be out of fellowship with a sister denomination because the latter was considering ordaining women. God's word is unchanging, and therefore so are the standards that it sets for its followers. There is one Authority, God himself, whose will is expressed through his Word and expounded by men of God. Liberal churches and the secular world disobey God's will, and the foundations of the family and traditional morality are crumbling as a result.

### Spirited Church

*Spirited Church* looks very different. It has its name advertised outside, but not its denominational affiliation. This is in fact United Methodist, one of the few largely liberal denominations surviving in the United States. Inside, the building has not been changed much from its original use as a car dealer's sales room. There is a stage with a cross at the front and a table with a big book at the back. The table is not used at all during the service.

The congregation arrives, informally dressed, at any time before or during the first half hour of the service. This is devoted to singing contemporary Christian songs projected onto a screen, accompanied by a full modern amplified band. The songs are interspersed with impromptu prayers by the choral leader, and periodically the congregation breaks into applause. Some members of the congregation may lift their hands in the air, clap, or dance, usually following the lead of the choral leaders at the front. Occasionally, an individual member of the congregation may 'speak in tongues', although the pastor keeps control of these ecstatic events. Then the pastor takes over for an hour, interspersing his sermon with occasional songs or calls up to the rail, as the Spirit moves. Finally, he invites all in need of prayer up to the rail, and they are prayed with individually.

The absence of any sign of denominational allegiance and the lack of a liturgy suggest that the worship of a sovereign God is not a dominant theme at Spirited Church. Rather, the emphasis, as with most charismatic churches, is on the individual allowing the Holy Spirit of God to lead and direct him or her. There is no communal ecstatic experience, but, rather, individuals may express their adoration of God and their joy in His presence in whatever way they feel appropriate. The pastor's address likewise suggests being open to the immediate leading of the Spirit, since at any point he may feel led to extemporary prayer or a direct appeal or reproach to the congregation. The invitation to be prayed for at the end of the service suggests an orientation towards addressing individual needs for wholeness and providing relief from problems.

Thus the setting and the ritual of Spirited Church re-inforce belief in an empowering God whose Holy Spirit directs individuals to surrender themselves to His leading. The overall approach is libertarian and enthusiastic. Worship should be emotional and fun. Whilst the individual has their own intimate relationship with God, however, the pastor insists to the congregation that there is little individual leeway in terms of values. Different views of the nature of baptism may be tolerated, he concedes, but the Bible is still the inerrant Word of God. He accuses some of being unwilling to demonstrate in an anti-abortion rally for fear of being seen, and distributes voting guides prepared by the far-Right Christian Coalition. The beliefs and values reinforced by Spirited Church's building and ritual are thus a blend of Biblical inerrancy, social conservatism, and individual freedom and expression. It is a fundamentalist church, but very different from Truth Church.

*Capstone Cathedral*

The *Capstone Cathedral* is different yet again. Shaped like a pyramid, the Cathedral is full of apocalyptic symbolism. There are seven layers of the pyramid, which represent the seven ages proposed by the pre-millennialist school of eschatology, which argues that we are now in the final era of human history. This will end with Christ's return to rapture the faithful into heaven before the Tribulation and the battle of Armageddon, after which He will return to rule for a thousand years. The upward tapering of the pyramid also represents the way in which the number of true believers is narrowed down before their rapture, led by God's mouthpiece and final prophet, Neal Frisby, the pastor of the Cathedral.

However, the design of the Cathedral also carries some less apocalyptic symbolism. It consists internally of a huge open auditorium, seating two thousand, which slopes towards a semi-circular stage in one corner of the base of the triangular pyramid. This design points towards the notion of performance by a star, upon whom all attention is fixed.

The ritual follows the sequence of a stage performance. Frisby's son warms up the audience with some solos, backed by guitar, drums, backing group, and electronic organ. He invites participation, orchestrating some synchronised clapping. Frisby himself then enters, and preaches what sounds to Randall Balmer like a stream of consciousness (Balmer, 2000, p. 73), randomly jumping from idea to idea. Then he invites all who seek healing or who can testify that they have received it to come to the front. There is no illness that he claims to be unable to heal, nor problem to solve. Some of the recipients of his prayers and 'laying on of hands' simply walk back to their seats, but others cry, shake, speak in tongues, jump up and down, or stagger away as though they have received an electric shock.

The setting and the performance direct attention to the performer himself. He is clearly a very important person indeed. If the medium is the message, then the message is that Frisby is a star, especially anointed by God as his final prophet. Frisby's production in his inner sanctum of scrolls dictated to him by God adds to his prophetic status (although his surrender to the temptation to specify the date of the apocalypse has not proved helpful). The audience is convinced by the performance, first that God through his prophet can cure their immediate ills, and second, that He will shortly return and give these powerless people the power and authority they lack in this earthly life.

At Truth Church, Spirited Church, and the Capstone Cathedral, different artefacts carry different symbolic meanings, which in turn re-inforce different beliefs and values. To the extent that the culture of each of these three local organisations changes and adapts, they survive and prosper. At the time when Tamney and Balmer investigated them, Truth and Spirited were flourishing numerically, whereas Capstone was languishing. This latter outcome may be the result of Frisby's increasing isolation from his social environment, a fatal mistake when a single individual is so central to organisational survival. All three churches, however, demonstrate the features of fundamentalisms, albeit from different traditions.

### Violence as a symbolic act

The assault of 9/11 destroyed two important buildings and killed many workers in the international finance sector. Furthermore, it devastated many families through the loss of a family member. It will take them many years to recover. However, the American economy, international trade, and individual organisations recovered relatively rapidly.

The effect of 9/11 was thus not so much economic as *symbolic*. The assault on the twin towers was not simply an action, an artefact of the sub-culture of al-Qaida. Rather, the action was deliberately symbolic (Juergensmeyer, 2003). The principal symbols of American power were attacked: commercial and financial institutions (the twin towers), the military (the Pentagon), and political power (the White House). Moreover, the assault carried different meanings for different audiences. These meanings were so powerful and convincing that many changed their beliefs and values, and created new artefacts in the form of new organisational structures and violent actions. Other artefacts had pre-dated 9/11, for example, bin-Laden's 1998 *fatwa* against America. But the dramatic action of 9/11 spoke louder than any words.

### The jihadist audience

What, then, did 9/11 say, and to whom did it speak? One of bin-Laden's audiences was *other jihadist organisations*. To them, the meaning was simple. The target of al-Qaida was now the USA in particular, and the 'far enemy', the West, in general (Gerges, 2005). Al-Qaida was thus leading the jihadi movement in a new strategic direction. It was breaking off much of its engagement with the 'near enemy', secular Muslim states such as Egypt, to concentrate on the real power that supports and upholds them. This new strategic direction threatened the other jihadist organisations, since it heralded an enhanced reputation for al-Qaida and an increase in funding and recruits. The superior attraction of a pan-Islamist organisation claiming to represent the entire *ummah* over locally based national groups such as themselves was worrying. And finally, al-Qaida's new strategic direction also threatened indiscriminate retaliation by a wounded superpower against all jihadis and those associated with them.

## The Muslim audience

A second audience for 9/11 were *Muslims everywhere*, whom al-Qaida was eager to construe as the *ummah*, and particularly eager that they too should construe themselves in this way. The first message to this audience was that al-Qaida represented them. They were daily humiliated and had lost their dignity, but al-Qaida could restore it. At least they could enjoy a symbolic empowerment over their oppressors. The second message to Muslims was that members of al-Qaida were, like them, faithful Muslims. The assault of 9/11 was totally in accord with the faith, as it was defensive in nature. Al-Qaida was defending the *ummah* against assault by infidels. Further, it was perfectly justifiable for the hijackers to kill themselves as well as their victims, although suicide is forbidden for Muslims. This is because they were martyrs in a holy war.

Indeed, the message to the faithful was that spiritual power works. It can conquer secular earthly power symbolically today, and will ultimately do so in every sense, despite continuing apparent defeat. Finally, 9/11 re-inforces the radical doctrine of *tawhid:* God is one, and the struggle against the infidel, although political and military, is nevertheless religious.

## The world audience

The third and largest audience for 9/11 was *the rest of the world*, but the Western infidels in particular. The first message for this audience was that we are at war with you. This is an astonishing and arrogant message, given that the victims were the only current world super-power and the assailants were a small group of jihadis. However, al-Qaida's definition of the post-9/11 situation was confirmed by President Bush, and so the attraction of this interpretation was immensely strengthened. With the definition of the situation as war, the additional implied message was that normal rules no longer apply.

Not only was this war; it was *cosmic* war. The struggle was between good and evil, Allah and the Great Satan. One incident, however spectacular, was treated as a symbol of cosmic conflict. To dignify 9/11 in this way is to imply that the action was spiritually inspired and supported, and therefore legitimate. It is also to recognise that the criteria for success in the struggle are divine and not human. The conflict may in human terms appear hopeless, but in the long term, Allah will triumph.

Further, the *manner* in which the 9/11 assault was conducted also sent a message. The fact that the hijackers were willing to die to achieve their objectives points to an entirely different world-view. They were proud to become martyrs, whereas infidels love their earthly lives too much to even consider martyrdom. To quote from the video-tape of a young martyr on another mission: 'Tomorrow is the day of encounter, the day of meeting the Lord of the Worlds ... [we will] make our blood cheap for the sake of God, out of love for this homeland and for the sake of freedom and honour of this people, in order that Palestine remains Islamic' (Juergensmeyer, 2003, pp. 71–72). Indeed, the suffering and glory of the 9/11 martyrs, who ritually purified themselves according to their instructions, contrasts profoundly with the moral decay of the infidel.

Of course, we can only infer that these meanings were intended by al-Qaida. However, it is clear that the 9/11 assault was entirely consistent with their public discourse before the event, including bin Laden's announcements of jihad and *fatwa* against America. Moreover, it is clear from the responses to the event that many of those meanings were drawn by the different audiences. The perception of meanings, however, needs to be distinguished from actions based upon those perceptions. Few jihadis agreed with al-Qaida's transfer of hostilities from the near to the far enemy and joined in the new war. Some Muslims sympathised with the aims of the action, but not with the means. And the infidels accepted the declaration of war and pursued it with disconcerting vigour (Gerges, 2005).

As far as al-Qaida itself is concerned, however, it is clear that the symbolic act of 9/11 affected the assumptions and values of its own sub-culture. The event itself and the American response to it confirmed their beliefs, both that they were fighting a cosmic war and not a series of local ones, and also that spiritual power could defeat the oppressor's technological might. It also confirmed the high value they attached to the traditional Muslim virtues of steadfastness, purity, and humility.

### Discipling or disciplining?

The way in which those with power in an organisation exercise control over other organisational members is a sub-cultural artefact that often carries considerable symbolic meaning. This was certainly the case in the *Philadelphia Church of Christ*, described by Watt (2002). This church was part of a movement called International Churches of Christ (Boston Movement), founded in 1979 by Kip McKean. Between 1979 and 1991, the movement grew from 30 members to nearly 38,000, and from one congregation, in Boston, to 103.

From the beginning of its existence, the movement had established a strong authority relationship between its leaders and other members. While the founder originally stated that 'church leaders could call people to obey and follow them in all areas of opinion' (Watt, 2002, p. 87), he had only slightly modified this position by 1991 to 'Christians are to obey their leaders in the work of the church'.

*The process of discipling, and the gendered allocation of roles*

Within the Philadelphia Church of Christ, the authority of leaders was supplemented by a process and structure known as '*discipling*'. Younger weaker Christians were partnered by older stronger ones of the same gender. These pairs were expected to meet face-to-face at least weekly, and to be in contact on a daily basis. The senior partner gave the junior advice about every aspect of his or her life, no part of which was allowed to remain private. Same-gender discipling partnerships were stipulated so that women would not exercise authority over men, and so that men would not be tempted into improper relations with women.

Special emphasis was placed upon advice regarding marital relationships, and when couples were experiencing difficulties, they were counselled regarding the supposed Biblical principles of marriage. These, typically of fundamentalisms, were taken to require deference by the wife to the husband's authority, which was derived from his Biblically ordained role as the head of the family. Where the counsellor thought that the big city environment was putting a strain on a marriage, the couple were even encouraged to move home to another location.

Every member was in a discipling relationship with another member, and the links went upward to the ministers of the church. There is no indication in Watt's account that the matters discussed within discipling pairs were treated as confidential. Entering into the discipling relationship was a necessary condition for becoming a member of the church. When the researcher engaged in discussion with a man who clearly wished to become his senior discipling partner, Watt's refusal to accept this person's interpretation of God's will for him resulted in him being discarded as membership material. The church's justifications for the practice of discipling were, first, theological: it is imitative of Biblical practice; and, second, practical: a structure of authority is the only way to get things done.

The second artefact relating to power and authority concerned the *allocation of positions* within the church according to gender. Women could not be ministers, but they were allowed to be counsellors. Female counsellors had complete licence to address groups of women and organise them into networks without male supervision. However, they did not speak in public in church when men were present. If they did, they were put down. Watt notes that a woman who asked a question was answered by condescending jokes. This is reminiscent of Balmer's observation (Balmer, 2000, p. 41) of a similar event at Dallas Theological Seminary, a fundamentalist college. One of the few female students asked a question about an obscure theological point, and was told to wait a while and a light might go on. If not, 'ask your husband at home'.

*Symbols of power*

These two cultural artefacts of Philadelphia Church of Christ, the discipling system and the gendered allocation of roles, were clearly symbolic. They contained meanings over and above their mere functional use. Discipling points to the authority of others over the individual in terms of belief and practice. Those others represent the church itself. Discipling suggests that there is no part of the individual member's life which is private and belongs to him or her. It all belongs to God, and is subordinate to God's will (which is interpreted and revealed by the church). The gendered allocation of roles carries the meaning that men and women are different according to God's plan, that they have different gifts, and that the man's position is superior, be it at home or at church.

There is clear evidence that these symbolic meanings were incorporated into members' belief and value systems. For example, women in the church unanimously and passionately agreed that the ordination of women was not in God's plan, and that God created very specific roles for men and women. The members of the church were happy to let its leaders tell them, without discussion, what the financial plan for the church should be. They believed them when they told them that their power was spiritual power, gained by following the church's teachings and thereby conquering the world for Christ.

*The Taliban*

A second example of artefacts of power and oppression comes from *the Taliban*. The name comes from the Arabic *taleb*, meaning student, and the Taliban were indeed former pupils at the *madrassahs*, the Islamic schools. There they were given a free education and nourishment. Their parents frequently could give them neither, being poor rural peasants. The understanding was that the boys might subsequently become jihadis, or, if not, undertake some other religious function. The education was entirely sheltered, and dominated by the *ulemas*, or religious teachers. Some boys entered at age 5, others at 12 or 13. Much of their time was spent learning the words of the Qu'ran in Arabic, not their native language. The curriculum of a *madrassah* visited by Stern (2003, p. 225) consisted of 14 subjects, all aspects of Islamic law.

All that the Taliban knew when they found themselves in 1996 in charge of Kabul, the cosmopolitan and (relatively) sophisticated capital of Afghanistan, was derived from this extraordinarily limited educational experience. As far as they were concerned, life consisted of religious morality, commerce, and war (Kepel, 2006). The apparatus of the modern state, with government departments managing the national business, was utterly foreign to them, and they immediately sent the civil servants off to receive a religious education. They conceived it to be their duty to ensure that the inhabitants of Kabul fully obeyed *sharia*, especially with respect to morality. They formed the

'Organisation for the commanding of good and the hunting down of evil', familiarly known as the 'Vice/virtue police'. Women had to wear *burkas*, and were not allowed to work, even in traditionally female occupations. Men were whipped if they were clean-shaven or had short beards only. Punishments were public spectacles, and included amputation and execution at the hands of the faithful.

The symbolic meaning of these actions by the Taliban was clear. Afghanistan was now a theocracy. The secularised city would have to abandon its immorality. The whole idea of modernisation was anathema. God's law was supreme, and the faithful (i.e. they themselves) were His agents. Punishment was as ordained by *sharia* law. It was meted out in public to demonstrate that wrongdoing was an offence against Allah, and therefore its punishment was a communal religious event.

Whether many of the Kabulis changed their beliefs or values as a result of these symbolic actions we do not know. However, their eager return to their former way of life after the defeat of the Taliban in 2001 suggests that their pre-existing attitudes towards modernity and theocracy were strengthened.

Common to the Truth Church, the Philadelphia Church of Christ, and the Taliban is the patriarchal belief in the inferior status of women. It is hardly surprising, therefore, that the artefacts of fundamentalist organisations tend to have masculine symbolic meanings. War, power, authority, control, punishment, orthodoxy, purity, and status are all stereotypically masculine preoccupations.

To conclude, I have demonstrated how a cultural model is appropriate for understanding fundamentalist organisations. In particular, I have sought to show that a model of cultural change can explain how fundamentalist believers adapt successfully to their changing environment and survive. This they do by adding symbolic meaning to their cultural artefacts: their actions, rituals, buildings, words, and so on. These meanings change or re-inforce their beliefs and values, which are expressed in new artefacts, and so the cycle continues.

## Summary

- Manifestations of fundamentalisms at the local level can best be analysed as organisations.
- Organisation theory offers several theoretical perspectives, but the most appropriate for fundamentalist organisations is the cultural perspective.
- This suggests that organisational artefacts become symbols, which carry meaning over and above the functional artefact itself.
- Such meanings impact upon basic assumptions and values in a dynamic process, which enables the organisation to adapt to its environment or to effect change upon it.
- According to the cultural model of organisation, leaders acquire and maintain their power by making artefacts meaningful.

- For example, they perform symbolic actions that carry implications for beliefs and values. Or, they provide a new perspective on the nature of the organisation and its relation with its environment. Or, they provide a framework for interpreting a current situation or event.
- This theoretical analysis is then illustrated by three examples: buildings and rituals as artefacts; violent assault (9/11); and processes of social control.
- The buildings and rituals of three different American Protestant fundamentalist churches point to different symbolic meanings: of the value and importance of correct doctrine; of the expression of enthusiastic emotion; and of the pastor as prophet and healer.
- 9/11 can be construed as a symbolic act, with a variety of messages for three different audiences.
- Finally, I considered control processes, within a Protestant church, and by the Taliban. The meanings attached to these processes affected the recipients' responses.

## Further reading

Balmer, R. (2000) *Mine Eyes Have Seen the Glory: A Journey into the Evangelical Subculture in America* (3rd edn.). New York: Oxford University Press.

Clegg, S.R., Hardy, C., & Nord, W.R. (1996) (eds.) *Handbook of Organisation Studies.* London: Sage.

Gerges, F.A. (2005) *The Far Enemy: Why Jihad Went Global.* New York: Cambridge University Press.

Haslam, S.A. (2001) *Psychology in Organisations: The Social Identity Approach.* London: Sage.

Hatch, M.J. (1997) *Organisation Theory: Modern, Symbolic, and Postmodern Perspectives.* Oxford: Oxford University Press.

Juergensmeyer, M. (2003) *Terror in the Mind of God: The Global Rise of Religious Violence* (3rd edn.) Berkeley, CA: University of California Press.

Kepel, G. (2006) *Jihad: The Trail of Political Islam* (4th edn.). London: IBTauris.

Morgan, G. (1997) *Images of Organisation* (2nd edn.). Thousand Oaks CA: Sage.

Tamney, J.B. (2002) *The Resilience of Conservative Religion: The Case of Popular Conservative Protestant Congregations.* Cambridge: Cambridge University Press.

Watt, D.H. (2002) *Bible-Carrying Christians: Conservative Protestants and Social Power.* New York: Oxford University Press.

Weick, K.E. (1979) *The Social Psychology of Organising.* Reading, MA: Addison Wesley.

## CASE STUDY: THE HOME-SCHOOL MOVEMENT AND ITS ORGANISATIONS

*The home-school movement provides a good example of why fundamentalist organisations are best understood from a cultural perspective. The artefacts of the different organisations constituting the movement gain symbolic meaning as a result of the efforts of the organisations' leaders. Some of these meanings re-inforce existing beliefs and values within the organisation, for example, the belief that the secular education system defiles and corrupts the young. Others change existing beliefs, for example, the belief that the public schools can be persuaded by fundamentalists to change their ethos and direction. The result of such a change is to gain support for the strategy of removing children from the public education system to Christian private schools or to home schooling. The case study thus exemplifies the model of organisation as a cultural change process, in which the various outcomes of organisational actions acquire symbolic meanings, which in turn change the beliefs and values of the organisation and hence its subsequent actions.*

## A growing phenomenon

Fundamentalist organisations do not consist only of local mosques, synagogues, or congregations, nor of groups of terrorists. They are also to be found engaged in a variety of para-church activities. One such movement is the American home-school movement. I will describe several organisations that are part of this growing phenomenon. These are analysed, once again, as sub-cultures. Their recent development demonstrates how the symbolic meanings of their artefacts have changed so as to allow the development of new beliefs and values (see pp. 113–115). This adaptability has enabled them to survive.

The cosmology of the Christian Right in America consists of a set of concentric circles (Lienesch, 1993). At the centre are the individual, and his (sic) family. Then the innermost circle is his local church congregation and his local community. Next comes the state and then the national levels of analysis, together with church denominations and other institutions that function at those two levels. Then the world scene appears, with particular reference to the Middle East, since that is the political arena to which the Bible refers. Finally, the world is subsumed into a supernatural cosmology, where spiritual powers intervene in world affairs. The Christian Right increasingly believes that it is their task to bring all these areas of their cosmology under the rule of God.

In the central sphere of *the family*, their rhetoric has been strident. All of their liberal demons: gays and lesbians, feminists, abortionists, evolutionists, and so on, have been attacked in the name of the family (Harding, 2000). All are seen as undermining that sacred institution, established by God, and continuously under threat from the secular world. Their main concern for their children is to ensure that they are kept pure from secular influences and follow in their parents' footsteps of faith (Danso, Hunsberger, & Pratt, 1997). Given that conservative Christians are more fertile than their liberal counterparts (Hout, Greely, & Wilde, 2001), they want to be sure to press home this numerical advantage.

They perceive the main obstacle in the way of developing more young conservative Christians to be the public school system. As long ago as the 1970s, fundamentalists were saying such things as 'The schools, with federal funding, are making a frontal attack on the Judaeo-Christian value system', and 'The federal government is trying to control minds and morals. They don't recognise that there are thousands concerned with looking for an absolute. The Bible should have a place, and be taught to children, as opposed to the humanistic approach' (Brown, 2002, p. 255).

The public schools, fundamentalists believe, are indoctrinating their children with secular values. Only just over 5% of Christian youth hold 'a Biblical world-view', they announce (Nehemiah, 2005). In an attempt to ensure that their children are brought up with the 'correct' world-view, they have adopted a two-pronged strategy. They have sought to put pressure on the public schools by infiltrating and taking over local school boards and influencing the curriculum. And they are increasingly either sending their children to explicitly Christian private schools, or else teaching them at home.

Whilst private schooling may be a relatively expensive option for middle-income families, home-schooling comes cheap indeed, and is becoming an increasingly popular alternative to the public schools. Moreover, if parents withdraw their children from public education in ever-increasing numbers, they believe that the state may be forced in the long term to withdraw from the provision of education altogether (Salai, 2002).

How big is the home-schooling movement in America? The best estimates come from the American government's National Household Education Surveys for 1996, 1999, and 2003 (Bauman, 2002; NCES, 2004). These show a rise from 636,000 through 850,000 to 1,096,000 students being educated at home. This latter figure constitutes 2.2% of the school-age population. However, these figures may be underestimates, as many home-schooling parents do not report the fact to the education authorities. A soundly based estimate of under-reporting is around 25%, so the true figure for 2003 may approach 1,400,000. The parents who choose home-schooling are likely to be middle-income, white, with larger families, and of higher educational attainment than average. One parent only is likely to be a full-time worker (Basham, 2001).

When they are asked why they chose home-schooling (Bauman, 2002), the most common reason parents give is that they believe that they can provide their children with a better education at home (given by 51% of parents). If we take standard measures of educational achievement as criteria, this belief has apparent foundation: home-schooled students typically score in the 70th to 80th percentile (Rudner, 1999). They are also more likely to go to college (Ray, 2003). However, the comparisons are not with a group controlled for other potential causal factors, such as parents' level of education, and so we cannot be confident that home-schooling is the reason for this superior performance. Explicitly religious reasons for educating their children at home were given by 33% of parents, whilst 30% cited a poor learning environment at school. Sizeable minorities cited objections to what the school taught (14%) and the need to develop their child's character and morality (9%), reasons that might be underpinned by religious beliefs. We can conclude that religious belief is certainly a strong, and possibly the major, reason for choosing home-schooling.

The growth in the numbers of home-schooled students over the last eight years is evident. The scope for further explosive growth is also clear. The presence at home of one of the parents is a strong predictor of the choice to home-school (61% of home students vs. 26% of state school students). Yet there are 10 million of the 36 million American mothers of children under 18 who do not work at all, with another 6.5 million who work part-time (Bauman, 2002). Thus there are millions more potential parent educators. Moreover, the legal regulation of home-schooling has become steadily less strict. In 1980, it was illegal in 30 states, and has only been legal in all 50 since 1993. At the time of writing, 41 states specify no minimum academic standards for parents who wish to home-school their children (Basham, 2001).

## Citizens for Excellence in Education (CEE)

The conditions thus favour an increase in home-schooling. But the main reason for expecting further and more explosive growth is that it has become a major political objective of the Christian Right. Several pressure groups have a general anti-public school agenda, one of which is NACE/CEE (National Association of Christian Educators/ Citizens for Excellence in Education). As befits an organisation devoted to the family, NACE/CEE is indeed a family ministry/business. Its Director is Robert Simonds, and it also employs his wife and daughter. Most of its finance comes from individual donations, but it also receives money from one of the Christian Right's main benefactors, the Coors Foundation (Public Eye, 2005).

Simonds has had a chequered history. A former mathematics teacher at a California community college, he was asked to resign after students complained of his religious proselytising (Brown, 2002, p. 259). Having founded the NACE, he was selected as a member of President Reagan's task force to implement the 'Nation at Risk' report, to remedy perceived deficiencies in the public schools. The CEE was then developed as an offshoot of NACE, with the aim of 'bringing public education back under the control of the Christian community' and taking 'dominion over our schools and our nation' (Boston, 2000, p. 247).

At its peak, NACE/CEE claimed to have established approximately 1700 chapters across America, and growing (NACE/CEE, 2004). It also claimed around 340,000 members. However, there is no independent verification of these figures, and they are likely to be exaggerated. The chapters sought to take over school boards, using infiltration techniques recommended in Simonds' book 'How to Elect Christians to Public Office'. They targeted such educational programmes as drug prevention, sex education, multi-cultural awareness, self-esteem enhancement and the teaching of evolutionary theory. They typically expressed an interest in improving the quality of education without making explicit their religious agenda, some not even using the NACE/CEE banner (Brown, 2000).

That such a fundamentalist agenda existed is evident from Simonds' position on the steering committee of the Coalition on Revival, a politico-religious pressure group arguing for a dominionist theology (see Chapter 7). It is also evident from much of his published work (see below), and from internal communications. 'There are 17,500 school districts in America', wrote Simonds in a direct mail shot. 'When we get an active Christian parents' committee in operation in all districts, we can take complete control of all local school boards. This would allow us to determine all local policy: select good textbooks, good curriculum programs, superintendents, and principals. Our time has come!' (Simonds, 2003).

Additionally, NACE/CEE claimed to have established nearly 900 Public School Awareness committees in fundamentalist churches. The churches were urged to be prepared to support home-schooling, and to host Christian private schools. The increased availability of education vouchers has enabled private schools to tap indirectly into government funds. Some, however, mistrusted federal intervention in any shape or form, especially when it comes bearing gifts.

Simonds found his support slipping during the 1990s, and made a move towards collaboration with more moderate groups in achieving public school reforms. However, this angered much of his remaining support, and in 1998, he signalled a change of emphasis. The effort from then on was to be directed towards support for exit from public schools, and away from attempts at their reform. 'Rescue within' was giving way to 'rescue from', under the banner 'Rescue 2010' (Simonds, 1998).

Public schools, he argued in his annual letter to his members, have refused to bend:

> Deception in our schools is the rule, not sincerity; arrogance, not cooperation. Therefore, after 15 years of sincere efforts to gain parental rights, a 'safe-passage' curriculum for our dear innocent children, the Lord has counselled me, and an impressive array of those associated in ministry have confirmed God's leading, that CHRISTIANS MUST EXIT THE PUBLIC SCHOOLS as soon as it is feasible and possible. The price in human loss, social depravity, and the spiritual slaughter of our young Christian children is no longer acceptable (and certainly never was!).
>
> Simonds (1998)

The first and foremost reason adduced by Simonds for this change of emphasis was that the public schools' teaching was now based totally on a humanist world-view rather than a Biblical one. Rescue 2010 aimed to fill current

Christian schools and to start a school in every church facility by 2010. But it also advocated home schooling for those who could not afford private schools.

In 2005, Simonds boasted considerable progress towards Rescue 2010's objectives (Simonds, 2005):

> 'Well beloved' [he writes endearingly], 'the good news for we (sic) who believe and trust the Lord is that we are now moving into the greatest area of God's twelve-year plan, Rescue 2010. Public school enrolment was predicted to increase as much as 25% in the next ten years (that was in February 1998 – the date CEE started Rescue 2010). Today (March of 2005) our CEE latest calculation shows an estimate of 6.48 million Christian children have been transferred out of America's unconscionable child-abusing public schools and into a good Christian school, a home school, or a private school . . . In 2004, our CEE parents, already working as volunteer activists, gave President Bush their support, and I believe it helped greatly to put him over the top. God blesses us in so many ways!

However, Simonds admits to a setback. The Southern Baptist Convention of summer 2004, representing 17 million Southern Baptists, refused to permit a vote on a proposal to encourage Southern Baptist parents to withdraw their children from public schools:

> Through the unchristian act of otherwise trusted Christian leaders of the largest Protestant denomination in the world, much harm to children's souls was done . . . It's hard to imagine what God may do to these leaders for turning away from the Gospel and all its teaching on Christian education for Christian children. His judgments on such horrendous sins as condemning tens of millions of children to an atheist, immoral, anti-God, anti-parent future separated from God forever are fearful. Woe to these deluded leaders who have chosen to follow mammon and abandon their children to the fire. God be merciful, please. Is there not an easier way to deal with this gross sin, O Lord?

The letter concludes with a plea for financial support:

> Rescue 2010 is now on the verge of success. We desperately need to plead with you, dear one, please help us win this battle for precious human (children's) souls. You will be glad you sacrificed for our godly 'little ones'.
>
> Simonds (2005)

### The Exodus Mandate

The subsequent effort to get the failed resolution adopted by Southern Baptist conventions at the state level in autumn 2004 was co-ordinated by the Exodus Mandate, a pressure group whose avowed aim is to persuade conservative Christians to remove their children from the public schools. Directed by E. Ray Moore, Exodus Mandate includes among its supporters the two sponsors of the resolution to the Southern Baptist convention, both home-schooling fathers. Moore also directs, as his main ministry/business, Frontline Ministries (Moore, 2004).

The success of the Exodus Mandate in gaining visibility for the anti-public-school movement is a demonstration of how an individual with media skills, working part-time, can affect public opinion. Moore is one of the first people to whom respected media organs such as the *Washington Times* go for a quote from the Christian Right perspective. Moore's publicity skills are evidenced in his choice of name for his organisation, resonating as it does with echoes of God rescuing his chosen people the Israelites from the tyrant Pharoah. Unsurprisingly, his book advocating withdrawal from the government system is entitled 'Let My Children Go' (Moore, 2002).

Moore's book, and the publications of his Frontline Ministries, clearly demonstrate that, like Simonds, his beliefs are derived not only from Christian fundamentalism in general, but also from its increasingly popular variant, dominionism. The *general fundamentalism* is evidenced in his argument that state education is mentioned neither in the Bible nor in the Constitution, and therefore cannot be right. There are echoes here of George W. Bush's association of God with the USA's manifest destiny in his second inaugural speech (see Chapter 2). The responsibility of parents and church to ensure a Godly education for their children is adduced from the quotation of numerous Biblical texts in isolation from their contexts. The treatment of the religion's holy book as the ultimate authority for belief and practice is, of course, one of the defining features of fundamentalisms. So is Moore's definition of the secular state as the enemy of the true faith.

The *dominionist emphasis* is evident from Moore's presentation of a choice between government and God, between a secular and a religious world-view. The withdrawal from the public schools is represented as the action of God's people in wresting back from secular authority the power to educate their children. They are asserting God's dominion over the innermost element of their world-view after themselves: their family. They are fulfilling the great commission of Christ: 'Go ye therefore, and teach all nations . . . to observe all things whatsoever I have commanded you' (Matthew 28.19,20) by first putting their own house in order.

On the other hand, dominionists still wish to subvert the public school system, so as to weaken their enemies the humanists:

> We need people to infiltrate institutions presently under the control of the Devil. We could start with the public schools. Of course, except in unusual cases, we should not send our own children to public schools; but courageous, Resistance-minded Christian educators need to secure posts in all levels of public education and reclaim their area for Christ.

Obviously, while under the present humanistic yoke, they may have to operate covertly for a while. They may not be able to publicly proclaim the Crown Rights of Jesus Christ. They should quietly subvert the humanistic system, however, by providing 'acceptable alternatives' (red-blooded Biblical Faith). If they become a little too bold and incite the ire of the humanistic administration or school board, they should cry 'Violation of academic freedom!' in tones appropriate to the cry of 'bloody murder!'

(Sandlin, 2005).

## The Nehemiah Institute

The idea of world-view is central to the case for withdrawal from the public schools. The proponents of withdrawal claim that all education is based upon a particular world-view, which underpins its beliefs, values, and practices. A secular, anti-God, world-view informs public school education, whereas a Biblical world-view is the basis for Christian private and home-school education. The two world-views are totally incompatible; there can be no compromise. The choice is between God and Satan.

Once again, some defining features of fundamentalism are evident here: the treatment of the secular world as the ultimate enemy; the treatment of the Bible as the ultimate authority; and the dualistic view of the world as divided between good and evil.

The particular dominionist emphasis is also apparent in the world-view assumption. Dominionist theology argues that there can be no common ground between the believer and the unbeliever (see Chapter 7). Those who argue for the Christian faith on the basis of reason are falsely assuming a degree of common ground, and the possibility of arguments for the existence of God based upon probability. Thus Christian educators should certainly not present a balanced perspective and give school students the intellectual tools to make their own decisions. On the contrary, they have failed if they have not confronted secularism head-on and inculcated a Biblical world-view into their students by the time they complete their formal education.

What might such a world-view look like? Fortunately, the American fondness for psychometric testing has enabled us to answer this question unequivocally. The Nehemiah Institute, director Dan Smithwick (2008), states: 'Our primary work is in providing a unique worldview testing and training service to private schools, churches, home schoolers, and other Christian ministries. Programs are designed for junior high through adult ages'. The aim of these programs is 'to aid in restoring our nation to a biblically-based society as it once was . . . We get our name from Nehemiah of the Old Testament who led the mission in rebuilding fallen Jerusalem. Today's "Jerusalem" for the church is the whole world' (Smithwick, 2008).

The Institute's programmes operate in three stages. First, in the Research stage, the PEERS test is administered. PEERS stands for politics, economics, education, religion, and social issues. The results allow respondents to be categorised into one of four major world-views: Biblical theism, Moderate Christian, Secular Humanism, or Socialism. Their scores are fed back to respondents, together with reports 'showing the strengths and weaknesses of the group as a whole ... The purpose of the research is to help individuals and organisations identify key areas where their views of life are contrary to Biblical reasoning. The test serves as a survey of the "damage to our walls" '.

In other words, a test of values and attitudes, in which there are, of course, no right or wrong answers, is being used to assess the extent to which respondents' values correspond with those of the test constructors and administrators. Where they do so they are 'strengths', and where they do not, they are 'weaknesses'.

The underlying ideology of the test constructors can be inferred from the test items:

- Society, not the individual, is chiefly responsible for social evils (strongly agree, tend to agree, no opinion, tend to disagree, strongly disagree).
- Private ownership of property is a necessary requirement for a nation to prosper (strongly agree, etc.).
- All people are conceived with a sinful nature, which, from birth on, creates desires in them to commit evil deeds.
- The Bible provides the foundation of civil law, and should be the primary source of instruction for establishing civil government in all nations.
- Capital punishment for certain crimes is a Biblical mandate, and should be enforced in our society.
- Civil government, at both the state and federal levels, should not have responsibility for the economic well-being of the citizens
- Traditional male and female roles are the result of special and distinct qualities with which men and women are born.

The next stage of the Nehemiah Institute programme is termed Rethinking:

> The value of PEERS testing is its ability to compare a student's worldview with that of their teachers or parents. The PEERS Test's item-by-item analysis makes it easy and time-efficient to zero in on the most problematic worldview areas. Based upon this data, parents and school administrators can take corrective action by enhancing the current curriculum or by placing more emphasis on particular issues.
>
> (Smithwick, 2008)

A handy way to achieve this latter objective is by giving the erring student position papers. Position papers are offered on test items 'most frequently missed' (i.e. where students most often disagree with the test constructors).

Here, in some detail, is the position paper provided for the test item:

'In a democratic society, citizens have a civil right to an education and this right must be protected and enforced by civil government'. The position paper carefully introduces the item as concerning political philosophy, and defines the terms 'civil right' and 'education' reasonably. It expands on the meaning of the statement constituting the item, also reasonably. It then leaps immediately into 'supporting scripture passages'. The following Biblical texts are quoted (out of context), and commented upon as follows:

> Exodus 20.3 You shall have no other gods before me.
> Comment: No person should pay homage, directly or indirectly, to any other person, idea, or institution, above the one God. All persons, ideas, and institutions must therefore be subservient to God and to the standards of God set forth in Scripture. This clearly implies that the state cannot usurp the place of God.
> Genesis 1.27 And God created man in his own image.
> Comment: God is creator, man is the creature, and thus God has all ultimate rights over man and man has no inherent rights.
> Proverbs 1.8 Hear, my son, your father's instruction, and do not forsake your mother's teaching.
> Comment: In Scripture the parents are given ultimate authority and the duty to educate their children.
> Proverbs 1.7 The fear of the Lord is the beginning of knowledge.
> Comment: True knowledge is rooted in reverence for God, and for His Word (see Psalm 119). A secularised government is incapable of meeting that ultimate standard of Godly education and, since all government in modern times is secular in the sense that it self-consciously severs Christianity from the state, then it should not be looked to for education or to enforce the 'rights' to it.
>
> (Smithwick, 2008)

After 'rethinking' the questionnaire item according to this position paper, the student should not find it too difficult to respond 'strongly disagree'.

The third and final stage of the Institute's programme is 'Rebuilding' (metaphorically rebuilding the 'walls of Jerusalem'). The purpose is the rehabilitation of the student by a course entitled: Developing a Biblical Worldview:

> The course is designed to lead an individual into thinking biblically about major areas of life with the goal of building a biblically-based culture . . . DBW includes a lesson on the Christian history of our nation and a lesson on major events of world history from a biblical point of view.
>
> (Smithwick, 2008)

## America's Providential History

One of the texts recommended by the Nehemiah Institute in the study of 'the Christian history of our nation' is 'America's Providential History' (Beliles & McDowell, 1991). This text has reportedly sold over 100,000 copies, and is used by home-schoolers, private, religious, and public schools, colleges, and seminaries. It begins as follows:

> The goal of 'America's Providential History' is to equip Christians to be able to introduce Biblical principles into the public affairs of America, and every nation in the world, and in so doing bring Godly change throughout the world. We will be learning how to establish a Biblical form (and power) of government in America and we will see how our present governmental structures must be changed. Since the principles we will be learning are valid in every society and in any time in history, they will be able to be applied throughout the world and not just in America. As we learn to operate nations on Biblical principles, we will be bringing liberty to the nations of the world and hence fulfilling part of God's plan for the nations.
>
> (Beliles & McDowell, 1991)

We may wonder how compatible this theocratic aim is with democracy. However, the authors have no trouble with this awkward concept:

> Even if Christians manage to outnumber others on an issue and we sway our Congressman by sheer numbers, we end up in the dangerous promotion of democracy. We really do not want representatives who are swayed by majorities, but rather by correct principles.
>
> (Beliles & McDowell, 1991, p. 265)

Instead, they promote a theocratic notion of liberty:

> When the Spirit of the Lord comes into the heart of a man, that man is liberated. Likewise, when the Spirit of the Lord comes into a nation, that nation is liberated. The degree to which the Spirit of the Lord is infused into a society (through its people, laws, and institutions), is the degree to which that society will experience liberty in every realm (civil, religious, economic, etc.).
>
> (Beliles & McDowell, 1991, p. 26)

In other words, believe and practise exactly what we believe and practise, as individuals and as nations, and you will be free. There are eerie echoes here of the theological writings of the radical Muslim clerics, Mawdudi and Qutb, whose ideas inspired the 9/11 hijackers (see pp. 185–194).

Naturally, the Puritan founders are the heroes of 'America's Providential History':

> The primary strength of the Puritans was their 'spirit of dominion'. They recognised the scriptural mandate requiring Godly rule, and zealously set out to establish that in all aspects of society.
>
> (Beliles & McDowell, 1991, p. 84)

The authors are clear how to work from the bottom up to achieve their theocratic aims:

> If Christians in every locality became a controlling influence in a political party after two years of serving there consistently, then every ungodly representative in the state legislatures and the Congress could be replaced within six years to work with a godly president.
>
> (Beliles & McDowell, 1991, p. 266)

Needless to say, the political programme of the theocratic right would abolish most functions of the state and hand them over to churches, since 'programs such as Social Security, and other welfare agencies, set up the State as provider rather than God'.

The authors also assert Christians' right to dominion over the natural world:

> Those men with a Christian worldview believe that God has provided all that they need and, consequently, they have faith to seek, find, and process abundant natural resources. As the natural resources available to man increase, his material welfare increases as well . . . A secular society will lack faith in God's providence, and consequently men will find fewer natural resources. The secular or socialist has a limited resource mentality and views the world as a pie (there is only so much) that needs to be cut up so that everyone can get a piece. In contrast, the Christian knows that the potential in God is unlimited, and that there is no shortage of resources in God's earth.
>
> (Beliles & McDowell, 1991, p. 251)

This book is a staple text for Christian home-schoolers and religious schools. It is not merely fundamentalist, but, rather, overtly dominionist in its religious ideology. As well as its authors, all the other influential movers and shakers in the anti-public-school movement mentioned in this chapter express similar beliefs. Smithwick of the Nehemiah Institute, for example, quotes the Director of the Coalition on Revival, Jay Grimstead, with approval:

> We affirm that the Bible is not only God's statements to us regarding religion, salvation, eternity, and righteousness, but also the final measurement and depository of certain fundamental facts of reality and basic principles that God wants all mankind to know in the spheres of law, government, economics, business, education, arts and communication, medicine, psychology, and science.
>
> (Smithwick, 2008)

However, the home-schooling movement does not confine itself to textbooks. Ensuring that it fights its secular opponents using their own weapons, it has established a web-site to oppose the editors of Wikipedia, the online reference site, which it claims to be biased in a liberal direction (Johnson, 2007). The new site is called Conservapedia, and its thrust may be discerned by comparing the Wikipedia and Conservapedia entries on dinosaurs:

> Wikipedia: Vertebrate animals that dominated terrestrial ecosystems for over 160 million years, first appearing approximately 230 million years ago.

> Conservapedia: . . . mentioned in numerous places throughout the Good Book. For example, the behemoth in Job and the leviathan in Isaiah are almost certainly references to dinosaurs.

Given this apparently general ideological direction, then, can we find a more specific statement of the dominionist position on education? The Coalition on Revival helpfully provides us with a formal set of statements of affirmation and denial (Coalition on Revival, 1995). Here is a sample:

- We affirm that in its most basic meaning, education is the triune God teaching His truth to mankind. We deny that education is solely mental or physical activity associated with learning the thoughts and experiences of other human beings.
- We affirm that education is the action or process by which a person comes to know and use God's truth, and that education is learning to think God's thoughts after Him and to see things as He sees them. We deny that education is merely the action or process by which a person acquires knowledge or skills.
- We affirm that the purpose of education is both to reveal God and to bring students into conformity with His revealed will. We deny that the sole purpose of education is to accomplish human perfection and understanding of the material world.
- We affirm that freedom of inquiry and academic freedom have a legitimate place in the pursuit of truth and in the framework of the learning and teaching process. We deny that academic freedom implies the right to disobey or contradict the Scriptures as the embodiment of God's truth in this world, or to violate a contractual agreement with an employer.
- We affirm that parents have a right to educate their children at home or in private schools that are free from control by civil government. We deny that civil government has legitimate authority to monitor, regulate, or directly control home schooling or private school education by such means as compulsory attendance laws, state curricula, state-wide student achievement testing, mandatory state teacher certification, or other intrusions into these areas of schooling.

## Sub-cultural symbols

The intense ambition of the dominionists, and at the same time their total intolerance of alternative perspectives, render them a frightening and alien social phenomenon to liberally inclined readers. And yet, this chapter has demonstrated a steady movement in America in the educational direction that they advocate. There are many and varied reasons for the increasing power of the Christian Right in the educational arena. Clearly, the movement away from the public schools and towards home-schooling has been in progress for at least the last 15 years. However, it is evident that the election of President George W. Bush for two terms provided very considerable added impetus. Bush's educational programme was supported by Congressional members of the Christian Right, such as Tom DeLay of Texas, who achieved power through the organisational skills of their religious supporters. Moreover, as I demonstrated in Chapter 2, the President's speeches contain the ideology that underpins his policies. There are indeed uncanny similarities between the second inaugural speech and the text of 'America's Providential History', as Yurica (2005) points out.

Perhaps the major cause of the home-school movement's increasing power, however, is the way in which its organisations have successfully adapted *their culture* to the changing American social and political environment. Discovering that it was not easy to take over school boards, and that even when they did so, parents and educators often rumbled their plans and rejected them at the next election, the CEE *changed its symbolism*. Instead of seeking to improve the public schools, it treated them as a fate worse than death from which children had to be rescued. Instead of potential, though flawed, vehicles for children's education, public schools were now to be seen as scenes of 'spiritual slaughter' where they were doomed to 'an atheist, immoral, anti-God, anti-parent future, separated from God for ever'.

This new symbolism taught fundamentalist parents to reconsider their perceptions of the public schools, and gave them a noble task, that of rescue. Once the change of belief and value had occurred, and the children had been brought out of the public system, the process of post-hoc justification soon kicked in. It must have been the right thing to do, runs the argument, because we have chosen to do it (Festinger, 1957). Thus the new artefact of home-schooling is established, and with it come new potential symbol systems, such as that contained in the textbook 'America's Providential History'.

As for *the Exodus Mandate*, its very title is its most notable cultural artefact. The symbolism of the exodus from Egypt, with God leading His chosen people out of slavery and into the promised land, resonated powerfully with people who already identified themselves as the new Israel. The same symbolic weight propelled *the Nehemiah Institute*. Rebuilding the fallen Jerusalem slips easily into 'restoring our nation to the biblically based society it once was'. As for the Institute's product, its training process of research, rethinking, and rebuilding, here we find a highly symbolic artefact. A profile of students' strengths and weaknesses, based upon a psychometric instrument that assesses values and attitudes, proclaims the aim of indoctrination. However, it gives this aim a spurious scientific justification, thus signalling that, like their difficulties with reading or mathematics, students' problems with their world-view can be addressed and fixed. Position papers and America's Providential History will do the trick.

Finally, we may note the *Coalition on Revival's* definition of what academic freedom is not. It is not the right to disobey or contradict the Bible, and it is not the right to violate a contractual agreement with an employer. Given that these two negative definitions occur in the same sentence, the idea that the Bible is a rule book for every aspect of life could not be symbolised more powerfully. The home-school movement is indeed propelled by organisations with some very powerful and adaptive sub-cultures of their own.

# 5   Small groups and fundamentalisms

## Some characteristics of small groups

### *What is a group?*

Organisations are the visible local face of fundamentalisms. However, perhaps their most powerful social engine is less visible. It is the small face-to-face groups of which local organisations are often constituted. Historically, it is evident that social, political, and religious movements have depended heavily for their success upon their small group structure. Examples are the Communist Party with its cells, the group meetings of Alcoholics Anonymous, John Wesley's Methodist Church with its classes, and the terrorist cells of al-Qaida.

Face-to-face groups are not the only form of group. We should not define 'group' in such a tangible way. If we continue with the theoretical approach we have adopted hitherto, that of social identity theory (Hogg & Abrams, 2003), then we must define groups in a much more subjective way. According to this approach, *a group is any category of persons to which individuals believe they belong* (Turner, 1982). We may wish to add a reality check on unbridled imagination: we may, for example, believe ourselves to be the reincarnation of the twelve apostles, but no-one else is likely to perceive us in this way. Hence, we may choose to insist that at least some other people who do not consider themselves members of such a category should believe that those who do are really members (Brown, 2000).

Given this more or less subjective definition of group, group membership can occur across all the levels of analysis that I have employed in this book so far. The categories of human being, Muslim, American, born-again Christian, jihadi, Southern Baptist, Gush Emunim, Philadelphia Church of Christ, and Finsbury Park Mosque, are all possible groups to which individuals may consider themselves to belong. On the basis of the present chapter, we may add such groups as study cell, house group, and worshipping family.

There are two reasons for paying particular attention to the small group level of analysis. The first is that much of the research and theorising that has been applied to groups in general has been based upon investigations of face-to-face groups. Thus, just as organisational theory illuminated the perspective on fundamentalisms from the organisational level of analysis in Chapter 4, so small group theory offers a different perspective and additional theoretical tools.

### Benefits of small groups

The second reason for the study of small groups is that they highlight several features that other levels of group analysis downplay. The first such feature is *the possibility of interpersonal relations*, which derives from the obvious fact that groups are face-to-face. Virtual groups such as chat rooms and blogs suffer from the disadvantage that self-presentation can be carefully constructed, or indeed, a totally imaginary self can be presented. Face-to-face groups are necessarily more personalised than larger or virtual groups. Personal identities as well as social identities inevitably become salient in interpersonal interaction within a small group, since people are acting as individuals and not just as members of the group.

However, for interpersonal relations to develop, the superordinate social identities that the group members share have to be established. Once we know that we are all born-again believers who attend Thomas Road Baptist Church, we can get to know and like other members of the group. This is because we perceive them to be similar to ourselves, and we generally like better those who are similar to ourselves (Byrne, 1969). We recognise everyone as 'one of us', and, safe in that recognition, we may confidently meet our needs for affiliation and esteem in our social relationship with our fellow members.

Another important feature of small groups is that they permit the development of deeply *nested social identities*. An individual may be at the same time an American, a born-again Christian, a Southern Baptist, a member of Thomas Road Baptist Church, and a Bible Study Group member within that congregation. The general BVNs of the more inclusive of these categories will subsume the more specific ones of the smaller categories. At the same time, these latter BVNs will ground the former in a local context and in members' own lived experience. For example, the general belief in constant supernatural intervention in everyday life derived from the born-again Christian identity will be fleshed out in the face-to-face group by the exchange of shared daily experiences of such intervention. The nesting of social identities is therefore a powerful reinforcement for fundamentalisms.

A further advantage of the face-to-face group is that other, potentially divisive, social identities can be defused. So, for example, within a church, synagogue, or mosque there may be marked differences in wealth or family circumstances. Social identities based on business success or on single parent status may become salient in members' minds, to the detriment of the social identity of the fundamentalist movement or the local organisation. One apparently counter-intuitive measure to prevent this is the formation of small groups consisting, for example, of business men or of single parents from among the congregation. This can prevent such differences becoming salient by removing them from the larger social situation and incorporating them as a nested identity. The individual accepts the social identity of a born-again Thomas Road Baptist Church single parent, rather than viewing themselves as a small group of single parents among all these married couples.

On the other hand, some pre-existing social identities may be very useful in helping a small group to become more cohesive. For example, members of al-Qaida cells are often recruited by relatives from the same family who already trust them (Sageman, 2004). Parental and marriage ties predispose American Protestants to join or change denominations (Musick & Wilson, 1995), and help to keep them there once they have joined.

We should also note that different levels of nested identity are likely to become *salient* in fundamentalists' minds in different situations. Salience is of major importance, since it is the currently salient social identity that directs action. In many situations, the identity 'member of a movement' (born-again Christian or jihadi, for example) will be salient. This is because comparison with, and hostility towards, the movement's general out-group are its dominant aims. Born-again Christians and jihadis may both be against secularism. However, in other situations, organisational identity may be salient. This is because the out-group is now another organisation, for example, Hizbollah, one of al-Qaida's rivals for leadership of the Islamic vanguard. In yet other situations where the small group itself has specific objectives, the social identity of the group may be salient, as it was in the 9/11 hijackings, to judge by Mohammed Atta's last message to his colleagues. Thus the small group is an essential feature if fundamentalisms wish to get specific things done at local level.

### Influence of the out-group

The nature of any group is largely determined by its relationship with its out-group(s). A group may constitute another group as its out-group because it has some conflict of interest with it (Sherif, 1966), or it may simply compare itself with the out-group in order to enhance the self-esteem of its members (Tajfel, 1981). Either way, the dynamic will be one of *differentiation*. The in-group will seek to make itself as different as possible from the out-group. To do so, it will create a stereotype of the out-group and a prototype of itself (Wright & Taylor, 2003). The *stereotype* is the belief that the out-group consists of people who all share certain characteristics, characteristics that firmly differentiate the out-group from the in-group. The *prototype* is a similar belief about one's own group: its members are characterised by a set of features that differentiate one's own group from the out-group.

The consequence is the *depersonalisation* of members of both groups. Their personal identities are submerged by their group identity. Both in-group and out-group become internally homogenised, and as different as possible from each other (Tajfel & Turner, 1986). This will result in an evaluative bias in favour of the in-group and against the out-group (Tajfel, 1981), which is likely to be expressed in discriminatory or hostile behaviour. The stereotyped beliefs will be about liberal theologians, or secular governments, or Arabs, or gays, or evolutionary scientists, and prejudice against these groups may precipitate hostile action.

Fundamentalist movements and organisations have been unremitting in their hostility to their out-groups. They have therefore used their small groups to tie adherents in to the BVNs of the movement and to strengthen their social identities as movement members. Movements can then become more differentiated from their out-groups, thereby more effectively providing the self-esteem and certainty that motivate their adherents.

## Group entry and conformity

### *A new social identity*

Joining a fundamentalist movement and/or organisation thus involves *acquiring a new social identity*, together with new out-group enemies from whom recruits have to firmly differentiate themselves as soon as possible. This means that the new identity cannot simply be an addition to the individual's existing array of social identities. He or she has not merely become a member of a sports club, whose social identity as member only becomes salient when they go to play a game and has little impact upon their other social identities. Rather, the fundamentalist social identity is at least partly defined by its out-group(s).

Any of the existing social identities that new recruits bring with them may fall into the category of the movement's out-group. If that out-group is as inclusive as 'secularism', then many of the recruit's existing social identities might be construed as out-group identities. To the extent that they are so construed, they are incompatible with membership of the movement, since one is discouraged from maintaining both in-group and out-group social identities simultaneously. Thus the more inclusive the out-group, the more of their existing social identities will have to be surrendered by the new recruit. They will be welcome as an American Republican patriot, a parent, and a spouse, but not as a supporter of Americans United for the Separation of Church and State who lives with their gay partner.

Socialising agencies such as Christian youth camps and Bible Colleges ensure that inappropriate BVNs and the social identities from which they are derived will be surrendered. Balmer (2000) reports the extent of this filtering out:

> If being a Christian . . . means abstaining from drinking, smoking, dancing, movies, and perhaps even bowling and roller-skating (because of their 'worldly' connotations), it doesn't take long for an evangelical high

school student to become a pariah among his or her peers – or, more frequently, a kind of cipher on the social scene. The options then become either finding a new support network – a church youth group, perhaps – or compromising your fundamentalist scruples in order to fit in with your peers.

(Balmer, 2000, p. 104)

Hence the entry of a newcomer into a fundamentalist movement has often been represented by its members as a dramatic throwing off of the old self and a putting on of the new: a classic conversion like that of St Paul on the road to Damascus. Various initiation rites signal this transformation. Al-Qaida recruits swear allegiance to Osama bin Laden in a one-to-one encounter (Sageman, 2004). Evangelical Christians give their testimony of how they were saved from a life of sin (Lienesch, 1993). However, although some do report their experience as a sudden and radical conversion, this is not true of many other converts (Rambo, 1993). Many clearly already have existing social identities which are compatible with a fundamentalist identity and predispose them to accept it. They are already patriotic conservative Americans, for example.

However, dramatic conversion is the preferred narrative for Protestant fundamentalists, since it is important to them to emphasise the difference of the fundamentalist social identity from other identities associated with their out-group (McGuire, 2002, p. 77). The new identity therefore has to be given some substance as soon as possible, because it needs to be strongly differentiated from such previous social identities. Hence even those personal stories that relate a sudden conversion may be post-hoc rationalisations, created and told aloud as the new member acquires the BVNs of the movement. It is, moreover, much more enhancing of one's self-esteem to say that one was persuaded by the power of the message and decided to believe and obey, than to say that one found oneself doing or saying something very different and subsequently discovered a reason for this novel action.

### The encouragement of conformity

It should be noted that the 'conversation' between preacher/witness and potential convert is certainly not a two-way dialogue. Researchers repeatedly report (e.g. Harding, 2000, p. 33 ff.) that the preacher/witness is not willing to listen to objections or difficulties. They feel impelled to tell the gospel story, and to back it up by recounting their own experience of conversion. The potential convert is invited to identify with this experience and make it their own; to permit God to work His miracle in their lives too. What we observe here is the rhetoric of persuasion rather than the dialogue of equals. This inequality is rationalised by the belief that this form of rhetorical persuasion is specifically required by God of his followers, echoing Christ's great commission to his disciples to preach the gospel and make converts. The pattern of *conformity to authority* is set from the start.

Differentiation from out-groups requires, above all else, *conformity* to the movement's BVNs, for it is only through conformity that homogeneity and cohesion can be acquired. BVNs are the instruments through which cohesive action can be motivated. Beliefs form the justification and legitimation for holding various value priorities and attitudes, which in turn justify and motivate the norms of behaviour that characterise the movement.

However, the process of conformity may occur equally often in the opposite direction. In other words, rather than being persuaded of doctrinal truths, and shown how to infer values, attitudes, and norms of behaviour from these beliefs, many new converts may begin their incorporation into the movement by adopting new forms of behaviour first (Spilka, Hood, Hunsberger, & Gorsuch, 2003, p. 355). In particular, they may find themselves using new language forms in which God features repeatedly (Harding, 2000). They subsequently acquire the beliefs and values required to explain and justify this behaviour to themselves and others. 'I must believe this', they tell themselves, 'otherwise why would I have said it?' (Bem, 1972).

### Explanations of conformity

The small group is the ideal environment for such a process. Having entered an ambiguous and unfamiliar social environment, the recruit is unsure how to behave. What is he or she expected to do or say, or should they stay silent and do nothing, as the new boy or girl on the block? The theory of *social comparison* (Festinger, 1954) suggests how they might discover how they should act. They should observe how others talk and act, infer how *they* understand the social situation, and then construct their own social reality. Clearly, it will be easier to make the correct inferences if all the others in the group appear to have the same BVNs. The more homogeneous the group, the less ambiguity for the newcomer.

However, a great deal of classic research shows that individuals conform to the judgements of others in the group, *even when there is absolutely no ambiguity* in the judgement to be made. Experimental subjects are willing to deny the clear evidence of their senses if they find others coming to a different conclusion (Asch, 1955). They cannot be in any doubt as to the correct answer, so the theory of social comparisons seems incapable of explaining the findings. A popular explanation is that people don't wish to appear different from others because they want *to avoid ridicule or rejection* (Deutsch & Gerard, 1955). If we assume that one of the motives for joining a small group is to meet one's need for affiliation, then it is important to avoid incurring such outcomes as ridicule and rejection. This normative explanation is indirectly supported by the repeated finding (Bond & Smith, 1996) that the greater the size of the majority, the more likely the individual is to conform. Clearly, it is less unpleasant to be ridiculed by one or two than by five or six.

A third explanation for conformity is the belief that *the outcomes of the task and the group's goal are important*. The aim of being God's agents in saving the world from Satan and combating all his works appears to be of great, indeed of cosmic, importance. This explanation therefore carries considerable weight in the fundamentalist case.

These three explanations for the individual's conformity in a small group are not mutually exclusive. They all point to the importance of *the new social identity*, as movement member, which the newcomer wants to incorporate into his or her self. The *social comparison* explanation indicates how important it is rapidly to grasp the BVNs of the small group and thence of the organisation and movement as a whole. One needs to know the nature of the social identity one is taking on, so that one can act and talk appropriately. Then others will confirm by their responses that the individual has indeed expressed his or her new identity acceptably. The *normative* explanation points to the likelihood that if the newcomer's behaviour has indeed been appropriate, then he or she will be accepted and liked (since they are just like us, and so we like them). The new social identity is already bringing its rewards of affiliation and self-esteem. And the same explanation fits the findings that *the importance of the group's task* aids conformity. A great aim adds a touch of quality to one's group social identity, and so to one's self-esteem.

### Roles, status, and self-esteem

The task of discovering how one should behave in the new group is made easier by the various *roles* that existing members play in the group, and the *signals of status* that go with them (Sherif & Sherif, 1964, 1969). In the Philadelphia Church of Christ (see pp. 121–123), Watt (2002) found that male gender was a signal of status. If the new member were female, she would soon learn her subordinate role. Similarly, the newcomer will see the respect shown to one individual, and the frequency with which that person initiates ideas and activities. He or she would infer that this was the leader of the group, and pay special attention to whatever that person did or said. For the leader represents the prototype of the group and, by inference, of the organisation and the movement that appointed them. The leader is the role model to follow.

Not only will the newcomer learn how to behave, and what to believe and value. He or she will also discover from other members' reactions how well they are doing in the task of exercising their new social identity. However, their possibly fragile self-esteem is not solely dependent on their success in this learning process. They are now able to share in the feelings of superiority over the out-group, and in their cosmic destiny as God's chosen agents, both of which are part of their new identity. Moreover, the new norms of behaviour serve to differentiate the group from its out-group more clearly, and so enable the newcomer to value herself as different and better.

## Conformity, commitment, authoritarianism, and deviancy

### Commitment and cohesion

However, group conformity is not only important as a socialising process for incorporating newcomers into the organisation or movement. It is also the means of creating a cohesive unit of people prepared for effective action (Mullen & Copper, 1994). Conformity to the movement's BVNs, and also to any specific BVNs derived from its nested identity, enables the small group to have its social identity firmly salient in the minds of all its members. Because the group sees itself as homogeneous and united in terms of its shared social identity, any interpersonal difficulties are less likely to intrude (Hogg, 1992). And as we like those who are like ourselves in terms of our BVNs, such interpersonal problems are less likely to occur anyway. Rather, the shared identity and personal ties *enhance commitment to the group* (Cosgel, 2001). Members withdraw from other commitments and relationships, and the competing social identities that these imply, and involve themselves ever more closely in the life of the group.

Furthermore, collaboration in a group task is in itself a source of cohesion, particularly when, as is always the case with fundamentalisms, that task is to oppose an enemy (Sherif, 1966). Even when apparent setbacks are encountered, their belief system permits them to rationalise such setbacks as pointers to ultimate success. In sum, the conformist small groups typical of fundamentalist movements are likely to be effectively mobilised in achieving their objectives.

### Conformity and personality

At this point, the objection may well be raised that the late-modern trend in Western societies is towards individualism and away from collectivism (Triandis, 1995). Surely, we may argue, people today are less susceptible to group pressures, particularly in such individualistic cultures as America. Yet the research that demonstrates conformity has largely been conducted in America, and fundamentalist movements are very strongly represented in that nation.

There appear to be two explanations for this anomaly. The first is that conformity to the movement's BVNs *meets fundamental psychological needs for self-esteem and meaning*. To the extent that the BVNs distinguish the movement's social identity from other categories, self-esteem is enhanced. And because they give a coherent account of the individual's experience and their place in history, the need for meaning is met. Hence there is no point in developing one's unique personal self, as one's fundamentalist social identity meets one's psychological needs.

The second explanation relates to *personality*. Recent advances in the psychometric study of personality have resulted in wide agreement that there are five basic factors of personality: extraversion-introversion, neuroticism-emotional stability, friendliness-hostility, conscientiousness, and intellect (Digman, 1990). There is no consistent evidence presently available that fundamentalists differ from others along any of these five factors. However, there is one specific personality construct where such differences have been found: *authoritarianism*.

The importance of the construct of authoritarianism derives historically from its use by Adorno, Frenkel-Brunswik, Levinson, and Sanford (1950) in an attempt to understand the Holocaust from a psychoanalytic perspective. Later scholars (e.g. Altemeyer, 1988, 1996) have identified, psychometrically, three elements of authoritarianism: submission, aggression, and conventionalism. The highly authoritarian individual is submissive to authority, aggressive towards out-groups, and holds tight to conventional values and norms of behaviour. Psychometric measures of authoritarianism are found to be highly correlated with measures of religious fundamentalism. These latter instruments ask such questions as whether one considers that one's own religious beliefs are uniquely true; whether this truth is opposed by evil; whether the religious practices of the past have to be followed; and whether only those of their persuasion have a right relationship with God (Altemeyer & Hunsberger, 1992).

Fundamentalism and authoritarianism measured in these ways are closely related, reaching correlations as high as .75 in one investigation (Wylie & Forest, 1992). The definition of authoritarianism includes the element of hostility towards out-groups, which can be operationalised as prejudiced attitudes towards them. When multiple regression analyses are conducted on measures of fundamentalism, authoritarianism, and prejudice against various out-groups, authoritarianism explains more of the variance in prejudice than does fundamentalism (Laythe, Finkel, & Kirkpatrick, 2001). However, the conviction of the correctness of their own beliefs may be a more powerful feature of fundamentalism; fundamentalists have few doubts (Hunsberger, Alisat, Pancer, and Pratt, 1996). In summary we may conclude that, at least among American Protestants, fundamentalists are likely to be more authoritarian than others, and that the combination of fundamentalism and authoritarianism renders them more likely to have few doubts and to be hostile to out-groups.

The first feature of authoritarianism is *submission to authority*. This is the most important determinant of conformity in the group setting. Once such submission is established and the movement's BVNs have been internalised, then absence of doubt and hostility towards the out-group ensure that conformity is firmly implanted.

Nevertheless, we should not conclude from the evidence that people become adherents of fundamentalist groups *because* they have an authoritarian personality. Correlation does not imply causality, and in the absence of longitudinal data, all that we can safely say is that authoritarianism and fundamentalism are related. It may be the case that, rather than already authoritarian people self-selecting into fundamentalisms, the inculcation of authoritarian BVNs during the process of group socialisation may make converts more authoritarian.

### *Conformity, deviance, and innovation*

Many late-modern secular organisations have found that strict conformity to the BVNs of the organisational culture is a doubtful blessing. Although it ensures efficient, co-ordinated, and motivated action, it also tends to prevent the flexible and creative solution of problems, especially novel ones. Further, it inhibits innovative ideas that might help the organisation to adapt to, anticipate, or even create, changes in its environment (Morgan, 1997). At the level of the small group, innovative (and therefore by definition non-conformist) ideas are likely to be proposed by *a deviant individual, or a few deviant allies.*

In many small groups, it is perfectly possible for deviants' proposals to stay latent in the minds of the conformist majority for a while, and have a delayed persuasive effect (Wood, et al. 1994). Group acceptance of a judgement by the majority, on the other hand, is likely to be much more immediate, and be the result of their superior power.

In fundamentalist groups, however, the movement, organisation, and group nested social identity is usually so strong that deviants from its BVNs are likely to be treated as being in error. One of the several reasons for this intolerance of deviants is that any example of deviance decreases the group's homogeneity, and hence its distinctiveness from its out-groups. We all need to be absolutely clear where we stand, particularly where the deviant 'heresy' is actually a part of the out-group's social identity. Moreover, we will all feel much purer and more virtuous if we have rooted out sinful error from our midst. Alternatively, if the deviant repents and requests re-acceptance, we will feel better for our act of forgiveness.

Some fundamentalist movements have institutionalised ways of dealing with deviancy. The Amesh, for example, engage in a practice that they (very honestly) term 'shunning' (Hood et al., 2005, pp. 146ff.). If a member of the church is engaged in what the leadership considers to be unrepentant sin, he or she is first approached privately. If the person continues in this deviant behaviour, he or she is confronted by a small group of witnesses. Continued unrepentant behaviour results in a public warning, while the final, and reluctantly taken, step in the disciplinary sequence is excommunication and shunning. All church members, including the individual's family, will avoid the deviant. They will not hold conversations with him or her, and will relegate the person to a separate table at meal times.

In a closed community such as the Amesh, this treatment is tantamount to social death. It is a withdrawal of the individual's central social identity and a denial of the need for affiliation. In the context of the generally peaceful and compassionate values of the Amesh, it demonstrates both the extraordinary importance placed by that movement on conformity to social norms, and also the low value placed on the individual in comparison with the integrity of the community.

Insistence on conformity renders grass-roots innovation less likely, and consequently fundamentalist movements tend to be dependent on their leadership for innovation. Where this is forthcoming, as it was from Jerry Falwell, from the multiple Gush Emunim leadership, from Osama bin Laden and Ayman al Zawahiri, and from the Ayatollah Khomeini, then the movement can adapt and survive. But the dependence on the leadership for innovation puts the movement at risk when that leadership becomes sclerotic (e.g. Neal Frisby, see pp. 118–119), or turns out to have feet of clay (e.g. the Bakkers).

## From group to individual

### *Conformity is not brainwashing*

The above theoretical account of small group processes within fundamentalist movements has been achieved without any recourse to such concepts as *'brainwashing'*. On the contrary, constructs from the classical theories of social psychology have proved sufficient for the purpose of understanding people whose BVNs appear very strange to a secular audience. There is no justification for a resort to the term 'brainwashing' as an explanatory concept. This has usually been used in association with the term 'cults'. Whereas sects are defined as splits from existing denominations, but still within the outer boundaries of religious and general cultural norms, cults are construed as novel forms of movement, often invented by a charismatic leader who may assume divine or semi-divine status and demands total commitment from his followers. As such, cults have attracted a great deal of opposition, to the extent that such opposition may itself be termed a movement (Spilka et al., 2003, pp. 401ff.).

'Brainwashing' refers to techniques of coercive persuasion that include total control and isolation, physical debilitation and exhaustion, confusion and uncertainty, guilt and humiliation, and the opportunity to avoid these outcomes by one means only: compliance (Anthony & Robbins, 1994). Brainwashing has generally proved successful in inducing temporary behavioural compliance, but not long-term changes in BVNs or in social identities. Those hostile to cults have argued that conversion to them is a consequence of brainwashing, rather than a voluntary action.

However, if coercive techniques are used in recruitment, they seem to be remarkably ineffective. Galanter (1989), for example, found that of people who voluntarily agreed to join an induction workshop run by the Unification Church (known as the 'Moonies'), the majority left within two days and most of the rest after nine days, leaving 9% of the original 104 attenders staying over 21 days.

Rather, other research on the Unification Church has suggested a combination of personal and social circumstances that are likely to lead to conversion to the cult (Lofland & Stark, 1965). Converts are likely to be people with a religious world-view who are unaffiliated to another church and who are experiencing some tension in their lives between their ideal and their actual experience. A turning point in their lives, for example a change of location or a loss of a job or a partner, leads them to search for a solution, and they have few social ties to help them through. Having encountered a member of the Unification Church, the potential convert is offered friendship by this individual and others, and/or by a small group. He or she has their needs for affiliation and acceptance met, and only then becomes a convert in the full sense as they take on the BVNs of the movement. This frequently followed a period of actually living with a group of adherents communally. Then, as Galanter (1989) observed, they felt happier (except when in contact with their unconverted family).

We can conclude that 'brainwashing' is not a useful explanatory concept when we are considering fundamentalist movements (few of which fall into the category of cults). Rather, an account based on the acquisition of a new social identity accords better with the evidence. The same dynamic interplay between a social entity and the individual that has been apparent in each chapter so far is also evidenced in the case of the small group.

This dynamic consists of the internalisation into the self of the cultural features of social groups, and the individual's re-creation and expression of these social groups in action. The cultural features are internalised as BVNs of the social categories to which individuals believe they belong, in other words, of their social identities. In the case of the small group, the group social identity is likely to be a nested identity subsumed within larger categories (born-again Christian, jihadi, etc.).

There are, of course, many social identities the BVNs of which are unrelated or inconsistent with each other, and individuals may be more or less willing to incorporate them into their selves. But, if people have internalised cultural and sub-cultural features into their selves in the form of the BVNs associated with nested social identities, then they will be motivated to action in support both of their selves and also of the social categories to which they believe they belong. Such action will constitute and re-constitute those categories.

The small group is the smallest of the social entities I will consider in this book. Although the small group identity may be nested within larger categories, it nevertheless constitutes a powerful psychological force. For, as I have argued, the small group and its associated identity nurture some of the social processes that are necessary for fundamentalisms to succeed. Specifically, *conformity* and *commitment* are vital, both to the distinctiveness and homogeneity of the movement and to its capability for action in its wider social environment.

Moreover, small groups often meet the need for *affiliation* in ways which larger social units cannot emulate. For example, Tamney (2002, p. 108) describes the 'Life Groups' which meet at 'Spirited Church'. Six couples, similar in age, meet for three hours weekly. They eat together, and chat, usually in same-gender groups. They then all get together, discover each others' current good news and problems, and pray for each other. This is followed by discussion of a passage from the Bible. 'Max', Tamney's interviewee, tells him that as a result he has made close friends from among the group, with whom he eats, plays, and discusses personal and spiritual issues.

The remaining chapters will be concerned with the *individual* level of analysis. The implications for individual identities have been drawn from consideration of the social context in the first part of this book. In the second part, the social identity of fundamentalist will be examined in terms of the beliefs, values, attitudes, and behaviour that derive from it.

## Summary

- Small groups are the smallest social category to be considered in the *cultural* analysis of fundamentalisms that has dominated this book so far.
- They thus form the most nested fundamentalist social identity, and reinforce the movement's BVNs.
- This is achieved by ensuring the conformity of members to BVNs that differentiate the movement from its out-groups.
- New entrants to a fundamentalist movement learn conformity by observing existing members' behaviour so as to avoid ridicule and gain acceptance, and by collaborating in important tasks, thus firming up their new social identity.
- Conformity to shared BVNs results in group cohesion and commitment, and is therefore vital to the movement's success.
- The difficulty of obtaining conformity in an increasingly individualised national culture is offset by the fact that some individuals are more authoritarian than others, and therefore more willing to conform.
- While the beneficial outcome of conformity for the movement is effective, co-ordinated, and motivated action, the downside is the absence of innovation.
- Movements have to rely on their leaders' capacity to adapt to their changing environment.
- There is no need to resort to the idea of 'brainwashing' in order to explain conformity and commitment to fundamentalisms. Rather, adequate explanations are available in the classic social psychological literature.

## Further reading

Altemeyer, B. (1996) *The Authoritarian Spectre*. Boston: Harvard University Press.
Brown, R. (2000) *Group Processes* (2nd edn.) Oxford: Blackwell.

154   *Religious Fundamentalism*

Harding, S.F. (2000) *The Book of Jerry Falwell: Fundamentalist Language and Politics.* Princeton, NJ: Princeton University Press.
Hogg, M.A. & Abrams, D. (2003) Intergroup behaviour and social identity. In M.A. Hogg and J. Cooper (eds.) *Handbook of Social Psychology.* London: Sage.
Martin, R. & Hewstone, M. (2003) Social influence processes of control and change: Conformity, obedience to authority, and innovation. In M.A. Hogg & J. Cooper (eds.) *Handbook of Social Psychology.* London: Sage.
Sageman, M. (2004) *Understanding Terror Networks.* Philadelphia: University of Philadelphia Press.
Spilka, B., Hood, R.W., Hunsberger, B., & Gorsuch, R. (2003) *The Psychology of Religion: An Empirical Approach* (3rd edn.) New York: Guilford.
Tajfel, H. (1981) *Human Groups and Social Categories.* Cambridge: Cambridge University Press.
Wright, S.C. & Taylor, D.M. (2003) The social psychology of cultural diversity: Social stereotyping, prejudice, and discrimination. In M.A. Hogg & J. Cooper (eds.) *Handbook of Social Psychology.* London: Sage.

## CASE STUDY: ISLAMIC TERRORIST CELLS

*The case of young Muslim citizens of Western nations acting as members of Islamic terrorist cells gives a good illustration of why cell groups are so powerful a unit within fundamentalist movements. Alienated as second- or third-generation citizens both from their immigrant parents' traditional religion and from the perceived cultural excesses and political hostility of their present environment, young Muslim men and women are in search of an identity. A social identity as a radical Islamist, a brother or sister, is strengthened by the powerful pull of conformity within a small group which regards surrounding society as an out-group. Conformity brings acceptance by like-minded others. It is also a necessary condition for successful collaboration in terrorist projects.*

### Affiliation, conformity, and commitment

Terrorist cells are by definition a very particular form of small group. Their purpose is to carry out specific assaults, a purpose that they have to try to conceal from others. However, they demonstrate the several key features of small groups. They are face-to-face groups in which alienated individuals can often meet their need for *affiliation* and comradeship; they ensure *conformity* to the BVNs of the movement or organisation of which they are part; and their mutual *commitment* and rigid *conformity* render them a *cohesive,* motivated, and reliable operational force, ready to die for the cause. The 9/11 hijackers and the London bombers of 7 July 2005 shared these common features. However, they also demonstrated some interesting differences, which have important implications for their social identities.

First, to what extent were the members of both groups *alienated individuals?* The careful demographic analysis by Sageman (2004), on which

Shahzad Tanweer © AFP/Getty Images

much of this case study relies, demonstrates that of 165 jihadis investigated, 115 (70%) joined the jihadi movement in a country where they had not grown up. A further 14 were second-generation nationals of France, the UK, and America (and note that Sageman's research was conducted before the Madrid and London bombings). Of these mobile individuals, almost all had left their families back in the land of their birth.

Foreign study and travel is fairly common for young men in the West, but its impact on Muslims is likely to be greater. The sudden absence of close Muslim family life and important extended family are more likely to result in feelings of alienation from the host culture and in the search for alternative ways to meet the need for affiliation. As for the London bombers, their alienation was from the British society of their birth. They were unable to feel part of a nation that was, in their view, persecuting their Muslim brothers and sisters in the Middle East. They, too, had a need to belong. They too needed a social identity.

This need for affiliation was typically met by young male friends from the same background. In Hamburg, where he was studying for his Masters degree, Mohammed Atta, the leader of the hijackers, was a member of a group of eight or nine who later formed the operational core of the 9/11 assault. In Leeds, the home city of the four London bombers, the group coalesced round its leader, Mohammed Sidique Khan. In both groups, initial bonds were cemented by an ever-increasing 'escalation of rhetorical militancy and condemnation of the West' (Sageman, 2004, p. 108). As Horgan (2005, p. 161) remarks: 'The process of becoming a terrorist involves a cumulative, incrementally sustained process of behaviours that culminate in increased, sustained and focused commitment to the group'.

Members of the group of London bombers are reported to have had intense discussions. Mohammed Sidique Khan and Shahzad Tanweer are reported to have stayed up all night discussing ideological matters (BBC, 2006a). This is exactly what would be expected if the group wished to distinguish itself more clearly from the surrounding culture from which it was alienated.

A recent autobiographical account by a young London Muslim (Husain, 2007) confirms this analysis. Born into a middle-class Muslim family, Husain is drawn gradually away from the gang culture of his East London school deeper and deeper into ever more radical Islamic groups. To quote:

> We thought we were making a new world. Our job was to mobilise the Muslim masses here. There was that feeling of being on the cusp of a new world order which would revive the glory days of Islam. For a 17-year-old who felt out of place in the UK, it was very attractive. Everywhere we went, we were the brothers to be respected. It was intoxicating.

As Sageman (2004, p. 155) observes:

> People may not be aware that they are being drawn into the clique. But once they become members, strong bonds of loyalty and emotional intimacy discourage their departure. This process is rarely a fully conscious one, as cliques do not start out as terrorist groups. They evolve in that direction as their mutual relationships deepen, in a spiral of greater loyalty, mutual devotion, self-sacrifice, and intimacy.

Ultimately, the group is willing to kill, but by then its world-view is so different from those of its surrounding culture that '. . . outsiders focus on the terrorists' willingness to kill, the insiders focus on their willingness to die'. There is no record of any hesitations immediately before the project among members of either 9/11 or 7/7 groups. The video records of the London bombers on their way to carry out their assaults show no hint of doubt. One was given a let-out when his bomb refused to detonate on the subway, but he boarded a bus instead in order to carry out his mission.

It would, however, be mistaken to conclude with Sageman that the actions of the 9/11 and the 7/7 groups are more attributable to their social bonds than to their BVNs (Sageman, 2004, p. 178) and we can disagree with his conclusion 'It may be more accurate to blame global Salafi terrorist activity on in-group love than out-group hate' (Sageman, 2004, p. 135). This conclusion represents a false dichotomy, one between group ties and religious beliefs. If we construe BVNs as *social* products, then they are an essential part of the social identity of the group and the movement of which it believes itself to be a part. Social bonds both strengthen, and are strengthened by, BVNs, and the more extreme these are, the more distinct and cohesive the group (Turner, 1982, 1985).

Thus the *need for affiliation* that the face-to-face group meets is not the only motivator. The group is also an ideal means for ensuring *conformity to the BVNs*. BVNs have two major functions for terrorist cells. First, they provide a world-view that explains and justifies their actions. And second, they arouse emotions, such as anger, which motivate them to action. All the evidence suggests that the members of both cells became more firmly fundamentalist in their beliefs before deciding to engage in terrorist actions.

For example, Mohammed Atta may have been radicalised to some extent at Cairo University, where the engineering faculty was a stronghold of the Muslim Brotherhood. His father had warned him against radicalism, so it was only when he arrived in Hamburg that he started taking religion very seriously, fasting, attending the radical al-Quds mosque daily, and praying (*Los Angeles Times*, 2002). By the time he wrote his instructions to his fellow hijackers, he was fluent in expressing the dualist Salafi variant of Islam promoted by Sayeed Qutb. That entire document is suffused with images of purification preparatory to the sacrifice of martyrdom and its subsequent rewards (Lincoln, 2002). The hijackers were urged to:

> shave excess hair from the body, and wear cologne . . . shower . . . Purify your soul from all unclean things . . . You should feel complete tranquillity, because the time between you and your marriage is very short. Afterwards begins the happy life, where God is satisfied with you, and eternal bliss, in the company of the prophets, the companions, the martyrs, and the good people who are all good company . . . Know that the gardens of Paradise are waiting for you in all their beauty, and the women of Paradise are waiting, calling out 'Come hither, friend of God'. They have dressed in their most beautiful clothing.
>
> Lincoln (2002)

Shahzad Tanweer, the London bomber, likewise became notably more religious in the last months of his brief life (Tumelty, 2005). He travelled to Pakistan in November 2004, in the company of Mohammed Sidique Khan. He went home to the rural village of his family's origin, with the purpose of learning the Qu'ran by heart at the mosque and the *madrassah*. His only visitor was Khan. On his return to Leeds in February 2005, he had grown a beard and prayed five times a day. He told his family how much he deplored British policy in Kashmir, Iraq, and Afghanistan, and how much he admired Osama bin Laden. Hasib Hussein, the third London bomber, became more devout after performing the *Hajj*, the pilgrimage to Mecca, and started wearing Islamic robes and growing a beard.

However, the most powerful evidence of the importance of religious belief as a motivator for the London bombings comes from the martyrdom videos of Mohammed Sidique Khan and Shahzad Tanweer. These are spoken in fluent English with a Yorkshire accent, and were released to Al Jazeera television station on 1 September 2005 and 6 July 2006, respectively. Khan's message insists: 'Our drive and motivation doesn't come from tangible commodities that this world has to offer. Our religion is Islam, obedience to the one true God and following the footsteps of the final prophet messenger'. Fundamentalist dualism is apparent in the distinction between 'this world', which is tangible, and 'our religion'. Khan also demonstrates the obsession with sacrifice and martyrdom, which is the ultimate expression of how little 'this world' matters to him: 'Our words are dead', he affirms, 'until we give them life with our blood'. The British bombers probably did not need to commit suicide to achieve their ends; they could have used detonators, as did the Madrid bombers of 2004. Martyrdom was as important to them as murder.

Khan then addresses the British people, holding them responsible for 'atrocities against my people all over the world', his Muslim brothers and sisters. He concludes ' We are at war and I am a soldier. Now you too will taste the reality of this situation'. Here again is the theological dualism of this tangible world and the world of the spirit, now expressed in us and them terms as the infidel army versus the army of Allah.

Tanweer's video echoes these themes. He accuses 'the non-Muslims in Britain' for having voted in a government that oppresses 'our mothers and children, brothers and sisters from the east to the west', and then brings in by way of iconic example 'the genocide of more than 150,000 innocent Muslims in Fallujah'. He too characterises the situation as one of war: 'And know that if you fail to comply with this [i.e. stopping support to America and Israel, and releasing Muslim prisoners], then know that this war will never stop and that we are willing to give our lives 100 times over for the cause of Islam'. In a chilling affirmation of the conflict of world-view inherent in fundamentalisms, Tanweer says: 'We love death the way you love life'.

We may conclude that both the need for affiliation and also the conformity to BVNs are each a necessary, but not a sufficient, condition for membership of a fundamentalist terrorist cell. The need for affiliation brings alienated young men together in the first place, and the increasingly extremist nature of their BVNs binds them cohesively in a common purpose.

### From 9/11 to 7/7: More local, but also more cosmic

There are, however, important differences between 9/11 and 7/7. It is clear that al-Qaida as an organisation was responsible for 9/11. Khalid Sheikh Mohammed, a member of the central staff of al-Qaida, was the operational director of 9/11 (Sageman, 2004). The group of friends, including Mohammed Atta, sought to go to Chechnya to fight in the jihad but were re-directed to America when the cell originally chosen for the 9/11 mission failed to gain entry. Thus they were selected for the task, although they had not necessarily been recruited into al-Qaida and formally selected as operatives. They were volunteers, like many would-be jihadis. Al-Qaida does not need to recruit; it has an abundance of volunteers. The al-Qaida network then ensured that the necessary finance was available. Ramzi bin al-Shibh, one of the group of friends who could not obtain a visa for America, was appointed to liaise between the operational leader, Atta, and the operational director, Khalid Sheikh Mohammed.

In summary, al-Qaida conceived, planned, and organised 9/11. It may have done so in an ad hoc and opportunistic manner, but this is typical of any networked organisation that needs to adapt rapidly. However, the same cannot be said with certainty of 7/7. In this case, two of the London bombers were later shown to have had connexions with five men convicted of an al-Qaida plot in 2007. Two organisations loosely connected to al-Qaida soon claimed responsibility for 7/7, but were known to have made false claims in the past. On 2 September 2005, Ayman al-Zawahiri appeared on the martyrdom video-tape of Mohammed Sidique Khan. He did not actually claim responsibility on behalf of al-Qaida, but implied it by saying that 7/7 was a response to Europe's rejection of the truce offered by Osama bin Laden in April 2004. Furthermore, the tape was edited; it did not show al-Zawahiri and Khan together at any point, but merely spliced in sequence. Of course, the ownership by al-Qaida of the martyrdom tape in the first place implies some degree of connexion, but what form this took is unclear. It is known that Khan visited Pakistan twice, in 2003 and 2004–5, and Shahzad Tanweer once. But there is no evidence of any meetings with al-Qaida operatives while they were there; we only know that they met each other.

The leader of the group of 7/7 may have had al-Qaida training and have received instructions to recruit a cell for a mission. However, the group appears to have been self-financed, and possibly even self-taught in technical matters. This degree of self-sufficiency implies strong leadership, and it seems likely that Mohammed Sidique Kahn, who was around ten years older than the others, played an instigatory role. Khan used local Muslim institutions, such as information centres, gyms, and adventure holidays to cement his relationship with the others, although there is no suggestion that these social and religious services were connected to terrorist activities. He also spent a lot of time in one-to-one discussions with Shahzad Tanweer. In March 2007, three men from Leeds were arrested on suspicion of providing support and funding for the bombings, but there is no indication at time of writing that they were links in the al-Qaida network.

The London bombings, then, probably represent a new development. They are likely to have been spontaneous actions by second-generation expatriate Muslims. However, as I argued in Chapter 1, this need not imply a diminution of al-Qaida's power. Rather, it suggests that the spread of jihadist fundamentalism has become so widespread among alienated expatriate youth that al-Qaida can claim at least indirect responsibility for almost any terrorist assault. Its media skills and previous operational successes have ensured that all such claims are given considerable credence. However, alienated local youth does not seem to have the same technical skills as hardened al-Qaida operatives; the attempts to bomb London on 21 July 2005 failed to cause casualties, and the only death in the 2007 car bombings was of one of the conspirators at Glasgow airport.

The existence and extent of a hard core of fundamentalist belief among British Muslims is revealed by an opinion poll conducted a year after the bombings (*The Times*, 2006). Respondents were a random sample of over 1000 adults from among the 1.6 million British Muslims. Some 13% believed that the bombers should be regarded as martyrs. However, 56% thought that the British government was not doing enough to combat extremism among Muslims; 65% thought Muslims needed to integrate more into mainstream British culture; and 79% said nothing would justify suicide bombings in Britain *against military targets* (let alone civilian ones). The picture that emerges is of a majority mainstream Muslim opinion hostile to jihadist ideology, but of a sizeable minority (perhaps approaching 200,000) who support it. Of course, there is a major gap between expressing an opinion and doing anything about it. But at the very least, the evidence suggests the existence of a potential pool of self-motivated and self-directed jihadis. Indeed, the British security services have recently stated that they are monitoring around 30 groups whom they consider to be dangerous.

These developments are all the more noteworthy given the history of Muslims in the UK (Kepel, 2006, pp. 185–198). Religious communities such as Muslims, Hindus, and Sikhs have traditionally been represented at local levels by their leaders. These secured for their people the services that they found most useful and appropriate, and provided a means of dialogue between people who wished to retain their ethnic and religious identity and British local and central government. Hence the loss of religious identity in a secular society had not been a big issue in Britain.

However, the declaration by the Ayatollah Khomeini of the *fatwa* against the British author Salman Rushdie for his book 'The Satanic Verses' sowed some ideological seeds. If the rule of Islamic law extended to countries that were hitherto considered not to be Islamic, then there certainly was a conflict between secular democracy and Islamic theocracy. In his martyrdom video, Mohammed Sidique Khan said 'Your democratically elected governments continually perpetuate atrocities'. The *fatwa* therefore prepared the ground for Osama bin Laden's exportation of jihad from its local origins to 'the far enemy' in America and Britain (Gerges, 2005).

The assault of 9/11 must therefore be seen as an initial marker of the instigation of global jihad. The London bombings are its logical extension. If the struggle is now between the *ummah* and the infidel, then it is an abstract and cosmic struggle. Both categories are abstract: the *ummah* is an imagined community and the infidel is an inclusive construct to include everyone else. Therefore the struggle is not locally rooted. It is the duty of the faithful to engage in jihad wherever they find themselves. The entire world, not just the Muslim world, is the arena for conflict.

## From nested to disconnected social identities

This development forces us to address the nature of the social identities of the jihadist groups. If we return to the concept of nested identities, then the early jihadis of the 1980s and 1990s were likely to have incorporated several levels of social identity into their selves. They were pious Muslims, for a start. They were jihadis, members of the vanguard of Islam and defenders of the *ummah*. They belonged to an organisation that was strongly associated with a particular locality (for example, al-Zawahiri brought a strong contingent of Egyptians from the Egyptian Islamic Jihad when he joined bin Laden's al-Qaida). Many had fought together as *mujahedeen* and retained an identity as comrades. And they had extensive clan and family identities, which served them well in their need for mutual trust. As far as the early jihadis were concerned, the enemy was primarily the secular government of whichever nation-state they lived in.

However, by 9/11 some of these nested identities had disappeared. These second-generation jihadis had not seen active war service. They were no longer tied to the country of their birth. They supported a movement, al-Qaida, but this was the one jihadi movement that had moved from a local to a global conception of its mission. And they had largely severed ties with their families. By 7/7, even more nested identities had been lost. There is no evidence that the London bombers believed themselves to be members of anything other than global Islam. They were rootless: they could conceive of themselves only as warriors in a cosmic war. The only local identity they had was a very local one indeed: their own little group.

This raises the question of how a single, all-embracing social identity, unsupported by any local nested identities, was sufficient to motivate the London bombers. One answer comes from social identity theory. Hogg (2003) argues that social identities do not have to be based upon categories of people who can be objectively identified. Rather, the category may be an abstract one, in this case, the *ummah*, or Islam. Further, the out-group can be similarly abstract: the infidel, or Satan. The more inclusive the out-group, then the more distinct from it the in-group has to become in order to sustain its differentiation from such a varied enemy. One way of maintaining this distinction is the persecution narrative of oppressor and victim, a narrative that became more convincing to many British Muslims after the invasions of Afghanistan and Iraq. The role of martyred defender of the *ummah* against the infidel oppressor is a cosmic identity to be rewarded by an entirely spiritual status. In the closed world of an intense group nourished on the internet by virtual religion, all ties to local reality, all local social identities, have been lost. Their roots are now in Paradise.

There is an interesting contrast here with the group known as the

Lackawanna Six (*Washington Post*, 2003; *New York Times*, 2003). These were Muslim Yemeni Americans, who had known each other from childhood. Attracted to jihadism by two charismatic al-Qaida recruiters, they became much more religious, refusing to watch television or go to the cinema, avoiding contact with women, and deploring the oppression of Muslims abroad. So far, so similar to the 9/11 and 7/7 groups. Soon they volunteered for training in Afghanistan. However, four of them left the course before the end, despite having the inspirational experience of meeting Osama bin Laden himself. They returned home and were less religious than they had been before they left. At their subsequent trial, they were not accused of any active plans to commit terrorist acts. One, al-Bakri, was described as an 'all-American kid' by an investigator. They had clearly retained a social identity as Americans, and when this came into conflict with that of jihadi, the incompatibility was sufficient to force them to abandon the latter. We may conclude that identities that are 'cross-hatched' in this way, rather than nested, may be difficult to hold simultaneously. The case demonstrates that being grounded in an intermediate-level identity, in this case that of American, may detract from the unique combined power of a small group and a cosmic identity. It is to the fundamental questions of self and identity that we turn in the next chapter.

# 6   A central identity

## Individuals and the social context: Personal and social identities

### The self and social identities

Many readers may find it strange that it is only at a point more than half way through this book that I am starting to write about *the individual*. After all, they may reason, all religion, including fundamentalist religion, is a matter of individual choice. We may choose whether or not to believe in God, and what to believe about Him (or Her). However, this perception that religion is a purely personal matter is likely to be culturally influenced. Most readers will be from late-modern Western cultures that increasingly emphasise individuality at the expense of collectivism. It is the individual's right to choose whatever best suits their needs, we believe.

Moreover, in several countries (e.g. America, France), there are legal requirements for the separation of church and state, and in others there is the tacit agreement that religion and politics do not mix, despite a residual connexion (e.g. the UK, the Netherlands). Christianity in the West has, in general, accommodated to the secular trend towards individualism. Indeed, it has started to embrace the secular idea of the individual as consumer who can be persuaded to choose from religious products aimed at segmented markets (Roof, 1999).

Students of the psychology of religion have taken the same approach. In general, they have tended to treat fundamentalism as being a particular individual orientation towards religion, a preference that appeals to some but not to others (Spilka et al., 2003). They have approached the topic from the classical psychological perspective of individual differences. Consequently, they have sought to relate measures of fundamentalist orientation to other individual differences such as attributional style (e.g. whether one tends to explain events in terms of personal action or situational constraints) or degree of authoritarianism.

Yet Muslims and Jews, particularly if they are from the Middle East, are likely to make very different assumptions. They will start with *the collective*. This may be evidenced on a grand inclusive scale (e.g. the *ummah*, referring to

Islam as a whole; or Israel, meaning God's chosen people, not the State of Israel). Or it will appear at a much more local level (e.g. the company of the faithful at their local mosque or synagogue). Either way, God and His people are the focus, not God and the individual believer. We may conclude that it is our own cultural background (if we are Western) that results in our possible surprise at the late arrival of the individual onto the pages of this book.

Of course, such expectations are matters of emphasis. It is clear that the constructs of '*the individual person*' and '*their social context*' are themselves culturally rooted ways of understanding the social world. It is also clear that, having distinguished person and context, we have to see them as being in a constant dialectical relationship with each other. At the end of each of the theoretical chapters so far, I have cautioned against the idea of social determinism. The social entities we have considered, from globalised culture, through national cultures and religious movements, to religious organisations and small groups, should not be construed as leaving the individual with no options. Conversely, the person cannot be perceived as an isolated individual, completely free to choose whatever identity they wish in the social market-place. Rather, *people both enact, and also are shaped by, their social environment*.

If the book had started with the individual level of analysis, it would probably have concentrated on the *psychological needs* that most people appear to share (once they have ensured their physical survival). For example, people need to have *a sense of self*, some notion of who they are as a person (Baumeister, 1999). Many seem also to prefer some degree of coherence and consistency within the self, such that they can recognise themselves as essentially the same person although they act differently in different social situations. To achieve a consistent sense of self, people impose some sort of meaning and structure onto their experience. Such meaning enables them to see themselves within a social, and perhaps also an historical, context. It also enables them to feel that they have some degree of prediction and control over how they act and what happens to them. They also feel the need to *affiliate* with other people, who provide them with elements for, and confirmation of, their selves. A sense of *self-esteem* may follow, and its achievement is a prime motivator of behaviour.

The issue of whether these psychological needs are prior to their social context is essentially a chicken-and-egg question. I have chosen to treat the social context first in this book for two reasons. First, I want to emphasise the social perspective in order to provide a counterbalance to the over-concentration upon individual differences by Western psychologists of religion. Second, I believe that fundamentalist believers are likely to have a greater preponderance of social elements of their selves in comparison with the uniquely personal element. In the West, this is certainly a counter-cultural direction to take.

To recapitulate: *the self* is a constantly changing mental construct that enables us to act and interact in our social environment. We adapt our idea of our selves as a result of reflecting on how we behave, and how others react to us and to what we say and do. The self is, in other words, a *reflexive construct*. The self has both personal and social elements (Hogg, 2003). The personal identity is how one perceives oneself as a unique individual. Social identities are several, and are one's beliefs about which social categories we belong to. The relative balance of personal and social elements within the self will vary across individuals, but in general we may expect to find a dominance of personal elements in individualistic cultures, where personal uniqueness and authenticity are highly valued.

It is one of the basic arguments of social identity theory that *the relation- ship between the social categories to which individuals perceive themselves to belong and other social categories is crucial.* This relationship profoundly affects the nature of the social identity that is internalised as part of the individual self. If the relationship is one of perceived threat, and therefore of hostility, then the in-group versus out-group dynamic will be established. The in-group will compare itself with the out-group, and seek to establish differ- ences between itself and the out-group. The more inclusive the out-group is perceived to be, the more different and extreme the in-group will tend to become. And, as has frequently been mentioned already, differences are easier to establish if the in-group perceives itself as homogeneous and separate from a stereotyped out-group. Individuals from both categories are depersonal- ised, and think of themselves and the others as examples of categories rather than as individuals. Social identity dominates personal identity.

Moreover, if one category membership is frequently used and very import- ant for an individual, then it is likely to be the salient social identity in many different social situations. As a major function of a social identity is to inter- pret social situations and direct and guide social behaviour, then the salience of one particular central social identity in an individual's mind will have a major effect upon their actions. If they have internalised the BVNs associated with the social identity in question, the effect will be to motivate, justify, and prescribe such actions.

In such a case, the social needs listed above are likely to be amply satisfied. If there is a single social identity that is central to the self, then possible conflict between different social identities is avoided. For example, 'member of a work organisation' and 'parent' are two social identities that often result in internal conflict. Likewise, if the BVNs of this central social identity have been internalised, and if they are coherent and structured, then the individual has a clear view of who they are, what they should believe, and how they should behave. If one perceives others in terms of prototypes and stereotypes, then one can happily predict how in-group comrades and out-group enemies are going to behave, and act so as to ensure that these predictions come true (Quinn, Macrae, & Bodenhausen, 2003). This certainly gives a feeling of predictability and control of one's social environment. And finally, if mem- bership of one category is so central an identity, then it would be strange if the individual does not maintain a close relationship with others who share it with them. This relationship is likely to meet needs both for affiliation and also for confirmation that one is right to hold the BVNs associated with this social identity. Self-esteem will be enhanced by being accepted, by realising how superior one is to the out-group, and by the content of the BVNs themselves (see below).

### Fundamentalist selves: Some hypotheses

The argument so far has emphasised that fundamentalist movements are likely to lead to strong and central social identities in the selves of their members. We can make some general statements about fundamentalist selves based on our analysis in the previous chapters of the different levels of social entity and the associated cultures to which they belong.

First, fundamentalists are more likely to have *a single dominant social identity*. All the levels of social analysis have pointed to the centrality to their selves of their social identity as believer. They may see themselves as involved in a cosmic global struggle, as representatives of a national or ethnic religious enclave, as loyal members of a movement or an organisation, as one of a group of pious friends or family, or as several of these congruent categories at the same time. But at whatever level of social analysis we seek to understand them, and whatever the mix of cultural and sub-cultural features they have internalised as BVNs, we may guess that their self-concept is likely to be dominated by their fundamentalist identity.

Moreover, we may also infer that *their social identity will completely over-shadow their personal identity*. We develop our personal identity by observing how we ourselves as individuals behave, and how others behave towards us. Fundamentalists will spend less time and effort on this sort of reflective activity, because they have developed somewhat depersonalised views of themselves. Their social identity tells them that they are primarily just like the other members of their category, and the opposite of the out-group, who are likewise similar to each other. Moreover, any feedback from others is likely to be taken as confirming the correctness of their social identity, particularly if it is hostile. Their practice of attributing the cause of events and outcomes to God or the Devil adds to their down-playing of their personal identity, as they have little to credit or debit themselves with. Hence there is little reason to reflect on one's self.

This being so, *there is unlikely to be much conflict or complexity within their selves*, as there are few other social or personal identities that matter much to them. On the contrary, they will have few doubts about who they really are.

Moreover, where the internalised BVNs of their movement are relatively uniform, as they normally are, we may expect *their views of their selves to follow a common pattern*. In other words, as the social category is homo-geneous, the self will also be similar to the selves of other category members.

The in-group versus out-group dynamic will not only provide them with a clear and simple identity, it will also give them *a strong sense of their place in history and their ultimate destiny* as victors through God's authority and control. Their needs for affiliation, certainty, and self-esteem will be more than adequately met, given these social and psychological conditions.

To what extent does the evidence support these generalisations? It is not difficult to exemplify individual fundamentalists' views of their selves from what they have said or written. It is harder to find controlled social scientific research studies. But, as I will try to demonstrate, what evidence we have confirms the hypotheses that:

- Fundamentalists' social identity as believer is the most central and dominant social identity that they possess.
- This social identity is very similar to that of other movement members.
- There are few occasions when they perceive any conflict or complexity within their selves.
- They have few existential doubts regarding who they are and what is their place in the social world, past, present, and future.
- They are confident that, in the long run, the Almighty is in control, despite currently feeling under threat.
- They seldom feel alone, but rather are valued highly by fellow believers.
- As a result of their social membership and the BVNs it brings with it, they have a high level of self-esteem.

The rest of this chapter looks at the fundamentalist self from these perspectives; subsequent chapters will examine their BVNs: the belief systems they espouse (Chapter 7), the values and attitudes they hold (Chapter 8), and the norms of behaviour to which they adhere (Chapter 9). Unfortunately, the present chapter uses evidence drawn almost entirely from Protestant fundamentalism. The reasons for this one-sided perspective are, first, that the psychological evidence derives almost exclusively from this population, and, second, non-Western fundamentalists are a lot less likely to write and talk about themselves. Hopefully the following case study of Sayeed Qutb redresses this imbalance a little.

## Stories about the self

### Evangelists' stories: Dramatic performances or accurate accounts?

There is, however, a methodological problem to be addressed. To what extent are we to believe what individual fundamentalists say about themselves as sound evidence of what they think about themselves? For example, it could be suggested that the sermons and books of fundamentalist preachers contain regularly recurring stories about their personal experiences, which they have to tell because it is expected of them. Their credentials as preachers depend upon them having such stories to tell. And their 'ministries' (or religious businesses) may benefit as a result.

One response to this justifiable caution is that, theoretically, re-occurrence of the same narrative is exactly what one would expect. If fundamentalist authors/preachers have internalised the social identity of the movement they represent, and, together with that identity, the uniform BVNs that it brings with it, then it is not surprising that they tell the same stories about themselves. They believe that there is a spiritual process, which all true believers have to undergo, and they are able to apply the story of that process as an honest account of their own experience.

Of course, we need to bear in mind, as Harding (2000) urges, that the main purpose of the autobiographies was not to provide their readers with an insight into their (the authors') selves. Their most likely aim was to witness to their readership, to tell the story of how God had worked in and through them despite their shortcomings, and to persuade the reader to join the author in telling the same story.

Randall Balmer (2000, pp. 3–4) tells a delightful tale of his first attempt as a little boy to witness to 'unbelievers' in an effort to win them for the Lord. His target was his friend and next-door neighbour, Stanley. 'Are you a Christian, Stanley?' he asked. 'Yes', was the monosyllabic reply, implying 'of course I am'. Yet the young Randall knew that this could not be true, since Stanley was a Roman Catholic. 'Are you sure?' he muttered weakly, before they resumed their baseball practice together.

Lienesch (1993) conducted an analysis of the autobiographies of several prominent American Protestant fundamentalists. They include Jerry Falwell, Jim Bakker, James Robison, Anita Bryant, Pat Boone, and Pat Robertson. The titles of these works are of interest: 'Strength for the Journey', 'Move that Mountain!', 'Thank God I'm Free', 'Mine Eyes Have Seen the Glory', 'A New Song', and 'Shout It from the Housetops'. Such titles point to the purpose of the writers of witnessing to the miraculous power of God in their lives.

Lienesch (1993) notes that *all these authors tell the same essential story*. It begins with 'the Holy Spirit moving within them', making them conscious of their sin and alienation. Next comes conversion itself, a process in which they are saved, or born again, by putting their faith in Christ and his sacrifice on the cross for their sins. Soon they become sanctified, made holy, as they take on a new way of living that involves obedience to, and trust in, Christ. In their case, this transformation was followed, often after a very brief interval, by a vocation to preach as well as to witness (the latter of these two tasks being the vocation of every believer). Sanctification and vocation are processes that are accompanied by revelations from God, often in the form of spoken instruction or dreams. In carrying out their vocation to preach, these famous fundamentalists defined their role in their society and their degree of engagement with it.

As Lienesch (1993, p. 50) puts it:

> For the authors of these autobiographies, conversion stands at the centre of their very selves, affording them autonomy and a sense of identity,

giving their lives meaning, offering them security and order in an otherwise insecure and disorderly world ... At the same time, conversion provides for them a conceptual core, a way of thinking that can be applied not only to oneself but also to society. Thus they are predisposed to think of themselves as saving society, and periodically they reach out to rescue society's soul.

What is most notable about these autobiographical accounts is the way in which the Biblical themes and stories, which are particularly favoured by fundamentalists, are so often used to 'pre-figure' or 'typify' the reported life events. Almost all of the authors report difficult relationships with wayward fathers, and imply that they too inherited some of their waywardness. Original sin clearly passes through the paternal line, however, as most of the mothers are saintly. But the authors' own sins turn out to be minor peccadilloes, which they seem to have to dredge up and magnify. Rather than having major misdemeanours to confess, they emphasise that, before their conversion, their lives were empty and that they felt insecure. Later, as they start their ministries, they liken their experience to the story of Christ being tempted by the Devil in the wilderness. Billy Graham is reported to have:

> walked alone through the mountain forest that night, struggling with his doubts and his feelings of inadequacy. As he sat on a rock with his Bible open, he finally decided to give up his questioning, admitting to God that he could not resolve all of his intellectual difficulties but surrendering, nonetheless, to the authority of the Bible, which he would simply accept by faith as God's Word.
>
> (Carpenter, 1997, p. 223)

In her interview with Melvin Campbell and her analysis of Jerry Falwell's autobiography and broadcasts, Harding (2000) detects a series of pre-figurings. Campbell tells her how he accidentally killed his son, but that God persuaded him to accept his death, just as Abraham was willing to sacrifice Isaac in the Biblical story. And so Campbell's story moves effortlessly on to the divine sacrifice at Calvary, and to the challenge to Harding to accept it, just as Campbell himself had accepted not only Christ's redemptive sacrifice but also the death of his own son.

Falwell's autobiography, likewise, tells stories of his life with pointers to Biblical characters and episodes. He got chosen as the preacher of the family, while his twin became the farmer, just like the story of Jacob and Esau. And, using the cunning of Jacob, he deceived his best friend and stole his girlfriend. He later identifies with Christ himself as he talks of the bitter cup he has to take, as Christ did in the Garden of Gethsemane. The bitterness refers to his various disappointments, failures, and scandals, and he begs his readers and listeners to share them with him.

### *God talk: Intimacy with the Almighty*

The same personal story of an intimate relationship with God is told by 'Lois', one of Tamney's (2002, pp. 98–9) interviewees. Lois says that she has been unhappy and depressed. She had sought to gain the respect of others by means of her material prosperity, but the pastor at 'Spirited Church' had persuaded her that she would find happiness by focusing on Jesus. Now that God is her focus, her life has changed in every way. Her only concern is to serve and obey God. And to help her discover how to do this, 'The Bible is the only truth you can find in this world'. She can feel the presence of the Holy Spirit at Sunday worship, and He can speak to her and give her guidance. 'We need to let God control our lives', she concludes, and this control is the source of her new-found happiness.

Thus an ordinary Protestant fundamentalist tells the same sort of story as the famous ones who have penned their autobiographies. It cannot be exaggerated how extraordinary to the modern mind these stories are. Indeed, psychiatrists have often considered experiences of God speaking as symptoms of mental illness. They are told in a unique form of discourse, which represents life experience as *a continuous dialogue between the individual and supernatural, spiritual beings*. These are usually God, either in His person as the Father, or as Christ, or as the Holy Spirit. Sometimes the conversation is with the Devil, or Satan.

These conversations are couched in biblical language, biblical both in style and content. They are surrounded by supernatural events: the Bible, for

Jerry Falwell                                          © Wally McNamee/Corbis

example, just happens to fall open at a page which contains God's message for the believer. While preachers may use examples from modern popular culture in their sermons (Watt, 2002; Tamney, 2002), they seem to conduct their 'private' conversations with God in biblical terms. And although fundamentalists often have carefully worked out and internally logical doctrinal positions, these conversations with God seem rather to follow highly figurative and allegorical turns.

Of course, we only know this because they have told us so. But it is worth noting that much of the ordinary conversation of believers in the church setting, or when they are witnessing to unbelievers, follows the same pattern. We may understand this in terms of *the salience of their social identity as born-again Christians*. In all situations where their born-again identity is salient, then the language of supernatural belief is spoken, since it is one of the BVNs attached to this identity. And since this identity is central to their selves, they will perceive many social situations in its terms. This explains why, on the London Underground recently, a businessman whom I had never met in my life before took out his Bible and started witnessing to me as I sat next to him trying to read my newspaper. So central was his born-again identity to his self that he perceived almost every social situation, including the normally anonymous Underground, as a witnessing opportunity.

Of course, this does not imply that fundamentalist believers 'put on a performance'. I am not arguing that they are engaging in some form of impression management (Goffman, 1959). The extreme sacrifices they make in following their strict and costly religion (Iannacone, 1994) argue against this interpretation. Rather, it is likely that they are acting in an entirely consistent way. They have adopted a supernatural belief system in which supernatural beings intervene in human affairs and converse with people. And they believe that the Bible is the only source of material with which to conduct these conversations (Hood et al., 2005).

It does not follow that they are being inconsistent if they do not use biblical language and concepts in every social situation. For, they believe, the Holy Spirit will guide them about what to say, and when and where to say it. In the terms of social identity theory, we might suggest that in some social situations, for example at their place of employment, other social identities are temporarily salient. But these are not necessarily incompatible with their born-again identity. Indeed, the work situation might easily be perceived to offer the opportunity for witness, if not in words then by actions.

Nor should we assume that all their stories are identical, although they do follow a common pattern. Needless to say there are variations due to individual and to sub-cultural differences. Pat Robertson only became aware gradually of his conversion, whilst the emotional Tammy Bakker raced to the front of the church even before the preacher could make his appeal (Lienesch, 1993). And the accounts of those from the charismatic Pentecostal tradition emphasise miraculous happenings much more than do those from Fundamentalists (Harding, 2000). (I use 'Fundamentalist' to refer to a specific sub-culture in American Protestantism, and 'fundamentalist' in the much broader social scientific sense defined in the Introduction.)

In sum, we should take fundamentalists' accounts of their experience and their selves at face value, unless we have strong grounds for not doing so. They see their selves primarily in terms of their relationship to a supernatural God. They are honestly expressing their supernatural world-view. This is probably different from that of most of my readers, but we should acknowledge that we are engaged in formulating a different construction of their reality. This does not invalidate their experience; it is, rather, a different account.

We are indebted to the naturalistic studies of scholars such as Harding and Watt, who actually placed themselves inside the supernatural conversations of fundamentalist believers. The ease with which Harding found herself explaining a near accident in supernatural terms (Harding 2000, p. 33) points to the essence of this difference. Harding had placed herself knowingly in the position of being witnessed to, fully aware that she was putting herself in the way of being converted. Yet she was already beginning to talk the talk in her mind, and could feel herself being drawn across 'the membrane between disbelief and belief'. Fundamentalists' accounts seek to draw others across that membrane, because their own perspective is God's revealed truth, and their purpose is evangelism. The purpose of this book, however, is to try to understand fundamentalists and fundamentalisms. And to further this purpose, we may conclude, in accordance with social identity theory, that the social identities of followers of born-again Protestant movements have a considerable similarity to each other and are central to their selves.

## Divine control

### Attributions of causality: God, the Devil, and oneself

The supernatural world-view of Protestant fundamentalism has God and the Devil intervening in the natural world, primarily but not entirely through people. We attribute the causes of events variously to ourselves, our efforts and abilities, to others, to the immediate situation, to global forces, to chance, to God or the Devil, or to any number of other potential determinants. When we do so, we are seeking to put a meaning onto our experience. We want to know why things happened. We may also be seeking a degree of control over outcomes which affect us, since if we know their causes we can perhaps predict and control them (Kelley, 1972). And we may, if we feel more in control, thereby add to our self-esteem (Steele, 1988) and reduce our anxiety.

What are fundamentalists doing when they make attributions to God or the Devil? The first and obvious conclusion is that they are *externalising psychological events that most other people would attribute to themselves.* 'I couldn't decide what to believe' we might say, or 'I was stupid and insensitive'. Or, alternatively, 'I really worked hard and I made it in the end', or 'I'm quite good with numbers, so I quickly spotted the mistake'. Fundamentalists, however, at least in their autobiographies, blame the Devil for temptations, or simply for putting obstacles in the way of God's purpose for them (Lienesch, 1993, p. 38).

So, for example, after his conversion Pat Robertson immediately doubts his new salvation, attributes this doubt to the Devil, and wrestles with him to the extent that 'By the end of the afternoon I had won, but I was physically and spiritually drained. It took days to completely recover'. Then the Devil makes his wife miscarry, so that he has to do household chores rather than become more zealously holy. The roof blows off Jim Bakker's studio in an attack by the Devil, who also tempts James Robison to lust after attractive women in his congregation.

Thus their Manichean world-view of a continuous cosmic struggle between God and Satan, good and evil, enables fundamentalists to externalise their own struggles. It is not they who feel like acting badly, and sometimes do. It is rather Satan, who enters into their souls and overcomes them with his crafty persuasion. Thus they both externalise the blame onto another 'person', and then internalise that other into themselves so that he can be held responsible for their innermost doubts and desires. Again, it must be emphasised that here fundamentalists are being entirely consistent with their supernatural and biblical world-view. In the biblical narrative, Christ Himself was tempted by the Devil, and cast out devils from other people.

Research on 'random' samples (usually of students!) shows that people are subject to the attributional bias of crediting themselves with favourable actions or outcomes, and blaming others, or external situations, for unfavourable ones. Clearly, our self-esteem benefits from this bias. Fundamentalists certainly tend to blame the Devil, although they do admit to being taken in by his wiles. Are they subject to the same self-serving bias on the credit side of the moral equation, or does their world-view lead them to credit God, not themselves, with the good things? The autobiographies generally suggest the latter, but the attribution is often a complex one, implying a combined responsibility. The individual had to trust God, Who then inspired them to set their sights higher, as they strove to achieve these ambitions. As Anita Bryant puts it (Lienesch, 1993, p. 41):

> I'm convinced that when you turn your business (sic) over to God entirely, He will not only send you the type of work that's best for your talents and your nature, but He'll help you begin to aim higher, so your ambitions will help you become more worthy of Him.

Lienesch notes that the autobiographies are shot through with this theme of effort and striving, of vaulting ambition to reach God's high targets for you (which usually seem to involve building up one's ministry/business). Thus the credit for success is *shared* with the Almighty rather than attributed entirely to Him.

Indeed, God is sometimes credited with the 'bad' things too. He permits Satan to tempt the preacher in order to test him out and refine him in the fire, or He allows him to fail in a part of his ministry in order to increase his faith. Trust in God, together with the belief that ' all things work together for good to them that love God' (Romans 8.36) results in the refusal to acknowledge that there might be a problem in the idea of a loving and omnipotent God permitting suffering.

As Hunsberger, Pratt, and Pancer's (1994) respondent puts it when presented with a scenario in which a believer's daughter dies in a car crash: 'This is entirely a question of faith. There is nothing else to find out about the situation. It just comes with your faith . . . It says in the Bible that God will not let anything happen to you that you can't handle. So there has to be a reason for it'.

The respondent's point is that this 'reason' is a spiritual one rather than a natural one. By definition, any event, however sad, has to be in God's plans for the believer.

In Hunsberger and colleagues' research, people differing on a scale measuring fundamentalist orientation were presented with various religious, ethical, and environmental issues to address. On only two of these issues did the more fundamentalist believers respond in a more simple, less complex, way than less fundamentalist ones. These were issues relating to God's overall control and to the legalisation of abortion. These are both essential elements of fundamentalist belief, to which there was a black and white answer. Thus the lack of complexity is likely to be located in the belief system rather than to be a general feature of fundamentalists' mental processes.

### More complex attributions

This belief that God is in control of the believer's experience is echoed by Tamney's (2002, pp. 134–135) respondents 'Ruth' and 'Edy'. Ruth says:

> I think that one of the very, very precious truths that He has impacted my life with, has been that your life – life is not fair, and it's not always going to be dependent, your happiness is not going to be dependent on all the good things that are happening to you, but that when you really walk close to the Lord and you study His Word, and you talk to Him in prayer, et cetera, that you can feel that inner peace and confidence in knowing that this is part of His plan for your life.

Edy has:

> . . . become more open to giving Him control . . . I think that He gives us free choice, yet He is sovereign and will work in the hearts that He chooses, and so He began to work in my heart, and I was receptive, . . . and I believe He is real in my life today and in His desire to work in and

through my life ... He wants to have control of my life instead of me wanting to control it ... I share my thoughts about what God is doing or what I am asking.

Edy goes to church, comments Tamney, in order to get together with God.

Ruth and Edy provide a *nuanced attributional account*. God has a plan for their lives, but they have to keep in constant personal touch with Him in order to fulfil it. The social identity of 'born-again believer' takes a very personal form for them: their selves seem to be constructed out of their relationship with God. But theirs is still a social rather than a personal identity. They are not referring to their authenticity and uniqueness as individuals, but to their relationship to God, which, they believe, they share with all true believers.

There is another benefit attached to attributions to God. If we believe that He is sovereign and in control, and if we believe that we are not only on His side but in an intimate personal relationship with Him, then *we ourselves gain vicarious control through Him*. Indeed, Protestant eschatological beliefs about the last days suggest that when Christ comes back to rule for a thousand years (the Millennium), born-again believers will act as His regents on earth (Boyer, 1992). This combination of beliefs: that God is in control, in our lives and in the world, and that the Bible tells us how He will exercise that rule in the future, is very powerful. It boosts self-esteem, and it tells us who we are, what our (favoured) place is in the world, and how to interpret the present as pointing to the future: God's future.

### *Attributions: Experimental evidence*

Experimental investigations provide confirmation that attributions to God and to the Devil are more frequent in more fundamentalist respondents (Lupfer, Brock, & DePaola, 1992). Fundamentalism was measured by a questionnaire assessing belief in the supreme authority of the Bible, the experience of born-again conversion, the duty to evangelise, and conservative social attitudes. The more fundamentalist the respondents, the more likely they were to hold God responsible for positive outcomes, and the Devil for negative ones. However, 90% of respondents' attributions were to secular rather than religious causes. Lupfer and colleagues speculate that this may be due to respondents giving naturalistic, secular explanations for more immediate and specific events, many of which may not appear to be in need of explanation at all. God is more likely to be invoked as being generally in charge.

This hypothesis is supported by research by Spilka and Schmidt (1983), who provided respondents with a much wider range of explanations. These scholars found that fundamentalist believers most frequently invoked the explanation that God *allowed* events to happen. Overall, we may conclude with Pargament, Kennell, Hathaway, Grevengoed, Newman, and Jones (1988) that Protestant fundamentalists generally attribute outcomes and the solution of problems to an active and interventionist God rather than to relatively passive believers. However, we should note that such Protestant fundamentalists as the reconstructionists (see Chapter 7) believe that God's rule requires His followers to work towards a theocracy now, rather than wait for His cosmic plan to unfold.

Given the centrality and the psychological benefits of the born-again social identity, we would expect fundamentalists to be very unwilling to let go of the BVNs attached to it. This is borne out by the evidence. In a classic research project, Festinger, Riecken, and Schachter (1956) examined what happened '*when prophecy fails*', specifically, when the end of the world failed to materialise on the appointed day. They predicted that, subject to certain conditions, the religious group concerned would re-affirm its beliefs and seek to make converts even more ardently than before. And so it turned out. Moreover, repeated failures of prophecies of the second coming of Christ on specific dates by Protestant fundamentalists in America do not seem to have permanently damaged the credibility or popularity of fundamentalist millennialism.

One explanation of these findings would attribute the believers' response to a specific psychological process. Festinger and colleagues, for example, suggested that belief and experience were so contradictory that cognitive dissonance was created. Believers felt the need to reduce this dissonance by ignoring or de-emphasising the experience. Others have simply supposed that it is a personal characteristic of fundamentalists that their belief systems are rigid and impervious to disconfirming evidence.

However, there are alternative explanations of a more social nature. Fundamentalist BVNs constitute, as we have seen, a totally different world-view. Explanations are supernatural, and fellow members may well come up with explanations that place the prophetic 'failure' within the context of God's plan for His people. This social construction of reality is perfectly acceptable to people who may have found the situation ambiguous and troubling (Dein, 2001) but whose trust in a supernatural God is unshakeable. They may, for example, claim that the prophecy has in fact been fulfilled, but in a spiritual rather than a physical sense; or that the failure was indeed a failure, but was simply God's way of testing their faith. A supernatural world-view in which the interventions of the Almighty reflect His holy ways rather than our sinful ones can easily explain the 'failed prophecy' findings.

### The world, the flesh, and the Devil

The main reason why the supernatural world-view is so powerful a part of the fundamentalist social identity is that it is sanctioned by the Bible. The authority of the Bible and personal trust in an omnipotent God are bed-rock beliefs, which cannot conceivably be threatened by an event that is merely a little hard to understand. Indeed, it may be argued, these difficulties are often raised by outsiders, whom the Devil is using to sow the seeds of doubt. Such assaults simply confirm the correctness of our faith: it must be true if the Devil is seeking to undermine it.

The dualist distinction between the supernatural world of the spirit and the sinful world of the flesh shapes the social identity of Protestant fundamentalists. They are to be found in the spiritual world, and their self is defined in terms of their relationship with God. The sinful world provides the 'other', the opposite with which the spiritual world can be compared and contrasted. The response to be predicted from social identity theory is one of hostility towards the out-group. The campaigns of the Moral Majority in the 1980s and the Christian Right in the last 15 years against various representative groups from the sinful world have seen this aggressive approach in action. Such campaigns serve to re-affirm the distinctiveness and cohesion of the in-group.

However, as Lienesch (1993, pp. 45ff) notes, there is often a dangerous ambiguity in attitudes towards the sinful world of the flesh. Preachers' autobiographies reveal that they are selective about which aspects of the sinful world they contest and which they engage with and participate in. In particular, they are often partial to political influence, financial rewards, and status gained by their own celebrity and their reflected glory from that of others. They sometimes chide themselves for the sin of pride, but in other passages treat their increasing wealth and prestige as indications of God's blessing. The recent growth of so-called 'prosperity theology', which invites believers to claim God's material blessings for themselves, shows that fundamentalists realise the need to rationalise their 'this-worldly' behaviour.

## Affiliation and self-esteem

### *Self-esteem and world-view*

Any social identity consisting of an in-group that is hostile to an out-group will enhance the self-esteem of its members (Tajfel, 1981). Mere membership of fundamentalisms, therefore, because they are built upon such opposition, will itself boost self-esteem. However, there are two other reasons why we might expect such an outcome. The first is *the totally different world-view that fundamentalists hold*; and the second is *the specific nature of the BVNs* that are part of their social identity.

The fundamentalist world-view supposes that God is constantly at work in the world, and that He has an intimate relationship with each and every believer. Believers, therefore, perceive themselves to be privy to God's will, which has been revealed to them in the holy book. As His redeemed disciples they do His will, which will ultimately prevail. Non-believers, however (i.e. non-fundamentalists), have an entirely different, worldly, perspective. Hence non-believers' criticisms of fundamentalist beliefs or actions indicate to the believers that they must be doing God's will. Such criticisms simply confirm fundamentalists in their belief that they are right, since if the Devil assaults us, we must be doing God's will. Conversely, if they start to be accepted or valued by 'the world', then they must be going against the will of God. Their self-esteem is therefore enhanced, both by the approval of like-minded believers *and* by the disapproval of 'the world'. Such self-esteem is bought at a psychological cost, however, for they thereby lose the main source of information upon which realistic views of the self and levels of self-esteem should be based: the reactions to them of a wide variety of others.

The ultimate outcome of contradictory world-views is that every triumph that is praised by 'the world' is in fact a failure; and, conversely, every apparent failure by fundamentalists is in fact a triumph. This is because spiritual and worldly values are directly opposed. Hence fundamentalists are guaranteed a high level of self-esteem. Their self-esteem is enhanced not only when they fail in terms of worldly criteria; this means they are fulfilling God's criteria. It is also increased when they succeed in worldly terms (e.g. when they help to elect President George W. Bush). This latter outcome can obviously be interpreted as the will of God, and hence as a source of holy pride.

### Self-esteem through social comparison

Self-esteem may also be enhanced by *the comparison of the self with the outgroup*, the world. Nowhere is this clearer than in the writings of Sayeed Qutb, the ideological inspiration of the jihadis:

> This message [from the Qu'ran] relieves him [the believer] of both [dejection and grief], not merely through patience and steadfastness, but also through a sense of superiority from whose heights the power of oppression, the dominant values, the current concepts, the standards, the rules, the customs and habits, and the people steeped in error, all seem low. . . .
>
> . . . The society may be drowned in lusts, steeped in low passions, rolling in filth and dirt, thinking that it has enjoyment and freedom from chains and restrictions. Such a society may become devoid of any clean enjoyment and even of lawful food, and nothing may remain except a rubbish heap, or dirt and mud. The believer from his height looks at the people drowning in dirt and mud. He may be the only one; yet he is not dejected nor grieved, nor does his heart desire that he take off his neat and immaculate garments and join the crowd. He remains the uppermost with the enjoyment of faith and the taste of belief.

(Qutb, 1981)

The superiority of the Muslim believer over the American male was brought home to Qutb when he visited the USA:

> This primitiveness can be seen in the spectacle of the fans as they follow a game of football, or watch boxing matches or bloody, monstrous wrestling matches . . . This spectacle leaves no room for doubt as to the

primitiveness of the feelings of those who are enamoured with muscular strength and desire it.

(Qutb, 1948)

Other comparisons are equally likely to boost self-esteem. For example, the fundamentalist Anglican vicar, Reverend David Banting, proclaims:

> We are in need of a second Reformation, but it will only happen by a fresh understanding of God's Word. The Scripture is essentially clear. Even a ploughboy can understand it. If the liberals are starting from their own experience, they are making God in their own image. The danger for the Christian church always comes from within, whether by persecution or apathy. It's false teaching which leads inevitably to false behaviour. You need sound doctrine and teaching to suit the congregation's itching ears.

(Bates, 2004, p. 23)

Deconstructing this paragraph, we may conclude that Banting believes that, in contrast to the liberals, he has the correct understanding of God's Word, whereas they are more stupid than a ploughboy (thereby succeeding in insulting both liberals and ploughboys, if any such still exist). He does not fall into the trap of creating God in his own image, whereas they do. He teaches the truth and acts it out, they behave and teach falsely. He meets his congregation's spiritual needs, they mislead theirs. All in all, he is right and they are wrong. Doubtless, the Reverend Banting does not suffer from a lack of self-esteem.

### *Self-esteem from BVNs*

The self-affirming effects of the supernatural world-view are reinforced by the more specific details of some of the fundamentalist BVNs. These will be described in subsequent chapters. Suffice it to note here the likely self-enhancing effects of such beliefs as:

- God is sovereign and rules over all
- God has chosen me, personally
- We are God's chosen people
- I am a soldier in God's army
- God will be victorious, and I will share in His victory
- God speaks to me personally, and I speak to Him
- He has revealed the truths of His Word to me
- His laws are plainly stated in His Word
- I know that what I am doing is God's will
- God has revealed to me what will happen to this world
- When He returns to rule, I will rule with Him

- I keep His laws, and He blesses me
- I am separate from others, holy and sanctified
- It is my duty to witness to them, so that they recognise their sin
- I live in accordance with God's spiritual values, not man's worldly ones

Experimental evidence supports the conclusion that fundamentalists are likely to have high self-esteem. Rowatt et al. (2002) compared students who scored in the top third of their sample on questionnaires testing general religiosity and religious fundamentalism with those who scored in the bottom third. The top third rated themselves more positively and less negatively than the bottom third.

The dynamic relationship of individual fundamentalists and their social context is clearly evident in their beliefs and feelings about themselves, their beliefs about God and the world, their values and attitudes, and their norms of behaviour. If the social context is construed as threatening and evil by the social category of believers, then this will be reflected in views of self and BVNs. This chapter has sought to demonstrate that fundamentalists see themselves operating in a cosmic war, in which they are God's soldiers and servants. As He is sovereign, and will ultimately be victorious, they suffer no lack of self-esteem. They use a different language and have a different world-view from those who reject God (that is, the more or less inclusive out-group against whom they fight). Their selves are impervious to the social feedback they receive from anyone other than believers, which, if it is critical, they treat as confirming their self-estimate. And as most of the feedback they do receive will be from fellow believers, and related to their own social identity as believers, they are likely to have selves dominated by that social identity.

## Summary

- The self is a reflexive construct: we base our view of ourselves on what we see ourselves doing and on how others react to us.
- It contains social and personal elements.
- If we believe that the social category to which we belong is threatened, then we will construe the situation as one of hostility between our in-group and an out-group.
- In order to strengthen the in-group social identity and differentiate it from the out-group, we perceive the members of both in-group and out-group as similar to other members, but different from the other group.
- Members of both groups are depersonalised; their personal selves are submerged in their group self.
- Fundamentalists appear to follow this pattern. Their social identity will be central to their selves, at the cost of their personal identity as unique individuals.
- However, there are psychological benefits in having a fundamentalist social identity.

- There is little internal conflict, and what there is can be externalised as the work of the Devil.
- The view of the self is clear and simple, allowing believers to know who they are, what they should believe, how they should act, and what their place is in God's plan for the world.
- They have a strong sense of control over what happens to them, because they believe that they can predict it.
- Evidence for these hypotheses can be found in the autobiographical accounts of famous Protestant fundamentalist preachers, interviews conducted with ordinary believers by ethnographic investigators, and experimental studies using questionnaires.
- The evidence suggests that:

  - Fundamentalist Protestants tell essentially the same story about their experience.
  - These stories should be taken at face value as accounts of what they believe; they are the BVNs of their born-again social identity.
  - They evidence a supernatural world-view based upon Biblical language, involving repeated dialogue with supernatural beings.
  - Central to their view of their selves is the relationship they believe they have with God.
  - This permits them to perceive God as in control of their lives and of history, a perception that allows apparently contradictory evidence to be ignored.
  - Their self-esteem remains at a high level relative to that of others, since they use spiritual rather than worldly criteria by which to evaluate themselves.
  - Moreover, they habitually compare themselves favourably with members of their out-group.

## Further reading

Baumeister, R.F. (1999) (ed.) *The Self in Social Psychology*. Philadelphia: Psychology Press.

Gerges, F.A. (2005) *The Far Enemy: Why Jihad Went Global*. New York: Cambridge University Press.

Harding, S.F. (2000) *The Book of Jerry Falwell: Fundamentalist Language and Politics*. Princeton, NJ: Princeton University Press.

Herriot, P. (2007) *Religious Fundamentalism and Social Identity*. London: Routledge.

Hogg, M.A. (2003) Social identity. In M.R. Leary & J.P. Tangney (eds.) *Handbook of Self and Identity*. New York: Guilford.

Hogg, M.A. & Abrams, D. (2001) Inter-group relations: An overview. In M.A. Hogg & D. Abrams (eds.) *Inter-group Relations: Essential Readings*. Philadelphia: Psychology Press.

Hood, R.W., Hill, P.C., & Williamson, W.P. (2005) *The Psychology of Religious Fundamentalism*. New York: Guilford.

Kepel, G. (2006) *Jihad: The Trail of Political Islam*. (4th edn.) London: IBTauris.
Lienesch, M. (1993) *Redeeming America: Piety and Politics in the New Christian Right*. Chapel Hill, NC: University of North Carolina Press.
Spilka, B., Hood, R.W., Hunsberger, B., & Gorsuch, R. (2003) *The Psychology of Religious Fundamentalism: An Empirical Approach*. New York: Guilford.
Turner, J.C. (1985) Social categorisation and the self-concept: A social-cognitive theory of group behaviour. In E.J. Lawler (ed.) *Advances in Group Processes: Theory and Research*. Vol. 2. Greenwich, CT: JAI Press.

## CASE STUDY: SAYEED QUTB: IDEOLOGUE AND MARTYR

*Social identities change over a life-time as people categorise themselves in new ways. The Islamist ideologue, Sayeed Qutb, illustrates well how mainstream believers can become revolutionary fundamentalists. Qutb's life story shows how fear for the future of his culture and religion, and anger at the failure of other Muslims to support them, resulted in a change of social identity. His actions, and more especially his writings, demonstrate that his later identity as revolutionary Islamist emphasised his in-group membership of true believers, and his radical and inclusive categorisation of other Muslims as well as infidels as the out-group. Abstract classes of person replace individuals in his perceptions of others, and he maintains his self-esteem by stressing his superiority in the eyes of Allah.*

### An unlikely hero

The iconic image of Sayeed Qutb shows a hunched, buttoned-up little man peering with an ambivalent expression through his prison bars. Yet this insignificant captive was to become 'the greatest ideological influence on the contemporary Islamist movement' (Kepel, 2006, p. 27). Ayman al-Zawahiri, al-Qaida's main ideologist and second in command to bin Laden, credits him with 'giving rise to the contemporary jihadist movement and dramatically and strategically changing its direction and focus' (Gerges, 2005, p. 5). He also describes him as Islam's most influential contemporary martyr (al-Zawahiri, 2001). Other Islamic biographers have praised him not so much for his revolutionary ideas as for his truly Muslim virtues: simplicity, stringency, and courage (Almond et al., 2003, p. 76).

How can we possibly infer the nature of this man's self? He is of another era and another culture, and left nothing in writing about himself other than a couple of family memoirs. He certainly did not tell a story that placed his life's work within a well-trodden literary and spiritual genre, as did the American evangelists reviewed by Lienesch (1993). Yet we can dimly discern how the huge social and political changes in the Middle East in the early and middle parts of the twentieth century impacted upon the life of this highly intellectual product of rural Egypt. And we can seek to infer from his actions and his writings how, in response to these changes, he continuously adapted his views of the world and of his own position within it.

The outlines of Qutb's life are clear (Kepel, 2005). Born in 1906, he grew up during the colonial era. The Muslim world was subject and oppressed. Its elites were used by the imperial European powers to help them govern, and acquired the technology and culture of modern Western societies. The vast rural masses, however, were mostly educated, if at all, according to time-honoured traditional Islamic practice in a *madrassah*. Qutb, born into a downwardly mobile pious village family in Middle Egypt, was educated in a secular primary school, but had learned the Qu'ran by heart by the age of 10. When he was 14, he moved to Cairo for secondary education, where he lived with his uncle. Next he enrolled in a teachers' college in 1929, and a full 10 years later in 1939, at the age of 33, qualified as a teacher with a BA degree. Qutb had thus made the transition from rural to urban life, and got himself onto the lower rungs of the bureaucratic ladder. Colonialism had not treated him too badly thus far.

Indeed, the not excessively stringent demands of his job allowed him to achieve in a second arena. He engaged in literary pursuits, writing some literary criticism, poetry, short stories, autobiographical accounts of his village childhood, a romantic novel, and literary commentary on the Qu'ran. Although his writing was rooted in his culture, he was familiar with European literature. However, what he was by now writing was sufficiently hostile to the colonialist government of King Farouk to persuade some influential friends, fearful for his safety, to arrange for him to be sent on a secondment to study educational theory and practice in America, which, after all, was not a colonial power, but rather had successfully freed itself from European rule.

Thus far we have no indication that Qutb was anything other than a normally pious Muslim, although he did address his co-religionists on the liner crossing the Atlantic. Moreover, his increasing interest in politico-religious issues is indicated by the publication of his first such book, 'Social Justice in Islam', in 1949, while he was in America (but probably written before he went). After a short spell in a college on the East Coast, he undertook Masters Degree studies at the University of North Carolina, living in the small town of Greeley. America, even as represented by this rural backwater where alcohol was still banned, was a huge culture shock for Qutb. Visiting a church social, he was astonished to note that:

> Every young man took the hand of a young woman. And these were the young men and women who had just been singing their hymns! Red and blue lights, with only a few white lamps, illuminated the dance floor. The room became a confusion of feet and legs: arms twisted around hips; lips met lips; chests pressed together.
>
> Qutb (1948)

In Qutb's book, 'The America I Have Seen', there is much, much more in this vein. For example:

> The American girl is well acquainted with her body's seductive capacity. She knows it lies in the face, and in expressive eyes, and thirsty lips. She knows seductiveness lies in the round breasts, the full buttocks, and in the shapely thighs, sleek legs – and she knows all this and does not hide it.
>
> Qutb (1948)

He concluded that Americans were: 'a reckless, deluded herd that only knows lust and money'.

It would be easy to engage in psychological speculation regarding Qutb's sexual health. However, it would be mistaken to do so. Every pious Muslim would have been profoundly shocked by Western cultural mores, even those such as Qutb who were familiar with Western literature. Some 40 years later, Mohammed Atta, leader of the 9/11 hijackers, asked for a Degas nude to be taken off the wall of his lodgings in Hamburg; withdrew from one-to-one help with his Master's thesis because the helper was female; and refused to shake hands with the female examiner of his thesis (*The Observer*, 2001). Cultural differences in the role of women and relations between the sexes, rather than individual dysfunction, are the explanation for Qutb's appalled response to his American cultural experience. He must have been deeply disappointed that this beacon of freedom from colonial mastery had turned out to be a den of vice.

Meanwhile, events were moving apace back in Egypt. The long colonial era was coming to an end. The nationalist revolution, spearheaded by the Free Officers, burst upon the scene in 1952, and good Muslims hoped that at last the nation would be governed according to Islamic principles (Kepel, 2005). Immediately upon his return to Egypt in 1951, Qutb had joined the Muslim Brotherhood. Founded in 1928 by the charismatic Hasan al-Banna, the Brotherhood was a reaction against colonialism (Lia, 1998). The movement sought to re-establish the political dimension of Islam, believing that colonial rule should be replaced by theocracies operating according to the *sharia*, the rules laid down in the Qu'ran. 'The Qu'ran is our constitution', they proclaimed, in opposition to the secular nationalists who wanted a democratic constitution. They appealed to the newly literate urban middle class as much as to the rural pious. Qutb joined up eagerly in 1951, losing his post in the government Education Department in the process.

Qutb soon rose in the ranks of the Brotherhood to become the head of its propaganda department (Choueiri, 1997). When the Revolutionary Council was established, the Brotherhood was exempt from the ban on political parties in the new one-party state (so much for democracy), being categorised instead as a social/cultural organisation. Indeed, Qutb was appointed Cultural Adviser to the Council. However, relations between the Brotherhood and the Council soon soured when it became evident that the Council was not going to establish an Islamic state. Deeply disappointed again, Qutb resigned that same year, and in 1954 the Brotherhood was banned. Soon a member of the Brotherhood tried to assassinate President Nasser, and Brothers were executed, imprisoned, or exiled. Nationalism had proved just as authoritarian as colonialism, and the government believed it had destroyed the Brotherhood for good. Anyway, they thought, the Brothers' *raison d'être*, the conquest of colonialism, had been achieved, and their message was irrelevant in the brand new nationalist and socialist era.

Little did they realise that Qutb, one of the now imprisoned Brethren, would develop, over the next 12 years until his execution in 1966, an Islamic critique of nationalism that would inspire the subsequent development of radical Islam. This inspiration resonated locally in the Middle East after the Egyptian defeat at the hand of Israel in 1967. It thundered globally when the 'far enemy', the Great Satan with whom Qutb became so disenchanted after his visit, was assaulted in 2001. How did the writings of this amateur literary dilettante come to exercise so powerful a hold on the imaginations of two generations of young men? How did his ideas succeed in spanning three great political and cultural movements of the twentieth century: colonialism, nationalism, and globalisation? And finally (and the real theme of this case study), how did he develop his idea of who he was in the light of his tumultuous and ultimately fatal experience?

## Jahilyaah: Muslims are not true Muslims

Qutb wrote a number of books in prison. The longest was a series of commentaries on the Qu'ran, 'Under the Aegis of the Qu'ran', which is the most popular commentary on the Prophet's magnum opus. Other books included 'This Religion', 'The Future of This Religion', 'The Characteristics and Values of Islamic Conduct', and 'Islam and the Problems of Civilisation'. However, easily his most influential work was 'Milestones along the Way' (Qutb, 1981). This included extracts from his commentaries on the Qu'ran, together with the contents of letters he wrote from prison. It is clear that President Nasser had not appreciated that the pen is mightier than the sword; otherwise he would hardly have permitted Qutb's constant ideological labour to see the light of day.

'Milestones', according to commentators on Qutb's writings, was written in a far more accessible way than the scholastic books of the *ulema*, the established clerical scholars. Young people with a traditional education could understand it, for it used the language and religious concepts of their culture. The quotations from 'Milestones' that follow suggest that the scholars' writings must indeed have been turgid. Like all fundamentalists, Qutb used the holy book selectively, introducing new meanings for old concepts, and some completely new concepts. And, like all fundamentalists, he became increasingly dualist in his thinking, with the cosmic struggle between us and them, the oppressed and the oppressors, coming to dominate his every sentence. It is no accident that, at his trial, much of the charge sheet was taken up by quotations from 'Milestones', for this long-winded theological exposition was political dynamite. It contained a series of unmistakeable challenges to those in power.

The first challenge was to the *ulema*, the guardians of traditional Islamic doctrine. Mainstream Islam is based on four sources of authority [as is the Anglican Communion, also under fundamentalist attack (Herriot, 2007, Chapter 5)]. These are: first, the Qu'ran; second, the *hadith* (stories about the Prophet's life recorded by those who knew him); third, analogous inferences from these two sources about how to address issues that are not dealt with in them; and, finally, the consensus of Islamic scholars. These latter two authorities are rejected by Qutb, who argued that the Prophet Mohammed was the last messenger from God. Any subsequent interpretation is usurping the authority of Allah, since the holy books provide all that man needs to know about the social order He desires:

> He who has created the universe and man, and who made man subservient to the laws that also govern the universe, has also prescribed the Shari'ah for his voluntary actions. If man follows Shari'ah, it results in a harmony between his life and his nature . . . Each word of Allah is part of the universal law, and is as accurate and true as any of the laws known as 'the laws of nature' . . . Thus the Shari'ah, given to man to organise his life, is also a universal law, because it is related to the general law of the universe and is harmonious with it.
>
> (Qutb, 1981, Chapter 5)

Here we can recognise the classic fundamentalist return to the holy book as the ultimate authority, and a challenge to all clerics who seek to spiritualise what it plainly says:

> These religious scholars, with their defeated mentality, have adopted the Western concept of 'religion', which is merely a name for 'belief' in the heart, having no relation to the practical affairs of life, and therefore they conceive of eligious war as a war to impose belief on peoples' hearts.
>
> (Qutb, 1981 Chapter 4)

The second challenge thrown down in 'Milestones' was far more dangerous. It was to *the nationalist rulers* of the Middle East. It was encapsulated in Qutb's use of the familiar term '*jahili*'. *Jahili* was originally used in the Qu'ran to describe the state of the world before the Prophet. 'Heathen', or 'unenlightened', might be an approximate translation. The term had then been used in the fourteenth century by ibn Taymiyya, a jurist who had declared in a *fatwa* that the faithful could indeed wage jihad against the conquering Mongols, even though these had converted to Islam. Jihad was justified because the Mongols had not followed the *sharia*, but rather the legal code established by Ghengis Khan. The precedent had thus been set long ago for permitting jihad against Muslims, and calling them *jahili*, heathen, in the process. An eighteenth-century Arab cleric, al-Wahhab, used the same tactics against Muslim tribes in the Arabian peninsula who, he alleged, had become idolatrous by substituting saints and shrines for the One True God. He waged war upon them, and even destroyed the tomb of the Prophet. Once again, the term *jahili* had been used to justify puritanical war against other Muslims. Finally, in the twentieth century, the Indian Muslim al-Ala Mawdudi, whose writings had a profound influence on Qutb, also used the term, this time to describe the government in newly independent India.

Hence, when Qutb used the concept of *jahili* as one of the two key ideas of his argument, he was making a historical reference with which his readers would be familiar. He was raising the dangerous spectre of Muslim against Muslim, as painful a reminder of the past as the failed revolt against the Romans was to the Jews (see pp. 95–97). After all, Islam had been split soon after its foundation by the schism between Sunnis and Shi'ites, a quarrel the longevity of which is evidenced today in the sectarian violence in Iraq. Further, Qutb was citing the failure to obey the *sharia* as justification for such jihad. No wonder that 'Milestones' was cited at his trial; the nationalist regime had just refused to establish a government based on the *sharia*.

On what basis are societies to be categorised as *jahili*, according to Qutb? The answer lies in his uncompromising interpretation of the Islamic declaration of faith: 'There is no God except Allah'. According to the principle of *tawhid*, this implies that unless one completely submits to the guidance of God, one is in effect worshipping another god or gods. As the guidance of God was finally revealed to the Prophet in the Qu'ran and fully detailed in the *sharia* law contained therein, it follows that any person or nation who does not obey *sharia* is failing to worship the true God. The *sharia* contains everything that anyone needs to know about faith, morals, values, standards, systems, and laws. The disobedient are worshipping other gods, and those gods are many and varied. They might consist of man-made legal codes, institutions of state, democratic forms of government, in fact, any elements of non-theocratic cultures. Because these are human creations, all those who live in states not governed by *sharia* are not only worshipping false gods, they are also in slavery to their human creators. They are submitting to another human being rather than to the law of God. Hence, paradoxically, only those ruled by a theocracy can be truly free.

Qutb is quite clear which societies and cultures are *jahili*. They are all those whose government is man-made rather than derived from God alone, thereby denying God's sovereignty. In other words, they are those who do not obey *sharia* law. As it is incumbent on true Muslims to obey *sharia* and thereby worship God, they are rejecting God by submitting to a *jahili* government.

Qutb (1981, Chapter 5) lists 'idolatrous' societies such as India, Japan, the Philippines, and Africa as *jahili*. He adds Jewish and Christian societies, which have 'distorted the original beliefs and ascribe certain attributes of God to other beings'. Further:

> their institutions and their laws are not based on submission to God alone. They neither accept the rule of God, nor do they consider God's commandments as the only valid base of all laws; on the contrary, they have established assemblies of men which have absolute power to legislate laws, thus usurping the right which belongs to God alone.

And now the real bombshell:

> Lastly, all the existing so-called 'Muslim' societies are also *jahili* societies. We classify them among *jahili* societies not because they believe in other deities besides God [like the idolatrous] nor because they worship anyone other than God [like the Jews and Christians] but because their way of life is not based on submission to God alone. Although they believe in the Unity of God, still they have relegated the legislative attribute of God to others and submit to this authority, and from this authority they derive their systems, their traditions and customs, their laws, their values and standards, and almost every practice of life. God Most High says concerning rulers: 'Those who do not judge according to what God has revealed are unbelievers'.
>
> (Qu'ran, 5, 44)

So Qutb threw down three challenges. The first was to the religious establishment, the usual first target of fundamentalist movements. The second was to nationalist governments of Muslim nations and their rulers, now condemned as unbelievers. And the third was to *all other nations in the world*. Mankind began as a single community, argued Qutb from the creation myth in the Qu'ran, but disobeyed God. God sent the Prophet and the Qu'ran in order to re-unify humanity in a single unified system of life. The Western world had subsequently divorced faith from practice, religion from society, and church from state. It was therefore responsible for preventing the re-unification of humanity under God and was a prime example of *jahili* society. Liberal democratic beliefs in rationality and autonomy, human rights, and the rule of law are *jahili* concepts. Ultimately, they result in a materialist society, because they are human rather than divine products, and therefore are guided by bodily instincts. Men legislate their own desires, rebelling against the sovereignty of God. The consequences for sexual behaviour had been only too evident to Qutb during his visit to America.

The first of Qutb's challenges, to the *ulema*, gained him an enthusiastic and youthful populist following; the second, to the nationalist state, was to cost him his life; but the third later provided the ideological inspiration and justification for the extension of the struggle into the whole world, and for the assault on the very citadel of the far enemy. His uncompromising dualism eventually led, long after his death, to conflict at the global level of analysis:

> Islam cannot accept any compromise with *jahiliyyah*, either in its concept or in the modes of living derived from this concept. Either Islam will remain, or *jahiliyyah*; Islam cannot accept or agree to a situation which is half-Islam and half-*jahiliyyah*. In this respect Islam's stand is very clear. It says that truth is one and cannot be divided; if it is not truth, then it must be falsehood . . . Command belongs to Allah, or else to *jahiliyyah*. The *Shariah* of Allah will prevail, or else people's desires.
>
> (Qutb, 1981, Chapter 7)

Thus the concept of *jahiliyyah* is basically part of another dichotomy used to justify an us-versus-them social conflict. The uncompromising duality is evident in several dichotomies in the above brief account of Qutb's theology: Islam versus *jahiliyyah*; the rule of God versus the rule of man; truth versus falsehood; God's law versus man's desires; and slavery under man versus freedom under God. Qutb's use of the concept of *jahili* set up the ideological basis for conflict between us and them; his re-definition of the concept of jihad prescribed how that conflict should be conducted.

## Eternal jihad and the cosmic conflict

For Qutb, the struggle between truth and falsehood is inevitably expressed in action, in a revolutionary conflict that will last till the end of time:

> Thus this struggle [jihad] is not a temporary phase but an eternal state, as truth and falsehood cannot co-exist on this earth. Whenever Islam stood up with the universal declaration that God's Lordship should be established over the entire earth, and that men should become free from servitude to other men, the usurpers of God's authority on earth have struck out against it fiercely and have never tolerated it. It became incumbent upon Islam to strike back and release man throughout the earth from the grip of these usurpers. The eternal struggle for the freedom of man will continue until the religion is purified for God.
>
> (Qutb, 1981, Chapter 5)

Throughout the history of Islam, the term 'jihad' has referred in general terms to the struggle in the cause of God. Qutb selected specific aspects of struggle, and emphasised them, in the manner of all fundamentalists. The struggle was to be on behalf of the oppressed against their oppressors: *jahili* societies and their institutions. Its aim was to free the oppressed from slavery, enslaved as they were both to these institutions and also to their own sinful selves. Both these forms of freedom would be achieved if humanity as a whole submitted to God's law, the *sharia*. So oppressive were *jahili* institutions that it was imperative to engage in immediate political struggle. The first task had to be political, rather than personal. Personal struggle could only be won, and the *sharia* obeyed in full, when the *jahili* institutions of state were replaced by Islamic ones. The *political* context for obedience to God had to be in place before the *person* could properly obey and enjoy the benefits of the Islamic community. Therefore of the two traditional Islamic forms of struggle, preaching and 'movement', the latter had to take priority. Preaching alone was unlikely to be sufficient to persuade the oppressors to give up their power, although it was necessary to provide a justification for jihad.

So what did '*movement*' entail, and who was to be responsible for conducting this form of struggle? Whilst preaching attacked *jahili* ideas, movement tackled material obstacles (*jahili* institutions). This might involve political violence, but Qutb did not stress the armed nature of the struggle, perhaps because to do so would put himself and others under yet more extreme threat from the authorities. Nevertheless, the Qu'ran rates oppression as an even worse sin than killing and, according to Qutb, all humankind is oppressed by *jahili* institutions. It is not surprising that both Muslim governments and the jihadists drew the conclusion that he was advocating universal violent revolution.

It was the duty of all obedient Muslims, the true *ummah*, to wage jihad against *jahili* institutions, argued Qutb. Everyone has the right to worship Allah and obey his law, and therefore it is true Muslims' obligation to free all those in slavery in *jahili* societies so that they can worship Him. According to the Qu'ran, every Muslim physically capable of waging jihad was obligated to do so; to refuse would be to admit that one was not a true believer. However, Qutb had a logical problem here, because, if all societies are *jahili*, as he alleged, then no true Muslims can exist. His call to jihad would then be an empty threat, since it was a call simply to an idealised *ummah*, which was only a distant hope. Therefore he had to argue that even those living under the *jahili* yoke of oppression had a duty to engage in jihad, to the extent of dying for their faith. Governments could understandably interpret this argument as fomenting revolution. However, Qutb could justify his definition of jihad as defensive and thus in accord with mainstream doctrine. Jihad according to Qutb's definition meant defending mankind against the systems which limit its freedom:

> ... this religion ... tries to annihilate all those political and material powers which stand between people and Islam, which force one people to bow before another people and prevent them from accepting the sovereignty of God.
>
> (Qutb, 1981, Chapter 4)

Al-Qaida was later to justify 9/11 in the same terms.

However, Qutb was not so hard-hearted as merely to urge the oppressed to save themselves. He borrowed from other revolutionary movements, notably communism, the concept of *the revolutionary vanguard*. The vanguard would lead the jihad by following the example of the Prophet himself. Following the *milestones* of the Prophet's life, the vanguard would: first, separate itself out from the *jahili* societies in which it found itself; second, create a pure Muslim enclave; third, develop this enclave into a Muslim state; and finally, from this base launch armed struggle against *jahili* societies, just as the Prophet attacked Mecca from his base in Medina.

Recognising, however, that these milestones might not be quickly or easily reached, Qutb offered consolations for the period of persecution, oppression, and suffering that would follow. Commenting on the verse in the Qu'ran that commands 'Do not be dejected or grieve. You shall be the uppermost if you are believers' (Qu'ran 13, 139), Qutb stresses that what the *jahili* world regards as defeat, true Muslims should consider to be victory:

> This verse means to feel superior to others when weak, few, and poor, as well as when many and rich. For God does not leave the believer alone in the face of oppression to whimper under its weight ... but relieves them of ... dejection and grief ... not merely through patience and steadfastness, but also through a sense of superiority from whose heights the power of oppression, the dominant values, the current concepts, the standards, the rules, the customs and habits, and the people steeped in error, all seem low.
>
> (Qutb, 1981, Chapter 11)

*Because true Muslims are so different, they can feel superior*, particularly if they demonstrate their difference by welcoming martyrdom:

> Conditions change, the Muslim loses his physical power and is con-quered, yet the consciousness does not depart from him that he is the most superior. If he remains a believer, he looks upon his conqueror from a superior position. He remains certain that this is a temporary condition which will pass away and that faith will turn the tide from which there is no escape. Even if death is his portion, he will never bow his head. Death comes to all, but for him there is martyrdom. He will proceed to the Garden, while his conquerors go to the Fire. What a difference!
>
> (Qutb, 1981, Chapter 11)

The belief that ultimately 'faith will turn the tide' refers to the promised return to the original Golden Age of the religion, an example of the millen-nial hope that inspires fundamentalist movements. Qutb's ultimate hope is of a return to the first community of mankind when God was truly worshipped as sovereign, and also to the generation of the Prophet, which briefly restored mankind to that condition of perfection, the ideal Islamic society. Needless to say, that society was characterised by its treatment of the Qu'ran as its only guide for belief and action, and by its complete separation from *jahili* society.

Qutb's ideology challenged the Muslim clerical establishment, Muslim governments, and ultimately, the world. Its extreme hostility to modernism, its dualist conceptual apparatus, its highly selective interpretation of the holy book, which it reveres as God's sole guidance for faith and practice, and its millennial hope, all point to its status as a paradigmatic fundamentalist text. But what does it tell us about the man himself?

## Maintaining self-esteem

There is no reason to suppose that Sayeed Qutb was anything other than a normally pious mainstream Muslim during his childhood, youth, and early manhood. The benefits of such mainstream belief for the self were considerable. It met the need for affiliation and shared social identity, and placed the believer within a historical and religious context that made sense of his or her present situation. The *social identity* of Muslims had, however, taken some savage blows. The glories of the Caliphate and the great empires had given way to the ignominy of colonial rule, and as a consequence the self-esteem derived from being a Muslim was diminished. Nevertheless, in terms of his *personal identity*, Qutb had much of which to be proud. He had made the transition from a rural peasant life to a coveted civil service job in the city. And he had made a name for himself in literary circles, displaying the erudition of a clever boy from an unsophisticated background.

He had never had the chance to contrast his own society at first hand with a non-Muslim culture. That opportunity came with his visit to America. He found the contrast so immense that his own social identity as a Muslim was reinforced, America and the West were stereotyped, and the in-group versus out-group dynamic was firmly established in his mind. As soon as he returned to Egypt he joined the Muslim Brotherhood, claiming that this was the day he was really born (Sivan, 1990, p. 22). The Brotherhood's brand of Islam was strict, and its BVNs moved Qutb in a more conservative direction. They certainly provided him with the strength of a nested identity: Muslim and Brother. The high hopes of the nationalist revolution were soon dashed, and the inclusiveness of the out-group was augmented by the addition of many apostate Muslims. As social identity theory would predict, this increase in out-group inclusiveness resulted in a more exclusive and distinctive in-group social identity, as a true Muslim. Such an identity has the benefit of enhancing self-esteem. One is a member of an exclusive category, distinguished by its superiority over the heathen *jahili*, the rest of the world.

However, Nasser's successful persecution of the Brotherhood and his own imprisonment and torture presented Qutb with a psychological problem. How could he maintain any self-esteem when the social identity of true Muslim, which by now was absolutely central and dominant in his self, was so threatened? After all, religion and politics, faith and action, were one and the same thing for all true Muslims, and by any ordinary reckoning, Islam was in decline. His solution, as we have seen, was to create an extra-ordinary reckoning. Contrary to all appearances, God would ultimately be victorious against all His (and Qutb's) foes: the millennial hope. And what appears at present to be suffering and oppression is in fact a victory for true Islam. To fight to the death is not defeat but glorious martyrdom, a necessary part of the eternal duty of jihad. Thus the believer could and should feel superior to others, as Qutb repeatedly affirmed. Self-esteem could remain intact.

To what extent did Qutb apply this analysis to himself? We only have occasional indirect clues from his writings. It is clear that he rejected one of his former sources of self-esteem based on his personal achievement: his literary work. He now treated it as a product of *jahilyyah*:

> Today too we are surrounded by *jahilyya*. Its nature is the same as during the first period of Islam, and it is perhaps a little more deeply entrenched. Our whole environment, people's beliefs and ideas, habits and arts, rules and laws, is *jahilyyah*, even to the extent that what we consider to be Islamic culture, Islamic sources, Islamic philosophy, and Islamic thought are also constructs of *jahilyyah*!
>
> (Qutb, 1981, Chapter 1)

This suggests that as his distinctive fundamentalist identity hardened, he needed to exclude from it elements, such as literature, which were associated with the out-group of apostate Muslims. After joining the Brotherhood, he never wrote anything other than religious doctrine (Kepel, 2005, pp. 68–69).

There are indications that he identified himself with the vanguard of true Muslims. Note the use of the first person plural in the following passage from 'Milestones' (Chapter 1):

> Our first task is to change society indeed, to alter the *jahilyyah* reality from top to bottom . . . To start with, we must get rid of this *jahilyyah* society, we must abandon its values and ideology, and must not enfeeble our own values and ideology by even one iota to bring them closer to it! Certainly not! Our paths diverge, and if we took even a single step toward it, our ethics would vanish and we would be lost.

And perhaps it is no accident that the milestones in the vanguard's revolution-ary strategy are pre-figured by those of the Prophet, a literary device used by the American evangelists in their autobiographies.

So we may discern a development in Qutb's self over the course of his life, as he adapted to momentous political changes and to the personal experi-ences to which they led. We can guess that the balance between social and personal identities within his self changed further towards the social over time. We may also infer that his identity as a Muslim became more central and important to him, and that it grew steadily more exclusive as he condemned more and more of his fellow human beings to *jahili* status. It is evident that this exclusiveness was his only real adaptive option if he was to maintain self-esteem as a Muslim, when it was Muslims who were imprisoning him.

Finally, Qutb refuses to recant, and reportedly goes smiling to his execution. The ultimate reward of martyrdom has been granted to him. His fundamentalist construction of the world and his place within it had enabled him to maintain his self-esteem in circumstances in which most people would be crushed. His writing and his martyrdom were all of a piece; he was hero and martyr not only to his own generation but to generations to come. They too would maintain their identity as oppressed Muslims for whom the ultimate victory was violent death.

# 7 Fundamentalist beliefs: Process and contents

## A shared belief process

### *Fundamentalist beliefs are explicit*

Fundamentalist movements have been analysed as sub-cultures throughout this book. I have argued that adherents identify themselves as true believers, and internalise as part of this social identity the BVNs that are themselves part of the movement's culture. In this chapter I address *fundamentalist beliefs*, which are the basis for their values, attitudes, and norms of behaviour.

Anthropologists, who have developed our methods of analysing cultures, have repeatedly stressed that one of their most difficult tasks is to discover a culture's assumptive and implicit beliefs. In other words, while people may be able to express many of their beliefs, there are others of which they are not conscious, but simply assume. These latter are often the most fundamental beliefs for their culture, and remain implicit and unspoken until the anthropologist researcher succeeds in accessing them, usually by participant observation.

Fundamentalist cultures appear to be an exception to this general rule. The fundamentalist movements of the three religions of the book are concerned to make explicit their beliefs. All of them emphasise the importance of *right practice and right belief*, Judaism and Islam stressing the former imperative, and Protestant Christianity the latter. Both right practice and right belief require explicit statement, the former of the law of God, and the latter of correct doctrine. Thus we may be optimistic that we can discover the core beliefs of fundamentalism from its written and spoken discourse.

However, this optimism begs an important question. We have shown different fundamentalist movements to be located within markedly different host cultures, and to demonstrate corresponding differences (see Chapters 2 and 3). Surely, we may argue, this necessarily implies that the beliefs of fundamentalisms will differ. Indeed, are not religions to be distinguished from each other primarily by the fact that their adherents hold different beliefs?

In line with the argument in the Introduction that we are justified in differentiating fundamentalist religious movements as a category from others because they share five common features, I propose that the opposite is the case. That is, there is a general process which all fundamentalisms use in making meaning and arriving at their world-view; and, moreover, their views on many of the core issues of belief are notably similar. That is not to say, however, that their belief systems are equally important to all fundamentalisms. As noted above, Christianity places a much greater emphasis on correct belief than do Judaism and Islam.

First, I will propose an overall schematic model of the process of arriving at a fundamentalist world-view (see Fig. 2), and then look at some shared positions on issues and some common modes of thinking.

### A process model

The basis for the model, from which all its other elements follow, are three core beliefs. These are: first, that there exists *a supernatural realm* or mode of existence, inhabited by supernatural beings, the chief of whom is God. The relationship of this supernatural world with the natural, social, and personal worlds is constant and intimate, with God intervening pervasively (see pp. 172–177). The second core belief is that God has revealed himself and his law in *the holy book*, which is the ultimate authority in matters of belief and practice (Ammerman, 1987). Clearly these two beliefs are related: a supernatural God exists, but people cannot know His will except through His word, the holy book. He may reveal His will by supernatural means, as when charismatic Christians open the Bible at random, and their eyes chance upon a verse that brings God's message to them personally. Fundamentalists' third core belief is that *their religion is under threat* from the secular world. It

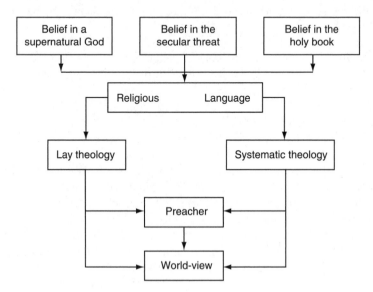

*Figure 2* Fundamentalist belief systems.

is this belief that is the primary difference between fundamentalist religious movements and non-fundamentalist ones.

From these three core beliefs there follows the essential and central element of the process of making meaning: *religious language*, or 'God Talk' (Tickle, 1997). This language genre, both spoken and written, refers continuously to the supernatural, and derives most of its terminology and figures of speech from its holy book. As the holy books were written by pre-modern people who held supernatural beliefs, they are ideal sources for the language needed to express such beliefs. This language is the primary means by which fundamentalist believers enact their faith. Once they are talking the talk, they then go on to walk the walk.

Because the holy book is the ultimate authority on matters of belief and practice, it sets boundaries around the range of meanings that adherents can make. The criteria for true doctrine or proper practice have all to be found 'intra-textually' (Hood et al., 2005), that is, within the holy book. Any other source of meaning can only be judged by the book's standards. It follows, given this restricted source of knowledge and truth, that it is not difficult to create internally consistent doctrinal positions. There is only one source within which the believer has to search for the truth, which also helpfully provides an appropriate language to express *a systematic theology*. Thus the boundaries imposed by the holy book around God enable the construction of systems within which God may be described (Boone, 1989).

Belief in the supernatural and the availability of a language to express that belief also permit the parallel development of *a lay theology*. This term refers to the working religious ideas that believers use in their everyday lives and conversations. These, unlike systematic theology, contain many inferences that are not justified in logical terms. They are, however, totally in accord with believers' experience, and thus moralistic and experiential language is apt to be mixed in with theology. As described in the previous chapter, attributions for the causes of events may be made in an apparently random way (see pp. 175–176). Moreover, lay theology frequently argues by analogy to stories from the holy book, relating them to features of the believer's experience.

Fundamentalist *preachers* succeed in developing the religious language so that it stays in tune with adherents' needs for meaning, while at the same time avoiding doing obvious violence to the systematic theology that legitimates their preaching. Preachers are thus the mediators for the believer between the formal and the informal systems of fundamentalist speech and thought.

Lay theology and systematic theology, interpreted and expressed by the movement's leaders and preachers, can then together provide *an overall world-view*. A world-view is a mental schema, an organised structure derived from their movement's BVNs, by means of which fundamentalist believers can make meaningful sense of their personal experience and the world. Once again, religious language provides the ideal means to describe and express this world-view. As one might expect, the world-view is not only used to provide meaning for believers. It is also a persuasive rhetorical device for recruitment and for confrontation with the out-group. Where the out-group consists essentially of the rest of the world, then the ultimate conflict of binary opposites can be fought: God's world-view versus the world's (Bruce, 2000, pp. 111–112).

This processual model is dynamically *self-reinforcing*. The holy book provides the basis for the religious language, but the religious language helps the holy book come to life for the adherent. The book is the source of the systematic theology, but any new theological ideas must be referred back to it to check that they are 'sound'. Belief in the supernatural permeates the religious language, but personal use of the language reinforces the belief; 'I have said it, so I must believe it'. Lay theology derives from the religious language, but it also motivates its use in order to express itself. And while both lay and systematic theology contribute to the world-view, the boundaries of that world-view limit what can be contained in the theologies. Thus *the fundamentalist belief process is impermeable and self-perpetuating*.

The contrast with non-fundamentalist religious world-views is profound (Hood et al., 2005, pp. 22–28). Non-fundamentalist belief systems and processes are not self-contained and self-reinforcing. Alternative textual sources exist in addition to the holy book, and are continuously being created. Peripheral beliefs from such sources may enter the belief system. Moreover, the resulting theologies are not absolute truths and dogmatic systems, but relative truths and contingent systems. Hence non-fundamentalist belief systems do not provide the ideological foundation for the in-group versus out-group social dynamic. They are not sufficiently differentiated from, and impervious to, other belief systems.

### Belief in the holy book

It is important to clarify further two of the elements of the process model I have described. First, misconceptions are frequent regarding fundamentalist *belief in the holy book*. Their belief is 'intra-textual'; in other words, the book contains all that the believer needs in order to learn the truth. However, the reader has to be open to God's revelation to him or her, which requires being in spiritual touch and constant dialogue with Him.

In general, God's truth is not difficult to grasp. He has revealed Himself clearly in His Word, and, as God cannot be in error, neither can His Word. Hence any apparent contradictions within the book have some theological explanation that God has not yet revealed. The book has to be internally consistent; God does not contradict Himself. Moreover, any contradiction with external sources of knowledge, for example, science, must by definition be resolved in favour of the holy book, since it, and it alone, is the ultimate criterion of truth.

However, fundamentalist readers do not always take the book 'literally', in the sense that they do appreciate that some passages are figurative and metaphorical. They consider, however, that the meaning is clear; God would not have made it difficult for ordinary believers to grasp His truth. Rather, the holy book says what it means and it means what it says, in accord with straightforward common sense. When it makes a propositional statement, that statement is to be treated as objective fact referring to external reality. Thus the various miraculous events described in all the holy books are objectively true, and to this extent, belief is literal. Jesus did physically rise from the dead. Allah did dictate the words of the Qu'ran to the Prophet verbatim through the mouth of Gabriel. It follows that the supernatural is constantly involved in the natural and social worlds.

The following statement of belief from the Baptist Bible Fellowship International (BBFI), exemplifies the fundamentalist approach to the holy book:

> We believe that the Holy Bible was written by men supernaturally inspired; that it has truth without any admixture of error for its matter; and therefore is, and shall remain to the end of the age, the only complete and final revelation of the will of God to man; the true center of Christian union and the supreme standard by which all human conduct, creeds, and opinions should be tried.
>
> Note 1. By 'The Holy Bible' we mean that collection of sixty-six books, from Genesis to Revelation, which, as originally written does not only contain and convey the Word of God, but IS the very Word of God.
>
> Note 2. By 'inspiration' we mean that the books of the Bible were written by holy men of old, as they were moved by the Holy Spirit, in such a definite way that their writings were supernaturally and verbally inspired and free from error, as no other writings have ever been or ever will be inspired.
>
> (BBFI, 2004)

### *Unique social identity, not impaired cognition*

Second, we need to address a specific psychological question. *Is there something different about the cognitive systems of fundamentalists that predisposes them to accept this closed system of belief?* Just as there was little evidence to show that fundamentalists differ from others in their personality characteristics, so too it seems unlikely that they have different cognitive processes.

For example, it might be proposed that their belief in the supernatural is part of a tendency to give credence to paranormal phenomena in general, such as extra-sensory perception and psychic healing. Rice (2003) indicates that, at least in America, fundamentalist belief and belief in the paranormal are not significantly correlated with each other. Or perhaps we might hypothesise that they are particularly reluctant to change beliefs despite contradictory evidence. This is certainly true of their religious beliefs (witness what happens when prophecy fails, p. 176), but there is no indication that the same is true of their beliefs in general. And there are, of course, perfectly logical reasons for refusing to change one's religious beliefs. If they are part of a consistent world-view that one believes to have been revealed by God, then to change them implies that God is a liar, or that His truth is not eternal and changeless. The new evidence has to be assimilated to the story, rather than the story accommodated to the evidence. The story is in principle unfalsifiable.

Finally, the dualistic, black-and-white nature of fundamentalist belief systems has led to the proposal that fundamentalists are more simple and less complex in their cognitive processes than others. Research by Hunsberger et al. (1996) demonstrates that American Protestants who score high on the fundamentalism scale have few doubts about their religious beliefs. Moreover, they demonstrate less complex thinking than others when responding to various dilemmas relating to those beliefs (for example, whether abortion should be legalised, life after death, or the existence of God). However, when the issues with which they were presented concerned non-religious ethical or environmental matters, there was no evidence of any relationship between fundamentalist belief and complexity of thought. The same conclusion seems to be clear: fundamentalists' religious beliefs are simple and non-negotiable because they have been revealed to them by God. The reason for their different mode of thought is not some general cognitive peculiarity, but rather is a direct consequence of the specific belief system which they have internalised.

The internalisation of their enclosed and self-perpetuating belief system is in turn a consequence of their acquisition of the fundamentalist movement's *social identity*. To the extent that this social identity is centrally important to their selves, it will be possible for them to develop a single and total world-view based upon its associated internalised BVNs. As I argued above, such a world-view enables the movement and its adherents to differentiate themselves from the rest of the world, and 'the world's world-view'. The ideological lines have then been satisfactorily drawn for in-group versus out-group conflict.

## A shared belief content

### God's plan for the world and the believer

Fundamentalists from different religions also appear to share similar beliefs about many of the basic existential questions which people have asked down the ages. The first cluster of such questions relates to *the self, the world, and the relationship between the two*. In Chapter 6, I argued that, for fundamentalists, the self is constituted largely of the social identity of true believer. This identity is so central to the self that it displaces such other normally central social identities as family member or citizen. It is salient for the believer in a wide variety of social situations, and therefore guides and directs social behaviour. Further, it dominates the self at the expense of the personal identity of the individual; the individual is first and foremost a believer, one of God's many servants, and only secondarily a unique individual.

As for the world within which they live, fundamentalists place their understanding of its present state within the overall context of God's historic plan for it. Jewish, Christian, and Islamic fundamentalists share a common perception of this plan. It runs in general terms as follows (Almond et al., 2003, pp. 52–56). In a golden age, at the beginning of time, God reigned, and God and man were in communion. Man broke this communion, succumbing to temptation by Satan. During the course of history, there have been times when the golden age was re-instated, as pure and simple as it was at the dawn of human history. For example, the life and works of the Prophet and immediately subsequent events (differing for Sunnis and Shi'ites), the restoration of the Jewish temple after the return from exile, and the spread of the early Christian church, were all examples of the golden age. So too, at least for Protestants, were more recent occasions, such as the Reformation, the Puritan settlements in America, and sundry subsequent religious revivals, such as the 'Great Awakening' in America.

However, the present age has plumbed new depths of depravity. The rot has really set in in modern times. True religion is threatened as never before by the Enemy, dressed up in a variety of garbs. Such a dire state of affairs indicates that the Almighty will surely soon intervene. The believer's duty is to fight back on God's behalf, with the ultimate aim of helping the Almighty to re-establish the golden age, when God will rule over all. This millennial hope is sure and certain: theocracy will ultimately come to pass.

The individual believer is therefore an instrument in God's plan for the salvation of the world. From 'the world's' perspective, he or she is deluded and duped by cults and their leaders, but from God's perspective (i.e. their own world-view) each one is a loyal servant of the faith, playing their part in the great spiritual movement of history. Persecution and ridicule is only to be expected, and is proof of their own belief. It is a spiritual, not a worldly reward that they will receive; they will gain a martyr's crown, or act as God's agents on earth when He returns to rule. Thus the self is placed in an honourable position within God's scheme of things. Needs for meaning and for self-esteem have been fully met by means of one's spiritual status.

The identification of the believer with God is thus all-embracing. The purpose of the believer's life is God's purpose. The Almighty is lord of all, and He will exercise His righteous sovereignty. The believer's task is to hasten the kingdom of the Lord.

### God is in control

This same set of beliefs explains why fundamentalist believers are so willing to *attribute the cause of events or actions to God* (see p. 175). It is God who is working out His plan for the world and for every individual within it, and every event and every action is to be understood as part of that plan (or as Satan's efforts to sabotage it through his agents, such as the United Nations, or feminists, or secular Jews).

Thus *the individual is defined by his or her relationship with God*. God has a plan for each person, which is part of His plan for the world. The believer will accept and obey that plan, unless he or she backslides, seduced by the world, the flesh, and the Devil. God will have endowed the believer with whatever qualities he or she needs to obey. God's plans for the individual and for the world are revealed through His word the holy book, read prayerfully or expounded faithfully. Thus understanding both oneself and the world is, for the fundamentalist believer, achieved by revelation by God to His spiritually attuned disciple. It is not a matter of human discovery or understanding.

The fundamentalist believer cannot therefore derive his or her self-esteem from their personal identity, their view of themselves as unique and authentic individuals who have consciously chosen to develop in this or that way, or who have reached some pinnacle of human achievement, or who have reached their own truth. Rather, self-esteem comes from the status of their relationship with God, and is shared with all the other adherents of their movement, who by definition are in a similar obedient relationship. As Tamney (2002) noted (see p. 79), a feeling of individuality in terms of a personal relationship with God can thus be compatible with fundamentalist adherence.

As it is obedience to the will of God that matters above all else, *death is to be welcomed*. It will bring the obedient believer into a closer relationship with God. By believing in such an anticipated reward, fundamentalists are actively denying the materialist world-view that dead bodies cannot come back to life, and re-affirming the truth of the stories of their holy book. God is the Lord of life and death.

As God is perceived as the sovereign creator, then *not only natural but also social phenomena are under His sovereignty*. Human institutions such as the family and the nation are in fact not human at all, but divine in their origin and purpose. Hence they, and they alone, are the 'natural', divinely ordained bases of social relationships. However, they must take the form prescribed by the holy book. Any other form is perceived as a perversion of them, and is not only unnatural, but also an assault on the Almighty Himself. Gays and feminists by definition have rejected God.

### Survey evidence

A typical response of a secular reader to the above account of the content of fundamentalist belief is to be amazed that any modern person could hold such a set of beliefs. To demonstrate that, on the contrary, they are widely held, I will now briefly review the survey evidence regarding the prevalence of specific Protestant beliefs in America. Similarly sophisticated polling data is not available for other religions (but see Norris & Inglehart, 2004).

All the following results are derived from large, random samples of adult Americans. The belief that 'religion is under attack in America' is agreed by 64% (Anti-Defamation League, 2005); 40% believe in a personal God, while another 41% regard God as a spirit or impersonal force (Pew Forum, 2004);

35% accept the Bible as the literal word of God, while a further 43% consider it to be God's word, but not literally so (Pew Forum, 2006). Thus each of the three key beliefs of the fundamentalist belief system is held by nearly half of the population of America (although it does not follow that the same proportion hold all three beliefs).

This overall estimate also applies to other beliefs that may be derived from these core beliefs. So, for example, 42% believe that humans and other living things have existed in their present form only (Pew Forum, 2006); 79% believe in Jesus Christ's second coming, and 33% that the time of his return is revealed in the Bible (Pew Forum, 2006). Thus the poll data show that acceptance of specific fundamentalist beliefs is widespread in America.

It is a somewhat different question to ask how many Americans are Protestant fundamentalists, as questionnaires have not consistently included items aimed at all of the five criteria. However, the Pew Forum (2004) has employed a highly conservative method of categorisation, as follows. First, Protestant respondents are divided into categories of Evangelical Protestantism and Mainline Protestantism according to the denomination to which they profess allegiance. So, for example, Southern Baptists fall into the first category, and United Methodists into the second. Next, each of these two categories is sub-divided into three: Traditionalists, Centrists, and Modernists. Traditionalists have high levels of belief in God, Satan, life after death, the Bible, creation science, and the falsehood of other religions. They have a heavy involvement in church attendance, financial support, prayer, bible study, and small group participation. They resist both societal and religious change. And they categorise themselves as fundamentalist, evangelical, Pentecostal, or charismatic. Thus of the six categories of Protestant believers so created, the most fundamentalist appear to be the Traditionalist Evangelicals. The two largest categories were Traditionalist Evangelicals (12.6% of the adult American population) and Centrist Evangelicals (10.8%). Thus even in terms of the most conservative estimates, belief systems and practice typical of fundamentalists are not the preserve of an isolated few.

### Core beliefs, dualism, and rationality

In summary, we can make three points about fundamentalist belief systems. First, *they depend upon the acceptance of three core beliefs*: belief in the supernatural and in the holy book, together with the central feature of fundamentalisms, the belief that they are under threat. The social identity of true believer could not be so central in the selves of adherents if they did not believe in a supernatural world where an omnipotent yet personal God forms and executes His plans. Such plans are for the whole of human history, past, present, and future. God through His word the holy book enables us to understand and know the past, interpret the meaning of the present in the light of the past and the future, and know what is to come in the last days. The attribution of divine causation derives both from a belief in the supernatural and also from a set of stories in the holy book that show how He works in the lives of men and women and in the affairs of the world. The belief that knowledge and understanding are revealed rather than discovered is implicit in the model of the conveyance of truth by a supernatural God through his book. The divine sovereignty over the natural world makes death lose its sting and the grave its victory, as the miraculous stories of the holy books clearly portray. And the only social institutions that humans should have are those modelled on the instructions in the holy book.

The second point to be made about fundamentalist beliefs is to re-emphasise their *dualist nature*. Their ideological function is to establish and legitimate the distinction between in-group and out-group, us and them. Dualism supports this function. It pervades fundamentalist beliefs at all levels. Their *beliefs about their beliefs*, for example, state that God has revealed the truth to them, that there is only one truth, and therefore that all who do not agree with them are wrong, in rebellion against God, and hostile to His true servants. The contest is between God's world-view and the world's, His servants and His enemies. Their distinction between *the natural and the supernatural* allows the supernatural explanation to trump the natural, since it is derived from the only authentic source of knowledge: the holy book. Hence they are in conflict with all who permit evidence from other sources to influence their beliefs and values. And their characterisation of *social institutions* of a certain form as divinely ordained and all others as mere human creations inevitably creates political conflict between social conservatives and reformers.

Finally, we must note that within the constraints of their world-view, *fundamentalist doctrine is entirely rational and coherent*. Once certain assumptions are made and accepted, tightly argued statements of systematic theology can be derived from them. As Bruce (2000, pp. 115–116) observes:

> The crucial test for abnormality is not whether a person's reasoning fits with ours, but whether it fits with their own. Bizarre though it may seem to an outsider, fundamentalism is perfectly consistent with the logic of the religious tradition from which it grows.

Or again (Bruce, 2000, p. 117):

> Fundamentalism is a rational response of traditionally religious peoples to social, political and economic changes that downgrade and constrain the role of religion in the public world.

Thus the assumption of a supernatural realm where God and Satan battle for the souls of men is a theological reaction to the threat that modernism poses to traditional religious belief. In its dualist emphasis on the battle of God versus Satan, this assumptive belief provides a rationale and a legitimation for hostility towards the perceived threat. Similarly, the assumption of an inerrant holy book through which God reveals His will to humankind provides an authoritative source for belief and practice. Such a source is in frequent and direct conflict with the multiple sources of secular knowledge. As we might expect, fundamentalist belief systems provide an ideological legitimacy for prosecuting this conflict. They are highly effective in radically changing adherents' values, attitudes, and norms of behaviour, and hence in mobilising them for political and social action. A fundamentalist world-view is a powerful weapon indeed.

## Different fundamentalisms, different beliefs

### *Belief versus practice and individual versus collective*

I have argued that the fundamentalisms associated with the three religions of the book, Judaism, Christianity, and Islam, share a common process of arriving at their world-view. I have also proposed that they hold similar beliefs regarding the basic existential issues facing humankind: the self, time past present and future, causation, knowledge and truth, life and death, social institutions, and so on. This is hardly surprising. They are not only all religions of the book, but they are also all monotheistic, they believe that the individual believer has direct access to God, and they possess sufficient tradition to enable fundamentalisms to claim to be the guardians of orthodoxy.

However, there remain some basic differences between these fundamentalisms in terms of their beliefs. I am not referring to obvious points of doctrinal detail, such as the specific nature of God's future rule, but rather to more general issues of emphasis. The first such difference relates to *the relative importance attached to different features of belief.* Many Protestant fundamentalists place great emphasis on correct doctrine. Holding fast to the truth means assenting to a set of theological propositions. These emphasise justification by faith rather than by works, the very essence of Reformation theology. The works follow the faith, as the believer becomes sanctified. Judaism and Islam, on the other hand, emphasise obedience to God's law as the main duty of the believer. Belief is important because it requires the adherent to acknowledge the unity of God. God requires the individual to do His will as expressed in the holy book in every area of their lives.

The danger of making such broad generalisations immediately becomes apparent when we arrive at the case study at the end of this chapter. This relates to the reconstructionists, a Protestant movement that emphasises the relevance of the whole Bible, including the Old Testament legal system, to the believer's life. However, it seems worth retaining the general distinction between believing a doctrine and obeying God's law.

Such a distinction may help in understanding the greater tendency to violence in Islamic than in Protestant fundamentalisms. Of course, explanations for this difference at the political, economic, and social levels of analysis are available, powerful, and legitimate. However, it is also possible to argue, as I have repeatedly hitherto, that belief systems themselves motivate action. They are not merely posthoc legitimisations of action undertaken for very different reasons. Thus the Islamic emphasis on obeying God's law renders completely predictable violent action by fundamentalists to overthrow states that fail to establish *sharia*. God's requirement is to impose *sharia* in every nation, argued Sayeed Qutb, who regarded all other legal codes as human rather than divine. These codes were designed to enslave, and, of course, it is right to rebel against slavery. It is important to note that Qutb insisted that freedom of religious belief would still be possible within an Islamic nation governed by *sharia*, thus emphasising the greater importance of obedience to law over doctrinal belief (Qutb, 1981, Chapter 5).

A second and related difference is the Protestant *emphasis on the individual*, relative to Jewish and Islamic *emphasis on the collective*. For Protestant fundamentalists the effects of the Reformed tradition and the individualistic American culture ensured that the individual's relationship with God was paramount. This was established through personal redemption and sanctification and maintained by worship and prayer (talking with God). Although religious experience is enjoyed in group as well as in individual settings, communal worship is construed by Protestants as God speaking to each individual through the communal experience (for example, singing worship songs or listening to a sermon) (Tamney, 2002). The Protestant fundamentalist theology of church as the body of Christ is not so well developed as in mainstream Protestant and Catholic denominations.

Fundamentalist Jews, on the other hand, emphasise the collective, the chosen people of God. For them, fulfilment is either, in the case of Gush Emunim, the full return to the promised land, or, for the Haredi, perfect obedience to every jot and tittle of the law. As for Islam, the collective *ummah* with its perceived suffering is a powerful motivator for alienated Muslim youth (see Chapter 5).

### Mode of engagement with the world

A third major difference in belief results in the differences between fundamentalisms in their *choice of strategy* (assault, engagement, or withdrawal). So, for example, Gush Emunim favour engagement, whereas Haredi withdraw to practise their piety. Evangelicals and Fundamentalists get engaged in politics, while Pentecostals and charismatics concentrate more on saving souls. Salafists urge jihad, while Sufis spiritualise. Underlying these different strategic choices are *different beliefs regarding God, His plan for the world, and the distinction between the spiritual and the material*.

For the *withdrawers*, God is omnipotent. His plan for the world has been determined, and human beings cannot affect it in any way. All they can do is to perfect themselves and/or save others from God's coming wrath. Their task is spiritual, the saving of their own souls and/or those of others. Politics and social affairs are part of the carnal rather than of the spiritual world. In

Protestant fundamentalism, these beliefs are associated with a *pre-millennial* theology of the last days. In other words, God has determined when He will rescue the faithful by rapturing them up to heaven, before the dreaded tribulation. Thus the only task left is to evangelise and rescue as many of the unsaved as possible from their fate (Boyer, 1992).

For *engagers and assaulters*, however, other beliefs are important. They believe that they are God's agents for the fulfilment of His plan for the world. The more faithfully they work on His behalf, the sooner His plans will come to fruition. They make little distinction between the spiritual and the material, believing that God rules in every sphere of life. Therefore political and social engagement is necessary to help achieve God's plan. For Protestant engagers and assaulters, the theology of the last days is *post-millennial*. God's sovereignty will be fully established before believers are taken to heaven, and it is their task to help its establishment in the here and now.

## Orthodoxy alive

### *Generative fundamentalist language*

One of the most important aspects of fundamentalist belief is that it succeeds in appearing to adhere strictly to traditional orthodoxy while in fact it is adapting to its environment. The model in Fig. 2 suggests a closed system of thought based upon an unchanging text. Yet, as I argued above, this closed system is in fact capable of generating new ideas. The main engine for such creative adaptation is the central element of the system: religious language.

Like all language genres, religious language is *generative*. Its users create new connexions, new meanings, out of its elements, by using generative rules. There are several ways of generating new meanings from within a language system. The first has already been mentioned: *the application of existing stories and themes to new personal, social, and political experience*. The elements of religious language include recurring types: the repentant sinner, the victorious warrior, the humble servant, the dutiful wife, the wise ruler, the fearless prophet, the disobedient son, the prudent merchant, the sinful woman, and so on. There are stories of victory and defeat, exile and return, deceit and treachery, arrogance and folly, sacrifice and reward, hope and fulfilment, loyalty and betrayal, sickness and healing, triumph and tragedy, death and revival. Above all, there are miraculous signs and wonders: divine appearances and pronouncements, miraculous healings, supernatural occurrences, dreams and portents, angels and devils.

These stories are related to each other and to believers' lives by means of some general rules. For example, a typological rule suggests that there must be at least some apparent similarities between the situations of a biblical story and a believer's experience if the story is to be taken to prefigure that experience. New meanings can come from old words and old stories, that is, from God's very word.

As Harding (2000) notes, skilful preachers use this figurative technique to enable their listeners to make new meanings for themselves. They leave a story in the air, for example, encouraging the believer to complete it in their own way. Thus the holy book, the source of the religious language and the stories and figures it contains, comes alive for the believer, and is 'forever new'. God speaks in the gaps, and the listener's lay theology becomes more confident. Each new trend or event can be interpreted in terms of the old stories. For example, Harding (2000, Chapter 4) notes how Jerry Falwell supports his plans to build a theological college on a Virginia hilltop by reference to biblical stories in which mountains feature. Thus the power of *the fundamentalist preacher* in this linguistic process is evident. It is he who can reconcile lay and systematic theologies of believers, and through them influence the world-view typical of the movement.

### Abstract ideas and their association

The second important generative mechanism of religious language derives from *the abstract and general nature of theological concepts*. Unless an idea is defined solely in terms of a limited and defined set of other ideas, as in mathematics, for example, its interpretation is open to change. Thus the concepts of jihad and *jahili* were redefined by Qutb in order to meet the ideological needs of a new situation: the establishment of secular but nominally Muslim nationalist governments in the Middle East. The Ayatollah Khomeini expanded the notion of the 'just jurist' so that he could apply it to himself and retain autocratic control of Iran. The new meanings for these concepts were not, however, imposed randomly. They actually drew from the existing meanings, which were deeply embedded in the religious culture. Thus the new meaning gained its power from the existing meaning, but enabled the fundamentalist movement to identify and mobilise against a new enemy, and to legitimate that mobilisation.

A third generative mechanism is combinatorial: *to associate two or more ideas that have hitherto been separate within the belief system*. So, for example, the theological godfather of the Protestant 'new evangelicalism' of the 1950s, Carl Henry, reconciled the Fundamentalist emphasis on prophecy and the imminence of the last days with the relevance of the gospel to every human situation, thus providing a dynamic for the urgent expansion of Protestant evangelicalism into modern American culture (Carpenter, 1997, Chapter 10). The prophecy idea provided the urgency, the relevance idea justified the expansion, and together the merged concepts motivated a major religious movement. Or consider the success of Jerry Falwell, a quarter of a century later, in associating the idea of the inerrancy of the Bible with the falseness of the dichotomy between the spiritual and the temporal (Harding, 2000, Chapter 5). Biblical inerrancy allowed the targets of the Moral Majority to be clearly identified. The assertion that God was sovereign in the temporal as well as the spiritual sphere justified political involvement. Once again, the association of two theological concepts provided the motivation and the justification for a major strategic project.

### *Values, attitudes, and behaviour*

A final creative use of religious thought and language is *the derivation of values, attitudes, and norms of behaviour* from beliefs. Two of the core beliefs of fundamentalisms, belief in the supernatural and the holy book, permit the generation of new value priorities, the identification of new attitudinal targets, and the development of new norms of behaviour.

So, for example, in terms of *values*, the upgrading of the importance of holiness and obedience in Protestantism emerged from a belief in the holiness and sovereignty of God and the power of His Holy Spirit working in the lives of believers. Likewise, the increased importance of jihad, struggle on behalf of Allah, derives from the dualist separation of the *ummah* from *jahili* nations.

As for *attitudes*, hostile attitudes towards categories of person may be generated from selective reading of the Bible, the inerrant word of God. Feminists certainly do not feature in its pages, but its social strictures permit them to be a legitimate target. America, similarly, does not appear in the Qu'ran, but hostility towards the Great Satan is constantly justified by reference to the Prophet's word.

Finally, new *norms of behaviour* may develop, providing means for differentiating the faithful from the wicked world and re-inforcing their social identity. Modes of dress, changes in ritual practice, manner of social intercourse, adoption or rejection of modern cultural artefacts and so on are all based on beliefs about what God wants and how He reveals those wants in the holy book. For example, the wearing of the *niqab* (see Chapter 9) is derived from, and justified by, a selective reading of the Qu'ran.

Thus there is an apparent contradiction between the closed belief systems of fundamentalists, seemingly set in stone, and their evident success in creating new meanings for their adherents, which are adapted to their current situation. I have argued in this chapter that the contradiction is only apparent. *Fundamentalist belief should be considered primarily as a process*, the process of forming and re-forming a world-view. This process is informed by three core beliefs, and driven by the generative properties of religious language and ideas. This is not to argue that the content of belief systems is unimportant. On the contrary, they are the engine for values, attitudes and norms of behaviour, and hence for the mobilisation of personal and, above all, communal action. Rather, it is to cast doubt on the fundamentalist perception of themselves as adhering to an historically fixed and unchanging doctrinal position. Instead, it may be more appropriate to consider them as making one or two basic assumptions, from which much else may be derived. After all, we may recall the extreme generativity of other relatively closed systems of thought. What Kuhn (1970) terms 'normal science' (i.e. science conducted within an agreed paradigm) is one example; formal logic and mathematics are others.

## Summary

- Jewish, Christian, and Muslim fundamentalisms share a common process whereby they arrive at a world-view. This process is dynamic, but occurs within a closed system.
- The elements of this system are core beliefs, religious language, lay and systematic theologies, and a unified world-view.
- Fundamentalisms also share common approaches to various belief issues. Questions regarding the self, the history of the world, and the place of the individual within it; the nature of causality; the nature of relationship with God; life and death; and social institutions, are all addressed in similar ways.
- Crucial to these beliefs are core beliefs in the supernatural, the holy book, and the threat of destruction; the dualist nature of fundamentalist thinking; and the internal rationality of their belief system.
- However, differences between fundamentalisms were also noted. These include the relative importance attached to acceptance of doctrinal belief and to obedience to God's law; the relative importance of the individual and the collective; and the justification of the distinction between the spiritual and the temporal.
- Finally, the apparent contradiction between rigid orthodox belief within a closed system and the evident successful adaptation of fundamentalisms to their social environment was addressed.
- It was argued that the closed system was in fact generative of new beliefs which can motivate and justify changing strategies and tactics.

## Further reading

Armstrong, K. (2000a) *The Battle for God: Fundamentalism in Judaism, Christianity, and Islam.* London: HarperCollins.

Boone, K.C. (1989) *The Bible Tells Them So: The Discourse of Protestant Fundamentalism.* New York: University of New York Press.

Boyer, P. (1992) *When Time Shall Be No More: Prophetic Belief in Modern American Culture.* Cambridge, MA: Harvard University Press.

Bruce, S. (2000) *Fundamentalism.* Cambridge: Polity Press.

Carpenter, J.A. (1997) *Revive Us Again: The Reawakening of American Fundamentalism.* New York: Oxford University Press.

Harding, S.F. (2000) *The Book of Jerry Falwell: Fundamentalist Language and Politics.* Princeton, NJ: Princeton University Press.

Hood, R.W., Hill, P.C., & Williamson, W.P. (2005) *The Psychology of Religious Fundamentalism.* New York: Guilford.

Tickle, P.A. (1997) *God Talk in America.* New York: Crossroad.

## CASE STUDY: RECONSTRUCTIONISM: THE THEOLOGY OF DOMINION

*Formal theologies contribute to fundamentalists' world-views, often as inter-preted for them by preachers or teachers. The Reformist Protestant reconstruc-tionist movement boasts a detailed theology characterised by its internal consistency. Like other fundamentalist theologies, it holds tight to certain core beliefs: in the supernatural realm, in the authority of the holy book, and in the threat to its continued existence. These beliefs serve to re-inforce its dualist dogma, according to which everyone else is in the wrong, holding a worldly rather than a godly world-view. Like the Islamic radicals, their hostility to the rest of the world results in a strategy of assault, although their dominion is to be acquired by political rather than violent means. The case study demonstrates the power of belief systems to re-inforce the reactionary and hostile activities of some fundamentalists.*

### Reconstructionism: An introduction

Systematic theology is an important element within the process model of fundamentalist belief formation (see Fig. 2, p. 198). It demonstrates how, within the closed system of fundamentalist belief, a coherent and rational account can be given once the system's core assumptions have been accepted. Moreover, it provides a structure that prevents lay theology from straying too far from orthodoxy. It also makes explicit the assumptions upon which the system is based, thus allowing the believer to reflect upon his or her faith. It re-inforces, and is re-inforced by, the religious language that is the engine for both lay and systematic theologies. And finally, it contributes powerfully to statements of world-view, which, again, believers may not have formulated explicitly.

*Reconstructionism* is a systematic Protestant Reformed theology developed in America in the latter part of the twentieth century. It perfectly exemplifies the capacity of the closed fundamentalist belief process to produce internally consistent doctrine that informs a totally dualist world-view. In order to give a flavour of reconstructionism, I will first quote a brief popular polemic account, before exploring the theology in greater detail:

> What is a world and life view? Simply stated, it is the way that one views the world and life as it exists in and around humanity. It is the way one views reality. Every person living has a world and life view. He may or may not be conscious of that view, but he lives his life in accord with that view. Either he sees God as totally sovereign in every sphere of life and every part of the world, or he makes man sovereign in some or all spheres of life. The two views are antithetical ... The Reformed Christian believes that Scripture addresses every area of life. As the late Cornelius Van Til stated, 'The Scripture is authoritative

in every area of life to which it speaks, and it speaks to every area of life.'

(Pugh, undated)

This exhortatory account is a popularisation of some serious theology. Highly academic theologians are responsible for reconstructionism's foundation documents. Its theology may be analysed in terms of certain key emphases, which, taken together, set it apart from the rest of conservative American Christianity. Reconstructionism is, according to one of its proponents (Sandlin, undated, b), Calvinist, Theonomist, Pre-suppositionalist, Post-millennialist, and Dominionist. Other theologies have some of these features; only reconstructionism has them all. The following, over-simplified, account hopefully succeeds in defining these five recondite terms, and in separating out their key elements from the abundant theological detail available in the lengthy foundation texts.

The distinctive feature of reconstructionist theology is that it pushes various propositions about God to their extreme meanings, and then draws a series of binary logical implications from these propositions. These implications are both for the rest of one's doctrinal beliefs and also for the Christian's and the church's behaviour in the economic, social, and political sphere. They are about the whole of life. The system of theology is starkly dualist (Bahnsen, 1987), which enables the implications to follow inexorably from the initial black-and-white assumptions. The believer is presented with a complete and internally coherent world-life view, uncompromising in its stern simplicity.

## Calvinist origins and the presupposition of God's existence

The first of the distinctive features of reconstructionism is that it is *Calvinist*. Calvin, the eminent Reformation writer and activist, emphasised the omnipotence of God (Dowey, 1994). God is in control of events. Individuals do not become saved from their sins because of their own efforts, but only by the grace of God. God chooses them as His followers; they do not choose God. He does all of the work in man's salvation.

God's sovereignty is absolute, and embraces His work in creation, providence, and ethics, as well as in the matter of the sinner's salvation. Hence God reigns now, and will continue to do so, in the end bringing all the nations under His rule. Calvin's emphasis on God's present rule is in marked contrast to much current American Protestant eschatology (doctrine about the last things), which places His reign in the near future. God's present reign means that His people can now enjoy the benefits of their relationship with their heavenly father who has chosen them as His children.

In addition to the sovereignty of God, Calvin also emphasised the importance of the Bible as the only authoritative source for belief and action. This principle of '*sola scriptura*' was, of course, in marked contrast to the authority of Mother Church, i.e. Roman Catholicism. It also went beyond the doctrines

Calvin                    © Hulton-Deutsch Collection/Corbis

of the more moderate Reformists, against whom Calvin was also in rebellion. Calvin's Biblical centrality was echoed by the theologian Cornelius Van Til, the father of reconstructionism. He affirmed that the Bible was the sole authority for belief and practice, and that there was no issue that it did not address.

Furthermore, Calvin emphasised the fundamental unity of scripture. He maintained that Christ's work in redeeming mankind, and establishing a new covenant of mankind with God, did not cancel out the old covenant with Israel as described in the Old Testament. Rather, the covenant with the patriarchs is so much like ours in substance and reality that the two are actually one and the same. It followed, therefore, that the sanctions against breaking the covenant with Israel described in the Old Testament are equally applicable in the Christian era. God, said Calvin, controls history just as He always has done. He causes His chosen people to prosper materially and spiritually when they obey His covenant; and He disciplines them when they break it so that they are brought back to the way of obedience. Covenants are between God and individuals, families, churches, and nations.

However, it was Calvin's actions as much as his preaching and writing that influenced reconstructionist theology. He organised the governance of the church and of the city of Geneva entirely according to Biblical principles (Naphy, 1994). These, as selectively interpreted by Calvin, were extremely strict: plays were banned, and psalms were sung in taverns. The Bible should be the sole basis, he argued, for church organisation, political organisation, and civil society itself. This insistence on God's sovereignty over every human institution forms the basis for another of reconstructionist theology's distinctive features, that of theonomy. Moreover, Calvin's active involvement in the governance of church and society inspired the Puritans of the Massachusetts Bay colony in their establishment of a theocratic society. The Puritans made profanation of the Sabbath, blasphemy, fornication, drunkenness, playing games of chance, and theatrical performances penal offences. These Calvinist colonists are major heroes in reconstructionist mythology, and are regarded as the spiritual forefathers of the true American Reformed church. Ever since the first generation of settlers, Reformed Christians believe, 'declension' (decline) has set in, and God's covenant has increasingly been broken.

Thus the first defining feature of reconstructionist theology, its Calvinist origins, provided it with an overwhelming sense of the sovereignty of God; a belief in the Bible as the sole authority in matters of doctrine and practice; and a relationship with God expressed as a covenant that God would always keep, but which his people frequently betrayed. However, Calvinism is but one of reconstructionism's defining features. The second is the reconstructionist insistence on the pre-supposition of God's existence.

*Pre-suppositionalism* is primarily the theological contribution of Cornelius Van Til. It takes Calvinist belief in the sovereign God of the Bible to its extreme logical limits. God is the creator of everything, runs the argument, and therefore His existence is the pre-supposition, the starting point, of the Christian world-view. Thus there is no point in seeking to argue for God's existence. It is a given, a foundation on which everything else is based. Either the individual, as a Christian keeper of God's covenant, holds a world-view based on this pre-supposition, or else he or she holds a false world-view founded upon human (and therefore sinful) pre-suppositions. Every world-view has its unquestioned and its unquestionable assumptions, its primitive commitments. Religious debate is always a question of ultimate authority (Van Til, 1976). Hence the traditional theological occupation of seeking to persuade a neutral agnostic to believe in God's existence (known as Christian apologetics) is misplaced. There is no such thing as neutrality. Rather, everyone knows God. Some, the covenant keepers, know Him and love Him; others, the covenant breakers, know Him and hate Him, rejecting His claim to sovereignty over their lives. The task is not one of rational persuasion, but rather of seeking to convict covenant breakers of their sin and urging their repentance. The true Reformed Christian is not involved in a discussion, but rather in a *conflict* between two opposing world-views.

According to Van Til, there are two forms of logic; God's divine logic and man's natural logic. While man believes that, for example, it is logically impossible for God to be both one person and three persons at the same time, this may be perfectly feasible in God's logic: 'Because man is unable to resolve a contradiction does not mean that God has the same inability. Because God is consistent with himself, man must be consistent, not fundamentally with man or with logic, but with God'. Indeed, the very existence of logic is proof of God's existence: 'The only proof for the existence of God is that without God you couldn't prove anything . . . Unbelievers can count, but they cannot account for counting'. Thus, when someone objects that there seems to be a certain circularity in this position, the reply comes back that the objection itself is proof of the existence of God! As Van Til (1976) says:

> I cannot even argue for belief in Him, without already having taken Him for granted. And similarly, I contend that you cannot argue against belief in Him unless you also first take Him for granted. Arguing about God's existence, I hold, is like arguing about air. You may affirm that air exists, and I that it does not. But as we both debate the point, we are both breathing air all the time.

There is obviously no point of dialogue with this theology. Either you are for God (and therefore us), or you are against Him/us. If the latter, then your unbelief is culpable, because you know Him but have rejected Him as sovereign lord and creator, and broken His covenant:

> Not believing in God, we have seen, you do not think yourself to be God's creature . . . Now if you actually are God's creature, then your present attitude is very unfair to Him. In that case it is even an insult to Him. And having insulted God, His displeasure rests upon you. God and you are not on 'speaking terms'. And you have very good reasons for trying to prove that He does not exist. If He does exist, He will punish you for your disregard of Him.
>
> (Van Til, 1976)

Thus any denial of reconstructionists' theological position ('God's truth') re-affirms the original us vs. you dichotomy. This antithesis is ordained by God, and therefore the continuing conflict between two opposing world-views is inevitable. 'The God-ordained "enmity" between belief and unbelief . . . cannot ever be successfully overcome' (Van Til, 1976).

The second distinctive feature of reconstructionism, then – presuppositionalism – adds emphasis to the Calvinist doctrine of God's sovereignty. Because He is lord of everything, there is no point in reasoned argument to seek to persuade others of God's claims. Rather, they are already rebels against Him, and there is inevitable and permanent conflict between the Biblical Christian world-view and the secular and sinful human world-view, the only two alternatives on offer. Of course, the Biblical Christian world-view is dualistic, as it assumes the existence of an opposing world-view.

## Theonomy and dominion

The belief in *theonomy*, the supremacy of the law of God, is the third distinctive feature of reconstructionism. It follows logically from the Calvinist emphasis on the Bible as the sole source of authoritative knowledge, and from the assumption of God's sovereignty over everything. If God is sovereign, then justice is to be found in His law, not in human law. Justice is not inherent in man after his fall from his initial innocence. Justice is found in the revelation of God Almighty. And that revelation of God and His law exists only in the Bible. Civil law, on the other hand, is a human creation, and therefore by definition sinful and derived from a secular world-view. Such notions as natural law, even though used by Calvin himself, are inadmissible. As for the idea of social contract, it is dismissed as the sinful product of Enlightenment philosophy.

As Rousas J. Rushdoony, the major proponent of theonomy puts it:

> Law is the will of the sovereign for his subjects. Thus Law represents the word of the God of the society. Now whose Law you have, He is your God. So if Washington makes our laws, Washington is our God. As Christians we cannot believe that. For centuries, God's law has functioned wherever God's people have been, whether in Israel or in Christendom. This is a new and modern thing that we turn to the state's law.
>
> (Rushdoony, undated)

The hostility to the state typical of the Christian Right in general is clearly demonstrated. Moreover, the virtuous covenant keepers are set against the sinful covenant breakers once again, since God's law is in fact His covenant with His people. To quote Rushdoony:

> The second characteristic of Biblical law is that it is a treaty or covenant ... The full covenant summary, the Ten Commandments, was inscribed on each of the two tables of stone, one table or copy of the treaty for each party in the treaty, God and Israel.
>
> (Rushdoony, 1973, p. 6)

The 'us' versus 'them' dualism is expressed as usual in the forceful terms of warfare:

> In brief, every law-order is a state of war against the enemies of that order, and all law is a form of warfare. Every law declares that certain

offenders are enemies of the law-order and must be arrested. For limited offences, there are limited penalties; for capital offences, capital punishment. Law is a state of war; it is the organisation of the powers of civil government to bring the enemies of the law-order to justice . . . Peace with God means warfare with the enemies of God. Christ made clear that allegiance to Him meant a sword of division (Matthew 10.34–36). In a sinful world, some warfare is inescapable. A man must therefore pick his enemies: God or sinful man? If a man is at peace with sinful men, he is at war with God.

(Rushdoony, 1973, p. 781)

Those who disobey God's laws have to be punished, whereas those who keep them will be blessed:

... God promises blessings both spiritual and material for those who, in the long term, obey His statutes. Through this inheritance of blessing, God multiplies and increases His covenant people, so that in turn, they may advance His purposes on earth. Just as crucial to understand is that within the same covenantal structures, God promises negative sanctions both spiritual and material for those who, in the long term, transgress and mock His Law. Thus through the covenantal curse, the wicked are disinherited in history. Through this dynamic of blessing and negative sanctions, the righteous accrue dominion in the earth.

(Ziegler, undated)

And what are these sanctions? They are, of course, those decreed in the Bible, including those in the Old Testament:

We want all moral laws of the Old Testament to be enforced according to biblical standards. Some may object: Isn't this harsh? Isn't this barbaric? No, in fact it will lead to greater liberty for the godly. We want the ungodly punished according to God's Law-Word because it is what God prescribes. We have been conditioned according to a humanistic world-view to reject Old Testament law as 'barbaric' or 'outdated'. God's law is not harsh, barbaric nor antiquated, because God is neither harsh, barbaric nor antiquated!

(Rogers, undated)

As God is unchangeable, runs the reconstructionist argument, and as He is revealed in the Bible as a whole, then the whole of the Bible expresses His nature and His law. The possibility that the Bible represents a developing view over time of the nature of God is not entertained. 'Theonomic ethics encourages the application of the whole word of God, including the Old Testament law (when properly interpreted and allowing for certain New Testament emendations) to the modern situation' (Gentry, 1997). Reconstructionists argue against the mainstream Protestant belief that sinners are saved by grace from the condemnation of the law. They certainly are saved by grace, the reconstructionists reply, but they are only sanctified by obedience to that law. They quote the reported words of Christ: 'Think not that I am come to destroy the law or the prophets: I am not come to destroy, but to fulfil [translated by reconstructionists as "confirm"]. For verily I say unto you, till heaven and earth pass, one jot or one tittle shall in no wise pass from the law, till all be fulfilled' (Matthew 5.17–18). The only parts of the Old Testament law that do not apply to Christians today are those ceremonial aspects of Judaism, which were types, or symbols, of Christ and which therefore became obsolete in the Christian era. The Old Testament civil code, however, which was binding on the Jews, is part of the moral law of God, and must be obeyed (Bahnsen, 1991). It is not only relevant to the situation of the people of Israel, but is universally applicable.

The implications of this assertion for the social, economic, and political institutions of state and society will be explored later (using a specific example, psychological counselling). It remains to examine what reconstructionists believe to be the functions of God's law:

> God's law is used for three main purposes: First, to drive the sinner to trust in Christ alone, the only perfect law-keeper. Second, to provide a standard of obedience for the Christian, by which he may judge his progress in sanctification. And third, to maintain order in society, restraining and arresting civil evil.
>
> (Sandlin, undated, b)

Or again:

> The law, then, first asserts principles, second, it cites cases to develop the implications of those principles, and third, the law has as its purpose and direction the restitution of God's order.
>
> (Rushdoony, 1973)

And that divine order must be restored everywhere. It is the divinely inspired foundation for personal ethics, civil morality, and free-market economics (Gentry, 1997):

> Revival and reformation are the consistent and persistent application of God's Law Word to all spheres of life. Biblical revival leads first to a return of doctrinal orthodoxy and fidelity to the Law of God. As a result of this 'reviving', conviction of sin and the public destruction of idolatry coextensive throughout society is evidenced. Finally a reconstruction of culture or Christian civilisation is erected, leading to national blessing, peace and prosperity.
>
> (Ziegler, undated)

Which brings us on to the fourth distinctive feature of reconstructionism, *dominionism*. Christians are mandated to exercise God's dominion. Clearly, if the sovereign Biblical God's law is binding on all humankind, it is His followers' duty to fight the battle against the enemy that rejects it.

Dominionism is defined as follows:

> The Christian Reconstructionist believes the earth and all its fullness is the Lord's: that every area dominated by sin must be 'reconstructed' in terms of the Bible. This includes, first, the individual; second, the family; third, the church; and fourth, the wider society, including the state. The Christian Reconstructionist therefore believes fervently in Christian civilisation. He firmly believes in the separation of church and state, but not the separation of the state or anything else from God. He is not a revolutionary; he does not believe in the militant, forced overthrow of human government. He has infinitely more powerful weapons than guns and bombs, he has the invincible Spirit of God, the infallible word of God, and the incomparable gospel of God, none of which can fail. He presses the crown rights of the Lord Jesus Christ in every sphere, expecting eventual triumph.
>
> (Sandlin, undated, a)

It is just as well that this statement stresses the absence of militancy, as some of the claims for dominion have a distinctly war-like tone:

> Christians have an obligation, a mandate, a commission, a holy responsibility to reclaim the land for Jesus Christ – to have dominion in the civil structures, just as in every other aspect of life and godliness. But it is dominion that we are after, not just a voice. It is dominion we are after, not just influence. It is dominion we are after, not just equal time. It is dominion we are after. World conquest. That's what Christ has commissioned us to accomplish. We must win the world with the power of the Gospel. And we must never settle for anything less ... Thus, Christian politics has as its primary intent the conquest of the land – of men, families, institutions, bureaucracies, courts, and governments for the Kingdom of Christ.
>
> (Grant, 1987, pp. 50–51)

However, we can rest assured that this will all happen in a thoroughly democratic way:

> You may ask, in a biblically reconstructed society: Who will be able to vote? Who will be able to rule? Elections will still be determined by popular vote of the people and legislation will still be voted on by representatives. Communities will have been reconstructed through personal regeneration so that the majority of the electorate will be Christian or

will hold to a 'Christian philosophy'. Therefore, the only people qualified to rule will be professing Christians who will uphold the moral law of God. This may be called a 'theonomic representative democracy' or a 'theocratic republic'.

(Rogers, undated)

The important emphasis, and one that has been part of Reformed theology ever since Calvin, is on the transformation of the structures of society, rather than of the individual only. 'Man is summoned to create the society that God requires' (Rushdoony, quoted in Duncan, 1994). The specific addition in the reconstructionist account is that this society is governed by Old Testament as well as Christian precepts.

The Church, according to reconstructionists, is the new Israel. God commanded at the beginning of time 'Be fruitful, and multiply, and replenish the earth, and subdue it: and have dominion over the fish of the sea, and over the fowl of the air, and over every living thing that moveth upon the earth' (Genesis 1.28). Man disobeyed God and broke the covenant, as did the nation of Israel later in history. Therefore God passed on the covenant commands and promises to the Church, which, in the reported words of Christ, was told: 'Go ye therefore, and teach all nations, baptising them in the name of the Father and of the Son, and of the Holy Ghost: Teaching them to observe all things whatsoever I have commanded you: and, lo, I am with you always, even unto the end of the world. Amen' (Matthew 28.19–20).

## Post-millennialism: Securing God's kingdom

The Christian's task, then, is to wrest control of the world back from Satan. God is sovereign, but His sovereignty is challenged by sinful man. When the church has succeeded in this mission, Christ's millennial rule on earth can begin, and all will be theocratic liberty, justice, and peace. Which brings us on to the fifth and final distinctive feature of Reconstructionism, its *post-millennial* eschatology.

American Protestant eschatology is a theological minefield. Many different accounts of the last days are eagerly disputed by millions of protagonists (Boyer, 1992). Recondite arguments of excruciating detail are pursued daily on the internet. The key distinction for our purposes is that between dispensational pre-millennialism and post-millennialism. The former was the dominant account during the twentieth century, but is being vigorously challenged by the post-millennial reconstructionists. In drastically simplified terms, pre-millennialists believe that human history is divided up into dispensations, or eras. Mankind is now in the church era, which is radically different from the previous era as a result of Christ's redemption of mankind. Various prophetic signs indicate that the church era is rapidly drawing to a close. True Christians will be raptured up into heaven to be with Christ, and the rest of the world will suffer horrendously before, in the end, Christ returns to rule on earth for the millennium.

The implication of this unusual set of beliefs was that Christians' duty in this sinful world was to be sanctified and separate; a strategy of withdrawal. However, they should seek to convert as many as possible, with the objective that more will avoid the dire consequences of being 'left behind' when Christ comes to rapture the faithful into heaven. The Christian's task, then, was to concentrate on evangelism and witness, especially one-to-one contact with sinners. It was not to change the world, since history is entirely under God's control. And before the millennial rule of Christ occurs, that history is going to be horrific.

This pre-millennial position is clearly unacceptable to reconstructionists for a variety of reasons. They stress the continuity of God's covenant across the Old and New Testament, not a major break between pre-Christian and Christian eras. They also want Christians to reconstruct the institutions of the world as God's agents, rather than leave it entirely to the Almighty. They want to be victorious on God's behalf, rather than defeatist in the face of secular dominance and fatalistic about the sufferings of the end times. Post-millennialism is therefore a much more appropriate eschatology for them, since it asserts that most of the biblical prophecies that are taken by pre-millennialists to foretell the end of the world have in fact already been ful-filled. Christ's kingdom is being advanced by his faithful followers now, and He will return in glory after they have reclaimed the world for Himself.

Not only does the post-millennial account serve to motivate adherents in general with its appeal to American optimism and activism, it also gained prominence, together with the rest of reconstructionist doctrine, at just that time when Republican strategists sought to marshal Christian conservatives to fight the 'culture wars' of the 1980s. The relationship between ideologies and the movements they support is certainly complex, but at the very least, this was a fruitful coincidence, which has formed the basis for the dominionist thrust of the Christian Right ever since.

## Reconstructionism and radical Islam

To sum up the argument proposed by the reconstructionists: The super-natural God of the biblical account exists, and there is no need to argue for His existence. It is simply a pre-supposition, which is in fact made by every-one. Indeed, the biblical God not only exists, but is sovereign over every aspect of life. The Bible as a whole reveals God to man, and is the sole authority concerning God's demands regarding belief and practice. Everyone knows God; some have rejected Him and broken His covenant with them; others have accepted Him and kept it. These are the only two categories of person, and they hold entirely incompatible world-views. Covenant keepers must acknowledge God's reign in every aspect of life. They must therefore follow His law as revealed in the Bible in their personal, family, church, and civil activities. Moreover, they must struggle with covenant breakers in order to assert His reign over every societal structure.

This theological position is an archetypal example of religious fundamentalism. First, reconstructionists are without doubt *reacting* against modernity. They hark back to the Puritans and the Reformation as times when God's law was obeyed. They view the Enlightenment as a key instance of human rebellion against God. Second, they see the world in *dualistic* terms, with God's people (themselves) as good, and everyone else as sinful. Third, they place such authority in the *holy text* that they allow no external factors to that text to affect their belief and practice. These include science and philosophy. Fourth, they are *selective* in the parts of the holy text to which they give doctrinal weight. For example, their doctrine of the requirements of the law as continuing largely unchanged despite Christ's redemptive work depends on a contentious selection of disputed texts. Finally, they have a strong *millennialist* element to their belief, permitting them to try to hasten the coming of Christ.

In terms of the model of fundamentalist belief process (see Fig. 2), it is clear that two core beliefs underpin reconstructionist theology: belief in a supernatural sovereign God, and attribution of final authority on every matter to the holy book. Biblical language permeates their discourse.

It is informative, and doubtless disturbing, to point up the eerie similarities between the reconstructionists and the radical Muslim clerics, Abu Mawdudi and Sayeed Qutb, whose ideas are the inspiration for today's militant Islamists (see Chapter 6). Mawdudi and Qutb created an ideology that pointed up as starkly as possible the difference between faith and secularism. Both advocated action against the secular enemy, in an effort to establish a theocracy. And both treated the Qu'ran as their justification, selectively redefining some of its concepts to justify conquering the evil world for God, rather than waging the struggle within the believer's own life or in defence of the faith.

Like the reconstructionists, the two Islamic clerics believed that the theocratic state offers perfect liberty:

> Islamic jihad does not seek to interfere with the faith, ideology, rituals of worship or social customs of the people. It allows them perfect freedom of religious belief and permits them to act according to their creed. However, Islamic jihad does not recognise their right to administer state affairs according to a system which, in the view of Islam, is evil. Furthermore, Islamic jihad also refuses their right to continue with practices under an Islamic government which fatally affect the public interest from the viewpoint of Islam.

> (Mawdudi, 1976, p. 28)

Qutb emphasised the implacable hostility between God and his (radical Islamic) followers and all human systems. In almost identical language to that of Van Til and Rushdoony, he wrote:

This religion is really a universal declaration of the freedom of man from servitude to other men and from servitude to their own desires, which is also a form of human servitude; it is a declaration that sovereignty belongs to God alone and that he is the Lord of all the worlds. It means a challenge to all kinds and forms of systems which are based on the sovereignty of man; in other words, where man has usurped the Divine attribute . . . In short, to proclaim the authority and sovereignty of God means to eliminate all human kingship and to announce the rule of the Sustainer of the Universe over the entire earth.

(Qutb, 1981, Chapter 4)

Both reconstructionists and radical Islamists believe themselves to be the only true followers of the Almighty who are obedient to his law. Everyone else falls into the category of apostate or unbeliever. Both groups therefore set themselves against the rest of the world, struggling to bring victory for divine sovereignty and law. To quote Gary North, a prominent reconstructionist:

The battle for the mind, some fundamentalists believe, is between fundamentalism and the institutions of the Left. This conception of the battle is fundamentally incorrect. The battle for the mind is between the Christian reconstruction movement, which alone among Protestant groups takes seriously the law of God, and everyone else.

(North, 1984, pp. 65–66)

What, then, are the detailed implications for everyday life of 'taking seriously the law of God'?

## A godly psychology

What would a reconstructionist nation look like? Would it be a replica of Calvin's Geneva or the Pilgrim Fathers' Massachusetts Bay Colony, with their stern Puritan governments? Would psalms be compulsory in taverns? Much popular attention has been directed towards the reconstructionists' recommendations regarding crime and punishment, which follow the Old Testament Judaic law. The stoning to death of incorrigible children, as recommended in the book of Deuteronomy (Chapters 17–22) is hardly likely to attract much support, even from their parents, despite Einwechter's (2003) advocacy for capital punishment of disobedient juveniles. However, the more important issue relates to the remorseless logic with which they pursue the implications of their core beliefs into every facet of modern life. The dominion mandate is to win every human institution for God.

To illustrate how this mandate is planned in detail in the case of even relatively minor societal institutions, I will consider the recommendations of the Coalition on Revival, a prominent dominionist pressure group, regarding the future of psychology and counselling. Psalms in taverns are to yield place to salvation by psychology. These recommendations clearly demonstrate the implications of dominionists' theological dualism for their practical pro-grammes. There are no concessions to the notion that there are different stakeholders involved in the modern professional-client relationship. Rather, professional practice is yet another arena in which the battle between God and secularism is to be fought out to the finish. To quote Scipione, Crabbe, and Payne (1989):

> Psychology and counselling, at their core, deal with the nature of man. What a practitioner does is inextricably bound to his system of assump-tions. Counselling theory and practice are by nature deeply theological. It is impossible to help people without implementing theological beliefs.
>
> Thus the Christian counsellor faces two demands. First, he must begin with the Word of God and a consistent grammatical, historical, and theological interpretation of it. He must not move from the study of man and his social context back to the Bible. A systematic understanding of the Word of God is his standard, not man and his social context.
>
> Second, his methodology must be consistent with a theological inter-pretation of man and man's social context. He cannot choose, or allow his counselee to choose, goals – or methods to achieve those goals – that violate Biblical principles.

But the Bible is not merely the source of the counsellor's theology. It is also his or her text book for professional practice:

> We affirm that the Bible gives specific practical directions for one's rela-tionship with God, others, and oneself, and that anything not specifically mentioned can be dealt with by Biblical principles correctly applied to the issues by deduction.
>
> We deny that any knowledge derived outside the Bible is necessary for the counsellor to complete his task of dealing with non-organically based problems, although it may be of supplementary value [it seems that the reconstructionists baulk at deriving the principles of brain surgery from the Bible]. Rather, the subject matter of counselling is precisely the same as that of the Bible and, therefore, the Bible completely equips us with the theory and principles of counselling.
>
> (Scipione et al., 1989)

Given that the mandate according to their interpretation of the Bible is to win over individuals and institutions for God, the counselee's perceptions are irrelevant:

> We deny that the counselee's perception of reality or his situation, unless that perception is Biblically accurate, has any bearing on the direction of

counselling except to be identified, explored, understood, and corrected by his counsellor.

(Scipione et al., 1989)

And how should his perceptions be corrected? There can be no other answer than by God's salvation:

We affirm that man's greatest concerns, not only for this life but also for eternity, should be to be regenerated by the Holy Spirit and to be forgiven through the sacrificial work of Jesus Christ. We deny that any other concern is measurable in comparison, and that counsellors may avoid evangelising their unsaved counselees ... the ultimate goal for all counselees is to be conformed to Christ's image.

(Scipione et al., 1989)

The process of correction will, of course, be a scene of spiritual struggle with the forces of darkness:

We affirm that creatures who have only a spiritual dimension exist, that some serve God faithfully (angels) and others are in active rebellion against God (demons), and that the latter may possess unregenerate persons and oppress or influence regenerate persons.

(Scipione et al., 1989)

The Christian counselee is in particular peril from such demons as those of homosexuality and alcoholism, and their need for repentance is urgent. Indeed, 'the several steps of church discipline are necessary for Christian counselees who fail to repent'. What is more, the Christian counselee cannot rely on the confidentiality of his dealings with the counsellor:

We affirm that Biblical authority within the family, the church, and the state may supersede the confidentiality of counsellors, but that strict confidentiality should be maintained when it does not conflict with Biblical mandates.

(Scipione et al., 1989)

These recommendations appear to conflict in several particulars with the code of practice of the American Psychological Association (APA). Clearly, however, the APA is a secular professional organisation, and therefore 'the enemy'. Instead, the document concludes with recommendations to purge the psychology and counselling departments of colleges and seminaries of all professors who fail to uphold 'the view of man, morality, and reality taught by the Bible'. All new appointees to such faculties should have to answer a questionnaire to ensure that they hold a biblical world-view, and agree with a statement of biblical inerrancy.

# 8 Fundamentalist values and attitudes

## Values and value systems

### *Values versus attitudes*

In the account of organisational culture in Chapter 4, I described Hatch's (1997) model (see Fig. 1, p. 114). This dynamic model suggested that basic organisational assumptions and beliefs generate values and attitudes, and thence behaviour and its outcomes, some of which achieve symbolic meanings. These then feed back into the belief system.

I will argue that, in similar fashion, the three basic beliefs of fundamentalists – that their faith is threatened by secular forces, that their sovereign and supernatural God constantly intervenes at the personal and societal level, and that their holy book tells them all they need to know about every aspect of their lives – inform the values and attitudes that they hold, and the actions in which they engage. Those actions and their outcomes then gain symbolic meaning, and feed back into their beliefs. Their values, attitudes, and norms of behaviour derive from their beliefs, and are part of their world-view (see Fig. 2, p. 196).

First, however, I need to establish the importance of *values and attitudes* to fundamentalist world-views, and then to distinguish between these two constructs. It is a historical fact that disagreements over the contents of religious beliefs have resulted in wars and persecutions, schisms and sects. Clearly, religious belief is not a dry intellectual exercise, but rather an activity that arouses the strongest emotions. Social psychologists have long maintained that such emotions are the expression of people's evaluations of all sorts of 'objects': beliefs, outcomes, social institutions, categories of person, and so on.

Most psychological research has distinguished simply between positive and negative evaluations. However, recent attempts have been made to associate particular emotions with particular beliefs (e.g. Mackie & Hamilton, 1993). So, for example, the belief that secular forces are threatening one's faith might lead to fear or anger, while the belief that homosexuals are breaking God's natural and holy law might result in disgust and contempt. The particular emotion aroused will affect the nature of the action that is contemplated: fear and anger may stimulate aggressive behaviour, whereas disgust and contempt might lead to avoidance.

However, the attempts to associate particular emotional responses with the 'objects' of evaluation are not yet well developed. What is generally accepted is the distinction between *beliefs* on the one hand, and *values and attitudes* on the other. The former refer to cognitions that something is true, whereas the latter always contain an evaluative component. Neither beliefs nor intentions are necessarily always present in the mind when an attitude is expressed (Fazio & Olson, 2003). The single defining feature of values and attitudes, then, is their evaluative component, positive or negative.

But what is *the distinction between values and attitudes*, and is it a justifiable and useful one? Both constructs refer to the evaluation of 'objects'. However, 'value' refers to a limited range of objects, whereas 'attitude' implies no such constraints. The only limitation to the number of attitudes is the number of 'objects' which individuals can distinguish and retain in their minds. In his classic research on values, Rokeach (1973, p. 5) proposed the following definition:

> 'A *value* is an enduring belief that a specific mode of conduct or end-state of existence is personally or socially preferable to an opposite or converse mode of conduct or end-state of existence. A *value system* is an enduring organisation of beliefs concerning preferable modes of conduct or end-states of existence along a continuum of relative importance.'

Note that Rokeach uses the term 'belief' in his definition, whereas it is the *evaluative* feature that is definitive. Values concern, above all, our standards: what we think ideally *ought* to be true, and what we would *prefer* to be the case.

### Rokeach on values

Rokeach refers to modes of conduct as *instrumental* values, and end-states of existence as *terminal* values, making the familiar philosophical distinction between means and ends. He maintains that both types of value are ideals. For example, each value is likely to be presented to children as an absolute: you should always be honest or obedient (instrumental values), children are told, or you should always aim for happiness or salvation (terminal values).

However, the messy business of taking action in complex social situations generally makes it difficult to maintain individual ideals. Different values seem to point to different solutions: pleasure and salvation notoriously conflict! However, the existence of a value *system* helps to alleviate such conflict. The basic feature of value systems is that they are organised into orders of priority, so in situations where values conflict, the values that the individual believes to be more important carry greater weight.

Rokeach argues for a cap on the number of possible values. He claims that the relatively limited number of basic human needs puts an upper limit on the number of values. Values, Rokeach affirms, are the cognitive transformations and justifications of needs, so that, as he charmingly puts it (1973, p. 20), 'a person can end up smelling himself, and being smelled by others, like a rose'. Further, we can only maintain in our minds a certain range of principles when we are seeking to guide and motivate our conduct, or to rationalise and justify it after it has occurred.

This does not imply, of course, that all our values are brought into play in any given situation. Rather, related clusters of values become activated in different social situations. For example, the statistical procedure of factor analysis revealed as the second most important factor in the sample of around 1400 Americans one that they labelled 'competence versus religious morality'. In this factor, the values 'logical', 'imaginative', 'intellectual', and 'independent' loaded positively, and 'forgiving', 'salvation', 'helpful', and 'clean' negatively.

Thus Rokeach's account fits admirably into the social identity theoretical framework that has informed this book. The value clusters that are activated in a social situation are those of that particular social identity that is salient in the situation. We might expect the social identity of believer to be salient in the fundamentalist's mind in most social situations, and therefore particular values to be activated; for example, the terminal value of salvation, and the instrumental value of obedient.

Rokeach boldly goes on to specify sets of 18 terminal and 18 instrumental values, which he claims to be relatively lasting and universal. Cultural differences, he argues, are in terms of value priorities rather than of the actual identity of the values held. Among the universal terminal values are an exciting life, a world at peace, equality, freedom, happiness, salvation, self-respect, social recognition, true friendship, and wisdom. Among the instrumental values are ambitious, clean, courageous, honest, independent, loving, obedient, polite, and self-controlled.

The research instrument employed by Rokeach was ordinal and ipsative: the task was for each individual to 'arrange them [the value sets] in order of importance to YOU, as guiding principles in YOUR life'. As Rokeach noted, the far more sophisticated methodology available for measuring attitudes has tended to downgrade the importance of values in social psychological research. However, where world-views are explicitly expressed and justified, as is the case with fundamentalisms, we would expect value systems to be of great psychological importance.

Indeed, there are tantalising hints from Rokeach's research regarding fundamentalist values. For example, the value 'salvation' has the highest test-retest reliability of any of the 36 values. In other words, respondents were less likely to change over time the ranked importance of this value than that of any other. Baptists, usually agreed to be towards the fundamentalist end of the Christian denominations, ranked salvation third on average, whereas other denominations ranked it between ninth and fourteenth, and non-believers and Jews rated it last. Those who attended church more frequently, and who rated religion as more important in their daily life, also ranked salvation, family security, helpful, and obedient more highly than did other respondents (Rokeach, 1969).

There is little other evidence on fundamentalist *values*, although inferences can be drawn from their leaders' writings. For example, Lienesch (1993) concluded that American Protestant fundamentalist leaders put a high priority on salvation, family security, obedient, and national security. Salvation, family security, and obedient also shine out from the Islamic writings of Mawdudi and Qutb. And salvation, national security, and obedience permeate the discourse of Jewish fundamentalists.

There is, on the other hand, a vast amount of evidence about fundamentalist *attitudes*, although nearly all of it has been conducted on American Protestants. Before reviewing this evidence, I will summarise the *distinction between values and attitudes*.

### Values versus attitudes again

First, values are considered to be *limited in number*, whereas attitudes are limited only by the number of attitude 'objects' that individuals can comprehend. Second, values are *psychologically more fundamental*: they concern more general principles, regulate attitudes towards a range of objects, and refer to long-term goals. They are apt to be more long lasting and stable than attitudes. So, for example, a high ranking given to the value of family security by fundamentalists would imply unfavourable attitudes towards feminism, divorce, homosexuality, and towards categories of person who held favourable attitudes regarding these three attitude objects. Attitude objects or evaluations may change, as new sub-cultures become prominent and threatening, but the underlying value will remain highly ranked.

The final distinction between values and attitudes relates to *function*. Recent research on the functions of attitudes suggests that they may serve to *express values*, particularly for those who are less concerned with how they appear socially to others (Maio & Olson, 2000). Those who are more concerned with social acceptance are likely to use attitudes to shape their social behaviour to become appropriate to the situation.

Another function of attitudes is *object appraisal*; that is, we can navigate our physical and social environment rapidly by knowing immediately what our pre-existing attitude is towards any 'object' (Fazio, 2001). So, for example, when presented with an advertisement for a specific sexually explicit film, an attitude is likely to be activated. This will help us to decide whether or not to go to see it. Moreover, we are also likely to respond with a more general category into which we place the film. For example, we may consider it to be pornography. Alternatively, we may respond by categorising the film as artistically erotic. Our more general attitudes towards these two categories will thus affect our specific attitude towards the film, and inform our decision.

However, there are possible down-sides to these attitudinal short-cuts to decisions. If attitude objects are invariably cast into existing categories towards which the individual has a pre-formed attitude, new and different features of the object may be missed, and new categories fail to be formed (Fazio, Ledbetter, & Towles-Schwen, 2000). If a new biology school textbook is immediately categorised as secular by fundamentalists, then the fact that it is not wholly supportive of evolutionary theory will fail to be appreciated.

Clearly, the psychological functions of values and attitudes differ. *Values* serve to inform and motivate our attitudes and actions, and to rationalise and justify them before and after we have carried them out. *Attitudes* express our value priorities, and provide us with rapid and cognitively economical short cuts to decision and action. The extensive research on American fundamentalist attitudes that I will now review should not deflect attention from the importance of values. Beliefs, values, and attitudes are all intimately related within the fundamentalist sub-culture and social identity.

## Attitudes: The evidence from polls

### *Fundamentalist attitudes: Smith's analysis*

There are two major sources of information regarding fundamentalist Protestant attitudes: the work of *survey organisations* ('pollsters'), and published *academic research*. Each has its own strengths and weaknesses. The attitudes selected for investigation by the pollsters are those that they or their clients find interesting, often the social or political issues of the moment. There exist, however, occasional data regarding the same attitude question asked over several years, thus permitting trends to be examined. Moreover, the size of pollsters' samples and their sophisticated random sampling process are far superior to those of much of the academic research (a lot of which is conducted on students). These advantages permit pollsters to separate out detailed subsets of respondents. The subset of Traditionalist Evangelicals, for example (see p. 203), is selected on criteria that are close to those for categorising a movement as fundamentalist, which I have followed in this book. However, pollsters are less likely to use the term 'fundamentalist' than are academics.

Academic research has the advantage of using questionnaire instruments that are psychometrically sound, having demonstrated adequate reliability and validity. Furthermore, academics tend to distinguish between beliefs, values, and attitudes, whereas all of these psychological constructs may be evidenced within a single poll questionnaire. Finally, academic research is designed to discover the relationships between constructs, whereas pollsters simply seek to describe the attitudes of the population under investigation at a particular moment in time.

However, the information from polls is extensive, technically reliable, and can be further analysed by interested parties. I will review two sets of poll data. The first is the statistical analysis by Smith (2000) of five polls conducted in 1996; the second is a variety of individual polls from the 2000s.

Smith (2000) controlled for the demographic variables of age, gender, educational level, income level, regional location, marital status, and whether respondents lived in the country or the city. He then conducted statistical comparisons of various sub-groups of respondents, in which Protestant sub-groups were compared with each other and with Americans as a whole. The sub-groups are distinguished on the basis of *self-reported category*, e.g. Evangelicals or Fundamentalists, of *denominational membership*, i.e. whether or not they are a member of a theologically conservative denomination, and sometimes of how conservative are their *theological beliefs*. (Note that 'Fundamentalist' and 'Evangelical' here refer to the American meanings of the terms as specific categories of Protestants. It is likely that many members of both these categories are fundamentalist according to the social psychological definition used in this book.)

Results demonstrate statistically significant differences on a range of attitudes between these conservative religious sub-groups, which I will term 'fundamentalists' for convenience, and the American population at large (i.e. the sample), termed 'Americans'.

- Around two-thirds of fundamentalists, but only one-third of Americans, agree that 'morals should be based on an absolute, unchanging standard'.
- Around half of fundamentalists, but only a quarter of Americans, agree that 'Christian morality should be the law of the land, even though not all Americans are Christians'.
- Fundamentalists agree more than Americans that the following groups have too much influence: gay rights groups, liberals, feminists, and atheists.
- Around one-third of fundamentalists, but only one-fifth of Americans, are opposed to homosexuals making a speech in one's community, teaching in a college or university, or having a book which they have authored available in a public library.
- Over a half of fundamentalists would not want a homosexual as a neighbour, whereas only a little over a third of Americans feel the same way.
- Nearly a half of fundamentalists would not want an atheist neighbour, compared to under a third of Americans.
- Around two-thirds of fundamentalists would not vote for a presidential candidate who is atheist or homosexual, whereas only around 40% of Americans would have similar voting intentions.

Smith (2000) argues that these responses do not do justice to the nuances of Evangelicals' attitudes, citing interview research to demonstrate that they are often conflicted on social issues, especially those regarding the role of women, the limits of politics, and the status of other religions. This is what one might expect, given that for many Americans their fundamentalist social identity may be central to their selves, but it is certainly not their only social identity. Only if they interpret the polling situation as an opportunity to witness, or in some other way that makes their fundamentalist identity salient, will their fundamentalist attitudes be uncontaminated by the attitudes associated with other identities. Of course, this theoretical explanation raises the alarming possibility for pollsters that the individual's expression of attitudes may vary depending upon which of their social identities is salient during their conversation with the pollster.

## *Fundamentalist attitudes: Surveys from the 2000s*

During the 2000s, a large number of nation-wide polls have been conducted by such organisations as the Pew Forum, Gallup, and Harris. Overall, there seems to be little overall change in fundamentalist attitudes in comparison to the 1990s. However, specific social issues have arisen, and been investigated, which provide a more nuanced picture. Moreover, Pew and Gallup have made more sophisticated distinctions between groups of conservative Protestants (see pp. 202–203). On the one hand, the percentage of Americans whom Pew Forum (2004) terms 'White Protestant Evangelicals' is 26%, and the sub-category of this group described as 'Traditionalist' still accounts for 13%. Gallup (2005), on the other hand, defines a category of 'Evangelicals' in terms of their adherence to all three of the following beliefs: their duty is to evangelise, the Bible is the actual word of God, and they have had a born-again experience. Of the American population, 22% fulfil these criteria. I will continue to use the term 'fundamentalists' of these categories of either major pollster.

We can summarise the attitude areas that have dominated the polls in the 2000s as concerning governance, pluralism, family, and issues of life and death. In terms of *governance*, the continuing existence of a strong theocratic strand within American fundamentalism is evidenced. When faced in 2006 by the Pew Forum with the question 'Which should have more influence on the laws of the United States – the will of the American people or the Bible?', 60% of fundamentalists responded that it should be the Bible. This compares with 16% of mainline Protestants, and 32% of the American people as a whole.

Associated with the Christian theocracy versus democracy debate is the area of *pluralism*. How do today's fundamentalist Americans respond to immigrants, and those of other religions? How wedded are they to the idea of America as a Christian nation, as exemplified, for example, by their desire to have a public display of Christian symbols? With regard to immigration, 49% say that legal immigration should be decreased, compared to 40% of Americans (Smith, 2006). In terms of the public display of Christian religious symbols, 89% of fundamentalists agree that 'it is important that religious symbols like the Ten Commandments be displayed in public buildings such as court houses', compared to 64% of Americans (Anti-Defamation League, 2005). With regard to other religions than Christianity, less than a third of fundamentalists have a favourable view of Islam, compared with 42% mainline Protestants (Pew Forum, 2005).

In the area of *the family*, the issue of homosexuality has dominated the polls. Longitudinal data regarding gay marriage is available from Pew (2006). Whereas approval among the general public has increased from 27% in 1995 to 39% in 2006, the attitudes of fundamentalists have until 2005 remained fairly consistent at between 12 and 14%. However, in 2006 there was a decrease to 56% from 65% in 2004 in those fundamentalists *strongly* opposed to gay marriage; 45% of fundamentalists agreed in 2004 with the statement 'Homosexuals should have the same rights as other Americans', up from 35% in 1992. The figures for the entire sample were 57% and 51%, respectively. There was little movement between 1999 and 2006 in fundamentalists' favorability towards gay and lesbian adoption (19 and 22%), whereas the approval of Americans in general rose from 38 to 46%. In terms of other issues related to the family, sex education in high schools is favoured by 87% of Americans but 72% of fundamentalists (Harris, 2005), and sexual abstinence before marriage by 63% of Americans but 91% of fundamentalists.

Finally, on issues of *life and death*, the issue of abortion dominated the polls. The following percentages are for those who either believe that abortion should always be illegal, or that it should only be legal in cases of rape, incest, and to save the mother's life: fundamentalists, 68%; Catholics, 43%; all Americans, 40% (Pew Forum, 2005). At the other end of the life-span, 45% of fundamentalists, but 68% of the general public, are in favour of withdrawing life support systems from those in a vegetative state (Harris, 2005).

In summary, the polls of the 1990s and 2000s have shown that fundamentalists have consistently been more theocratic, less pluralist, more concerned to limit sexual activity to heterosexual marriage, and more pro-life in their attitudes than the general American public and than other religious groups.

## Stereotypes and prejudice: Research and theory past and present

### Past understanding of prejudice

The academic research on both religious attitudes in general and fundamentalist ones in particular has tended to concentrate upon one subset of attitudes: *prejudices*. There may be several reasons for this emphasis. The first is the influence of the early history of the psychology of religion, which sometimes tended to accept the Freudian view of religious belief as an immature and neurotic reaction to the experiences of life. Hence those seeking to explain religious belief looked for characteristics of the person that were correlated with degree of attachment to religion. In the area of attitudes, infantile and neurotic tendencies would be likely to be expressed in prejudice, for prejudice was assumed to be an irrational way of expressing fear and rage. Hence religious people would be hypothesised to be more prejudiced than others. Their neurotic personality would predispose them to religion and its prejudiced attitudes.

A second reason for the academic emphasis on prejudice is the general tendency of psychologists to concentrate on individual differences as both independent and dependent variables in their research. The research task then becomes one of establishing the relationships between different theoretical constructs that represent individual differences. The history of research in this tradition is well reviewed by Spilka et al. (2003, pp. 457ff). Whether degree of prejudice is positively related to degree of religiosity was one of the early research issues. When the results were not clear-cut, the question became whether the relationship was linear or curvilinear, with those who were moderately religious perhaps being more prejudiced than those who were extremely so. Then the issue developed into a consideration of religious styles or orientations. Were there some ways of believing that were more associated with prejudice than others? Grave difficulties with the technical qualities of the measures of these religious orientations made progress difficult in answering this question. And at this point, fundamentalism makes its entry into this research literature. It is treated as one of the religious orientations that may be more highly associated with prejudice than others.

Thus in the psychological research literature, fundamentalism is generally defined as an *individual difference*, a particular style or mode of belief. There is little attention to the *social context* from within which the individual develops and applies this orientation. Hence a whole range of potential social context variables tend to be ignored, and theoretical models limited to internal mental constructs. Before I review the research literature in this tradition, however, it is necessary to clarify the concept of prejudice, and its related construct, stereotype.

### Prejudices as functional attitudes

In ordinary language, and indeed in much of past psychological research, the term '*prejudice*' has had a negative meaning. It has been used to refer to *negative* attitudes towards categories of people, and it has been treated as socially and psychologically undesirable. How to understand and then reduce prejudice has been a major pre-occupation, and the implicit objective, of research.

However, more recent definitions of prejudice and stereotypes have been more value-neutral. For example, Wright and Taylor (2003, p. 433) define *stereotypes* as 'the beliefs, shared by members of one group, about the shared characteristics of another group'. *Prejudice* is 'a socially shared judgement or evaluation of the group, including the feelings (affect) associated with that judgement'. Thus, in accordance with these definitions, beliefs that specify the characteristics of another group (stereotypes) are likely to activate evaluations of those characteristics according to one's instrumental value priorities. The overall evaluation of the other group will depend upon whether the preponderance of such evaluations is in the positive or negative direction.

One can, therefore, have positive as well as negative prejudices. They are, literally, 'pre-judgements'; attitudes, whether favourable or unfavourable, which, like other attitudes (see pp. 230–231), enable us to make rapid judgements about attitude 'objects'. In this case, the objects are social objects, other individuals, whom we categorise and evaluate. Rapid judgements of this sort enable us to make immediate social judgements and take immediate social action. They also serve to motivate and justify such action.

For example, I may judge that the people to whom I have just opened my front door are Jehovah's Witnesses. I believe that Jehovah's Witnesses are likely to seek to convert me to their religious movement. I also believe that it is very difficult, if not impossible, to engage in dialogue with them. I have strong attitudes against trying to convert people to a religious movement, and also against one-way religious communication. I feel hostile, both at any attempt to convert me in this way and because my privacy has been violated and my current activity interrupted. I do not engage them in conversation but bid them good-day and close the door.

As soon as I opened the door I had categorised these visitors as Jehovah's Witnesses, applied my stereotype, evaluated them on the basis of my stereotypical beliefs, felt hostile, and taken social action (terminated the encounter). By taking that action I had re-inforced my stereotype and prejudice, having given myself no opportunity for receiving any evidence to the contrary. I could then justify my doubtless abrupt action in closing the door by referring to my stereotypical beliefs. And I could congratulate myself for having avoided a painful and time-wasting experience by my rapid and accurate social judgement when I opened the door.

It is also worth noting that despite the above definitions, there is a sense in which we can have stereotypes and prejudices *about ourselves*, and the categories to which we believe we belong (our social identities). I have already referred to these self-stereotypes as '*prototypes*' (see pp. 91–92). I have also noted that both prototypes and stereotypes are likely to result in *depersonalisation*. In the above example, the people who are the object of my social judgement are simply Jehovah's Witnesses; that is all I am willing to know about them. I am not concerned about them as individual persons. Similarly, I may, as Prime Minister Margaret Thatcher famously did (Young, 1989), stereotype someone who belongs to the same political category as myself as simply 'one of us'.

### Prejudices have social origins

The origins of stereotypes and prejudice are to be found not only in the individual human mind but also in the cultures and sub-cultures to which people belong and which they embrace (Moscovici, 1981). Prejudices are likely to be derived more from the BVNs of cultural and sub-cultural social movements and groups than from individual experiences. Indeed, individual experiences of others' behaviour are often the outcomes of self-fulfilling prophecies; stereotyped people respond to our prejudiced behaviour in exactly the way in which we have set them up to behave (Snyder, 1992). Hence cross-cultural and inter-group conflict is a possible outcome of negatively prejudiced attitudes and behaviour, just as inter-group co-operation is a possible outcome of positive prejudice. The use of the phrase 'culture wars' to describe the activities of the Moral Majority in America in the 1980s reflects the outcome of fundamentalist (and doubtless secular) negatively prejudiced attitudes.

Theory and research (Taylor & Moghaddam, 1994) has pointed out that conflict can primarily result from *different stereotypical beliefs* held about one's own category and the other category by each party. Or, it can primarily derive from *different evaluations of stereotypes*, which both parties share. In the above example, my stereotype of Jehovah's Witnesses includes the beliefs that they want to convert me and that they do not engage in dialogue. Their self-stereotype may be that they are obeying God's will in witnessing to Him. Each party's stereotypes are totally different. So are our prejudices. My prejudice against them is based on my negative evaluation of being the object of a uni-directional conversion attempt, while their positive prejudice about themselves is that it is a very good thing indeed to be obeying God's will. Thus, in the above example, both parties' stereotype and prejudice are totally incompatible. However, if we return to the account of reconstructionist theology at the end of Chapter 7, the same might not be true in that instance. Many non-fundamentalists might agree with the reconstructionists' self-stereotype as holding a theocratic world-view that is incompatible with other world-views. However, they would feel highly unfavourable to a theocratic outcome, whereas it is what reconstructionists are fighting for. Conflict can occur because of different stereotypes, or because of different evaluations of the same stereotype.

Thus, in summary, we may now view stereotypes and prejudice not as unique and unfortunate social psychological facts, but rather as *examples of more general social psychological phenomena: beliefs and attitudes*. Like other attitudes, they enable us to make rapid judgements about attitude objects so that we can decide how to behave. In the case of stereotypes and prejudice, the function is the same, but the object is specifically people. And, as is also the case with other beliefs and attitudes, stereotypes and prejudice are difficult to change in the light of disconfirming evidence, since this is unlikely to be obtained.

## Academic evidence regarding fundamentalist attitudes

### *The RF scale*

Although the academic research uses a different index of fundamentalism from the pollsters, the results are compatible. Much of the research is based upon Altemeyer and Hunsberger's (1992) definition of fundamentalism, and the instrument used to measure it. They define fundamentalism as:

> ... the belief that there is one set of religious teachings that clearly contains the fundamental, basic, intrinsic, essential, inerrant truth about humanity and deity; that this essential truth is fundamentally opposed by forces of evil which must be vigorously fought; that this truth must be followed today according to the fundamental, unchangeable practices of the past; and that those who believe and follow these fundamental teachings have a special relationship with the deity.
>
> (Altemeyer & Hunsberger, 1992, p. 118)

Their instrument, the RF (religious fundamentalism) scale, assesses the extent to which respondents fit this definition. The items sample the four definitional criteria enumerated above. They are, therefore, assessing both beliefs and attitudes. Although the RF scale samples some of the defining criteria of fundamentalism according to the definition preferred in this book, it omits the central criterion: that it is modernism that is the enemy and the threat. Moreover, we do not learn from the instrument the extent to which respondents identify with a fundamentalist movement.

Much of the research has investigated the relationships between religious fundamentalism as measured by the RF scale and other constructs. In particular, relationships of religious fundamentalism with right-wing authoritarianism and with religious orthodoxy have been explored. Relatively high correlations have been obtained with measures of both these constructs. Indeed, it is unclear to what extent the three constructs and their measures are conceptually independent of each other. Statistical regression analyses that seek to separate out their relative contibution to the relationship with measures of prejudice against particular groups do, however, show that even when the effects of right-wing authoritarianism and religious orthodoxy are taken out, some of the variance in measures of prejudice is still accounted for by religious fundamentalism (Laythe, Finkel, Bringle, & Kirkpatrick, 2002).

It is perhaps more useful to consult the helpful table in Spilka et al. (2003, p. 472). This summarises the results of the studies carried out between 1990 and 2003, which related religious fundamentalism to negative attitudes towards various groups. Statistically significant correlations were obtained between religious fundamentalism and negative prejudice in every study conducted on prejudice against gays/lesbians, women, communists, and religious out-groups. In the case of ethnic/racial prejudice, five studies found significant correlations, but six failed to do so (i.e. any correlations were statistically non-significant). Overall, 31 studies found relationships and six did not. This differs markedly from the results for respondents with other religious orientations. For example, for those with a Quest orientation, which involves a questioning and open attitude to religious issues, 13 studies showed positive attitudes towards these groups, and eight failed to find significant correlations.

### Why are fundamentalists more prejudiced?

Thus, taking the survey and the psychological evidence together, it is clear that those Americans who probably fulfil the five criteria of fundamentalist allegiance described in the Introduction are more likely than others, including other religious people, to hold negative prejudice towards certain categories of person. The evidence is clear for gays and lesbians, and for atheists and religious out-groups, but not so clear-cut for ethnic groups. However, the survey evidence also reveals a range of social attitudes on which fundamentalists hold more conservative views than other religious Americans and than other Americans in general. These issues relate to abortion, euthanasia, sexual behaviour, sex education, the public display of Christian symbols, and immigration. These attitudes are not, of course, prejudices, but rather, conservative attitudes, as prejudices are by definition attitudes about categories of person.

How can we explain these results? Are people who are generally prejudiced and conservative attracted to fundamentalist movements? Do fundamentalist movements make their adherents generally prejudiced? Or are there specific BVNs, which adherents hold because they are adherents, some of which are prejudices? The latter explanation is favoured by Batson, Schoenrade, and Ventis (1993). Batson and colleagues point to the absence of consideration of the social context in psychological investigations of prejudice in religious people. They argue that whereas some religious movements oppose negative prejudice, others ignore it, or even advocate it. For example, Duck and Hunsberger (1999) found that students reported that their churches mostly taught that racial prejudice was wrong, but did not proscribe prejudice towards gays and lesbians. Batson and colleagues tread carefully when suggesting that some movements may actually prescribe rather than proscribe prejudicial attitudes, and that therefore it should come as no surprise when their adherents demonstrate prejudices. However, there is every reason why fundamentalist movements should encourage, and their adherents should hold, certain negative prejudicial attitudes.

### Prejudices and core beliefs

This is a controversial position to take, but it follows inexorably from the belief system typical of fundamentalist movements. Fundamentalists believe as their core assumption that they are under threat from secular forces, and must therefore resist. Hence the *in-group versus out-group social dynamic* is ever present in their ideologies and actions. Whereas some extreme fundamentalist movements aggregate their secular enemy into one category (for example, 'infidels' or 'the world'), most choose various out-groups, the identity of which depends upon the larger social context and their leaders' promptings.

Hence the core definitive feature of fundamentalisms, their perception of threat, predisposes them to hold negative prejudicial attitudes towards categories of people. This is why conservative attitudes regarding issues such as homosexuality or abortion so easily become prejudices against gays or abortionists. To use fundamentalist terminology, hostility is directed not just towards the 'sin', but also against the 'sinner'. Indeed, research demonstrates that fundamentalists have particularly negative attitudes towards gays, even when they are celibate (Fulton, Gorsuch, & Maynard, 1999). These researchers argue that such hostility is over and above what is required to be consistent with their theological doctrine. Similarly, Batson, Floyd, Meyer, & Winner (1999) found that particularly devout believers were less likely than others to help gays in trouble, even when helping them would in no sense promote homosexuality.

However, this still leaves open the question of why fundamentalists hold especially conservative attitudes regarding certain attitude 'objects', but not regarding others. Reference to Fig. 2 (p. 196) provides an answer. In sum, it is because their holy book appears to tell them that such 'objects' are regarded with disapproval by their sovereign God, whose servants they are. Thus, while the most definitive fundamentalist belief (that they are under threat) is the source of prejudice against people, the other two basic beliefs (in a sovereign supernatural, yet personal, God, and in His word the holy book) determine the choice of object of that prejudice.

Moreover, all three core beliefs are interwoven in complex ways. The holy book tells them that their God disapproves of certain sorts of behaviour and ordains that these should be punished. Their God is a sovereign and yet a personal God, so they are under an obligation to carry out His commands. And the categories of person who deserve punishment are part of the hostile secular world, which is engaged in a cosmic war against the Almighty.

However, it is only when formal and lay theologies interpret the holy book in a fundamentalist way, and when fundamentalist leaders and preachers propagate these interpretations, that individual adherents are confident in their prejudices and other attitudes. As I have already argued (pp. 90–91), there are any number of actions proscribed in the holy books, and the choice of out-groups is a strategic matter for leaders. They, after all, have the authority to interpret the holy book in a selective way.

Yet it would be a mistake to conclude that the choice of objects of negative attitudes and prejudices is determined solely by the leaders of fundamentalist movements. For example, it is no coincidence that homosexuality in particular, and sexual activity outside marriage in general, is regarded with hostility by many different fundamentalist movements. Rather, it is clear that *certain attitudes and prejudices follow logically and consistently from the core beliefs of fundamentalisms.*

Fundamentalist prejudice against gays provides a good example of the process at work. The pressure for gay rights is one of the outcomes of the powerful thrust of modernism in asserting individual rights in general. It therefore represents the secular enemy who threatens the survival of the true faith. Moreover, on a surface, 'common sense' reading, various passages in the Bible explicitly forbid homosexuality and prescribe severe punishment for it. 'Common sense' interpretation of these passages is taken as correct, as in fundamentalist belief the Bible is God's word spoken directly to the believer. In fact, biblical scholars suggest that the meaning of these passages is anything but clear-cut, given that they were written in a different social context (Bates, 2004, Chapter 3). However, reason fundamentalists, given that God has revealed His condemnation of homosexuality, and that He has commanded that they should be punished, then it is perfectly logical and right that we should feel hostile towards them and act accordingly. We are, after all, servants of a sovereign God, who holds us all personally to account for our obedience to His commands.

Some important values are clearly implied by the three core fundamentalist beliefs. From Rokeach's (1973) lists of 18 instrumental and 18 terminal values (see pp. 228–229), a high ranking for *obedience* and for *family security* would be expected. From these general values, a set of more specific attitudes and prejudices follows. The high importance attached to obedience implies a positive attitude towards proposed action against God's enemies. And to safeguard the family, it is necessary to disempower those categories of person who seem to threaten it: gays, lesbians, feminists, and all who encourage sexual activity outside marriage.

The extent to which such attitudes and prejudices find their expression in action is the subject of the next chapter. Such actions are likely to achieve symbolic status and to feed back into the belief system, as suggested in Fig. 1 (p. 114). For example, the actions taken to oppose gay marriage, and to support the public display of Christian symbols, the saying of prayers in public schools, and the repeal of the abortion laws have, with the help of the media, enabled these issues to achieve iconic status for American fundamentalists. The consequence is that they are now a necessary part of fundamentalist belief, even in fundamentalist churches that have adapted to a degree to late modernity (Tamney, 2002).

We must conclude that although people with certain pre-existing values, attitudes, and prejudices may be attracted to fundamentalist movements, the main reason why fundamentalists are particularly hostile to certain features of their social environment is that these attitudes follow inexorably from their basic beliefs. It is clear that they are correct in proclaiming that they have a coherent and internally consistent world view, in which beliefs, values, attitudes, and actions are all of a piece. It is also clear from a social psychological perspective that such a system of BVNs is part of their social identity.

## Summary

- The BVNs of individual adherents of fundamentalisms are subject to a dynamic process of change.
- Values and attitudes are an integral part of this process. Values, particularly, justify and motivate behaviour and arouse emotions.
- Values are similar to attitudes in that both involve evaluations of 'objects'. They differ from attitudes in that they are limited in number, consisting of a select range of instrumental and terminal 'objects'.
- These are more psychologically important than attitudes, playing the role of general principles from which attitudes follow, and of which they are an expression.
- Values are organised into systems, according to their order of priority for the individual, and different values are salient in different social situations.
- Extensive evidence about the attitudes of American fundamentalist Protestants is available both from survey and from academic research.
- Both sources demonstrate that fundamentalists have more negative attitudes towards certain 'objects' than do other Christians and the American people in general.
- These objects include homosexuality and homosexuals, atheism and atheists, and abortion.
- The academic research treats fundamentalism as a particular religious orientation typical of many believers. The RF scale, developed to measure the extent of this orientation, has been found to be highly correlated with right-wing authoritarianism and religious orthodoxy, and to predict prejudice against categories of person.
- The explanation for fundamentalist prejudice may be found at the social group rather than the individual level of analysis.
- Prejudices are likely to feature among the BVNs of fundamentalist sub-cultures, rather than resulting from general individual prejudice or a specific individual orientation.

## Further reading

Altemeyer, B. & Hunsberger, B. (1992) Authoritarianism, religious fundamentalism, quest, and prejudice. *International Journal of the Psychology of Religion*, 2, 113–133.
Fazio, R.H. & Petty, R.E. (2007) (eds.) *Attitudes: Their Structure, Function, and Consequences: Key Readings*. New York: Psychology Press.
Lawrence, B.B. (1989) *Defenders of God: The Fundamentalist Revolt Against the Modern Age* pp. 120–152. Columbia, SC: University of South Carolina Press.
Rokeach, M. (1973) *The Nature of Human Values*. New York: Free Press.

Smith, C. (2000) *Christian America? What Evangelicals Really Want.* Berkeley, CA: University of California Press.

Snyder, M. (1992) Motivational foundations of behavioural confirmation. In M.P. Zanna (ed.) *Advances in Experimental Social Psychology* Vol. 25. San Diego, CA: Academic Press.

Spilka, B., Hood, R.W., Hunsberger, B., & Gorsuch, R. (2003) *The Psychology of Religion: An Empirical Approach* (3rd edn.) 445–447. New York: Guilford.

Wright, S.C. & Taylor, D.M. (2003) The social psychology of cultural diversity: social stereotyping, prejudice, and discrimination. In M.A. Hogg & J. Cooper (eds.) *Handbook of Social Psychology.* London: Sage.

## CASE STUDY: FRIENDS OF THEIR ENEMY'S ENEMY: THE NETUREI KARTA

*Prejudices are positive or negative attitudes towards categories of person. We would therefore expect fundamentalists to have negative attitudes towards their dominant out-group. This is because they are characterised by a dualistic world-view which results in an oppositional social dynamic. The ultra-orthodox Jewish fundamentalist sect, the Neturei Karta, demonstrate perfectly how their hostility towards their primary out-group, Zionist Jews, results in unexpectedly favourable attitudes and actions to Arabs and Muslims, towards whom they might be expected to be hostile. Thus their simple dualist world-view dominates the overall direction of their attitudes.*

## The Haredim

To anyone with the slightest familiarity with the politics of the Middle East, it seems inconceivable that a group of Orthodox Jewish rabbis and their followers would enjoy cordial social relations with the late Yasser Arafat of Palestine, Louis Farrakhan of the Nation of Islam, Abu Hamza the radical Muslim cleric, and President Mahmoud Ahmadinejad of Iran. Yet this political engagement is precisely what the Neturei Karta Jewish fundamentalist movement has maintained in the last few years, culminating in its astonishing attendance at the International Conference to Review the Global Vision of the Holocaust, a meeting of Holocaust revisionists held in Iran in 2006 (BBC, 2006b).

How could these events possibly happen? Orthodox Jews have a variety of attitudes towards Muslims and Arabs but it would be hard to find many that could be described as cordial. A typical Jewish fundamentalist attitude towards Arabs can be discerned in the case study of the Gush Emunim movement in Chapter 3. I will argue that, given the history and belief system of the Neturei Karta, their attitudes towards Muslims and Arabs are entirely logical and consistent.

The *structure* of Judaism is incredibly complex, and a grossly simplified account will have to suffice for the purpose of seeking to understand the

A Neturei Karta demonstrator      © Ron Sachs/CNP/Corbis

Neturei Karta and their counter-cultural attitudes. The main divisions of Judaism are between Reform, Conservative, and Orthodox. Orthodox Judaism sub-divides into Modern Orthodox and Haredi, the latter also being known as ultra-orthodox. Disliking both these labels, Haredim prefer to be called 'true-Torah' Jews, a preference that points to their fundamentalist credentials. The Haredim in turn sub-divide into Agudat Israel (founded in 1912) and Edah HaChareidis. The former participate in the democratic processes of the state of Israel while disavowing Zionism. Zionism can be defined as a political movement and its associated ideology arguing that the land of Israel should become the homeland of the Jewish people. This participation has given Agudat Israel considerable influence, since they have frequently held the balance of power in the Knesset between major political blocs (Sprinzak, 1998). The Edah HaChareidis, however, are profoundly hostile to Zionism and the secular state. The most extreme of the several movements that form the Edah HaChareidis is Neturei Karta (founded in 1935), many of whose members are descended from Jews who emigrated to Israel from Hungary and Lithuania. Neturei Karta is thus the fundamentalists' fundamentalism.

The complex *structure* of Judaism, and its theological variety, can only be understood in the light of the *history* of Jewry. Having briefly reviewed the long historical background when describing Gush Emunim in the case study in Chapter 3, I will concentrate here upon the more recent history, from the Enlightenment onward. In essence, this history is the story of the accommodation of Judaism to gentile modernism, of the sacred to the secular (Lawrence, 1989, Chapter 6). It is, in other words, a reprise of the central and definitive feature of fundamentalisms everywhere: the belief that religion is under threat from secularism. Those believers who refuse to accommodate to modernism form fundamentalist movements, and, in the case of Judaism, these are the Haredim. This name means 'those who fear God', i.e. the truly pious. They constitute some 6% of the Jews now living in Israel.

The Enlightenment resulted in many institutions that threatened the traditional Jewish faith. The formation of *the nation-state*, for example, and the concomitant network of economic, political, and social institutions, provided great opportunities for Jews, as for others. Who could have imagined that Benjamin Disraeli would become Prime Minister of the United Kingdom, a nation not noted historically for its pro-semitic sentiments?

Inevitably, Jewish observance suffered. Social and commercial life in the Western city made it impossible to keep to the letter of the law, and it was impractical in the modern world to establish exclusive ghettos. Given that Judaism is a religion primarily of orthopraxis, doing the right thing, rather than of orthodoxy, believing the right thing, this increasing laxity was a serious development. Moreover, the emphasis of the Enlightenment on the freedom of mankind to follow the dictates of reason and throw off the irrational burden of tradition likewise threatened the integrity of the law. For the law had been handed down from the time of Moses in an uninterrupted line of traditional authority. Jews who succumbed to the siren voices of the Enlightenment were called '*maskil*', enlightened Jews. Thus was born the divide between Reformed and Orthodox Judaism.

The Jews of Eastern Europe were the last to succumb to the Enlightenment, sheltered as they were in ghettos where it was still possible to live an Orthodox religious life. Moreover, they were far less accepted by their host communities than were their brethren in the West. However, many of them felt themselves drawn back out of exile to their true home, the holy city of Jerusalem. They soon discovered that they were still in spiritual, although not physical, exile when the state of Israel was established. Since the nation-state was one of the dominant expressions of modernism, such a secular development was to be deplored, argued the Haredim. Additionally, many of the social movements they found flourishing in Israel, including *socialism and Zionism*, were actively hostile to traditional religion.

Particularly deceitful, they felt, was the effort by the Israeli government to incorporate the Orthodox faith as civil religion. As Lawrence (1989 p. 139) observes, the new nation-state 'embraced them despite their opposition to its existence'. The government recognised the regulation of social behaviour, such as Sabbath observance and marriage, as a rightful prerogative of religion. Further, various concessions regarding religious education were made, and religious scholars were excused military service in the Israeli Defence Force. Some of the 'truly pious' Haredim were determined not to compromise with this transparent effort to incorporate them. However, for many the opportunity for political influence and government support for their religious institutions proved too tempting. Further, the annexation of Judaea and Samaria in the Six Day War needed a religious justification, which some groups, for example, Gush Emunim, were willing to provide.

The historical scene was thus set for the ultimate defence of the tradition, the battle for the true faith for which only a few, the pure and holy, were prepared. The archetypal conditions for a classic fundamentalist movement were in place.

## A classic fundamentalism

The Haredim in general constitute just such a general movement (Heilman & Friedman, 1991), with Neturei Karta demonstrating many common features with other specific Haredi movements, but having one or two distinctive features.

First, the Haredim place the classic fundamentalist emphasis on *the holy book*. In their opinion, however, the unchangeable written law of God, given to Moses, has to be supplemented by the oral law. God's commands are interpreted authoritatively by religious leaders, so that the faithful know how to put them into practice in their worship and in the rest of their lives (Soloveitchik, 1993). If followed completely, the law as interpreted (the '*halacha*') can enable spiritual and moral perfection. The *halacha* contains detailed and intricate rules for worship and conduct, which have been developed down the centuries in a continuous tradition of rabbinical interpretation.

The law was given by God so that His chosen people, the Jews, could fulfil their side of their exclusive and unbreakable covenant with Him. Haredim consider non-Orthodox versions of Judaism to be heresies, because they deny some of these basic beliefs. For example, just as fundamentalist Protestants could not tolerate the application of modern scholarship to the Bible, so the Haredim regard higher criticism of the Talmud as heretical. (The Talmud is the most authoritative book of rabbinic scholarship).

The Haredi *view of history*, past, present, and future, is intimately bound up in this view of God's law. The history of the Jews is one of exile, since they broke their covenant with God by failing to keep the law. He punished them with exile, but at least they succeeded in maintaining the religious tradition by developing in their host countries autonomous communities governed according to the *halacha*. They presently remain in spiritual exile, whether or not they have returned to the land of Israel, persecuted either by gentile nations abroad or by apostate Jews in Israel. They will continue to live in exile until God decides to send the Messiah and establish the true Jewish Commonwealth, His universal rule (Almond et al., 2003, pp. 62–63).

This history and eschatology is, of course, entirely at odds with a secular Jewish perspective, which largely ignores the tradition, treats exile as a historical misfortune, and regards Jewish national history proper as starting with the foundation of the state of Israel in 1948. It is also at odds with the fundamentalist activism of Gush Emunim, who exalt the commandment to occupy the land, at the expense of all other religious obligations. Gush, like the American post-millennialists, believe that they can hasten the chosen people's redemption; Haredim, like the pre-millennialists, leave it to the Almighty, realising, however, that He will only redeem them if Jews are obedient.

These theological beliefs clearly facilitate an *in-group versus out-group* dynamic. A religion based on orthopraxis inevitably includes only those whose lives are devoted to obeying God's law. Any who have a different view of what God's law is, or who make little effort to obey, are by definition outsiders. They are unobservant apostates, not 'true-Torah Jews'. Rather, virtue lies in obeying the strictest interpretation of the rules, as provided by such holy twentieth-century rabbis as Rabbi Abraham Karlitz, known as 'the Hazon Ish'. Lawrence (1989, p. 134) gives as an example of strictness the Hazon Ish's re-calculation of the size of olives. The amount of unleavened bread consumed at the Passover meal was to be the size of an olive, according to a sixteenth-century guide to the *halacha*. However, olives had got smaller since the sixteenth century, and therefore the amount of unleavened bread had to be equivalent to the size of more than one olive. The appropriate calculations were provided for the faithful to follow.

Clearly the function of such revered leaders is to maintain the boundaries, to differentiate the faithful from the rest more clearly by giving them the opportunity to be different. By their own scrupulous obedience, such leaders are providing a prototype for the in-group, a model of what it really means to be a 'true-Torah Jew', rather than a 'Jew by birth only'.

However, perhaps the most obvious fundamentalist feature of the Haredim is their insistence on their distinctiveness and *separation* from others. In terms of the three strategies of engagement with the world described in Chapter 3 – assault, engagement, and separation – the Haredim's fundamental stance is *separation*, with occasional forays out from the fortress to engage with the world on religious matters. Indeed, this description is not merely metaphorical. Literally, the Haredim periodically sally forth from their urban ghettos to protest against violations of the *halacha*. Emerging from the Meah Shearim district of Jerusalem, they stone cars travelling on the Sabbath, and force women wearing Western dress to move to the back of the bus as it approaches 'their' area (Westervelt, 2007).

The notion of boundaries around the faithful to protect them against the pollution of the secular world, a veritable 'wall of virtue', is central to their belief and practice. They have to bear witness to 'purity in the midst of pollution' (Lawrence, 1989, p. 137). The idea of enclave echoes their history of exile and ghetto life in foreign lands. To ensure that they remain distinctive and separate, they exercise complete control over the education of their young. From *heder* infant school, through *yeshiva*, devoted to study of the *halacha*, to *kollel* (higher religious education for married men), the main purpose is to prepare their young for study of the Torah.

So central and important an activity for the entire community is such study assumed to be that education for any other purpose is regarded as inferior. It may be necessary for commercial or professional employment, but ambition to participate and excel is not approved. *Kollel* permits young married males to fulfil the requirement of the *halacha* to spend their lives in study, while their wives often soil their hands with secular labour in order to support their spouses' pure and holy existence. *Yeshiva* and *kollel* are often supported financially by rich private backers, so there is minimal dependence on the state. Employment within Haredi communities is frequently the result of a complex network of family and social ties, so that as few as possible have to go out into the secular world to earn their living.

The Haredim are also distinguished from others by their visible observance of a host of *specific rules*. If one's religion stresses orthopraxis, and if it lays down detailed rules of overt conduct, then such distinctiveness is inevitable. However, it also clearly serves the function of emphasising the barriers, of defining the unique identity. Dress, beards, and ringlets for men, and long skirts and sleeves for women, are obvious signs of difference, harking back as they do to the holier days of the eighteenth and nineteenth centuries. More profound, however, are the limitations on their contact with secular culture. Television, theatre, and cinema are forbidden, as are mixed social gatherings. Such social institutions represent the insidious attempts of the enemy to subvert the faithful and to blur the *halacha* distinctions between what is lawful and what is not. They must be avoided at all costs, otherwise True-Torah purity will be defiled.

## Neturei Karta

The Neturai Karta represent the most extreme fringe of the Haredim movement. Their name means 'Guardians of the City', and derives from a story in the Talmud. Two rabbis on a tour of inspection asked to see the guardians of a city, and were shown some armed men. They responded that these were not the true guardians, who were, in fact, the scribes and the scholars. There could be few more effective names than this, for it points to their sole purpose in life: to defend the Torah and the pure Judaic tradition. As they say in their mission statement: 'Neturei Karta International is dedicated to the propagation and clarification of Torah Judaism. Its only loyalty is to G-d and His revelation' (Neturei Karta International, undated). And their anthem runs:

'G-d is our King; We are His servants; The holy Torah is our Law; We are loyal to it'. God is spelt G-d because it is not permitted to refer to the Almighty explicitly.

However, immediately after these two statements of belief, there follows a clear identification of the enemy. In the mission statement we read:

> One of the basics of Judaism is that we are a people in exile due to Divine decree. Accordingly, we are opposed to the ideology of Zionism, a recent innovation, which seeks to force the end of exile. Our banishment from the Holy Land will end miraculously at a time when all mankind will unite in the brotherly service of the Creator. In addition to condemning the central heresy of Zionism, we also reject its policy of aggression towards all peoples. Today this cruelty manifests itself primarily in the brutal treatment of the Palestinian people. We proclaim that this inhuman policy is in violation of the Torah.
>
> (Neturei Karta International, undated)

Or, more briefly in the anthem: 'We do not recognise the heretic Zionist regime; Its laws do not apply to us; We walk in the ways of the Torah'.

These statements make clear both the identity of the enemy and the grounds for enmity. Zionism and the State of Israel are heretically usurping God's prerogative. It is only God who can bring Israel out of exile and into redemption. The state seeks to use the true and traditional religion of Israel for its own political purposes, which are certainly not to ensure obedience to *halacha*. It is seeking to defile God's truth by transforming it into civil religion. And in any event, the Talmud forbids strife with gentiles in order to form a Jewish state.

These anti-Zionist attitudes led Neturei Karta into a series of highly *political actions*, designed to capture headlines and create difficulties for the Israeli government and for Jews everywhere. One of their Rabbis, Moshe Hirsch, served as Minister for Jewish Affairs in Yasser Arafat's Palestinian cabinet. Two Neturei Karta members participated in a prayer vigil for Arafat as he lay dying in hospital in Paris. Rabbi Moshe Ber Beck met with Louis Farrakhan, leader of the Nation of Islam, in New York. Rabbi Yosef Goldstein testified in court on behalf of Abu Hamza, the radical Muslim cleric, in London. In defence of President Ahmadinejad's call for Israel to be wiped from the pages of history, Rabbi Yisroel Dovid Weiss argued that the President's statements were not indicative of anti-Jewish sentiments. Other members of Neturei Karta later agreed that they shared Ahmadinejad's aspiration for the disintegration of the Israeli government. At the Teheran holocaust conference of 2006, Neturei Karta spokesmen praised the President for distinguishing between Judaism and Zionism, and expressed their solidarity with his anti-Zionist policies. As a result of these actions, even other Haredim groups joined the United Orthodox Communities in condemning Neturei Karta and, in some cases, urging the excommunication of its members.

The astonishing favourable attitude held by the Neturei Karta towards Muslims and Arabs can, however, be explained by reference to their *basic beliefs*. The derivation may run something like this:

- The true faith, of which we are guardians, is under secular threat:

    – Zionism, of which the State of Israel is the expression, is the main carrier of this threat
    – Therefore we are hostile to Zionism.

- God is omnipotent, and He will decide when He will redeem His covenant people by sending their Messiah:

    – The State of Israel is seeking to set up an earthly kingdom, thereby usurping God's authority
    – Therefore we are hostile to Zionism.

- God has revealed His law to us, and we keep it:

    – Others, especially Zionists, do not keep it
    – They are disobeying God, and thereby delaying redemption
    – Therefore we are hostile to Zionism.

The three core fundamentalist beliefs (see Fig. 2, p. 196) thus lead inevitably to a hostile attitude towards Zionism. This attitude is mediated through *key values*. Clearly, *salvation*, in the spiritual sense of redemption, is ranked highly in their value system, in contrast to national security. The spiritual is far more important than the temporal. The miraculous redemption of Israel easily trumps the occupation of Palestine. Indeed, Neturei Karta claim to wish to hand over Palestine to the Palestinians. Moreover, the value of *obedience* is also likely to have a high priority for them, as is the instrumental value *clean*. To obey God is to keep clean from secular defilement and to achieve spiritual perfection. Zionism is antithetical to spiritual perfection.

The final link in the logic now becomes apparent. If the most hostile attitude of all is reserved for Zionism, the 'internal' enemy, then by comparison, other out-groups are lesser enemies. However, when these are the enemies of Zionism, they can even become friends, on the basis that *my enemy's enemy is therefore my friend*. Extreme hostility to co-religionists is also apparent in other fundamentalisms. Radical Islamists initially concentrated their aggression on the nationalist governments of nominally Muslim countries. The first target of Protestant fundamentalists was liberal Christians. However, there appears to be no comparable example of such profound animosity towards the internal enemy that the external enemy becomes one's friend. Perhaps Neturei Karta is unique.

The general theme of this case study, however, is to point to the logical connexions between the beliefs, values, and attitudes of fundamentalist movements. Taken individually, their attitudes towards various issues and categories of person may appear irrational. However, taken within the context of their overall world-view, such attitudes are perfectly logical. It is the success of fundamentalist movements in developing such world-views in the minds of their adherents which is the most important psychological issue to be addressed.

# 9 Fundamentalist behaviour: Its effects on Them and Us

## Reinforcing fundamentalist beliefs

### Behaviour consistent with BVNs

Fundamentalists' actions and behaviour certainly grab our attention, just as they are intended to. From 9/11 on through subsequent violent assaults, terrorist activities have dominated the media when they have occurred. Other actions, for different reasons, have impinged on our awareness, for example dramatic acts of 'healing' by televangelists, or angry demonstrations against the ordination of gay bishops. And we cannot help noticing fundamentalists' regular daily habits, such as the wearing of eighteenth-century dress by Haredim and Amesh believers. Unusual and unexpected actions do indeed often speak louder to us than words, for we use them to infer actors' beliefs and motives. And, as I will argue, they perform exactly the same function for fundamentalists themselves.

Fundamentalists' behaviour is not only aimed at making an impression on *us*. It also serves two other psychological purposes which relate to *them*. These are, first, to *effect change in fundamentalist world-views*, or, second, *to reinforce them as they are*. Behaviour often has a powerful symbolic force, which makes subsequent adjustment of beliefs, values, and attitudes imperative. For example, the assault of 9/11 led many young Muslims to believe that the traditional distinction between *Dar ul-Kufr*, the land of unbelief, and *Dar ul-Islam*, the land of Islam, was no longer relevant. Since there was nowhere where Islam truly ruled, as Osama bin Laden argued, the whole world was now *Dar ul-Harb*, the land of war.

In contrast, the wearing of eighteenth-century dress in the twenty-first century has a different sort of symbolic meaning. It is not *challenging* existing fundamentalist beliefs, but rather *reinforcing* them. Such behaviour re-affirms the separation of the faithful from the apostates and the heathen. 'We are very different', the Haredim are saying, speaking not just to the rest of the world but to themselves also, 'and furthermore, we have been different like this for a very long time'.

This distinction, between behaviour that is *consistent* with existing fundamentalist BVNs and reinforces them, and behaviour that is *inconsistent* and changes them, provides the structure for the first half of this chapter. We should immediately note, however, that there are many occasions when behaviour is inconsistent with BVNs, but BVNs do not change. I will start by considering *consistent behaviour*.

Of course, the fact that an action is consistent with the entire fundamentalist world-view, comprising beliefs, values, and attitudes, does not imply that the fundamentalist actor has gone through a *conscious rational process* in arriving at the decision to act in this way. On the contrary, the actor may respond to a person or a situation in an *automatic* way. He or she may be making an immediate response to the stereotype, e.g. of a gay person, which the presence of such a person has activated in their mind (Quinn, Macrae, & Bodenhausen, 2003). No conscious reference to values or core beliefs is required. If a conscious rational process of decision-making *is* to occur, there has to be both the opportunity and the motivation for such deliberation (Fazio, 1990). For example, one may need to make the best choice because the outcomes of making a mistaken one would be costly. Such decisions require the acquisition of data and the opportunity and capacity to evaluate it properly. In such situations, fundamentalists will refer to their holy book or its interpreters, and seek to gain evidence about what they should do from its pages. Fundamentalists' conscious decisions may thus be more theory-driven than data-driven.

However, the fact that a fundamentalist's response to a gay person is automatic and unconscious does not necessarily imply that their attitude towards gays is not originally derived logically from core beliefs and values. Nor does it imply that the believer is unaware of this derivation. On the contrary, he or she is likely to be able to give a reasoned post-hoc justification for their prejudiced behaviour. So, for example, prejudiced behaviour against gays is likely to be justified by reference to the core belief in the holy book as the word of God, which apparently treats homosexuality as a sin. The specific finding that Protestant fundamentalists are more likely than both other Christians and also non-religious people to engage in domestic violence (Brinkerhoff, Grandin, & Lupri, 1992) is likewise explicable in terms of biblical injunctions to apply physical discipline.

### Reinforcing core beliefs

The function of symbolic behaviour to *reinforce the three core beliefs* is evident. For example, distinctive dress fortifies the belief that the faithful are living in a hostile secular world, from which they are separate. The use of religious language and the practice of talking to God reinforces belief in a personal but supernatural God who intervenes in human affairs. And the regular performance of religious rituals emphasises the importance of obeying God's laws as revealed through the holy book and its interpreters.

This reinforcement of core beliefs by behaviour that is consistent with them operates psychologically in at least three ways. In the first place, *believers may infer their belief from their behaviour* (Bem, 1972). 'I have prepared myself for martyrdom, so I must believe that I am fighting the secular enemy on Allah's behalf'; or, 'I frequently talk to God, so I must believe He exists'. When people are constructing their self-concept, they use the evidence of their own behaviour to help them do so.

Second, they may observe that others within the movement, whom they admire and use as role models, behave in the same way as they do (e.g. read the Bible daily). Furthermore, these prototypical adherents appear to approve of them behaving in this way (e.g. welcome their quotation of biblical proof texts in conversation). The *behaviour becomes normative*, 'the right thing to do', and therefore by definition expresses correct beliefs (Martin & Hewstone, 2003). We *are* in a fight against evil, and the holy book *is* indeed God's word to guide and support us in that battle.

Third, *the more costly and effortful their behaviour*, the more strongly people hold the beliefs, values, and attitudes which support and justify that behaviour (Aronson & Mills, 1959). For example 'I have exchanged my comfortable Jerusalem apartment for a rough border settlement, so God's command to acquire all the land of Eretz Israel in order to bring about Israel's redemption must be paramount'. The same applies to what the fundamentalist does *not* do. For example, 'as a truly observant Jew, I refrain from watching television, theatre, and cinema. I hear that these are attractive activities, but since I reject them I am thereby ever more strongly convinced that they are nothing but the insidious tools of the Devil'.

Of course, one of the reasons why fundamentalists' behaviour reinforces beliefs, values, and attitudes is because *it is very difficult for that behaviour and its outcomes to falsify or challenge belief*. For example, the Islamic martyr, or indeed anyone else, may never know whether he or she has attained a high rank in paradise. All that we can say with confidence is that martyrs' expectations follow logically from their core religious beliefs. For them, belief in a literal war to the death with the secular world, and in a God who demands allegiance even unto death, justifies violent suicidal behaviour.

### *Ritual as the reinforcement of beliefs: Speaking in tongues*

I will conclude the consideration of fundamentalist behaviour as a *reinforcer* of belief with a more detailed account of how a particular example of fundamentalist ritual behaviour serves that function. Religious ritual, like other forms of ritual, is organised, patterned, repetitive, and above all, *symbolic* behaviour. We immediately think of Muslim prayer or Christian communion as examples of religious ritual. Muslim physical prostration at prayer symbolises the sovereign authority of Allah, whereas Christian consumption of bread and wine represents the centrality of Christ and His death.

Like other forms of ritual, religious ritual often performs a variety of useful personal and social functions. It symbolises enduring meanings and values, providing a counter-balance to existential uncertainty and unpredictable change. It allows a structure for the expression of emotions that can be considered difficult or dangerous in other social contexts (Pargament, 1997). And it maintains the cohesion of the religious group, as they have all collaborated in the enactment of the ritual, playing their appropriate roles as they do so.

The particular ritual I will explore is a practice of the Pentecostal and Holiness denominations and of charismatic groups in other Christian denominations. It is known technically as 'glossolalia', or, colloquially, as 'speaking in tongues'. It normally occurs in the context of church worship, and consists of individual worshippers, or sometimes more than one at a time, giving utterance to ecstatic sounds that phonologically resemble speech but from which no discernible semantic or grammatical content can be derived.

An account of such an event can be found in Cox (1995, pp. 83–85). A large congregation was prepared for glossolalia by a leader who spoke of the Holy Spirit hovering over the building, waiting and 'eager to pour down a blessing into the hearts of every single one who was present. He added that if we received the Lord that night there would surely be "signs following" '. Sure enough, as people knelt at their seats, accompanied by helpers who had one arm around them, the other extended heavenwards, signs indeed followed:

> People cried out, called, moaned, and wept. Blacks and whites and men and women knelt together . . . Then, individuals would stand, extend both arms to the heavens and cry out in phrases that sounded to me a little like Jesus's last words on the cross, 'Eli, Eli, lama sabacthani', but in a different order and with many other syllables mixed in.
>
> (Cox, 1995, p. 85)

It will immediately be objected by charismatic believers that such events constitute the exact opposite of religious ritual. They are evidence of the Holy Spirit breaking down the barriers of formal religion and speaking directly through His servants. People are acting spontaneously, and 'speaking through the heart'. However, there are several reasons to disagree with this objection.

First, it is clear that glossolalia is in fact a normative practice that is encouraged within regular worship. The prior events of the service consciously lead up to its occurrence, as in the example quoted. Second, it is used as an initiation rite for new converts. To speak in tongues is to demonstrate that one has received 'the baptism of the Holy Spirit', a requisite for full acceptance within the denomination. And third, there is no evidence that those who engage in glossolalia are in any sense psychologically different or impaired. According to Cox (1995), they are remedying a cultural and personal 'ecstasy deficit' common in modern life. Hence it is likely to be a socially induced activity rather than the outcome of some personal abnormality. In sum, glossolalia is an organised, patterned, often repeated, and, as I will show, a deeply symbolic event.

Those who have engaged in glossolalia describe the experience as crossing a barrier, overcoming one's limitations, and entering a sacred and ecstatic state in which God speaks through you (Holm, 1987). This post-hoc construction of the event suggests that it involves overcoming inhibitions and experiencing intense excitement, possibly but not necessarily while in a trance state.

The real significance of glossolalia is its function of reinforcing core fundamentalist beliefs. First, the experience is taken as evidence that *God is real and personal*, so real and personal that He speaks directly through his servants. The remarkable sounds uttered are not the production of the individual; they are the evidence of God's Holy Spirit, working supernaturally in the believer through the 'gift of tongues'.

The experience is also accepted as confirmation of *the Bible as the inerrant word of God*. The account of the day of Pentecost in the Bible (Acts of the Apostles 2.4) reads: 'And they [the disciples of Christ] were all filled with the Holy Ghost, and began to speak with other tongues, as the Spirit gave them utterance'. People of different nationalities are reported to have heard them speak in their own language. Clearly, some form of ecstatic speech was prevalent in the early Christian church, for St Paul enumerates 'divers kinds of tongues' and their interpretation as among the spiritual gifts bestowed on the church (I Corinthians 12). Indeed, it seems to have been considered a particularly prestigious gift, for in his famous encomium to love, Paul lists it first as the most likely to usurp the position of love as the supreme gift: 'Though I speak with the tongues of men and of angels, and have not charity [love], I am become as sounding brass or a tinkling cymbal'. He cautions (14.2) that 'he that speaketh in an unknown tongue, speaketh not unto men, but unto God: for no man understandeth him; howbeit, in the spirit he speaketh mysteries'.

The point for Pentecostalists, however, is that speaking in tongues is characterised in the Bible uniquely as a gift of the Holy Spirit bestowed at Pentecost. Hence their own repeated experience of that same divine gift proves that the Bible is as true today as it was then. And, as a bonus, it reinforces their claim, typical of fundamentalist movements, that they are returning to the pure and original form of worship which was practised at the foundation of their faith.

So we may conclude that this particular example of religious ritual serves the purpose of reinforcing two of the three core beliefs of all fundamentalist movements. Behaviour that is entirely consistent with the movement's doctrinal emphasis reinforces adherents' belief in that doctrine.

## Preserving fundamentalist beliefs

### *Coping with inconsistent behaviour*

There are many occasions when believers (and not just fundamentalist believers) behave in ways that are inconsistent with their BVNs; a considerable amount of research aims to discover just how consistent or inconsistent they are. This research is helpfully reviewed in Spilka et al (2003, Chapter 13). There is no clear evidence of a negative relationship between religiosity and cheating, but there is for one between religiosity and drug-taking, extra-marital sexual activity, and criminal behaviour. However, we should remember that correlation does not imply causality. Religion might not result in a decrease in these behaviours. Rather, more law-abiding and rule-observing people might be more attracted to religion than less law-abiding people. Further, much of this research relies on self-reports of behaviour, and fervent believers might have more at stake than others when it comes to admitting their errant ways. Such statistics as the frequency of divorce among Evangelicals in America indicate that overall, religious people periodically behave in ways inconsistent with their beliefs.

Moreover, it seems possible that fundamentalists, following as they do a more demanding form of religion with more detailed prescriptions and proscriptions, may be more likely to experience such inconsistencies.

What effect does this have upon fundamentalists' beliefs, values, and attitudes? Are they constantly having to adapt their beliefs and values because their behaviour so often falls short? The answer appears to be negative.

The reason is that there exists a range of possible strategies on which they can draw to account for their apparent aberrant actions while keeping their BVNs intact. One such strategy has already been described (pp. 172–177). It is the opportunity for *external attribution* for such actions. They themselves are not primarily responsible for their violation of values, or their failure to keep to God's commands. Such sin can be explained as the work of the Devil, or of God putting one to the test (Lienesch, 1993). If one succumbed, it was a matter of momentary weakness rather than evil intent. The belief in super-natural powers of good and evil, far more powerful than the believer, can serve to finesse the failure to obey God's law. There is no need to adapt one's BVNs, despite one's sinful ways.

This would explain why the evidence is mixed regarding possible debilitating feelings of guilt and fear of punishment as a consequence of fundamentalist belief. One might expect that the inevitable failure to achieve the high stand-ards set would increase such feelings and decrease self-esteem. However, the problems of maladjustment predicted by Kirkpatrick, Hood, and Hartz (1991) are not supported by a great deal of evidence, and some research (e.g. Sethi & Seligman, 1993) indicates that, on the contrary, fundamentalists are in general optimistic about their lives in comparison to others. Clearly, there exist a variety of psychological processes for minimising the inconsistency between actions and ideals.

### Self-consistency and self-esteem

Which brings us to the key theoretical point about the relationship between behaviour and belief: *that behavioural consistency or inconsistency involves the self* (Aronson, 1999). The most basic reason for changing one's beliefs as a result of one's actions is to re-establish a degree of internal consistency between elements of the self, and so maintain one's self-esteem.

Different individuals will achieve such consistency in different ways, depending upon the nature of their selves. If I have a strong *personal identity* as a unique individual, and am not dominated by a single social identity, then I can continuously adapt my self to remain consistent with my actions and others' responses to those actions. There are few social constraints upon my so doing. Indeed, I may even re-invent my self. Likewise, if my self is constructed mostly of a wide *variety of social identities*, I can increase the relative importance and salience of a different social identity. So, for example, even if I fall short of being a fully observant Jew, I can increase the centrality of other social identities, for example as business person, family member, or pillar of the local Jewish community. In both these cases, my self remains consistent to a degree, and my self-esteem is preserved.

If, however, I have *one central fundamentalist social identity* and believe myself to be first and foremost a Bible-believing Baptist or a true-Torah Jew, but know myself to have behaved inconsistently with that social identity, the self is in trouble, and self-esteem is threatened. As the fundamentalist identity in question dominates the self, and as its BVNs are highly internally consistent and prescribed, then consistency really does matter to the fundamentalist.

One way to deal with such an inconsistency would be to change aspects of the BVNs associated with the social identity (Visser & Cooper, 2003). For example, the believer could question whether the strict social rules enjoined by Baptists or Haredim are actually really God's will. After all, as a loving God, He surely would not ask the impossible of His followers.

However, there are ways of avoiding such a heretical outcome. Rather than eliciting a change in beliefs, inconsistent behaviour can even be used to re-inforce them. For example, for the televangelists mired in scandal in the 1990s, their misbehaviour was turned into an opportunity to re-affirm the forgiving grace of God. And, to repeat the attributional example quoted above, the evil agency of the Devil can serve as a justification for such sinful lapses. This use of inconsistent behaviour to actually re-inforce belief systems is made possible by the complexity of the lay and formal theologies that contribute to the fundamentalist world-view. The televangelists were able to emphasise the doctrine of free grace for the sinner at the expense of teachings regarding personal holiness.

Alternatively, if the fundamentalist believer already enjoys high self-esteem, their unshakeable self-affirmation can *act as a buffer* against any change in the self and the belief system as the result of a lapse. The lapse need not be attributed externally, but rather to some unimportant aspect of the self (Aronson, Blanton, & Cooper, 1995), for example, a personal quirk or a quasi-medical condition. Or a fundamentalist in a position of leadership might argue that so important is his contribution to the movement that one or two weaknesses in his character are of no account.

## Changing fundamentalist beliefs

### Changing belief: Conversion and leadership initiatives

There are clearly many ways of reconciling inconsistent behaviour with fundamentalist social identity and BVNs without changing the identity or its BVNs. What, then, is different about those situations where BVNs *do* change as a result of behaviour? It will be informative to review two such situations.

The first is the process of *fundamentalist conversion*. We should note that the classic fundamentalist account of a sudden radical transformation is not evidenced in a high proportion of conversion accounts. However, where it does occur, there is a profound change of the self, and the espousal of often entirely different BVNs from those held previously. The process, however, is likely to start with the convert making an initial behavioural commitment, for example, an oath of allegiance to a sheikh, or a response to a gospel appeal. This and other behaviour that initiates subsequent change in the self and in BVNs is itself novel, as it involves engaging in the role behaviour prescribed by the fundamentalist movement. In particular, using religious language that assumes the truth of the three core beliefs leads to subsequent internalisation of these and other BVNs, as Harding (2000) has emphasised.

Perhaps, then, behaviour that is to lead to belief change needs itself to be a change: novel, broad ranging, and internally consistent behaviour. Such behaviour is unlikely to occur in a social vacuum. Rather, it follows from normative prescription of role behaviour by a social movement or institution.

A second instance of change of BVNs following behavioural change is to be found in the consequences of *leadership initiatives for change*. When a charismatic leader, who has exemplified a movement's prototype, has built up sufficient 'idiosyncrasy credit' (see pp. 92–93), he has the authority to change normative practice within the movement. Followers will rapidly conform their behaviour to the new direction he sets. They may not initially internalise the change of identity or BVNs that his initiative implies. However, the authority he carries results in a sufficiently radical change of behaviour, which in turn results in internal change.

Some examples of such leadership initiatives have already been quoted in Chapters 3 and 4. However, they bear repeating, because they clearly demonstrate how it is possible to engineer change in movements that place a great value on tradition and continuity. These leaders include Jerry Falwell, the Ayatollah Khomeini, and Osama bin Laden. Falwell will serve as an example.

### Jerry Falwell and the Moral Majority

In the 1980s, the late Jerry Falwell, and others, persuaded disparate movements within American Protestant fundamentalism to collaborate to form the Moral Majority and to engage in joint political activity (Harding 2000, Chapter 6). The primary social identity of these believers had hitherto undoubtedly been that of their movement: I am a Fundamentalist (Falwell's own religious identity), an Evangelical, or a Charismatic (or Pentecostal). These movements had previously been mutually hostile. Fundamentalists despised Evangelicals as having compromised on doctrine in order to attract and retain modern Americans. And both Fundamentalists and Evangelicals tended to dismiss Pentecostals as lacking in any sort of intellectual structure and pandering to the emotions. Furthermore, in true in-group versus out-group style, each of the three movements emphasised those beliefs and values that distinguished it from the others. Fundamentalists insisted on total inerrancy of Scripture, Evangelicals on the overwhelming importance of evangelism, and Pentecostals on the necessity of receiving the ecstatic gifts of the Holy Spirit.

Falwell and his colleagues persuaded these disparate groups to collaborate on a joint political project: to change what they regarded as permissive legislation, to combat the moral decay of American society, and, ultimately, to get one of their number, Pat Robertson, elected to be President of the United States. Such political work required whole-hearted involvement and costly commitment (Balmer, 2000, Chapter 8). Behavioural collaboration on the ground allowed the three movements to embrace the new superordinate social identity of 'the Moral Majority'. This did not result in a loss of their identities as Fundamentalists, Evangelicals, or Pentecostals. Rather, it subordinated those identities to a common purpose: to take the secular enemy on at his own game, in the political arena. Each of the three movements retained its identity under the common umbrella, and differentiated itself by contributing in different ways to the effort according to its strengths. Evangelicals provided their penetration of the academic, business, and political communities, Pentecostals their fervour and enthusiasm, and Fundamentalists their access to rich backers.

The collaboration resulted in changes in the beliefs and values of each movement. A basic value of the Fundamentalists had been one of separation from the secular world. This sank in their order of priority, to the extent that winning the world's institutions for God has become the main aim of a considerable group of them, led by the reconstructionists. The Pentecostals, too, gave up their exclusive emphasis on personal holiness. As for the Evangelicals, a core element of their eschatology had been the pre-millennialist belief, similar to that of the Haredim, that God has chosen the time when He will rescue His people and send the Messiah. There is therefore little left for the believer to do in this world other than to rescue the unsaved from the dreadful fate that will befall them on the day of judgement. This pessimistic diagnosis was emended to allow the possibility that the faithful could at least ameliorate the apocalyptic horror and hasten the day by fighting the moral decay afflicting America. The political adventures of the Moral Majority needed an eschatological justification.

Thus Falwell succeeded in engineering a political movement that required a change of behaviour in its participants. They not only engaged in novel activities, they engaged in them together, despite their different religious identities. As a consequence of this behaviour, they changed some of their beliefs, values, and attitudes, and acquired a new superordinate religious identity that, under a sequence of different labels, has continued to this day.

## The creation of the out-group

### Inviting a hostile response

It is perfectly possible to create an imaginary out-group whose existence no-one except its creator, the fundamentalist in-group, recognises. There has been a history of such shadowy scapegoats in Protestant fundamentalism, for example, the New World Order (Boyer, 1992). However, it is far more effective to create an out-group consisting of real people, which can act so as to affirm its own social identity, in contrast to the fundamentalist identity.

Such a 'real' out-group performs several functions. Its existence permits the fundamentalist in-group to reinforce its core belief that the secular world is out to destroy it. It enables the in-group to create stereotypes against a category of persons and feel prejudice against it. This in turn allows the in-group to re-emphasise its distinctiveness. Moreover, a homogeneous in-group prototype can be developed in contrast to the out-group stereotype. The self-esteem of in-group members and group cohesion are thereby enhanced.

However, it helps immensely if the out-group actually acts in ways that confirm the in-group's stereotype of it. Behaviour that is clearly contrary to God's will serves to confirm secular society's godlessness and, by contrast, fundamentalists' own righteousness. Therefore we might expect much fundamentalist activity to be aimed at eliciting such behaviour. Instead of fighting for righteousness, fundamentalists are sometimes not too upset when they stir up sin.

The most obvious example of this reasoning is 9/11. Osama bin Laden must have known that President Bush's most likely response to the assault on America would be to make war, and that such a war would bring added suffering to Muslims. The consequence of supposedly fighting on their behalf would be, he knew, their increased misery. However, he succeeded in inciting America to act in a way that precisely confirmed jihadist stereotypes of the great Satan who persecutes the *ummah*. A 'war on terror' can easily be represented as a war on Islam.

A similar example of violent action aimed at eliciting a punitive response is the murder of an abortion doctor by Reverend Paul Hill in 1994. As the date of Hill's execution for murder drew nearer, his friend Reverend Michael Bray sought to portray the execution as the martyrdom of a just and merciful man. Hill was 'called by God to the sacrificial, public witness he made', wrote Bray (Juergensmeyer, 2003, p. 169). In other words, God wished his 'disciple' to be killed so that the strength of the secular government's support for legal abortion would be made crystal clear.

Other fundamentalist activities are not murderous, but certainly stimulate a hostile response in others. For example, recent funerals of American armed forces personnel killed on service in Iraq have been marred by demonstrations by a fundamentalist sect. The demonstrations are against gays, but the justification for conducting them at military funerals is that the government that sent troops to Iraq is the same government that tolerates gays. This indirect and twisted logic points clearly to the real motive behind the choice of military funerals as the site for a demonstration. The demonstrators wished to create as much outrage as they possibly could. The same motive may be discerned in the actions of Islamists demonstrating in London and elsewhere, who carried placards calling for the death of people whom they believed to be dishonouring the Prophet.

### *Acting differently*

However, there are many less violent or extreme ways of stimulating a hostile reaction. For example, behaving peaceably but differently, and cultivating an unusual appearance, are not only ways of signalling separation. They are also implicit challenges to dominant cultural norms. They invite the response that they themselves imply: a stereotype of the other. Thus there are two outcomes of such fundamentalist behaviour. First, they can confirm their own stereotype of the out-group, because they have managed by their own actions to persuade the out-group to behave in ways which confirm it. And second, they can stimulate the out-group to form its own stereotype of them, thus ensuring the continuation of hostilities. Each can now regard the other as its out-group. This is a big advantage for fundamentalists, because otherwise they might be ignored as fringe eccentrics. The grandeur of cosmic conflict is infinitely preferable to the obscurity of private eccentricity.

## Responses to fundamentalist behaviour

### *Political and personal responses*

The above behavioural examples are quoted as attempts to reinforce the core fundamentalist belief that there is a conflict between sacred and secular for survival, and to set up such a conflict whenever possible. The questions remain: how *do* we respond to fundamentalist activity, and how might we best respond to it in the future? Note that fundamentalists have already succeeded in distinguishing themselves as a separate social identity, which is why I used the first person plural 'we' in the previous sentence. There is already an 'us and them' distinction in my mind, and perhaps also in the minds of my readers, although this is a presumption on my part. Some of my readers may be fundamentalists, and they will have translated my frequent 'we's' and 'us's' into 'they's' and 'them's' and made the reverse translation as well. Thus the existence of this book strengthens, doubtless by only an infinitesimal amount, the social identity of fundamentalists.

However, books about fundamentalists exercise minimal impact compared to the responses of secular states to fundamentalist aggression. I have repeatedly argued that President Bush and Prime Minister Blair played right into Osama bin Laden's hands by declaring their response to be a 'war on terror' (and making actual war). This response confirmed bin Laden's construction of the situation as a cosmic war between the infidel West and God's people. It enabled him to represent himself as the champion and protector of the *ummah* against the forces of evil. There is an interesting contrast with Prime Minister Brown's response to the attempted car bombings in London and Glasgow in June, 2007. He refused to talk of war, and spoke of the bombers as a tiny criminal element to be carefully distinguished from the large body of loyal British Muslims.

There are, of course, many other forms of fundamentalist behaviour to which we respond. Many of these deliberately challenge taken-for-granted features of secular modernity. For example, the right of a woman to choose whom she marries, or the right of individuals to travel on the Sabbath or dress how they wish, are constantly challenged by fundamentalists. Yet these are freedoms that are simply assumed in Western cultures. Likewise, the broadly accepted authority of science in understanding natural phenomena is opposed by fundamentalist creationism and 'intelligent design'. So oppositional and contrary to secular modernism are the positions taken by fundamentalists that in this book I have agreed with them that theirs is a totally different world-view. However, I have not concurred with their binary distinction between their own world-view and that of 'the world', designed to strengthen their categorisation of their out-group as everyone other than themselves. There are many different alternative world-views to theirs.

My own ambivalent response to fundamentalist behaviour reflects that of many other non-fundamentalists. The initial liberal instinct is to bend over backwards to welcome sub-cultural diversity and the multiple and different social identities that it implies. Such a response is doubtless partly a reaction against the prejudice and xenophobia that still disfigure our increasingly pluralist societies, particularly in times of economic hardship. However, very soon the contradictions between fundamentalist BVNs and those of different social identities become apparent. Perhaps the most intractable of these is the fundamentalists' stated desire for theocracy.

So, for example, in their search for a superordinate social identity to unite the disparate elements of British society in the face of fundamentalist violence, Prime Ministers Blair and Brown have chosen 'being British' and 'the British way of life'. Yet this identity assumes the importance of the rights of all citizens under the rule of (secular) laws agreed by those same citizens. All those fundamentalists who want theocracy and reject the Enlightenment, not just those who plant bombs, will immediately reject efforts to promote such an identity.

Thus responses to the big political issues raised by fundamentalist behaviour are in their political and intellectual infancy. The recognition that 'the war on terror' is better perceived as a 'struggle for hearts and minds' than as the dropping of bombs is a small start. But almost every response so far attempted has only succeeded in reinforcing fundamentalists' favoured construction of the world as a cosmic battle between good and evil, God and His enemies. This is not a surprising outcome, for as fundamentalists have already discovered for themselves, it is far easier to represent a complex situation in dualist black and white terms than to address its complexity.

### The liberal dilemma

And complex indeed it is. For example, when does the value of freedom of religious worship clash with the right of the citizen to safety under the protection of the state? Or, putting the question more specifically, when does radical fundamentalist preaching become incitement to violence? And when do practices that fundamentalist movements claim are an integral part of their religion become so damaging to adherents that the state itself should step in to protect them? How should the state respond to the practice of female circumcision, for example? What about parents' refusal to permit their child medical treatment necessary to save his or her life? To what level, if at all, should parents be allowed to inflict pain upon their children in the name of discipline? How should we react to arranged marriages to which the prospective bride is opposed? What if women are prevented from receiving higher education in order to avoid their being corrupted?

However, fundamentalist behaviour does not only impinge upon the great political issues of freedom and justice. It also affects our daily lives. How do we as individuals react to attempts to convert us? What do we do when our children or grandchildren are taught creationism in a science lesson? How, if we are liberal Christians, or mainstream Muslims or Jews, do we respond when fundamentalists organise politically in order to win control of our denomination? These more personal questions point up the same moral dilemmas as are faced at the political level. How is it possible, for example, to show another individual respect when you believe that their world-view is not only profoundly simplistic, but also potentially dangerous?

But the personal is also the political. If I construe fundamentalists as an out-group, and act accordingly in my dealings with them, then I am re-inforcing their own in-group identity. I may be enhancing my self-esteem by contrasting myself as a liberal and enlightened modern person with these 'blinkered fanatics'. However, this self-esteem is bought at a cost: increased inter-group conflict. And, ironically, conflict is involved in any case, for the high value I place on peace and the avoidance of conflict is itself in conflict with the high value fundamentalisms place on conflict! Any tentative answer in this book to the question 'how *should* we respond' must await the theoretical summary of the next and final chapter.

## Summary

- Fundamentalists' behaviour may either reinforce their existing beliefs or result in a change in them.
- When their behaviour carries symbolic meaning and is consistent with their existing beliefs, its function is always to reinforce them.
- Consistent behaviour is not always consciously derived from the core beliefs that mandate it. However, fundamentalists can usually justify their actions in terms of their beliefs.
- The reinforcement of beliefs by behaviour that is consistent with them occurs through three psychological processes: the inference of belief from behaviour; the development of normative behaviour; and the justification of the cost of the behaviour.
- A frequent form of behaviour that reinforces fundamentalist belief is religious ritual. The phenomenon of 'speaking in tongues' is described by way of example.
- Behaviour is often inconsistent with belief. However, such inconsistency does not necessarily imply a subsequent change in belief.
- A range of strategies enables the avoidance of belief change. These include external attribution of responsibility for one's action, and taking advantage of the ambiguity of doctrine.
- Such strategies are motivated by concern for the self. The preservation of consistency within the self, and hence of self-esteem, is crucial.
- Nevertheless, there are many occasions when behaviour results in a change in beliefs. Examples are fundamentalist conversion and behavioural change initiated by the movement's leadership. Falwell's formation of the Moral Majority is described as an example.
- Behaviour is also used to buttress belief when fundamentalists act in such a way as to provoke retaliatory hostility by out-groups.
- Fundamentalists need out-groups in order to identify themselves as the in-group defending the faith.
- Non-fundamentalists have hitherto reacted mostly with retaliatory hostility, as fundamentalists planned.
- Such simple reactivity is an inappropriate response to an extremely complex set of issues, with belief and value conflicts at their core.

## Further reading

Aronson, E. (1999) Dissonancy, hypocrisy, and the self-concept. In E. Harmon-Jones & J. Mills (eds.) *Cognitive Dissonance: Progress on a Pivotal Theory in Social Psychology.* Washington, DC: American Psychological Association.

Cox, H. (1995) *Fire from Heaven: The Rise of Pentecostal Spirituality and the Reshaping of Religion in the Twenty-first Century.* Reading, MA: Addison Wesley.

Fazio, R.H. (1990) Multiple processes by which attitudes guide behaviour: The MODE model as an integrative framework. In M.P. Zanna (ed.) *Advances in Experimental Social Psychology,* Vol. 23. San Diego, CA: Academic Press.

Harding, S.F. (2000) *The Book of Jerry Falwell: Fundamentalist Language and Politics.* Princeton, NJ: Princeton University Press.

Pargament, K.I. (1997) *The Psychology of Religion and Coping.* New York: Guilford.

Quinn, K.A., Macrae, C.N., & Bodenhausen, G.V. (2003) Stereotyping and impression formation: How categorical thinking shapes person perception. In M.A. Hogg & J. Cooper (eds.) *Handbook of Social Psychology.* London: Sage.

Spilka, B., Hood, R.W., Hunsberger, B., & Gorsuch, R. (2003) *The Psychology of Religion* (3rd edn.) 416–444. New York: Guilford.

Visser, P.S. & Cooper, J. (2003) Attitude change. In M.A. Hogg & J. Cooper (eds.) *Handbook of Social Psychology.* London: Sage.

Wulff, D.M. (1997) *Psychology of Religion: Classic and Contemporary Views* (2nd edn.) New York: Wiley.

## CASE STUDY: DIFFERENT PERSPECTIVES: JACK STRAW AND THE *NIQAB*

*Fundamentalist actions serve different functions. For the believer, they can reinforce beliefs, values, and fundamentalist identity. They can also serve to reinforce the distinctiveness of the in-group, and its distance from out-groups. The Islamic niqab, or full veil, performs both these functions. It reinforces belief and identity, with its wearers emphasising their renewed feelings of Muslim modesty, and it certainly differentiates them from others. This case study examines the effect of wearing the niqab not only on the wearer, but also on a variety of others who react to this religious action. Hostility, incomprehension, solidarity, and political opportunism are among the responses. Public religious behaviour is therefore a symbolic action that is personal, social, and political as well as religious.*

## A chance encounter?

Jack Straw is an experienced and politically agile British Member of Parliament who has succeeded in achieving high Cabinet rank in the governments of both Prime Ministers Blair and Brown. He represents the constituency of Blackburn in Lancashire, where about 25% of the electorate are Muslims. Here is a column he wrote in his local newspaper, the *Lancashire Telegraph,* (Straw, 2006).

The niqab                                    © Phil Noble/Reuters/Corbis

'It's really nice to meet you face-to-face, Mr Straw', said this pleasant lady in a broad Lancashire accent. She had come to my constituency advice bureau with a problem. I smiled back. 'The chance would be a fine thing', I thought to myself but did not say out loud.

The lady was wearing the full veil. Her eyes were uncovered but the rest of her face was in cloth.

Her husband, a professional man I vaguely knew, was with her. She did most of the talking. I got down the detail of the problem, told them that I thought I could sort it out, and we parted amicably.

All this was about a year ago. It was not the first time I had conducted an interview with someone in a full veil, but this particular encounter, though very polite and respectful on both sides, got me thinking. In part, this was because of the apparent incongruity between the signals which indicate common bonds – the entirely English accent, the couple's education (wholly in the UK) – and the fact of the veil. Above all, it was because I felt uncomfortable about talking to someone 'face-to-face' who I could not see.

So I decided that I wouldn't just sit there the next time a lady turned up to see me in a full veil, and I haven't.

Now, I always ensure that a female member of my staff is with me. I explain that this is a country built on freedoms. I defend absolutely the right of any woman to wear a headscarf. As for the full veil, wearing it breaks no laws.

I go on to say that I think, however, that the conversation would be of greater value if the lady took the covering from her face. Indeed, the value of a meeting, as opposed to a letter or phone call, is so that you can – almost literally – see what the other person means, and not just hear what they say.

Straw goes on to say that 'ladies' have never refused this request, and recounts a more recent encounter. He admits that he was surprised when on this occasion his constituent told him that it was her own decision to wear the veil, and he asked her about the religious justification for it. However, he also asked her to consider his own concern that:

> Wearing the full veil was bound to make better relations between the two communities more difficult. It was such a visible statement of separation and of difference. I thought a lot before raising this matter, and still more before writing this. But if not me, who? My concern could be misplaced. But I think there is an issue here.
>
> (Straw, 2006)

There is not enough space here for a full deconstruction of this carefully crafted piece. However, I will comment on three of its features. The first is the use of paragraphing, for full dramatic effect. There are two particularly brief paragraphs in the piece. The first reveals ('shock, horror') that the 'lady' was wearing a full veil; and the second claims that he did something about it ('good for you, Jack' is the expected response). The second feature worth comment is the not-so-subtle sequence 'I defend absolutely the right of any woman to wear a headscarf. As for the full veil, wearing it breaks no laws' (translation: 'I don't defend absolutely the right of any woman to wear the full veil'). Finally, at the end 'My concern could be misplaced. But I think there is an issue here'. Straw knew perfectly well that there was an issue there, and what would be the consequences of raising it.

So to whom was Straw addressing his piece? It would be naïve to suppose that it was just the readership of the *Lancashire Telegraph*. He would know, despite his subsequent expressed surprise (Ward, 2006), that the piece would be picked up by the national media, eager for a story, and, in the case of the tabloids, for the excuse for some more xenophobia. Basically, Straw was writing for the media, and in particular, for those commentators with the ability to keep the issue on the boil for as long as possible. And what really was 'the issue'? It was, for Straw, certainly not his difficulty in communicating with his constituents. Rather, it was the issue of 'Britishness'. For ultimately, Straw's central identity is as a politician. And for British politicians, the recent examples of 'home-grown' terrorism have led to the perception of a need for greater cohesion, less separation, and the re-evaluation of the idea and practice of multi-culturalism.

Moreover, Straw would have known that the piece would flush out a variety of responses from groups whose opposition it would be politically advantageous to enjoy; radical Muslims, for example, and liberal feminists. And he would have hoped for the vocal support of his political allies in the government.

## What happened next

Straw was not disappointed in any of these hopes. The story took off and ran in the British media, attracting, for example, leading articles in the *Guardian* and the *Observer*, as well as tabloid coverage. It even crossed the Atlantic to the august pages of the *New York Times* and *Time Magazine*. So immediate was its impact in Britain that Straw was able to command more media attention by responding the following day to outspoken *Muslim* objections. The Lancashire Council of Mosques said that he had misunderstood the issue, and that his statement was very insensitive, unwise, ill-judged, and misconceived (Ward, 2006). Straw felt emboldened to say that he personally would rather that veils were discarded completely, and to re-affirm that he wanted 'to put out on the table something which is there in any event' (Sturcke, 2006).

Muslim representatives made a variety of points in the media (although it is in order to ask to what extent they *are* representative). An imam from the Muslim Council of Britain said:

> On the one hand he [Straw] says this is a free country. On the other, he is denying that free choice to a woman who chooses to wear the veil.
>
> (Bunyan & Wilson, 2006)

To call upon people to give up cultural and religious customs and practices is calling for cultural assimilation, he argued, and is equivalent to saying that one culture is superior to another. Another Muslim Council spokesperson said, confusingly but revealingly:

> This country is supposed to celebrate diversity. That is the wonderful thing about this country: that it accepts, that it is tolerant. Women who wear the veil are making the statement that they are separate from society and that is why they wear it.
>
> (Bunyan & Wilson, 2006)

More vigorously, yet another Muslim Council spokesperson said:

> This is going to do great damage to the Muslim community, again we are being singled out by this government as the problem. Women have

a right to wear a veil, and this is just another example of blatant Muslim-bashing by this government.

(Taylor & Dodd, 2006)

Similarly outspoken responses were drawn from *feminists*, who nevertheless were understandably split down the middle. Some argued that the veil represented patriarchal oppression, and that there were some forms of oppression and intolerance which a liberal democracy should not tolerate. Wrote one:

Only someone who has paid scant attention to the great feminist debates about the female body could assert that wearing the veil is merely a matter of personal choice. The *niqab* affects me and other women who don't wear it because it represents a return to medieval religious notions of female modesty, which deny women access to public space on the same terms as men . . . As for the notion that wearing the veil is 'their' culture, it seems to me this is a complete misreading of what's happening in this country. Some young Muslim men and women are adopting a much more conservative religious identity than their parents, of which the veil is a powerful visual symbol.

(Smith, 2006)

And again:

While middle-aged male Muslims queue up to defend the right of women to wear the *niqab*, most Muslim women in Britain today are far from being in a position to make free, informed choices about their lives, least of all about what to wear.

(Sarda, 2006)

This writer goes on to point out that Muslim women are more likely to be economically inactive, have the highest unemployment rate of any group in Britain, and be disproportionately concentrated in low-pay sectors of the economy (Sarda, 2006).

Other feminists, however, argued for a woman's right to choose what she wore, whatever that represented. It was understandable that women wanted to wear the opposite of the over-sexualised fashions of today, they said (Bunting, 2006). Indeed, according to one male commentator, by wearing the veil, Muslim women were striking a blow for their independence (Sardar, 2006). These latter feminists also insisted, however, that women had a similar right to refuse to wear dress that someone else sought to force them to wear. They quoted examples of attempts to enforce on women the wearing of strict Muslim dress in Afghanistan and Iran:

David Edgar [a liberal commentator] demands that we 'defend to the death' the right of Muslim women to wear the *niqab*. Let's trust, then, that Britain will not ban it. It is because I find the *niqab* repellent that I do not believe it should be outlawed. I would far rather 'defend to the death' the right of women living under Islamicist rule to choose what they wear.

(Lustig, 2006)

Not surprisingly, *Muslim women* whose views were quoted also expressed diverse views. One, who herself wore neither headscarf (*hijab*) nor veil (*niqab*), took a standard liberal line regarding human rights:

He [Straw] may be entitled to his opinion about whether the veil is a 'visual statement of separation and difference', but what right does he have to ask any woman to remove her veil? A woman may put on as many layers of clothing as she likes. That is her human right.

(Rauf, 2006)

Another Muslim woman, wearing a full veil, said:

OK, it's religion first, but modesty comes into it a lot for me. I started using the full veil eight months ago and it's done so much for my self-respect. It's comfortable, I feel protected, and I happily eat out at McDonald's in it. I've devised this special way of getting the food up behind the material'.

(Wainwright, Branigan, Vasagar, Taylor, & Dodd, 2006)

And the story elicited immediate response from Straw's *fellow politicians*. Allies immediately supported him, including members of parliament from neighbouring constituencies. The recent political context for Straw's article had been the Labour Party Conference, at which the issue of multi-culturalism had been belligerently raised by John Reid, Home Office Minister. Britain would not be bullied by Muslim fanatics, he had said, having warned Muslim parents that their children were being targeted by extremists 'looking to groom and brainwash your children for suicide bombing'. Political supporters clearly realised that they were expected to keep the issue prominent. However, two colleagues in the Cabinet later backed off slightly, perhaps after noting the degree of hostility aroused by Straw's speech. Ruth Kelly and Peter Hain said that they would not ask a constituent to remove her veil.

However, parliamentarians with a large proportion of Muslim constituents were much less supportive. For example, Khalid Mahmood MP said:

The debate has turned Islamophobic. It is Jack's fault for raising it. He knows what offence would be caused and what issues would be attached on the back of it. It plays into the hands of extremists on the far right, such as the BNP [British National Party], and on the Muslim side.

(Branigan & Dodd, 2006)

And, said Shahid Malik MP, 'You can't have a real debate on issues when one part of the community feels it is being targeted'.

So *what were the outcomes*? Jack Straw did himself no harm, moving onward and upward and achieving high office in the new government of Gordon Brown in June 2007. Individual Muslim women wearing the *niqab* reported harassment. Said Asma Patel:

> People are now staring at me in the street all the time and making remarks. Last Friday I was in the market when a man came up to me and said 'You won't be keeping that veil on for long'. This sort of thing didn't happen before.
>
> (Ward, 2006)

A journalist, Zaiba Malik, wore a *niqab* for the first time to see how she would be received. She reports:

> A man in his 30s, who might be Dutch, stops in front of me and asks: 'Can I see your face?' 'Why do you want to see my face?' 'Because I want to see if you are pretty. Are you pretty?' Before I can reply, he walks away and shouts 'You fucking tease!'
>
> Then I hear the loud and impatient beeping of a horn. A middle-aged man is leering at me from behind the wheel of a white van. 'Watch where you're going, you stupid Paki!' he screams. This time I'm a bit faster. 'How do you know I'm Pakistani?' I shout. He responds by driving so close that when he yells 'Terrorist!' I can feel his breath on my veil.
>
> (Malik, 2006)

Of course, these reported incidents are not firm evidence of the consequences of Straw's article. But thoughtful commentators remarked that, while it was probably a good idea to discuss the issues of multi-culturalism, separation, and cohesion, the example of the *niqab* was the wrong way to bring them to the media's attention. The fact that Muslims suffer from relative poverty and discrimination is likely to be a more potent cause of alienation and separation than their cultural and religious practices, especially those of the tiny minority of Muslims who wear the *niqab*. Recognition of these economic and social causes makes it less likely that Muslims will be blamed for that separation. A woman Muslim member of Birmingham City Council remarked:

> It's not a neutral conversation. Non-Muslims start from a perception that 'we have all been victimised as a majority by this awkward minority. They start from a hostile stance and the Muslims start from a defensive stance.'
>
> (Cowell, 2006)

Approximately 1.6 million Muslims live in the UK, constituting about 3% of the population.

## Meanings and contexts

So how is it that a single behaviour, wearing the *niqab*, can have so many different meanings for different people? For *Straw*, it connotes the separation between different communities within the UK. To *Muslim women* who wear it, it carries a range of meanings, including modesty, religious obedience, security, and self-affirmation. For *feminists*, it symbolises either the right of women to appear in whatever way they wish, or else the subjugation of women to a patriarchal authority that women have fought hard battles to overcome. For *journalists*, it represents a good story, pressing appropriate buttons in the consciousness of their readerships, be those buttons womens' rights, religious freedom, fears for security, or xenophobia. And for *politicians*, the issue becomes a banana skin on which it is easy to slip as they try to negotiate their path between the varied attitudes of their constituents and the demands of their political party.

Such remarkably different constructions of the wearing of the *niqab* can only be properly understood if we explore the various contexts from within which the issue arose. The first is *the British political context*, both historical and immediate. The 1950s and 1960s were a period of considerable immigration into the UK from countries formerly part of the British Empire, especially the West Indies and Pakistan. The immigrants were not primarily professionals, but poorer people who were willing to undertake unpopular and poorly paid work.

From the start, it was the British government's policy to recognise and welcome cultural differences, although that did not prevent the immigrants' initial, but now decreased, experience of discrimination and prejudice. Muslims tended to live together in certain areas where suitable work was available, for example, the cotton mill towns of Lancashire. They were given considerable freedom at the local level to develop and maintain cultural practices, especially of worship. Religious leaders represented Muslims to authorities at local and national level, and generally encouraged the use of the democratic process. The first generation concentrated on establishing themselves in their new land and earning a living. The support of their extended family, which often lived in their immediate neighbourhood, was an added advantage.

Throughout the 1990s, governments continued with the policy of multiculturalism, dealing with senior Muslims who represented others on various bodies, usually unelected. Yet strains were beginning to show. A report on riots in Bradford in 2001 described the white working-class and the Muslim communities as 'living parallel lives'. Far-right parties such as the British National Party were beginning to make inroads on the Labour Party vote in white areas. The second generation of immigrants, born in the UK, were more aggressive in asserting their rights, and less happy to be represented by conservative imams and local dignitaries.

Then came the assault of 9/11 in 2001, and the subsequent American and British invasions of Afghanistan and Iraq. A proportion of British Muslim youth became politically radicalised, partly because America and the UK had attacked Muslim nations, and partly because radical Islamic clerics had found a useful base in England. The multi-cultural tradition had permitted the development of what Sageman (2004), among others, has called Londonistan. Firebrands such as Abu Qatada and Abu Hamza used mosques, such as the Finsbury Park mosque, as centres for spreading jihadi teachings, raising finance, and recruiting volunteers for jihad.

If they had not been aware of the influence of radical Islam before, the assault of 7 July 2005 on Londoners rendered it impossible for the British government now to ignore it. Indeed, all of the four individuals found guilty of the failed London attack of 21 July 2005 had attended the Finsbury Park mosque at some stage. The rise of the phenomenon of the home-grown terrorist added a whole new dimension.

The government was aware of the danger of scapegoating the Muslim population in general with associated guilt for these crimes. Indeed, there was still the temptation to deny the idea that the Muslim faith, albeit an extreme fundamentalist version of it, had much connexion with them. The close association of Muslim religion and culture rendered this an extremely sensitive political issue. For example, an editorial in the *Guardian* (17 October 2006) on the topic of Straw's article argued that:

> Many whose commitment to Islam is fervent, even extreme . . . nonetheless reject violence. . . . Rather, Islamist terrorists are criminals.

What seems absent from the *Guardian*'s comment is any perception of the process of the radicalisation of young Muslims (see Chapter 5), whereby the espousal of extreme religious beliefs is a necessary condition for the subsequent and ultimate step: the commitment to violent jihad.

Prime Minister Blair's government recognised that separation and alienation of Muslim youth made their recruitment to the jihadi ranks far easier. They stopped certain radical imams from preaching jihad. Instead, however, of addressing two of the other reasons for this alienation (relative Muslim poverty and aggressive British foreign policy), the government sought to establish a greater sense of British identity and community. Among the key values of Britishness to be emphasised were tolerance, freedom, and justice under the (secular) law. These proposed aspects of a British social identity are typical of Western democracies developed under Enlightenment values of pluralism and human rights. They are incompatible with radical fundamentalist Islam.

It was in this domestic political context that Straw made his seemingly spontaneous reaction to the *niqab*. We cannot, however, ignore *world politics*, where Muslim dress has had different meanings. In colonial Egypt in the late nineteenth century, for example (Armstrong, 2006), the British consul-general had sought the abolition of the veil, and therefore wearing it was an act of anti-colonial assertion. However, its significance changed in such theocratic nations as Iran, where in April 2007 a police crackdown on 'incorrect' observation of Islamic dress codes (showing hair, for example) resulted in the arrest of thousands of women in Teheran. In France, on the other hand, the wearing of any form of Muslim dress in schools has been expressly forbidden in the interests of the historic post-Revolution policy of *laïcité*, the removal of all religious symbols from the public sphere. What is clear is that in the Middle East the full veil is a symbol of extremist belief imposed by fundamentalists who have the power of at least partially theocratic states behind them. In the UK, the same is likely to be true; that is, the full veil is mandated by fundamentalist Muslim movements.

This brings us to the second crucial contextual area: *religion*. As usual when we examine a holy book for an explanation of a specific religious ritual or action, there is ambiguity. The key passage in the Qu'ran (24, 30ff) reads as follows:

> Enjoin believing men to turn their eyes away from temptation and to restrain their carnal desires. This will make their lives purer. Allah has knowledge of all their actions.
>
> Enjoin believing women to turn their eyes away from temptation and to preserve their chastity; to cover their adornments (except such as are normally displayed); draw their veils over their bosoms and not to reveal their finery except to their husbands, . . . [there follows a long list of other relatives].

Different Islamic scholars give different interpretations of this passage, and there are different practices in different regions of Islam. However, the important point is that in Britain the wearing of the *niqab* has become a highly visible symbol of difference. It signifies a strong identification with Islam among some of the second generation of British Muslims. As a Muslim mother said:

> When our mums and dads came here, it was all work, work, work for them, no time to study and no mosques. Now we have lessons in English, Urdu, and Arabic and women are learning what their religion really asks them to do.
>
> (Wainwright et al., 2006)

Or again, the journalist who wore the *niqab* for the first time comments:

> My parents only instructed me to cover my hair when I was in the presence of the imam, reading the Qu'ran, or during the call to prayer. Today

I see Muslim girls 10, 20 years younger than me shrouding themselves in fabric. They talk about identity, self-assurance, and faith. Am I missing out on something?

(Malik, 2006)

For the second and third generations of British Muslim women, wearing the *niqab* is indeed an assertion of their devotion to their religion and the modesty it seeks to enforce. For example:

I certainly don't agree with Jack Straw, because my religion demands that I wear this. I have taken the full veil for 16 years now, and I am much more comfortable wearing it. It is a matter of modesty as well as religion. I hope that it will not put other people off. Once they talk to me and get to know me, I think that problem disappears.

(Wainwright et al., 2006)

## So what does it signify?

The significance of this case study is profound, and brings out many of the theoretical points that have been made in the present and previous chapters.

The starting point is a *specific behaviour*: the wearing of the *niqab* by a constituent consulting her member of parliament. Right from the start there is an apparent anomaly. A person wearing the garment decreed by fundamentalist and theocratic groups at the extreme edges of her Muslim faith is actively engaging in the political processes of a Western democracy.

There is no doubt that the specific behaviour is one of the *behavioural norms* that are part of the social identity of fundamentalist Islam. It is enforced in those countries ruled by theocratic governments. Those norms reflect *fundamentalist values*: they are the natural implications of a high value placed on female modesty and a hostility to any behaviour that could remotely be construed as the expression of sexuality. This value, in turn, follows from a *core belief* in the importance of obeying a sovereign God who has commanded such modesty in His holy word. 'My religion demands that I wear this', says the woman in the last quotation above.

The behaviour serves the purpose of powerfully *reinforcing the fundamentalist social identity*. As Straw observes, it separates and distinguishes the wearer from others. It indicates to her and others that she, at least, is strictly obedient. Moreover, the hostile behaviour of some others towards her reinforces and confirms this distinction. The fundamentalist dynamic towards the establishment of in-group and out-group is given added impetus, and the potential for conflict is increased.

Yet there is much more than this going on. For a start, the wearer's embrace of two apparently contradictory identities (theocratic fundamentalist and democratic citizen) immediately adds dimensions of symbolic meaning to her behaviour. It becomes part of the political domain, and is used by a politician for his political purposes. Almost by definition in a modern society, it consequently becomes *mediated* behaviour. With the construction put upon it by Straw, it is mediated at one remove to the readers of the *Lancashire Telegraph*. It passes through several more lenses as it becomes the 'story' of the week. And later, Straw's use of it becomes the story, followed by the uses that are made of Straw's use ('political storm brews')!

Yet these complexities are still explicable in terms of *social identities.* The woman was behaving as citizen, Muslim, and woman. Which of these identities was salient in the social episode of the consultation is a matter of speculation. One commentator (Sardar, 2006) blames Straw vehemently for putting down a *woman* who was actually asserting her independence by going to see her MP. Straw is really suggesting that he believes it was her fundamentalist *Muslim* identity that was salient. However, there is no reason to deny the salience of her role as local *citizen* in a democratic society. She may even have construed herself as *British*.

Indeed, there is no need to suppose that the single social identities of citizen, Muslim, woman, or Briton are the only alternatives. Combinations of these identities to form composite identities might equally well have been salient. For example, Muslim woman, or woman Muslim, depending on where the emphasis lay; or Muslim citizen, or British Muslim, or British Muslim woman. These composite identities may well be more than simply the sum of their parts; they may be more central and salient to the self than each of their parts (Crisp & Hewstone, 2006).

Clearly, living as part of a modern society usually results in the internalisation of several social identities, not all of which are compatible with each other. The image of the Muslim woman trying to eat a McDonald's hamburger through her *niqab* is at once both comic and deeply symbolic. The core theoretical issues raised in this case study concern culture and identity. How are cultures related to each other? How are social identities related to each other? And how are the relationships between cultures related to the relationships between identities? Religious fundamentalisms need to be analysed in these broad terms. The final chapter rashly makes the attempt to do so.

# 10 Fundamentalism is very different

## Cultures and sub-cultures

### *What cultures and identities have in common*

Throughout the first nine chapters I have introduced explanatory concepts from the social sciences piecemeal. They have made their appearance in the argument as seemed appropriate and helpful in understanding fundamentalism at different levels of analysis, from the global, through the local, to the personal level. There has been little structured theoretical account, and this chapter is a very preliminary attempt to provide one. In the belief that there is nothing so practical as a good theory, I will conclude by pointing up some implications for relationships with fundamentalists.

Two broad theoretical concepts have dominated the account: culture and identity. *'Culture'* has been used to analyse the context of fundamentalisms and fundamentalisms themselves, and *'identity'* to seek to understand fundamentalists. Clearly, therefore, the relationship between the social and the personal, the key to analysing the fundamentalist phenomenon, is encapsulated in the relationship between the two concepts.

I have repeatedly referred to three features of both culture and identity. The first is that we need to construe them as *dynamic processes* as well as structures of elements. A culture is dynamic in the sense that its artefacts (which include its behaviours and rituals) acquire symbolic meanings which feed back into its core belief system (see pp. 111–114). In exactly the same way, social identities may change as the behaviour to which they lead accrues symbolic meaning and thereby affects beliefs.

The second feature to note is that the analysis is in terms of *cultures and identities*, not culture and identity. The idea of in-group versus out-group, us versus them, has been a constant refrain throughout this book. Yet even fundamentalists do not possess only their in-group identity. They too live in increasingly pluralistic societies, in which it is becoming more and more difficult to live a mono-cultural life (Deaux, 1996; Brewer, 2000). The Haredim in their urban ghettoes (see Chapter 8) and the Amesh in their rural retreats (pp. 150–151) still make a monumental effort to do so, but theirs is consciously a strategy of separation rather than one of engagement or assault.

The third and final key feature is that both cultures and identities may be consciously changed by *purposeful action* at the individual or group level. They may also change *incidentally* as a consequence of other societal and institutional changes that are themselves purposeful. So the frequently cited example of the Moral Majority represented an institutional change *consciously* engineered by a small group of political and religious conservatives which resulted in cultural and social identity change in American Protestantism. And the rapid development of globalisation has resulted in an increase in uncertainty, which has *incidentally* provided an opportunity for fundamentalist cultures to flourish and for fundamentalist social identities to provide certainty (see Chapter 1).

### *How are cultures organised?*

If cultures and identities have to be considered in their plurality, *how are they organised?* I have consistently talked of cultures and sub-cultures, which implies a *hierarchical relationship* between super-ordinate and subordinate cultures. However, social scientific analysis is unlikely to perfectly parallel biological sciences, where species and sub-species are categorised hierarchically. Rather, such a neat and tidy relationship is but one among several possible, as cultures are fuzzy in outline and definition.

In some cases, the hierarchical relationship does apply, because all the cultures within the hierarchy contain the same core beliefs; one may be termed a sub-culture of the other because it differs on non-core beliefs and other features. Other sub-cultures will likewise share the core, but differ in different ways. So, I have argued that fundamentalism is a general culture because it shares certain core beliefs. However, fundamentalist parts of different religions are sub-cultures, because, although they all share these core fundamentalist beliefs, they differ along other BVNs: Jewish, Christian, and Muslim fundamentalisms are sub-cultures. Similarly, within Christian Protestant fundamentalism, certain core beliefs are shared, for example, the supreme authority of the Bible. However, Protestant fundamentalist movements differ in other features, for example, reconstructionism stresses Reformed doctrine whereas Pentecostalism emphasises the ecstatic fruits of the Spirit. Reconstructionism is therefore a sub-culture of fundamentalist Protestantism, and a sub-sub-culture of fundamentalism.

It is important to note, however, that cultures themselves exist in a context of social change. Biological hierarchies, in contrast, only need to accommodate to the long slow march of evolution. It may be the case that change in a highly superordinate culture will indirectly impact on a sub-culture much lower down the hierarchy. Indeed, I gave an example of global culture change increasing uncertainty and thus increasing the popularity of dogmatic movements such as reconstructionism. However, it is far more likely that detailed cultural change occurs under the influence of more proximal super-ordinate cultures. Increasing theological conservatism in the Southern Baptist Conference, for example, will result in changes in the cultures of individual districts and churches.

However, there are other relationships than hierarchies possible between cultures. First, cultures may simply *overlap*, that is, they may share some central features but not all. American culture and Protestant fundamentalist culture share some core elements, as is clear from Chapter 2. Belief in God, for example, is a shared element, but the belief that secular modernism is seeking to destroy religion is not. And second, cultures may be separate from and *independent* of each other, sharing very few elements or none at all. Reconstructionist culture and football culture are examples.

The *relationships* between cultures may change as well as the cultures themselves. For example, the Haredim regarded themselves as part of Israel before the establishment of Israel as a nation state, but as separate from its secular culture thereafter.

## From culture to identity: Differentiation and representation

### *Social categorisation*

If culture is analogous at the social level of analysis to social identity at the individual level, how are the two constructs related? How do the cultural BVNs of a fundamentalist movement become internalised as BVNs that are part of an individual's specific social identity? The consistent answer throughout this book has been that this internalisation results from *the process of categorisation*. This can occur as a matter of assignment by others, and/or of assertion by the individual (Daniel, 2002). I may apply the social category of 'born-again' to myself, or I may have it assigned to me by my family or by the individual who witnessed to me and helped me get saved (Harding, 2000). Indeed, as Brown (2000) observes, I probably need to get social validation from others for my assumed membership of the category in order to use it to guide my social behaviour.

It is extremely useful if there is already a *label* for the category to which I assign myself or am assigned. The probability that such a label exists is partly a function of whether a recognisable culture supports or implies the category. For example, when a culture is based on an institution, such as the nation or religion, than labels are immediately available: American, or Muslim. But essentially, categories are *social representations*: individuals' constructions of themselves or others. Such social representations themselves have social origins: cultures, and the groups that maintain and enact them. Hence we might expect categories to be organised in a similar way to cultures.

However, there is a further step to account for: how do categories applied to the self or to others become fully blown social identities or stereotypes? In other words, what is the process between, first, calling oneself born-again or jihadi, or being called these things by others; and, second, defining who one is, how one should be evaluated, and how to think, feel and act according to this social identity?

### The organisation of social identities

The process is primarily one of *differentiation*. One seeks to differentiate oneself in positive ways from relevant other groups, thereby enhancing self-esteem and reducing uncertainty. Once such differentiation has occurred, once boundaries have been established, then the self is capable of being defined in terms of this social identity. In other words, that particular social identity can become salient, and social situations can be perceived in its terms. In-group conformity and cohesion, and stereotyping and discrimination against perceived out-groups, often follow. Oneself and others are depersonalised: perceived primarily as prototypical or stereotypical exemplars of categories rather than as individuals (Turner, 1985).

Social identities become salient in the mind when they are important to the individual, and when they are well-practised and therefore easily accessible. Most social situations can be construed in terms of important and accessible social identities.

How then does the individual *organise* his or her several social identities? If the organisation of identities resembles that of the cultures that produce them, then one of its forms should be hierarchical. Indeed, one of the great social psychologists, Gordon Allport, proposed (1979) that all social identities were organised in this way, based on the size of the group from which the identity was derived. From small to large, and core to periphery, these groups were family, neighbourhood, city, state, nation, racial stock, and mankind, with the smaller the group, the stronger the identification. However, a moment's reflection on the contents of the first nine chapters suggests that this hypothesis is unlikely to be consistently supported. Size of group *per se* is hardly likely to determine strength of identification. Mohammed Atta, the 9/11 hijacker, was far more strongly identified with radical Islam than with his family (Herriot, 2007). Rather, we need to ask which psychological needs are being met, and how effectively, by any particular social identity.

Brewer (1991, 1993) proposed that group size is indeed of importance, as Allport suggested, but only in so far as it is related to meeting different psychological needs. The need for *assimilation* into the group, that is, for belonging, or affiliation, is important in itself. However, it is also important as a source of self-esteem (if others welcome and include us, we think better of ourselves). On the other hand, there are also needs for *differentiation*. We need our group to be different from other groups in order to clearly distinguish ourselves from others, to know for certain who we are and how much better we are than them. Thus, a fairly large group may still meet this need, providing it remains sufficiently homogeneous to be clearly distinguishable from out-groups. Although a large group identity certainly adds to status and self-esteem, however, it may not adequately meet assimilation needs. This is because it may not offer the opportunity for face-to-face relationships.

This is where the hierarchical organisation of American fundamentalist Protestant culture and of its derived social identities becomes useful as one explanation for its success. Fundamentalist Protestantism and its denominational sub-cultures provide large categories, which have status in American society and give self-esteem and clear meaning for the self, the world, and daily life. The local congregation and the house-group, on the other hand, meet the need for assimilation and belonging. In contrast, the terrorist cells described in Chapter 5 appeal to the need for belonging and face-to-face approval felt by alienated young British Muslim men. However, they also have to identify with the nebulous and inclusive category of 'Islam' or 'the *ummah*' to meet their need for certainty.

Thus, hierarchical organisation of social identities can benefit the individual, because it meets both of the key needs of the self, for self-esteem and for certainty. However, the key to understanding individuals' organisation of their social identities is to realise that that organisation is *their own subjective representation* of their selves. It does not consist of categories imposed by observers, nor can it be directly inferred from the organisation of cultures. Some social identities may well be hierarchically represented, whereas others may overlap, and others again may be totally separate and distinct from each other. However, the evidence has to be derived from individuals' self-perceptions, or from behaviour from which self-perceptions may be inferred. *The organisation of self-identities is psychologically based.*

How, then, may individuals represent the relationships between their various social identities other than as hierarchies? What do they make of the fact that they believe themselves to be Muslims, Britons, women, and citizens simultaneously (see Chapter 9)? Some people have highly complex representations of these relationships (Roccas & Brewer, 2002). For all we know, the woman constituent interviewed by Jack Straw (pp. 267–278) may have thought of herself in that particular situation as a female Muslim British citizen, a composite social identity in which some elements were probably more important to her than others.

Other people, however, may have far simpler representations. A fundamentalist may perceive his or her fundamentalist identity, as an Islamic jihadi or a true-Torah Jew or a Reformed Protestant, as totally dominant, with all other social identities, such as parent and citizen, completely subordinated to it. The Americans who educate their children at home (see Chapter 4) and who seek to elect born-again believers to democratic institutions (see Chapter 7) are likely to represent their social identities in this way. Or some may perceive their social identities as overlapping each other in a relatively undifferentiated mass, another form of simple representation.

## Differentiation: The key

### Being different

There are, clearly, a variety of different bases for representing social identities. The centrality, or *importance*, of any identity is one, and its *salience* is another. We may recognise some social identities as having an immediate accessibility, perhaps because we use them often and are familiar with them. However, the most important basis for representing identities is the degree of *differentiation* that they provide.

Differentiation is absolutely crucial. This is because the extent to which needs for self-esteem and certainty are met depends upon the degree of differentiation that an identity provides. As groups and the identities they provide become more different, they are evaluated more differently. Any out-group becomes less favourably evaluated, and any in-group more so. In the interests of achieving greater differentiation and distinctiveness, proto-types and stereotypes of in-group and out-group respectively are developed.

Prototypes make clear the characteristics one should have oneself, giving certainty about the sort of person one should be and is in the process of becoming. Stereotypes give an instant way of judging the characteristics of another whom one perceives as a member of an out-group category, and predicting how they will behave. To the extent that members of in-group and out-group conform to their prototype and stereotype, the two categories are more differentiated from one another. This is because there are no members of either group who share some of the characteristics of the other. Boundaries are clearly drawn. In pluralist societies where inter-group boundaries are typically fuzzy, adding to uncertainty about who one is and how one should behave, high differentiation is an attractive alternative option (Hogg, 2001).

When out-groups appear to be becoming increasingly similar to the in-group, the latter increases its bias against them (Jetten & Spears, 2004). Paradoxically, the more alike an out-group appears to be to the in-group, the greater the hostility. This is a counter-intuitive finding, as similarity between people usually results in positive inter-personal attitudes. Differentiation has to be the central aim of the in-group for this paradox to occur. The strength of its social identity is the in-group's major concern. Perhaps this is why some of the greatest fundamentalist hostility is reserved for 'apostates' of their own faith. Conversely, those who are most different to the in-group provide it with a means of self-definition: we are the opposite of them. Thus atheists such as Dawkins (2006) are the sort of out-group that fundamentalists welcome.

### Staying different

How, then, do in-groups succeed in differentiating themselves clearly from out-groups? The development of *prototypes and stereotypes* has already been cited as an effective tool in differentiating the in-group. Another useful method is to *choose the out-group* carefully. Any category or group that is as close as possible to the exact opposite of the in-group's prototype is in line for out-group status. Clearly, such a choice, for example, of atheists, differentiates the fundamentalist in-group very clearly.

There are, however, certain consequences of choosing a much more inclusive out-group, for example, 'evil', 'Satan', or 'the secular world'. When the out-group is so varied and ambiguous, some of its members will inevitably share some of the characteristics of the in-group, thereby threatening the in-group's distinctiveness (Haslam, Oakes, Turner, & McGarty, 1995). The only way to preserve distinctiveness in this case is to become yet more different. It is no accident that al-Qaida and the reconstructionists, among the most extreme of the Islamic and Protestant fundamentalisms, have the most inclusive and ambiguous out-groups.

Another method of ensuring differentiation for the in-group is to *strengthen inter-group boundaries*. For example, one can emphasise the difference in BVNs between the in-group and out-groups. So the reconstructionists incorporated their BVNs into 'the biblical world-view', and contrasted it point by point with 'the secular worldview' (see pp. 211–226). The Haredim have dress and appearance norms that set them apart from other Jews and from gentiles. Another way to strengthen boundaries is to ensure that in-group members have as few other social identities as possible that might be shared with out-group members. This is why fundamentalist movements prefer their adherents to separate themselves as much as possible from secular institutions, providing sanitised Christian or Muslim alternatives when involvement is unavoidable. Christian schools and universities, Muslim *madrassas*, and Jewish *yeshivot* and *kollel* are all attempts to maintain bulwarks against secular education and culture.

A final means of enhancing differentiation is to *emphasise the threat* that the in-group is facing from the out-group. Threat has the advantage of arousing fear and anger, strong motivations for fight or flight. Threat to the self, and to a specific social identity within the self, may be directed at self-esteem and certainty (Hogg & Hornsey, 2006). These are the two needs that social identities, especially highly differentiated ones, are designed to meet. Hence any threat to self-esteem or certainty is likely to increase the salience and differentiation of a social identity.

### Making the most of threats

The first and most obvious form of threat is to the social identity itself, if the existence or status of the group on which the identity is based is in danger. The central and defining feature of all fundamentalisms is the perception that they are threatened by the secular world. If the *status* of the group is threatened, it is *self-esteem* that is primarily at risk. The status of conservative Protestantism in America was diminished by the Scopes 'monkey' trial and, as a result, conservatives withdrew to organise and re-group. Billy Graham's subsequent visits to the White House worked wonders for their self-esteem. In Israel, the status of ultra-orthodox Jews was likewise diminished when the state of Israel was established, and they withdrew further into their enclaves, re-emphasising their distinctiveness. In Islam, twentieth-century nationalist governments immediately disabused the faithful of the notion that they would restore the theocratic glory of pre-colonial Islam. They were doomed to suffer continued humiliation at the hands of the infidel, an unbearable loss of self-esteem that resulted in radical ideologies and violent action.

When the *existence* of the group is threatened, however, the threat is primarily to *certainty*. If the group social identity is central to my self, and is threatened, then it is I myself who am existentially threatened. I am no longer confident about who I am, about my place in the world, about my core beliefs and values: all are in danger. The very essence of my meaning and purpose in life is at risk. Thus, when such a threat is perceived, the typical response is to draw the boundaries in tight, withdraw behind the ramparts, and sally forth as a yet more distinctive, cohesive, and committed band against a stereotyped enemy.

This response to an existential threat requires great homogeneity in the in-group, informed by a prototype of the ideal member to which all members need to aspire and approach. Any individuals who fail to do so will be treated as deviants and expelled. Potential new recruits will be subject to stringent scrutiny (Yzerbit, Leyens, & Bellour, 1995). Leaders will be accepted who exemplify the prototype. They will be expected not only to act as models, but also to enforce group homogeneity. The key to differentiating the in-group from others is to have a strong and clear prototype (Pickett & Brewer, 2001).

The perception of threat is central to fundamentalisms. The previous nine chapters are full of examples of the different ways of dealing with this perceived threat. All involve differentiation, the establishment of a distinctive social identity. Some fundamentalisms signal their differences loud and clear by their distinctive dress and symbolic behaviour. Others proclaim their own unique doctrines and denounce their enemies as apostates or infidels.

However, we may ask the question: to what extent are fundamentalists' perceptions of threat justified? Are they really under threat to their existence, or is the threat more symbolic in nature (Stephan & Stephan, 2000)? And does it matter if the threat is perceived rather than real, if the consequences are the same? There is probably no single answer to these questions. The threat to individual jihadis' lives from the military of various nations is obviously real, but whether this is a real threat to the jihadi movement is another question. Aggressive tactics may succeed in removing jihadis at the individual level, but result in the acquisition of angry young recruits to the movement who welcome martyrdom.

There is no existential threat to such Protestant groups as the reconstructionists, because American democracy guarantees freedom of worship. Yet if the three core beliefs of fundamentalism really are under attack from secularism in America, to what extent is fundamentalism itself threatened? If we accept that their core beliefs are a basic element of fundamentalists' social identity, then surely that identity is threatened by secularism. And if the identity is threatened, so is the social movement. We should probably conclude that both real and symbolic threats lead to differentiation of the fundamentalist social identity; but that real threat is more likely to result in violent response.

## Fundamentalism: the most distinctive social identity

### *Ways of ensuring fundamentalists' distinctiveness*

The above theoretical overview points directly to one basic conclusion: *all of the factors that predict a powerful and distinctive social identity are present in the case of fundamentalisms*. Not only are they present; they are present in spades.

Fundamentalist movements have well-developed prototypes and stereotypes that enhance differentiation from out-groups. From the 'good soldiers', the steadfast martyrs who carried out 9/11 (Herriot, 2007 Chapter 4) through the 'biblically sound' Anglicans who are seeking to gain control via the issue of gays (Bates, 2004), to the 'true-Torah' Jews who alone are truly observant (see Chapter 9), the picture is the same. A prototype of the group member provides a unique differentiation from everyone else. Charismatic leaders exemplify and enforce the prototype, quashing dissent and expelling deviants. Because of the absolutist nature of the prototypical BVNs, those who cannot subscribe to even a relatively insignificant B,V, or N leave and create new movements. The immense variety and profusion of fundamentalist sects in all religions bears paradoxical witness to the homogeneity of the original movement.

Homogeneity of the in-group prototype enables differentiation in another way for fundamentalisms. It permits them to choose their out-group so as to be most distinct from themselves. They can select an out-group that best exemplifies the opposite BVNs to their own, thereby pointing up the difference between themselves and others. Defenders of the *ummah* require a major enemy: the Great Satan. Champions of Christian morality need gays and pornographers. True-Torah Jews choose the flesh-pots of Tel Aviv against which to rail.

Their stereotypes of their chosen out-group allow fundamentalists to make social judgements of out-group members. These judgements result in actions that expect a response in accordance with the stereotype. These self-fulfilling prophecies are fulfilled, the stereotype is confirmed, and differentiation is reinforced. In particular, fundamentalists are able to use out-groups' hostile responses to them as confirmation of the rightness of their own prototype. If as a Haredi you consider that driving on the Sabbath is a typical behaviour of a non-observant Jew (see Chapter 9), then the driver's angry response to your well-aimed stone simply confirms that he is wrong and you are right.

Religious Fundamentalism

Moreover, your choice of target and the degree of hostility of your action towards a fellow Jew indicate something more: that differentiation from the less observant is your main concern. This is because other Jews are more of a threat to your distinctiveness, because they are more like you than the gentiles. The contrast between the Haredim and the other major Jewish fundamentalism, Gush Emunim (see Chapter 3), is notable. The Gush do not regard other Jews as their major out-group because distinctiveness is not their most major concern. Arabs are their chosen enemy.

### Boundaries and threats

Fundamentalist absolutism is another powerful driver towards extreme differentiation. If you are the only true believers, then everyone else is the out-group. However, if you do actually treat the whole of the rest of the world as your out-group you have a problem, because inevitably there are some out there who are quite like you. The rest of the world is, after all, a fairly inclusive category! The only way to ensure that you are different is to become uniquely extreme. Reconstructionists and al-Qaida believe that the whole of the rest of the world is in error. For the reconstructionists, the distinction is between the Biblical world-view and the secular world-view, the former of course consisting solely of their own world-view. As for al-Qaida, there are no truly Muslim nations, and therefore they are the only true revolutionary vanguard fighting the war against both apostate Muslims and infidels. As a consequence of their inclusive out-groups, these two movements are forced to become far-out extremists to keep themselves sufficiently different.

Throughout this book, the emphasis of fundamentalisms on maintaining their boundaries has been repeatedly exemplified. Unique language and practice, unusual BVNs, and prohibitions on secular associations ensure that adherents are not at risk of being contaminated. Different strategic approaches to contact with the world (see pp. 89–90) imply different ways of maintaining boundaries. Those movements that favour a strategy of *separation*, such as the Haredim and the Amesh, draw defensive boundaries. They seek to establish a clear defensive wall against secular encroachment. Those *engaging*, on the other hand, face a different problem. By definition, they are involved in the political process, and therefore compromise is always a likely outcome. The history of American fundamentalisms in the twentieth century is one of repeated periods of engagement, followed by separation as they re-affirm their identity. The final strategy, of *assault*, requires less boundary maintenance. The out-group is always demonised, thereby increasing in-group differentiation. And their various forms of aggression enable adherents to justify only hostile contact. No form of dialogue or co-operation is ever contemplated; the only communication is of threats.

The *perception of threat* was discussed above as the prime motive for differentiation. It is the central definitive feature of fundamentalisms. Hence, fundamentalisms are likely to be highly differentiated. Fundamentalists perceive threats to their self-esteem and to the certainty of their belief and value systems. Threats to self-esteem may be largely historically based. Fundamentalists' constant nostalgia for a golden age of pious purity reflects some more recent losses of status and self-esteem. Within the last two centuries, Islam has lost its empires and its status, despite its numerical growth. And in the twentieth century, both Orthodox Judaism and Protestant orthodoxy faced major secular challenges to their high social standing. By differentiating themselves and portraying themselves as suffering and downtrodden minorities, fundamentalisms have made the most of this loss of status. The role of minority fighting for its rights is a good strategic choice in the late-modern era, providing both justification and motivation. The unpopularity of theocracy when fundamentalisms cease to be minorities, as in Afghanistan with the Taliban, indicates the benefit of continued minority status.

The current context for fundamentalisms, the process of *globalisation*, which takes modernity to its ultimate conclusion, contributes immensely to their attractiveness and growth. Uncertainty threatens the self, in different ways in wealthy and poor nations. Perceived powerlessness and insignificance damage self-esteem. And fundamentalisms, with their unique capacity for differentiation, meet the needs for certainty and self-esteem very successfully. Far from being surprised at their success, we should rather recognise and understand their achievement in attracting so many adherents. If we do so, a meaningful choice may be made from among the various options open to us regarding how best to relate to them.

## Some social scientific solutions

The heading of this section includes the word 'solutions', and thereby implies that there is a problem with fundamentalism. Few would deny that we face a problem in dealing with fundamentalist violence, but it should by now be evident that relatively few fundamentalists are violent. Many ideologies have been used and misused to motivate and justify violence. What characterises fundamentalism is that it is reactive and oppositional: it needs enemies, and thrives on conflict. But should we be concerned about political, social, and moral conflict as such? Many would argue that conflict often results in a new synthesis, in which some equilibrium is achieved between conservative and progressive elements in society. It could also be argued, however, that the issues facing the human race are now so profound that energy spent on ideological disputes is energy wasted. And from a liberal perspective, the problem of how to deal tolerantly with intolerant people is an eternal dilemma. Given these reservations, we may still seek solutions to the real daily issue of how to behave as societies and as individuals towards fundamentalists. After all, many may feel that they have been constituted as an out-group by fundamentalists' aggressive self-differentiation.

### The societal response: hostility

The most frequent response to fundamentalists has been one of *hostility*. If my analysis is correct, most of us find help in deciding who we are by comparing ourselves with those who we are not. Fundamentalists provide a very useful out-group for comparison purposes, just as secularists provide a comparison group for them. When fundamentalists attack us symbolically, verbally, or physically, we typically return their hostility. Whether it be George W. Bush declaring war on 'terror', or Richard Dawkins belabouring them for 'hatred of women, modernity, rival religions, science and pleasure; love of punishment, bullying, [and] narrow-minded bossy interference in every aspect of life' (Dawkins, 2006, p. 326), we are providing them with a comparison group against which to firm up their difference.

A more subtle way of being hostile is to seek to undo them through a Trojan horse strategy. In other words, efforts are made to foment schism, to encourage deviants, and thereby to make the movement's leadership so totalitarian and repressive as to be intolerable to adherents. However, a brief scan of religious history indicates that the new sects so formed are usually more extreme and fundamentalist than before (see pp. 74–77). The same outcome is likely when attempts are made to seduce their leadership into the ways of the secular world. The leadership may be disgraced, but they are replaced by a new and sterner breed.

Social scientists have come up with ways of reducing inter-group bias and conflict; some of these might be thought appropriate to fundamentalisms. These strategies consciously seek *to decrease the strength of the in-group identity by reducing its degree of difference*. Various strategies have been proposed to persuade the in-group to develop additional social identities, thus reducing the differentiation that is gained by possessing one central, dominant, and highly distinctive one.

### Introducing new categories

The first of these strategies seeks to provide a salient super-ordinate category that both in-group and out-group can share (Gaertner & Dovidio, 2000). For example, both Muslims and Christians might be encouraged to construe themselves as British (see Chapter 9). However, the immediate and obvious threat to distinctiveness involved in any super-ordinate category, together with the difficulty of making it stick, makes this solution problematic.

One way of ameliorating this problem is to ensure that the in-group and out-group retain their distinctive social identities while still taking on the super-ordinate category (Hewstone & Brown, 1986). This might be achieved by ensuring that each group makes its own unique contribution to a communal effort, especially if that effort is against a common threat. Group boundaries and distinctiveness are thus preserved in a context of mutual inter-dependence.

However, it is still likely that a fundamentalist in-group will regard itself as superior to the out-group, and the latter's contribution will be down-played. A specific cause of such a continuing superiority complex may be found in the nature of the super-ordinate identity selected (Mummendey & Wenzel, 1999). If this identity contains elements only of the in-group's prototype, then the out-group will continue to be denigrated, for it will be perceived as deficient in those terms. A famine-relief organisation that proclaimed God's concern for justice for the poor would enable religious partners to continue to feel superior to secular contributors. The super-ordinate identity has to contain features of both groups' prototypes if it is to be accepted. So, for example, if two religious movements were to unite in a humanitarian endeavour, the super-ordinate category would have to contain those elements of each which stressed their concern for justice and compassion. In other words, the need is to craft 'an understanding (or developing meaning) of the super-ordinate that recognises and values the sub-groups' (McGarty, 2006, p. 33).

Inevitably, however, these strategies give rise to the perception of threat to the identity and to the desire to maintain one's positive distinctiveness, even though inter-group bias is often successfully decreased. Other strategies have sought to avoid this trap, and one such is known as the *crossed categorisation* approach (Deschamps & Doise, 1978). Here, sub-groups are formed that consist of members of the in-group and members of the out-group, respectively. However, these two groups are 'cross-cut' along the dimensions of another unrelated category. For example, Afro-Caribbean versus white ethnicity might be cross-cut with gender to give four groups: Afro-Caribbean men, white men, Afro-Caribbean women, and white women. In this way, bias can be shifted from one dimension to another as each becomes more or less salient according to the situation. Afro-Caribbean men may respect Afro-Caribbean women more, for example, if both feel the need to differentiate themselves from white men and women.

However, this solution, too, fails to appreciate the importance of social identities. It is only when the strength of *existing social identities* is taken into account that cross-categorisation stands a chance of success. If, in the above example, gender is central and important to individuals, but ethnicity is not, then cross-cutting these two categories is futile (Crisp, 2006).

## New categories or a new context?

### *Fundamentalism is too central an identity*

Thus the maintenance of distinct social identities has been proposed, in one form or another, paradoxically as a way of reducing bias and conflict. However, there are several reasons why these strategies are unlikely to be effective in the case of fundamentalisms.

The first, and most obvious, is that any secular attempt to influence fundamentalists for change *is bound to be interpreted as a hostile attack*. Further, it is important, and very difficult, to specify at what levels of bias and conflict direct policy intervention is justified. Freedom of religious belief and practice is a cornerstone of democratic and certain other societies. Finally, the conflict-resolution models are based upon the assumption that there are two distinguishable categories of person between whom differences may be decreased. This is certainly true of, for example, fundamentalists and liberals in the Anglican Communion who are in conflict over gay bishops. However, in the violent conflicts in which intervention is clearly justified, there is no such clarity. While the in-group, such as al-Qaida, defines itself clearly and exclusively, their out-group is in effect the whole of the rest of the world, for in terrorist attacks, anyone may be killed, including fellow Muslims.

Another difficulty with strategies based on manipulations of categories becomes apparent as soon as we recognise that interventions are not going to work if they *use the policy-maker's categories*. It is only when the categories used are part of individuals' repertoire of social identities that they can be effective. This being so, fundamentalists are extremely unlikely candidates for successful interventions of this sort. They are likely to have one central, important, and frequently salient social identity, that of their movement. Other social identities are likely to be represented as subordinated to this one, for example, those of parent and citizen. Such subordinated identities are likely to add to this distinctiveness: not only are they Evangelicals, but also home-schoolers and supporters of fundamentalist candidates for local and political office. These additional characteristics add to their fundamentalist distinctiveness, rather than providing alternative modes of categorisation. All of them may simply coalesce with the core fundamentalist identity to create a self that is reliably distinguished from all other possible selves.

Several other reasons why interventions are unlikely to be successful with fundamentalists have recurred throughout this book. First, they are likely to have their personal needs for self-esteem and meaning more than adequately served by fundamentalism. *Why should they go elsewhere?* Second, more practically, there is considerable social utility to fundamentalists in having simple stereotypes to apply in social situations so that one can *respond rapidly*. Third, fundamentalists' extraordinary commitment to their central social identity [described by Iannacone (1994) as 'strict religion'] leaves *little time or energy* for the other activities that the salience of other social identities would imply.

How, then, *should* we relate to fundamentalists? Certainly it seems that both reactive hostility and also explicit policy intervention based on social scientific analysis are likely to be counter-productive in this particular instance. If we accept that *a different context* would offer alternative and more attractive ways of meeting psychological needs, what sort of contextual changes are required? For example, it could be argued that *more pluralist societies* offer more alternative social identities. However, it is possible, on the basis of the evidence reviewed in this book, that increased pluralism would simply provide more out-groups by which fundamentalists could differentiate themselves, and create more uncertainty to which fundamentalisms offer the answer.

Another alternative is to hope that the *personal*, as opposed to the social, identities of fundamentalists can be made more salient (Brewer & Miller, 1984). When social contexts are personalised, and people believe that they are dealing with unique individuals rather than with representatives of another category, the salience of the fundamentalist identity will decrease, as will derogatory stereotypes (Vanbeselaere, 1991). In other words, *de-categorisation* occurs.

However, it is difficult to imagine fundamentalists being willing to risk such a degree of social intimacy. Their boundaries are usually drawn too tightly for deep personal contact, and they are encouraged to marry within their movement. And this solution appears to be based upon one-to-one relationships, which may or may not percolate up to social institutions. Perhaps the only opportunity for de-categorisation might occur in situations of extreme common threat, for example, to the future of Planet Earth. Yet even this example demonstrates the possibility of alternative constructions of the situation based on different world-views. For ecologists, the survival of the planet and its inhabitants is indeed at risk; for some fundamentalists, the multiple indications of dangerous climate change are signs that the millennial return of the Lord is nigh.

### Changing the context

To conclude, instead of seeking only to change fundamentalists, we need to change ourselves and our society. Fundamentalisms thrive on opposition, and we have been only too willing to provide that opposition. Just as fundamentalists have defined their religion in contrast to our secularism, so we have done the reverse. We have defined our modernism (or our post-modernism) in contrast to their fundamentalism. Instead of assaulting their barricades, thereby encouraging them to build them higher and to sally out ever more ferociously, we should blur the boundaries. If, for example, mainstream religion can be recognised as a potentially powerful ally in promoting peace, justice, and personal well-being in the world, we would be diminishing fundamentalisms by our indifference to them, rather than building them up by our hostility.

Of course, this does not imply that we should not attempt to catch and punish according to the law those who plan or commit terrorist offences (defined as violent and indiscriminate assaults aimed at inducing terror for political or religious purposes). We can never be indifferent to such attacks upon the rule of law and the safety of the citizen; on the contrary, we should pursue them with the utmost rigour as they represent an appalling personal, civil, and political threat. However, terrorists should be treated as criminal offenders rather than as representatives of particular religions. Whilst fundamentalist religious beliefs may have motivated and justified their actions, it is the action rather than the belief that constitutes their offence. Fundamentalist belief systems should be construed as social and psychological outcomes of historic and contemporary cultural processes, held by infinitely more people than are ever likely to engage in terrorist activity.

Ultimately, our solution to the 'problem' of fundamentalism has to be societal. The unique contribution of the social sciences is to point out how successful fundamentalisms are in meeting the central human needs for self-esteem and certainty, and to suggest reasons for that success. However, it is the task of everyone, personally and institutionally, to seek to bring about an economic and political context that provides greater transactional, procedural, and interactional justice for all. Such a context would enhance self-esteem and reduce uncertainty, so decreasing the attraction of reactionary movements such as fundamentalisms. Transactional justice would result in equity, procedural justice in transparency, and interactional justice in respect. Equity, transparency, and respect go a long way towards meeting the personal and social needs of human beings. To fight for justice is likely to be more rewarding than to fight against fundamentalism.

How likely are we to succeed in diminishing the threats posed by fundamentalism? There are few current indications of any decrease in the attractiveness of fundamentalisms. Rather, certain trends argue that they may increase in membership. If we assume that fundamentalists are usually already religious people who become attracted to an extremist version of their faith, it follows that there is more chance of people becoming fundamentalists in those parts of the world where religion in general is maintaining or enhancing its power. Norris and Inglehart (2004) demonstrate that these areas are: first, agrarian societies, and second, those societies in which there are major differences in wealth between the richest and the poorest. These two contexts are precisely those in which justice issues are most pronounced. If we further assume that the experience of injustice is fertile soil for fundamentalisms, and then factor in the tendency of agrarian societies to have higher birth rates than industrial and post-industrial societies, the conclusion seems inescapable. Unless we champion justice for all we are worth, the future favours an increase in fundamentalism.

## Summary

- The key theoretical concepts in this book have been culture and identity.
- Both are dynamic processes, both are enacted in several forms by individuals, and both can be consciously changed.
- Cultures are sometimes organised hierarchically into sub-cultures, but they may also overlap with, or be independent of, each other.
- Cultures become internalised as social identities through the process of categorisation. However, in order to become a central and salient social identity, a category has to become sharply differentiated from other categories.

- Some categories may be organised hierarchically, and identities so organised are likely to meet the needs of affiliation, self-esteem, and certainty.
- Fundamentalists are likely to represent their fundamentalist identity as central and super-ordinate to all other identities.
- This is because they have highly differentiated this identity from all others by a variety of methods. These include the development of prototypes and stereotypes, the careful choice of out-group, the maintenance of strong boundaries, and above all an emphasis on the secular threat to their existence.
- As a result of this extreme distinctiveness, efforts to apply successful methods of conflict reduction that involve the introduction of additional social identities are likely to fail.
- It is concluded that only a global increase in the various forms of justice will meet needs for self-esteem and certainty.
- Improving justice can reduce the attractiveness of fundamentalisms and counteract the effect of certain trends which favour fundamentalisms.

## Further reading

Brewer, M.B. (1993) The role of distinctiveness in social identity and group behaviour. In M.A. Hogg & D. Abrams (eds.) *Group Motivation: Social Psychological Perspectives*. London: Harvester Wheatsheaf.

Crisp, R.J. & Hewstone, M. (2006) (eds.) *Multiple Social Categorisation: Processes, Models, and Applications*. Hove, UK: Psychology Press.

Deaux, K. (1996) Social identification. In E.T. Higgins & A.W. Kruglanski (eds.) *Social Psychology: Handbook of Basic Principles*. New York: Guilford.

Gaertner, S.L. & Dovidio, J.F. (2000) *Reducing Intergroup Bias: The Common Ingroup Identity Model*. Philadelphia: Psychology Press.

Hewstone, M. & Brown, R.J. (1986) (eds.) *Contact and Conflict in Intergroup Encounters*. Oxford: Blackwell.

Hogg, M.A. (2001) *Self-categorisation and Subjective Uncertainty Reduction: Cognitive and Motivational Aspects of Interpersonal Behaviour*. New York: Cambridge University Press.

Hogg, M.A. & Abrams, D. (2001) (eds.) *Inter-group Relations: Essential Readings*. Philadelphia: Psychology Press.

Oskamp, S. (2000) (ed.) *Reducing Prejudice and Discrimination*. Mahwah, NJ: Lawrence Erlbaum.

# Bibliography

Adams, G. & Markus, H.R. (2004) Toward a conception of culture suitable for a social psychology of culture. In M. Schaller & C.S. Crandall (eds) *The Psychological Foundations of Culture*. Mahwah, NJ: Lawrence Erlbaum.

Adorno, T.W., Frenkel-Brunswik, E., Levinson, D.J., & Sanford, R.N. (1950) *The Authoritarian Personality*. New York: Harper & Row.

Akbar, M.J. (2002) *The Shade of Swords: Jihad and the Conflict between Islam and Christianity*. London: Routledge.

Albert, S. & Whetten, D.A. (1985) Organisational identity. In L.L. Cummings & B.M. Staw (eds.) *Research in Organisational Behaviour*, 7, 263–295. Englewood Cliffs, NJ: Prentice-Hall.

Al Jazeera (1999) 10 June.

Allport, F.H. (1924) *Social Psychology*. Boston, MA: Houghton Mifflin.

Allport, G.W. (1979) *The Nature of Prejudice*. Reading, MA: Addison-Wesley.

Almond, G.A., Appleby, R.S., & Sivan, E. (2003) *Strong Religion: The Rise of Fundamentalisms around the World*. Chicago: University of Chicago Press.

Altemeyer, B. (1988) *Enemies of Freedom: Understanding Right-Wing Authoritarianism*. San Francisco: Jossey Bass.

Altemeyer, B. (1996) *The Authoritarian Spectre*. Boston, MA: Harvard University Press.

Altemeyer, B. & Hunsberger, B. (1992) Authoritarianism, religious fundamentalism, quest, and prejudice. *International Journal of the Psychology of Religion*, 2, 113–133.

Al-Zawahiri, A. (2001) *Knights Under the Prophet's Banner*. London: Al-Sharq al-Awsat.

Ammerman, N.T. (1987) *Bible Believers*. New Brunswick, NJ: Rutgers University Press.

Anthony, A. (2006) *The Observer*, 13 August.

Anthony, D. & Robbins, T. (1994) Brainwashing and totalitarian influence. In U.S. Ramachdran (ed.) *Encyclopaedia of Human Behaviour*, Vol. 1. New York: Academic Press.

Anti-Defamation League (2005) *American Attitudes Toward Religion in the Public Square*. Washington, DC: ADL.

Aran, G. (1986) The roots of Gush Emunim. In P.Y. Medding (ed.) *Studies in Contemporary Jewry*. Bloomington, IN: University of Indiana Press.

Aran, G. (1991) Jewish Zionist fundamentalism: The Bloc of the Faithful in Israel

(Gush Emunim). In M.E. Marty & R.S. Appleby (eds.) *Fundamentalisms Observed*. Chicago: University of Chicago Press.

Armstrong, A. (1991) *Muhammad: A Biography of the Prophet*. London: Victor Gollancz.

Armstrong, K. (1993) *A History of God*. London: Heinemann.

Armstrong, K. (2000a) *The Battle for God: Fundamentalism in Judaism, Christianity, and Islam*. London: HarperCollins.

Armstrong, K. (2000b) *Islam: A Short History*. London: Phoenix.

Armstrong, K. (2006) My years in a habit taught me the paradox of veiling. *The Guardian*, 26 October.

Aronson, E. (1999) Dissonance, hypocrisy, and the self-concept. In E. Harmon-Jones & J. Mills (eds.) *Cognitive Dissonance: Progress on a Pivotal Theory in Social Psychology*. Washington, DC: American Psychological Association.

Aronson, E., Blanton, H., & Cooper, J. (1995) From dissonance to disidentification: Selectivity in the self-affirmation process. *Journal of Personality and Social Psychology*, 68, 986–996.

Aronson, E. & Mills, J. (1959) The effect of severity of initiation on liking for a group. *Journal of Abnormal and Social Psychology*, 59, 177–181.

Asch, S.E. (1955) Opinions and social pressure. *Scientific American*, 193, 31–55.

Ashforth, B.E. & Mael, F.A. (1989) Social identity theory and the organisation. *Academy of Management Review*, 14, 20–39.

Bahnsen, G. (1987) At war with the word – the necessity of biblical antithesis. Online. Available: http://www.salemreformed.org/AtWarWiththeWord.html

Bahnsen, G.L. (1991) *No Other Standard: Theonomy and its Critics*. Tyler, TX: Institute for Christian Economics.

Bainbridge, W.S. (1997) *The Sociology of Religious Movements*. New York: Routledge.

Balmer, R. (2000) *Mine Eyes Have Seen the Glory: A Journey into the Evangelical Subculture in America* (3rd edn.). New York: Oxford University Press.

Balz, D. & VandeHei, J. (2005) Bush speech not a sign of policy shift, officials say. *Washington Post*, 22 January.

Baptist Bible Fellowship International (2004) 'Statement of belief'. Online. Available: http://www.bbfi.org

Bartlett C.A. & Ghoshal, S. (1990) *Managing Across Borders: The Transnational Solution*. Boston, MA: Harvard Business School Press.

Basham, P. (2001) Home schooling: From the extreme to the mainstream. *Public Policy Sources*, 51. Vancouver, BC: The Fraser Institute.

Bates, S. (2004) *A Church at War: Anglicans and Homosexuality*. London: IBTauris.

Batson, C.D., Floyd, R.B., Meyer, J.M., & Winner, A.L. (1999) 'And who is my neighbour?' Intrinsic religion as a source of universal compassion. *Journal for the Scientific Study of Religion*, 38, 445–457.

Batson, C.D., Schoenrade, P., & Ventis, W.L. (1993) *Religion and the Individual*. New York: Oxford University Press.

Bauman, K.J. (2002) Home schooling in the United States: Trends and characteristics. *Education Policy Analysis Archives*, 10, 26.

Bauman, Z. (1987) *Legislators and Interpreters: On Modernity, Postmodernity and Intellectuals*. Cambridge: Polity Press.

Bauman, Z. (1992) *Intimations of Postmodernity*. London: Routledge.

Baumeister, R.F. (1999) The nature and structure of the self: An overview. In R.F. Baumeister (ed.) *The Self in Social Psychology*. Hove, UK: Psychology Press.

BBC News (2006a) Online. Available: http://news.bbc.co.uk

BBC News (2006b) *Why are Jews at the 'Holocaust denial' conference?* 12 December. Online. Available: http://news.bbc.co.uk

Beaman, L.G. (2003) The myth of pluralism, diversity, and vigor: The constitutional privilege of Protestantism in the United States and Canada. *Journal of the Scientific Study of Religion*, 42 (3), 311–325.

Beliles, M.A. & McDowell, S.K. (1991) *America's Providential History* (2nd edn.) Charlottesville, VA: Providence Foundation.

Bem, D.J. (1972) Self-perception theory. In L. Berkowitz (ed.) *Advances in Experimental Social Psychology*, Vol. 6. New York: Academic Press.

Berger, P. & Luckmann, T. (1966) *The Social Construction of Reality: A Treatise in the Sociology of Knowledge*. New York: Doubleday Anchor.

Berger, P. & Luckmann, T. (1967) *The Social Construction of Reality*. Garden City, NY: Anchor.

Bibby, R.W. (1978) Why conservative churches are growing: Kelley revisited. *Journal for the Scientific Study of Religion*, 17, 129–137.

bin Laden, O. (1996) Declaration of Jihad against the Americans occupying the land of the two holy mosques. *Al Islah*, 2 September.

bin Laden, O. (1998) Text of Fatwa urging Jihad against Americans. *Al Quds Al Arabi*, 23 February.

bin Laden, O. (2004) To the Muslims in Iraq in particular and the Nation in general. *Al-Sahab*, 27 [quoted in Gerges 2005, pp. 251–252].

Blanchard, C.M. (2006) *Al Qaeda: Statements and Evolving Ideology*. Washington, DC: Library of Congress.

Bond, R. & Smith, P.B. (1996) Culture and conformity: A meta-analysis of studies using Asch's line judgement task. *Psychological Bulletin*, 119, 111–137.

Boone, K.C. (1989) *The Bible Tells Them So: The Discourse of Protestant Fundamentalism*. New York: University of New York Press.

Boston, R. (2000) *Close Encounters with the Religious Right*. New York: Prometheus.

Boyer, P. (1992) *When Time Shall Be No More: Prophecy Belief in Modern American Culture*. Cambridge, MA: Harvard University Press.

Branigan, T. & Dodd, V. (2006) Muslim leaders 'risking voluntary apartheid' as veil row escalates. *The Guardian*, 16 October.

Brewer, M.B. (1991) The social self: On being the same and different at the same time. *Personality and Social Psychology Bulletin*, 17, 475–482.

Brewer, M.B. (1993) The role of distinctiveness in social identity and group behaviour. In M.A. Hogg & D. Abrams (eds.) *Group Motivation: Social Psychological Perspectives*. London: Harvester Wheatsheaf.

Brewer, M.B. (2000) Reducing prejudice through cross-categorisation: Effects of multiple social identities. In S. Oskamp (ed.) *Reducing Prejudice and Discrimination*. Mahwah, NJ: Lawrence Erlbaum.

Brewer, M.B. & Miller, N. (1984) Beyond the contact hypothesis: Theoretical perspectives on desegregation. In N. Miller & M.B. Brewer (eds.) *Groups in Contact: The Psychology of Desegregation*. San Diego, CA: Academic Press.

Brinkerhoff, M.B., Grandin, E., & Lupri, E. (1992) Religious involvement and spousal violence: The Canadian case. *Journal for the Scientific Study of Religion*, 31, 15–31.

Brown, R.J. (2000) *Group Processes* (2nd edn.) Oxford: Blackwell.

Brown, R.M. (2002) *For a "Christian America"*. Amherst, NY: Prometheus Books.

Bruce, S. (2000) *Fundamentalism*. Cambridge: Polity Press.

Bruce, S. (2002) *God is Dead: Secularisation in the West*. Oxford: Blackwell.

Bruner, J. (1990) *Acts of Meaning*. Cambridge, MA: Harvard University Press.

Bryman, A. (1996) Leadership in organisations. In S.R. Clegg, C. Hardy, & W.R. Nord (eds) *Handbook of Organisation Studies*. London: Sage.

Bunting, M. (2006) Straw's storm of prejudice. *Guardian Weekly*, 14 October.

Bunyan, N. & Wilson, G. (2006) Take off your veils, says Straw. *Daily Telegraph*, 6 October.

Byrne, D. (1969) Attitudes and attraction. In L. Berkowitz (ed.) *Advances in Experimental Social Psychology*, Vol. 4. New York: Academic Press.

Carpenter, J.A. (1997) *Revive Us Again: The Reawakening of American Fundamentalism*. New York: Oxford University Press.

Casanova, J. (1994) *Public Religions in the Modern World*. Chicago: Chicago University Press.

Castells, M. (1996) *The Rise of the Network Society*. Oxford: Blackwell.

Choueiri, Y.M. (1997) *Islamic Fundamentalism*. London: Pinter.

Clarke, T. & Clegg, S. (1998) *Changing Paradigms: The Transformation of Management Knowledge for the 21st Century*. London: HarperCollins.

Coalition on Revival (2005) The Christian Worldview of Psychology and Counselling. Online. Available: http://www.reformation.net

Coleman, S. (2000) *The Globalisation of Charismatic Christianity: Spreading the Gospel of Prosperity*. Cambridge: Cambridge University Press.

Cosgel, M.M. (2001) The commitment process in a religious commune: The Shakers. *Journal for the Scientific Study of Religion*, 40, 27–38.

Cowan, R. & Norton-Taylor, R. (2006) At the receiving end of al-Qaida campaign. *The Guardian Weekly*, 27 October–2 November.

Cowell, A. (2006) For multiculturalist Britain, uncomfortable new clothes. *New York Times*, 22 October.

Cox, H. (1995) *Fire from Heaven: The Rise of Pentecostal Spirituality and the Reshaping of Religion in the Twenty-first Century*. Reading, MA: Addison-Wesley.

Crisp, R.J. & Hewstone, M. (2006) (eds.) *Multiple Social Categorisation: Processes, Models, and Applications*. Hove, UK: Psychology Press.

Crisp, R.J. (2006) Commitment and categorisation in common ingroup contexts. In R.J. Crisp & M. Hewstone (eds.) *Multiple Social Categorisation: Processes, Models, and Applications*. Hove, UK: Psychology Press.

Cullison, A. (2004) Inside al-Qaeda's hard drive. *Atlantic Monthly*, 294 (2), 55–70.

Daniel, G.R. (2002) *More than Black? Multiracial Identity and the New Racial Order*. Philadelphia: Temple University Press.

Danso, H., Hunsberger, B., & Pratt, M. (1997) The role of parental religious fundamentalism and right-wing authoritarianism in child-rearing goals and practices. *Journal of the Scientific Study of Religion*, 36, 496–511.

Dawkins, R. (2006) *The God Delusion*. London: Bantam Press.

Deaux, K. (1996) Social identification. In E.T. Higgins & A.W. Kruglanski (eds.) *Social Psychology: Handbook of Basic Principles*. New York: Guilford.

Dein, S. (2001) What really happens when prophecy fails? The case of Lubavitch. *Sociology of Religion*, 62, 383–401.

Demerath, H.J. (2003) Civil society and civil religion as mutually dependent. In

M. Dillon (ed.) *Handbook of the Sociology of Religion*. Cambridge: Cambridge University Press.

Deschamps, J.C. & Doise, W. (1978) Crossed category membership in intergroup relations. In H. Tajfel (ed.) *Differentiation Between Social Groups*. London: Academic Press.

Deutsch, M. & Gerard, H.B. (1955) A study of normative and informational social influence upon individual judgement. *Journal of Abnormal and Social Psychology*, 51, 629–636.

Digman, J.M. (1990) Personality structure: Emergence of the five-factor model. *Annual Review of Psychology*, 41, 417–440.

Dowey, E.A. (1994) *The Knowledge of God in Calvin's Theology* (3rd edn.) Grand Rapids, MI: W. B. Eerdmans.

Duck, R.J. & Hunsberger, B. (1999) Religious orientation and prejudice: The role of religious proscription, right-wing authoritarianism, and social desirability. *International Journal for the Psychology of Religion*, 9, 157–179.

Duncan, J.L. (1994) *Moses' Law for Modern Government: The Intellectual and Sociological Origins of the Christian Reconstructionist Movement*. Paper presented to the Social Science History Association, Atlanta, GA.

Durham, R. (2000) *The Christian Right, the far right, and the boundaries of American conservatism*. Manchester: Manchester University Press.

Einwechter, W. (2003) Authority of the Old Testament in the State. *Christian Statesman*, May–June. Online. Available: http://www.natreformassn.org/statesman/03/otinstat.html

Eisenstadt, S.N. (1999) *Fundamentalism, Sectarianism, and Revolution: The Jacobin Dimension of Modernity*. Cambridge: Cambridge University Press.

Ekman, P. & Davidson, R.J. (1994) *The Nature of Emotion*. New York: Oxford University Press.

Etkes, D. & Friedman, L. (2006) Who leads the settlers? *Settlements in Focus*, 2, 10.

Farris, A., Nathan, R.P., & Wright, D.J. (2004) *The Expanding Administrative Presidency: George W. Bush and the Faith-Based Initiative*. New York: The Nelson A. Rockefeller Institute of Government, State University of New York.

Fazio, R.H. (1990) Multiple processes by which attitudes guide behaviour: The MODE model as an integrative framework. In M.P. Zanna (ed.) *Advances in Experimental Social Psychology*, Vol. 23. San Diego, CA: Academic Press.

Fazio, R.H. (2001) On the automatic activation of associated evaluations: An overview. *Cognition and Emotion*, 15, 115–141.

Fazio, R.H., Ledbetter, J.E., & Towles-Schwen, T. (2000) On the costs of accessible attitudes: Detecting that the attitude object has changed. *Journal of Personality and Social Psychology*, 78, 197–210.

Fazio, R.H. & Olson, M.A. (2003) Attitudes: Foundations, functions, and consequences. In M.A. Hogg & J. Cooper (eds.) *Handbook of Social Psychology*. London: Sage.

Festinger, L. (1954) A theory of social comparison processes. *Human Relations*, 7, 117–140.

Festinger, L. (1957) *A Theory of Cognitive Dissonance*. New York: Row Peterson.

Festinger, L., Riecken, H.W. & Schachter, S. (1956) *When Prophecy Fails*. Minneapolis: University of Minnesota Press.

Folger, R. and Cropanzano, R. (1998) *Organisational Justice and Human Resource Management*. Thousand Oaks, CA: Sage.

Fukuyama, F. (1992) *The End of History and the Last Man*. London: Penguin.

Fulton, A.S., Gorsuch, R.L., & Maynard, E.A. (1999) Religious orientation, anti-homosexual sentiment, and fundamentalism among Christians. *Journal for the Scientific Study of Religion*, 38, 14–22.

Gaertner, S.L. & Dovidio, J.F. (2000) *Reducing Intergroup Bias: The Common Ingroup Identity Model*. Philadelphia: Psychology Press.

Galanter, M. (1989) *Cults: Faith, Healing, and Coercion*. New York: Oxford University Press.

Gallup, G. (2005) *Who are America's Evangelicals?* Washington, DC: Gallup Polls.

Gentry, K. L. (1997) Dispensationalism in transition: Challenging traditional dispensationalism's 'code of silence'. Online. Available: http://reformed-theology.org/ice/newslet/dit/dit01.97.htm

Gerges, F.A. (2005) *The Far Enemy: Why Jihad Went Global*. New York: Cambridge University Press.

Giddens, A. (1991) *Modernity and Self-Identity: Self and Society in the Late Modern Age*. Cambridge: Polity Press.

Glock, C.Y. & Stark, R. (1965) *Religion and Society in Tension*. Chicago: Rand McNally.

Goffman, E. (1959) *The Presentation of Self in Everyday Life*. New York: Anchor Books.

Goffman, E. (1971) *Relations in Public*. London: Allen Lane.

Goffman, E. (1974) *Frame Analysis*. Cambridge, MA: Harvard University Press.

Goodstein, L. & Kirkpatrick, D.D. (2004) Conservative group amplifies voice of protestant orthodoxy. *New York Times*, 22 May.

Grant, G. (1987) *The Changing of the Guard*. Fort Worth, TX: Dominion Press.

Greider, W. (1997) *One World, Ready or Not*. London: Penguin.

*Guardian* (2006) Guardian Unlimited, Agencies Report, 27 July. www.guardian.co.uk

Habermas, J. (1987) *The Philosophical Discourse of Modernity*. Cambridge, MA: MIT Press.

Hammond, P.E. (1976) The sociology of American civil religion: A bibliographical essay. *Sociological Analysis*, 37, 169–182.

Harding, S.F. (2000) *The Book of Jerry Falwell: Fundamentalist Language and Politics*. Princeton, NJ: Princeton University Press.

Harris (2005) *The Harris Poll* #78. www.harrispollonline.com

Haslam, S.A. (2001) *Psychology in Organisations: The Social Identity Approach*. London: Sage.

Haslam, S.A., Oakes, P.J., Turner, J.C., & McGarty, C. (1995) Social categorisation and group homogeneity: Changes in the perceived applicability of stereotype content as a function of comparative context and trait favourableness. *British Journal of Social Psychology*, 34, 139–160.

Hatch, M.J. (1993) The dynamics of organisational culture. *Academy of Management Review*, 18 (4), 657–663.

Hatch, M.J. (1997) *Organisation Theory: Modern, Symbolic, and Postmodern Perspectives*. Oxford: Oxford University Press.

Heilman, S. & Friedman, M. (1991) Religious fundamentalism and religious Jews: The case of the Haredim. In M.E. Marty & R.S. Appleby (eds.) *Fundamentalisms Observed*. Chicago: University of Chicago Press.

Herriot, P. (2001) *The Employment Relationship: A Psychological Perspective*. London: Routledge.

Herriot, P. (2007) *Religious Fundamentalism and Social Identity*. London: Routledge.

Hewstone, M. & Brown, R.J. (1986) Contact is not enough: An intergroup perspective on the 'contact hypothesis'. In M. Hewstone & R. Brown (eds.) *Contact and Conflict in Intergroup Encounters*. Oxford: Blackwell.

Himmelfarb, G. (1999) *One Nation: Two Cultures*. New York: Random House.

Hochschild, A.R. (1983) *The Managed Heart: Commercialisation of Human Feeling*. Berkeley, CA: University of California Press.

Hofstede, G. (1980) *Culture's Consequences: International Differences in Work-related Values*. Beverly Hills, CA: Sage.

Hogg, M.A. (1992) *The Social Psychology of Group Cohesiveness: From Attraction to Social Identity*. London: Harvester-Wheatsheaf.

Hogg, M.A. (2001) Self-categorisation and subjective uncertainty reduction: Cognitive and motivational facets of social identity and group membership. In J.P. Forgas, K.D. Williams, & L. Wheeler (eds.) *The Social Mind: Cognitive and Motivational Aspects of Interpersonal Behaviour*. New York: Cambridge University Press.

Hogg, M.A. (2003) Social identity. In M.R. Leary & J.P. Tangney (eds.) *Handbook of Self and Identity*. New York: Guilford

Hogg, M.A. & Abrams, D. (2001) Inter-group relations: An overview. In M.A. Hogg & D. Abrams (eds.) *Inter-group Relations: Essential Readings*. Philadelphia: Psychology Press.

Hogg, M.A. & Abrams, D. (2003) Intergroup behaviour and social identity. In M.A. Hogg & J. Cooper (eds) *Handbook of Social Psychology*. London: Sage.

Hogg, M.A. & Hornsey, M.J. (2006) Self-concept threat and multiple categorisation within groups. In R.J. Crisp & M. Hewstone (eds.) *Multiple Social Categorisation: Processes, Models, and Applications*. Hove, UK: Psychology Press.

Hogg, M.A. & Mullen, B.A. (1999) Joining groups to reduce uncertainty: Subjective uncertainty reduction and group identification. In D. Abrams & M.A. Hogg (eds.) *Social Identity and Social Cognition*. Oxford: Blackwell.

Holland, D., Lachicotte, W., Skinner, D., & Cain, C. (1998) *Identity and Agency in Cultural Worlds*. Cambridge, MA: Harvard University Press.

Holm, N.G. (1987) Sunden's role theory and glossolalia. *Journal for the Scientific Study of Religion*, 26, 383–389.

Hood, R.W., Hill, P.C., & Williamson, W.P. (2005) *The Psychology of Religious Fundamentalism*. New York: Guilford.

Hopfl, H. & Maddrell, J. (1996) Can you resist a dream? Evangelical metaphors and the appropriation of emotion. In D. Grant and C. Oswick (eds.) *Metaphor and Organisations*. London: Sage.

Horgon, J. (2005) *The Psychology of Terrorism*. London: Routledge.

Hout, M., Greely, A., & Wilde, M.J. (2001) The demographic imperative in religious change in the United States. *American Journal of Sociology*, 107 (2), 468–500.

Hunsberger, B., Pratt, M. & Pancer, S. (1994) Religious Fundamentalism and integrative complexity of thought. A relationship for existential content only? *Journal for the Scientific Study of Religion*, 33, 335–346.

Hunsberger, B., Alisat, S., Pancer, S., & Pratt, M. (1996) Religious fundamentalism and religious doubts: Content, connections, and complexity of thinking. *International Journal of the Psychology of Religion*, 6, 201–220.

Hunter, J.D. (1991) *Culture Wars: The Struggle to Define America*. New York: Basic Books.

Hunter, J.D. (1994) *Before the Shooting Begins: Searching for Democracy in America's Culture War*. New York: Free Press.

Huntington, S.P. (1996) *The Clash of Civilisations and the Remaking of World Order*. New York: Simon & Schuster.

Husain, E. (2007) *The Islamist: Why I Joined Radical Islam in Britain, What I Saw Inside, and Why I Left*. London: Penguin.

Iannacone, L.R. (1994) Why strict churches are strong. *American Journal of Sociology*, 99, 1180–1211.

Institute of Management (1996) *Managing the management tools*. London: Institute of Management.

Institute on Religion and Democracy (IRD) (2004) Commentary: Methodism and Patriotism, 29 November. http://www.ird-renew.org/news

Jaspers, K. (1965) *The Origins and Goal of History*. New Haven, CT: Yale University Press.

Jenkins, S. (2006) *The Guardian*, 8 September.

Jetten, J. & Spears, R. (2004) The divisive potential of differences and similarities: The role of intergroup distinctiveness in intergroup differentiation. In W. Stroebe & M. Hewstone (eds.) *European Review of Social Psychology*, Vol. 14. Hove, UK: Psychology Press.

Johnson, B. (1963) On church and sect. *American Sociological Review*, 28, 539–549.

Johnson, B. (1993) The denominations: The changing map of religious America. In Roper Centre, *The Public Perspective*. Storrs, CT: University of Connecticut Press.

Johnson, B. (2007) Conservapedia – the US religious right's answer to Wikipedia. *The Guardian*, 2 March.

Juergensmeyer, M. (2003) *Terror in the Mind of God: The Global Rise of Religious Violence* (3rd edn.). Berkeley, CA: University of California Press.

Juergensmeyer, M. (2005) Religious antiglobalism. In M. Juergensmeyer (ed.) *Religion in Global Civil Society*. New York: Oxford University Press.

Karmon, E. (2006) Al-Qaida and the war on terror after Iraq. *Middle East Review of International Affairs*, 10(1), 1–15.

Katzman, K. (2005) *Al Qaeda: Profile and Threat Assessment*. Washington, DC: Congressional Research Service, Library of Congress.

Kelley, D.M. (1972) *Why Conservative Churches are Growing*. New York: Harper & Row.

Kelley, H.H. (1972) Causal schemata and the attribution process. In E.E. Jones, D.E. Kanouse, H.H. Kelley, R.E. Nisbett, S. Valins, & B. Weiner (eds.) *Attribution: Perceiving the Causes of Behaviour*. New York: General Learning Press.

Kepel, G. (2005) *The Roots of Radical Islam*. London: Saqi.

Kepel, G. (2006) *Jihad: The Trail of Political Islam* (4th edn.) London: IBTauris.

Kirkpatrick, L.A., Hood, R.W., & Hartz, G.W. (1991) Fundamentalist religion conceptualised in terms of Rokeach's theory of the open and closed mind: New perspectives on some old ideas. In M.L. Lynn & D.O. Moberg (eds.) *Research in the Social Scientific Study of Religion*, Vol. 3. Greenwich, CT: JAI Press.

Kuhn, T. (1970) *The Structure of Scientific Revolutions*. Chicago: University of Chicago Press.

Lasch, C. (1980) *The Culture of Narcissism*. London: Abacus.

Lasch, C. (1985) *The Minimal Self*. London: Picador.

Lawrence, B.B. (1989) *Defenders of God: The Fundamentalist Revolt Against the Modern Age*. Columbia, SC: University of South Carolina Press.

Laythe, B., Finkel, D., & Kirkpatrick, L.A. (2001) Predicting prejudice from religious fundamentalism and right-wing authoritarianism: A multiple regression approach. *Journal for the Scientific Study of Religion*, 40, 1–10.

Laythe, B., Finkel, D.G., Bringle, R.G., & Kirkpatrick, L.A. (2002) Religious fundamentalism as a predictor of prejudice: A two-component model. *Journal for the Scientific Study of Religion*, 41, 623–625.

Legge, K. (1995) *Human Resource Management: Rhetorics and Realities*. London: Macmillan.

Levinger, M. (1985) We and the Arabs. *Nekuda*, 36, 27 November [quoted in Lustick, 1988, Chapter 5].

Levitt, M.A. (2002) The political economy of Middle East terrorism. *Middle East Review of International Affairs*, 6(4), 1–15.

Lewis, B. (2001) *What Went Wrong: Western Impact and Middle Eastern Response*. New York: Oxford University Press.

Lia, B. (1998) *The Society of Muslim Brothers in Egypt: The Rise of an Islamic Mass Movement, 1928–1982*. London: Ithaca Press.

Lienesch, M. (1993) *Redeeming America: Piety and Politics in the New Christian Right*. Chapel Hill, NC: University of North Carolina Press.

Lincoln, B. (2002) *Holy Terrors: Thinking about Religion after September 11*. Chicago: University of Chicago Press.

Lofland, J. & Stark, R. (1965) Becoming a world-saver: A theory of conversion to a deviant perspective. *American Sociological Review*, 30, 862–875.

*Los Angeles Times* (2002) 27 January.

Lupfer, M.B., Brock, K.F., & DePaola, S.J. (1992) The use of secular and religious attributions to explain everyday behaviour. *Journal for the Scientific Study of Religion*, 31, 486–503.

Lustick, I.S. (1988) *For the Land and the Lord: Jewish Fundamentalism in Israel*. New York: Council of Foreign Relations.

Lustig, V. (2006) Letter to *The Guardian*, 13 October.

Mackie, D.M. & Hamilton, D.L. (1993) *Affect, Cognition, and Stereotyping: Interactive Processes in Group Perception*. San Diego, CA: Academic Press.

Maio, G.R. & Olson, J.M. (2000) *Why We Evaluate: Functions of Attitudes*. Mahwah, NJ: Erlbaum.

Malik, Z. (2006) Even other Muslims turn and look at me. *The Guardian*, 17 October.

Martin, R. & Hewstone, M. (2003) Social influence processes of control and change: Conformity, obedience to authority, and innovation. In M.A. Hogg & J. Cooper (eds.) *Handbook of Social Psychology*. London: Sage.

Mawdudi, A.A. (1976) *Jihad in Islam*. Lahore: Islamic Publications.

McGarty, C. (2006) Hierarchies and minority groups: The roles of salience, overlap, and background knowledge in selecting meaningful social categorisations from multiple alternatives. In R.J. Crisp & M. Hewstone (eds.) *Multiple Social Categorisation: Processes, Models, and Applications*. Hove, UK: Psychology Press.

McGuire, M.B. (2002) *Religion: The Social Context* (5th edn.) Belmont, CA: Wadsworth.

Moore, E.R. (2002) *Let My Children Go*. Columbia, SC: Gilead Media.

Moore, E.R. (2004) Salt and Light, the great commission and who's responsible for educating your children. http://www.exodusmandate.org

Morgan, G. (1997) *Images of Organisation* (2nd edn.) Thousand Oaks, CA: Sage.

Moscovici, S. (1981) On social representation. In J. Forgas (ed.) *Social Cognition.* London: Academic Press.

Moscovici, S. (1988) Notes towards a description of social representation. *European Journal of Social Psychology*, 18, 211–250.

Mullen, B. & Copper, C. (1994) The relation between group cohesiveness and perform-ance: An integration. *Psychological Bulletin*, 115, 210–227.

Mummendey, A. & Wenzel, M. (1999) Social discrimination and tolerance in intergroup relations: reactions to intergroup difference. *Personality and Social Psychology Review*, 3, 158–174.

Musick, M. & Wilson, J. (1995) Religious switching for marriage reasons. *Sociology of Religion*, 56, 528–552.

NACE/CEE (2004) http://www.nace-cee.org

Naphy, W. (1994) *Calvin and the Consolidation of the Genevan Reformation.* Manchester: Manchester University Press.

NCES Issue Brief 1 (2004) *One Million Homeschooled Students in the United States in 2003.* Washington: US Department of Education: Institute of Educational Sciences, document NCES 2004–115.

Nehemiah (2005) Position paper Q23. http://www.nehemiah.org

Neturei Karta International (undated) Anthem of the Neturei Karta. http://www.nkusa.org

*New York Times* (2003) 12 October.

*New York Times* (2005) 21 January.

Newman, D. (1982) *Jewish Settlement in the West Bank: The Role of Gush Emunim.* Occasional Papers, 16. University of Durham: Centre for Middle Eastern and Islamic Studies.

Niebuhr, H.R. (1929) *The Social Sources of Denominationalism.* New York: Henry Holt.

Noon, M. & Blyton, P. (1997) *The Realities of Work.* London: Macmillan.

Norris, P. & Inglehart, R. (2004) *Sacred and Secular: Religion and Politics Worldwide.* New York: Cambridge University Press.

North, G. (1984) *Backward Christian Soldiers? An Action Manual for Christian Reconstruction.* Tyler, TX: Institute for Christian Economics.

*Observer* (2001) 23 September.

Office of the Director of National Intelligence (2005) *Letter from al-Zawahiri to al-Zarqawi.* Washington, DC: 11 October. www.fas.org/irp/news/2005/10

Ohmae, K. (1995) *The End of the Nation State.* New York: Free Press.

Olson, D.V.A. & Perl, P. (2001) Variations in strictness and religious commitment among five denominations. *Journal for the Scientific Study of Religion*, 40, 757–764.

Pargament, K.I. (1997) *The Psychology of Religion and Coping.* New York: Guilford Press.

Pargament, K.I., Kennell, J., Hathaway, W., Grevengoed, N., Newman, J., & Jones, W. (1988) Religion and the problem-solving process: Three styles of coping. *Journal for the Scientific Study of Religion*, 27, 90–104.

Percy, M. (2002) *Fundamentalism, Church, and Society.* London: SPCK Press.

Pew Forum (2004) *The American Religious Landscape and Politics, 2004.* Washington, DC: The Pew Forum.

Pew Forum (2005) *Trends 2005.* Washington, DC: The Pew Forum.

Pew Forum (2006) *Many Americans Uneasy with Mix of Religion and Politics.* Washington, DC: The Pew Forum.

Pickett, C.L. & Brewer, M.B. (2001) Assimilation and differentiation needs as motivational determinants of perceived in-group and out-group homogeneity. *Journal of Experimental Social Psychology*, 37, 341–348.

Public Eye (2005) Christian Reconstructionism. Theoretic Dominionism gains influence. http://www.publiceye.org/magazine/v08n1

Pugh, F. (undated) The necessity of a Reformed world and life view. http://www.forerunner.com/puritan/PS.Worldview.html

Puttnam, R.D. (2000) *Bowling Alone*. New York: Simon & Schuster.

Quinn, K.A., Macrae, C.N., & Bodenhausen, G.V. (2003) Stereotyping and impression formation: How categorical thinking shapes person perception. In M.A. Hogg & J. Cooper (eds.) *Handbook of Social Psychology*. London: Sage.

Qutb, S. (1948) *The America I Have Seen*. Reprinted in K. Abdel-Malek, (ed.) (2000) *America in an Arab Mirror: Images of America in Arabic Travel Literature: An Anthology*. Basingstoke: Palgrave Macmillan.

Qutb, S. (1981) *Milestones along the Way*. New Delhi: Markazi Maktaba Islami and Cedar Rapids, IO: The Mother Mosque Foundation. Also online at: http://www.youngmuslims.ca/online_library/books/milestones

Rambo, L.R. (1993) *Understanding Religious Conversion*. New Haven, CT: Yale University Press.

Rauf, A. (2006) The social problems masked by the veil. Letter to *The Guardian*, 7 October.

Ravitsky, A. (1996) *Messianism, Zionism, and Jewish Religious Radicalism*. Chicago: University of Chicago Press.

Ray, B.D. (2003) *Facts on homeschooling*. Salem, OR: National Home Education Research Institute.

Reich, R. (1991) *The Work of Nations*. New York: Random House.

Reicher, S.D. (2001) The psychology of crowd dynamics. In M.A. Hogg & R.S. Tindale (eds.) *Blackwell Handbook of Social Psychology: Group Processes*. Oxford: Blackwell.

Rice, T.W. (2003) Believe it or not: religious and other paranormal beliefs in the United States. *Journal of the Scientific Study of Religion*, 42, 95–106.

Rieff, P. (1966) *The Triumph of the Therapeutic*. Harmondsworth, UK: Penguin.

Riesebrodt, M. (1993) *Pious Passion: The Emergence of Modern Fundamentalism in the United States and Iran*. Berkeley, CA: University of California Press.

Rifkin, J. (2000) *The Age of Access: How the Shift from Ownership to Access is Transforming Capitalism*. London: Penguin.

Robertson, R. (1992) *Globalisation: Social Theory and Global Culture*. London: Sage.

Roccas, S. & Brewer, M.B. (2002) Social identity complexity. *Personality and Social Psychology Review*, 6, 88–106.

Rogers, J. (undated) What is theonomy? Online. Available: http://www.forerunner.com/theofaq.html

Rokeach, M. (1969) Value systems in religion. *Review of Religious Research*, 11, 3–23.

Rokeach, M. (1973) *The Nature of Human Values*. New York: Free Press.

Roof, W.C. (1999) *Spiritual Marketplace: Baby Boomers and the Remaking of American Religion*. Princeton, NJ: Princeton University Press.

Rothschild, M. (2005) The hidden passages in Bush's inaugural address. *The Progressive*, 21 January.

Rowatt, W.C., Ottenbreit, A., Nesselroade, K.P. & Cunningham, P.A. (2002) On being holier-than-thou or humbler-than-thee. A psychological perspective on religious-ness and humility. *Journal for the Scientific Study of Religion*, 41, 227–237.

Rudner, L.M. (1999) Scholastic achievement and demographic characteristics of home school students in 1998. *Public Policy Sources*, 51. Vancouver, BC: The Fraser Institute.

Rugman, A. (2000) *The End of Globalisation*. London: Random House.

Rushdoony, R.J. (1973) *The Institutes of Biblical Law*. Nutley, NJ: Craig Press.

Rushdoony, R.J. (undated) *An Interview with R.J. Rushdoony*. www.chalcedon.edu

Ruthven, M. (2000) *Islam in the World* (2nd edn.). London: Penguin.

Sageman, M. (2004) *Understanding Terror Networks*. Philadelphia: University of Philadelphia Press.

Salai, S. (2002) School's Out. *Washington Times*, 7 August.

Sandlin, A. (undated, a) Join the resistance. Online. Available: http://www.forerunner.com/puritan/PS.Join_the_Resistance.html

Sandlin, A. (undated, b) The creed of Christian reconstructionism. Online. Available: http://www.chalcedon.org

Sandlin, A. (2005) www.AndrewSandlin.net

Sarda, K. (2006) Letter to *The Guardian*, 7 October.

Sardar, Z. (2006) Jack Straw's thinly veiled abuse of power. *New Statesman*, 16 October.

Scarborough, R. (2003) Drugs money sustains al-Qaeda. *Washington Times*, 29 December.

Schaller, M., Conway, L.G., & Crandall, C.S. (2004) The psychological foundations of culture: An introduction. In M. Schaller & C.S. Crandall (eds.) *The Psychological Foundations of Culture*. Mahwah, NJ: Lawrence Erlbaum.

Schein, E. (1985) *Organisational Culture and Leadership*. San Francisco: Jossey-Bass.

Scipione, G.C., Crabbe, L., & Payne, E. (1989) *The Christian Worldview of Psychology and Counselling*. Sunnyvale, CA.: The Coalition on Revival, Inc.

Sennett, R. (1998) *The Corrosion of Character: The Personal Consequences of Work in the New Capitalism*. New York: Norton.

Sethi, S. & Seligman, M.E.P. (1993) Optimism and fundamentalism. *Psychological Science*, 4, 256–259.

Sheridan, M. (2006) *Sunday Times*, 30 July.

Sherif, M. (1966) *Group Conflict and Cooperation*. London: Routledge and Kegan Paul.

Sherif, M. & Sherif, C.W. (1964) *Reference Groups*. New York: Harper & Row.

Sherif, M. & Sherif, C.W. (1969) *Social Psychology*. New York: Harper & Row.

Sherkat, D.E. (2001) Tracking the restructuring of American religion: Religious affiliation and patterns of religious mobility. *Social Forces*, 79, 1459–1493.

Simonds, R. (1998) Rescue 2010 Strategy. Online. Available: http://www.nace-cee.org

Simonds, R. (2003) Citizens for Excellence in Education/National Association of Christian Educators. Online. Available: http://www.zeppscommentaries.com

Simonds, R. (2005) President's Report. Online. Available: http://www.exodusmandate.org

Sivan, E. (1990) *Radical Islam: Medieval Theology and Modern Politics* (2nd edn.) New Haven, CT: Yale University Press.

Smith, C. (2000) *Christian America? What Evangelicals Really Want*. Berkeley, CA: University of California Press.

Smith, G.A. (2006) *Attitudes toward immigration: In the pulpit and the pew*. Washington, DC: Pew Forum.

Smith, J. (2006) Letter to *The Guardian*, 13 October.

Smithwick, D. (2008) Online. Available: http://www.nehemiahinstitute.com/aboutus.php

Snyder, M. (1992) Motivational foundations of behavioural confirmation. In M.P. Zanna (ed.) *Advances in Experimental Social Psychology*, Vol. 25. San Diego, CA: Academic Press.

Soloveitchik, H. (1993) The new role of texts in the Haredi world. In M.E. Marty & R.S. Appleby (eds.) *Accounting for Fundamentalisms*. Chicago: Chicago University Press.

Spilka, B., Hood, R.W., Hunsberger, B., & Gorsuch, R. (2003) *The Psychology of Religion: An Empirical Approach* (3rd edn.) New York: Guilford.

Spilka, B. & Schmidt, G. (1983) General attribution theory for the psychology of religion: The influence of event-character on attributions to God. *Journal for the Scientific Study of Religion*, 22, 326–339.

Sprinzak, E. (1981) Gush Emunim: The tip of the iceberg. *The Jerusalem Quarterly, 21*. www.geocities-com/alabasters_archive

Sprinzak, E. (1998) *The Ascendancy of the Religious Right in Israel*. Oxford: Oxford University Press.

Stark, R. & Bainbridge, W.S. (1985) *The Future of Religion*. Berkeley, CA: University of California Press.

Stark, R. & Finke, R. (2000) *Acts of Faith: Explaining the Human Side of Religion*. Berkeley, CA: University of California Press.

Steele, C.M. (1988) The psychology of self-affirmation: Sustaining the integrity of the self. *Advances in Experimental Social Psychology*, 21, 261–302.

Stephan, W.G. & Stephan, C.W. (2000) An integrated threat theory of prejudice. In S. Oskamp (ed.) *Reducing Prejudice and Discrimination*. Mahwah, NJ: Lawrence Erlbaum.

Stern, J. (2003) *Terror in the Name of God*. New York: HarperCollins.

Stiglitz, J. (2002) *Globalisation and its Discontents*. London: Penguin.

Straw, J. (2006) *Lancashire Telegraph*, October 5th.

Sturcke, J. (2006) Straw: I'd rather no-one wore veils. *Guardian Unlimited*, 6 October. Online. Available: http://www.guardian.co.uk/politics/2006/oct/06/immigrationpolicy.religion

Tajfel, H. (1981) *Human Groups and Social Categories*. Cambridge: Cambridge University Press.

Tajfel, H. & Turner, J.C. (1986) An integrative theory of social conflict. In S. Worchel & W. Austin (eds.) *Psychology of Intergroup Relations*. Chicago: Nelson Hall.

Tamney, J.B. (2002) *The Resilience of Conservative Religion: The Case of Popular Conservative Protestant Congregations*. Cambridge: Cambridge University Press.

Taylor, D.M. & Moghaddam, F.M. (1994) *Theories of Intergroup Relations: International and Social Psychological Perspectives* (2nd edn.). Westport, CT: Praeger.

Taylor, F.W. (1911) *The Principles of Scientific Management*. New York: Norton.

Taylor, M. & Dodd, V. (2006) Take off the veil, says Straw – to immediate anger from Muslims. *The Guardian*, 6 October.

Taylor, P. (2006) A reason to hate. *The Guardian*, 1 September.

Telhami, S. (2006) Success by Hezbollah overshadows al-Qaida. Online. Available: http://www.mercurynews.com

Temple University (2002) www.tntemple.edu

Thomas, T.L. (2003) Al Qaeda and the internet: The danger of 'cyberplanning'. *Parameters*, Spring, 112–123.

Tickle, P.A. (1997) *God-Talk in America*. New York: Crossroad.

*The Times* (2006) 3 July.

Triandis, H.C. (1995) *Individualism and Collectivism*. Boulder, CO: Westview Press.

Troeltsch, E. (1981) *The Social Teachings of the Christian Church*. Chicago: University of Chicago Press.

Tumelty, P. (2005) An in-depth look at the London bombers. *Terrorism Monitor*, 3, 15.

Turner, J.C. (1982) Towards a cognitive redefinition of the social group. In H. Tajfel (ed.) *Social Identity and Intergroup Relations*. Cambridge: Cambridge University Press.

Turner, J.C. (1985) Social categorisation and the self-concept: A social-cognitive theory of group behaviour. In E.J. Lawler (ed.) *Advances in Group Processes: Theory and Research*, Vol. 2. Greenwich, CT: JAI Press.

Turner, J.C. & Haslam, S.A. (2000) Social identity, organisations, and leadership. In M.E.Turner (ed.) *Groups at Work: Advances in Theory and Research*. Hillsdale, NJ: Lawrence Erlbaum.

US Director of National Intelligence (2006) www.dni.gov

Van Til, C. (1976) *The Defence of the Faith*. Philadelphia: Presbyterian and Reformed Publishing Co.

Vanbeselaere, N. (1991) The different effects of simple and crossed categorisations: A result of the category differentiation process or of differential category salience? In W. Stroebe & M. Hewstone (eds.) *European Review of Social Psychology*, Vol. 2. Chichester, UK: Wiley.

Visser, P. & Cooper, J. (2003) Attitude change. In M.A. Hogg & J. Cooper (eds.) *Handbook of Social Psychology*. London: Sage.

Wainwright, M., Branigan, T., Vasagar, J., Taylor, M., & Dodd, V. (2006) Dangerous attack or fair point? Straw veil row deepens. *The Guardian*, 7 October.

*Wall Street Journal* (2005) 21 January.

Ward, D. (2006) Straw warns of widening cultural split in constituency. *The Guardian*, 14 October.

*Washington Post* (2003) 29 July.

Watt, D.H. (2002) *Bible-Carrying Christians: Conservative Protestants and Social Power*. New York: Oxford University Press.

Weaver, A.J. & Seibert, N. (2004) Follow the money: Documenting the Right's well-heeled assault on the UMC. *Zion's Herald*, January.

Weber, M. (1919/1946) *From Max Weber: Essays in Sociology*. In H.H. Gerth & C. Wright Mills (eds) New York: Oxford University Press.

Weber, M. (1922/1993) *The Sociology of Religion*. Boston, MA: Beacon Press.

Weber, M. (1947) *The Theory of Social and Economic Organisation*. London: Oxford University Press.

Weick, K.E. (1979) *The Social Psychology of Organising*. Reading, MA: Addison-Wesley.

Westervelt, E. (2007) Jerusalem's 'Rosa Parks' fights 'modesty patrols'. NPR, 26 June.

Wheatcroft, A. (1995) *The Ottomans: Dissolving Images*. London: Penguin.

Wheatcroft, A. (2004) *Infidels: A History of the Conflict between Christendom and Islam*. London: Penguin.

Whitaker, B. (2006) *The Guardian*, 27 July.

White House (2001a) *President George W. Bush's Inaugural Address*. Online. Available: http://www.whitehouse.gov/news/inaugural-address.html

White House (2001b) *Guidance to Faith-Based and Community Organisations on Partnering with the Federal Government*. Washington, DC: The White House.

White House (2004) *America's Compassion in Action*. Washington, DC: The White House.

White House (2005) *President Bush Sworn-in to Second Term*. Online. Available: http://www.whitehouse.gov/inaugural

Willmott, H. (1993) Strength is ignorance; slavery is freedom: Managing culture in modern organisations. *Journal of Management Studies*, 30(4), 515–552.

Wood, W., Lundgren, S., Ouellette, J.A., Busceme, S., & Blackstone, T. (1994) Minority influence: A meta-analytic review of social influence processes. *Psychological Bulletin*, 115, 323–345.

Worchel, S. (2003) Come one, come all: Toward understanding the process of collective behaviour. In M.A. Hogg & J. Cooper (eds.) *Handbook of Social Psychology*. London: Sage.

Wright, L. (2006) *The Looming Tower: Al Qaeda's Road to 9/11*. London: Allen Lane.

Wright, S.C. & Taylor, D.M. (2003) The social psychology of cultural diversity: Social stereotyping, prejudice, and discrimination. In M.A. Hogg & J. Cooper (eds.) *Handbook of Social Psychology*. London: Sage.

Wuthnow, R. (1988) *The Restructuring of American Religion: Society and Faith since World War II*. Princeton, NJ: Princeton University Press.

Wylie, L. & Forest, J. (1992) Religious fundamentalism, right-wing authoritarianism, and prejudice. *Psychological Reports*, 71, 1291–1298.

Young, H. (1989) *One Of Us: A Biography of Margaret Thatcher*. London: Macmillan.

Yurica, K. (2005) The despoiling of America. www.yuricareport.com

Yzerbyt, V.Y., Leyens, J-P., & Bellour, F. (1995) The ingroup overexclusion effect: Identity concerns in decisions about group membership. *European Journal of Social Psychology*, 25, 1–16.

Ziegler, J. (undated) Imprecatory prayer – the church's duty against her enemies. Online. Available: http://www.forerunner.com/puritan/PS.Prayer.html

# Author index

Abrams, D. 57, 141, 154, 181, 295
Adams, G. 48
Adorno, T.W. 149
Akbar, M.J. 83
Albert, S. 115
Alisat, S. 149
Al-Jazeera 32
Allport, F.H. 85
Allport, G.W. 282
Almond, G.A. 2, 43–6, 50, 52, 54, 58, 73, 86, 89, 93–4, 107, 182, 201, 247
Altemeyer, B. 85, 149, 153, 238, 242
al-Zawahiri, A. 182
Anthony, A. 31
Anthony, D. 151
Anti-Defamation League 202
Appleby, R.S. 2, 58, 94
Aran, G. 98, 100
Armstrong, K. 10, 30, 50, 58, 81–2, 84, 94–5, 210, 276
Aronson, E. 255, 259–60, 267
Asch, S.H. 146
Ashforth, B.E. 110

Bahnsen, G.L. 212, 218
Bainbridge, W.S. 75–6, 94
Balmer, R. 116, 118, 122, 125, 144–5, 168, 261
Balz, D. 63–4
Baptist Bible Fellowship International 199
Bartlett, C.A. 38
Basham, P. 128
Bates, S. 179, 241, 287
Batson, C.D. 239–40
Bauman, K.J. 127–8
Bauman, Z. 9, 17, 28
Baumeister, R.F. 18, 86, 95, 164, 181
Beaman, L.G. 59

Beliles, M.A. 134–6
Bellour, F. 286
Bem, D.J. 146, 255
Berger, P. 85, 111
Bibby, R.W. 79
bin Laden, O. 30, 34
Blanchard, C.M. 30–1, 37
Blanton, H. 260
Blyton, P. 15
Bodenhausen, G.V. 165, 254, 267
Bond, R. 146
Boone, K.C. 197, 210
Boston, R. 110, 128
Boyer, P. 24, 67, 89, 175, 207, 210, 220, 262
Branigan, T. 272
Brewer, M.B. 87, 279, 282–3, 286, 295
Bringle, R.G. 238
Brinkerhoff, M.B. 254
British Broadcasting Corporation 156, 243
Brock, K.F. 175
Brown, I. 127–9
Brown, R.J. 141, 153, 281, 290
Bruce, S. 22, 28, 73, 198, 204, 210
Bruner, J. 47, 58
Bryman, A. 91
Bunting, M. 271
Bunyan, N. 270
Byrne, D. 142

Cain, C. 48
Carpenter, J.A. 45, 90, 169, 208, 210
Casanova, J. 57–8
Castells, M. 10, 12–13, 28
Choueiri, Y.M. 184
Clarke, T. 14, 33
Clegg, S.R. 14, 33, 125
Coalition on Revival 137

Whitaker, B. 35
White House 62–5, 69–70
Wilde, M.J. 126
Williamson, W.P. 25, 181, 210
Willmott, H. 36, 112
Wilson, G. 270
Wilson, J. 143
Winner, A.L. 240
Wood, W. 150
Worchel, S. 84, 95
Wright, L. 29

Wright, S.C. 68, 143, 154, 235, 243
Wulff, D.M. 267
Wuthnow, R. 45, 53
Wylie, L. 149

Young, H. 236
Yurica, K. 138
Yzerbit, V.Y. 286

Zanna, M.P. 243, 267
Ziegler, J. 217–18

# Subject index